An A–Z of Counselling Theory and Practice

PB

An A–Z of Counselling Theory and Practice

THIRD EDITION

William Stewart
Freelance counsellor and trainer
Eastleigh, Hampshire, UK

First published in 1992 by Chapman & Hall
Second edition published in 1997 by Stanley Thornes (Publishers) Ltd

Third edition published in 2001 by:
Nelson Thornes Ltd
Delta Place
27 Bath Road
CHELTENHAM
GL53 7TH
United Kingdom

  03 04 05 06 / 10 9 8 7 6 5 4 3

A catalogue record for this book is available from the British Library

ISBN 0 7487 5710 4

Page make-up by Acorn Bookwork

Printed and bound in Spain by GraphyCems

Contents

FOREWORD

Neil Morrison, Director, Institute of Counselling, Dixon Street, Glasgow, UK

The third edition of this easy to read, comprehensive and interesting work is enhanced by new material, rationalization of subjects and engaging articles. It is comprehensive in its holistic approach to the counselling field and includes the spiritual and transpersonal. The work generates interest and actively engages the reader to reflect on what is presented.

Examples of counselling skills and practice flesh out the topics for the reader and put them into context. It is this practical approach that is refreshing and engaging for the person dipping into or looking at various topics. In this way it is an excellent companion for the counselling student or practitioner.

This enhanced edition will engage, inform and inspire students and qualified counsellors alike. It is an excellent book for counselling courses and programmes and an asset to the counsellor's library.

PREFACE TO THE THIRD EDITION

In the eight years since the publication of the first edition, I have been amazed and gratified by how well this book has been received. Students of counselling have found it particularly helpful, but I have been particularly pleased that many counsellors have told me how much they have benefited from dipping into it. One counsellor said that she always had it to hand when counselling, so that she could refer clients to specific parts that she considered might help them.

In creating a third edition a decision has to be made as to what new material to include and what to leave out. I have carried out a major restructuring of the book, rationalizing many of the subjects by bringing together related articles rather than scattering them throughout the book.

Many of the older, more fringe, articles have been removed, to be replaced with other articles more pertinent to counselling. Wherever appropriate I have added examples of counselling skills to emphasize the 'practice' part of the book. There are several new articles. Many of the references have also been rationalized. I have deleted some of the older references and added new ones.

It is my hope that readers will find this third edition sufficiently different, particularly the new articles.

William Stewart
Eastleigh, September 2000

NOTE ON SOURCES

Some of the principal and secondary references listed in the bibliography are old and many are out of print, but they should still be obtainable through libraries. Many books may have been published since a particular reference I have included; however, my aim is not to produce a bibliography of topics but to refer you to certain sources. There has been no attempt to keep the articles to a uniform length. Some articles are long, generally those that deal with a particular theory or one of the principal areas of counselling practice.

ABOUT THE AUTHOR

William Stewart spent 20 years in the Royal Army Medical Corps and gained experience in general and psychiatric nursing in the UK and abroad. He was commissioned in 1968 as a specialist officer in mental health and pioneered social work in the armed forces. Following his training as a psychiatric social worker he established a private counselling and counselling training practice.

On retiring from the RAMC in 1974 he worked as Senior Nurse (Allocation) in the Southampton University Hospital's Combined School of Nursing until 1987.

Twenty years ago he was one of the early pioneers of counselling within the health care professions. In 1987 he was invited to set up the Student and Staff Counselling service (part-time Student Counsellor/Lecturer) at St George's and Roehampton College of Health Studies, and St George's School of Radiography, London. In addition to providing a counselling service for students and college staff, he taught a variety of interpersonal skills within the College. He retired from that post in 1991.

Since 1992 he has been a distance learning tutor for the Institute of Counselling, Glasgow, and has written three texts for them.

In addition to *An A–Z of Counselling Theory and Practice*, William Stewart has written many other counselling and self-help books, and several devotional books, published privately for charity.

For several years he has been a supervisor of other counsellors.

LIST OF SUBJECTS

Items marked with an asterisk are either new or significantly revised for the third edition.

'A' type personality
Abreaction
Action plans
Advice
Aggression
Alienation
Alter ego
Altruism
Ambivalence
Analytical psychology
Anger
Anima and animus
Anomie
Anorexia nervosa
Anxiety
Apathy
Apprehension
Approval
Assertiveness
Atonement
Attachment
Attending
Attitude
Authoritarianism

Befriending
Behaviour therapy
Bibliotherapy
Blame
Body-image
Bonding
Brain-storming
Brief counselling*
Bulimia nervosa
Burnout

Catharsis
Challenging
Child abuse

Sadness
Scapegoating
Self*
Self-disclosure
Self-fulfilling prophecy
Sex therapy*
Sexual harassment
Silence
Six category intervention
Stages of Freudian psychosexual development*
Stereotypes
Stigma*
Stress management
Suicide
Summarizing
Supervision
Sympathy

Tavistock method
Telephone counselling
Therapeutic hour
Tolerance
Touch
Transactional analysis
Transference and counter-transference*
Transpersonal psychology
Trust

Values

Working through
Wounded healer

A

'A' TYPE PERSONALITY (*see also*: Stress management)

The type A behaviour pattern was first described by two cardiologists, Meyere Friedman and Ray Rosenman, and related to myocardial infarction. Type A behaviour is an ingrained pattern of behaviour observed in people who struggle to obtain something from their environment as quickly as possible. What they strive for is often not clear and may be in conflict with other things or persons.

Type A behaviour characteristics

- Extreme competitiveness and hostility
- Striving for achievement
- Aggressiveness (sometimes very repressed)
- Haste
- Impatience and anger
- Restlessness
- Hyperalertness
- Explosiveness of speech and interrupting when others are speaking
- Tension in facial muscles
- Feelings of being under pressure of time
- Feelings of being under the challenge of responsibility
- Deep commitment to a vocation or profession. Other aspects of life may be neglected.

A high proportion of 'A'-type men develop coronary heart disease. The cardio-vascular system seems particularly sensitive to 'A'-type behaviours.

People who are high on type A behaviours, although outwardly self-confident, have been shown to be prey to constant feelings of self-doubt. It would seem that this might be one of the reasons why such people push themselves to accomplish more in less time.

In contrast, type B people do not exhibit these characteristics; they are able to relax without feeling guilty, they achieve what they have to, without feelings of being pushed and without agitation that they will not get it done; they are generally more patient and are not easily aroused to anger.

Although there are links between type A behaviour and coronary heart disease, there is no agreement as to why this should be. It is possible that it is not the competitive spirit but anger, hostile feelings and persistent annoyance that place the type-A person at risk. A further factor might be if the person is a smoker.

Modifying type A behaviour

A counselling programme that concentrates on the following is the most promising, particularly in the reduction of hostility and the urgency. This programme may be of benefit to people who have suffered coronary attacks.

- Education
- Relaxation training
- Cognitive therapy
- The use of imagery
- Behaviour modification
- Emotional support.

Further reading

Friedman, M. (1969) *Pathogenesis of Coronary Artery Disease*, McGraw Hill, New York.
Friedman, M. and Rosenman, R. (1974) *Type 'A' Behaviour and Your Heart*, Knopf, New York.

ABREACTION (*see also*: Catharsis)

The living again of painful emotional experiences in psychotherapy. Abreaction involves bringing repressed unconscious or preconscious material into conscious awareness. Abreaction does not eliminate the causes of conflict but it may open the way for further exploration of feelings and experiences.

Freud evolved the 'cathartic method' from hypnosis and in the early days of psychoanalysis abreaction was considered therapeutic in itself, whether or not the patient understood the significance of the repressed experience.

While there is no doubt that when a client experiences the release of hitherto forgotten experiences the relief is dramatic, abreaction is not the main purpose of counselling, mainly because it is a technique that involves working with the unconscious rather than with the conscious.

ACTION PLANS (*see also*: Goals and goal-setting)

Creating action plans is Stage 3 in the Egan model of counselling (see Goals and goal-setting).

There is more to helping than talking and planning. If clients are to live more effectively they must act. When they fail to act, they fail to cope with problems in living or to exploit unused opportunities. Attaining goals cannot be left to chance.

Three steps in Action are:

- Discovering strategies for action
- Choosing strategies and devising an action plan
- Implementing plans and achieving goals.

A goal is an **end**; a strategy is a **means** for achieving a goal. Many people fail to achieve goals because they do not explore alternatives. Brainstorming ways of achieving a goal increases the probability that one of them or a combination of several, will suit the resources of a particular client.

Planning helps to initiate, and give direction to, action. Clients and the counsellors will know that the goal has been reached only when the clients feel sufficiently free from the forces that have been restraining them to take constructive action. The aim is to help the client discover, then harness, inner resources that have been locked in. Increased self-awareness and insight are often the keys that will release these resources.

The stages of the action plan:

1. Thinking it through – inadequate thinking through may spell disaster
2. Carrying it out.

Goals should be:

- Stated as accomplishments or outcomes rather than means or strategies
- Clear and specific
- Measurable or verifiable
- Realistic
- Genuine
- In keeping with the client's overall strategy and values
- Set in a realistic time frame.

Further reading

Egan, G. (1988) *Change-agent Skills*, University Associates, San Diego, CA.

ADVICE

The dictionary definition of advice is opinion, judgement (as it appears to me), probability, careful thought, consideration, deliberation, recommendation regarding a course of conduct, information or notice given or action to be taken.

Advice is generally considered inappropriate in person-centred counselling and most humanistic and holistic approaches. It may be more appropriate and acceptable when working with the very young, with people who are disturbed or helpless or in essentially practical issues.

Directive therapies – behaviour therapy, cognitive therapy, crisis intervention and brief therapy – rely on advice-giving, although not in the lay understanding of the term – 'this is what I think you should do'. The advice so given is aimed at helping the person deal with the problem to achieve a goal.

It is useful to distinguish between advice on how the client's life should be lived and instruction about specific aspects of the therapeutic process.

Counsellors who offer a lot of advice run the risk of increasing the dependency of the client. Advice should always be 'this is what is possible', not 'this is what you should do'. The stronger the emotional content of the issue the less appropriate is advice.

There are occasions when counsellors put strength behind the advice; when they 'advocate' some course of action, e.g. seeking a medical opinion.

Further reading

Burnard, P. (1999) *Counselling Skills for Health Professionals*, 3rd edn, Stanley Thornes, Cheltenham.

AGGRESSION (*see also*: Anger; Competition versus co-operation)

Aggression is a variety of behaviour patterns in which (in human terms) a person shows a tendency to approach in attack rather than flee from something perceived as a threat. It is almost impossible to arrive at a concise definition of aggression.

Aggression is viewed as:

- A motivated state
- A personality characteristic
- A response to frustration
- An inherent drive
- The need to fulfil a socially learned role.

In everyday terms, 'aggression' refers to acts of hostility and violence and meets with disfavour, yet there are contradictions. We speak approvingly of an athlete running an aggressive race or of the successful entrepreneur who conducts an aggressive sales campaign.

Competition, dominance, rivalry and victory, all characterize aggression. Many murders or serious violent assaults appear to be instances of hostile aggression or explosive outbursts resulting from an argument or perceived threat. The majority of people who commit aggressive acts are more likely to commit them against people known to them, usually family members.

Passive aggression is a mechanism whereby the individual deals with conflict and stressors by expressing anger and aggression indirectly towards others. The person presents a facade of overt compliance, which masks the underlying feelings, often of resistance, resentment and hostility. The hostility is never entirely concealed. Hostile or destructive feelings and intentions may also be expressed through passive or submissive behaviour. **Passive aggressive** characters usually direct such behaviours toward others on whom they feel dependent or to whom they feel subordinate. Manifestations of passive aggression include:

- Lack of interest
- Withdrawal
- Negativism
- Obstructionism
- Insufficiency
- Procrastination
- Sabotage
- Perfunctory behaviour
- Errors of omission
- Indifference
- Foot-dragging
- Lack of initiative
- Literalness in compliant behaviour that frustrates the outcome
- Dumb insolence.

The individual denies any hostile or negative intent, although there may be periodic angry outbursts.

Caregivers on the receiving end of such behaviour as wrist-cutting often feel they have been the victims of sadistic behaviour. Understanding the feelings, coupled with a matter-of-fact approach to the act, is often more productive than treating the behaviour as perverse. 'Time out' may be one way of breaking the pattern of the client who persists in self-defeating behaviour.

The clients to be wary of, when they express anger towards others, are:

- Those who lack perspective – they may misinterpret events.
- Those who want to hurt specific people, in unspecified ways.
- Those who have a history of episodic aggression.
- Those unable to express anger toward another person on whom they are dependent.

Further reading

Lion, J. R. (1995) Aggression. In: *Comprehensive Textbook of Psychiatry*, 6th edn (eds H. J. Kaplan and B. J. Sadock), Williams & Wilkins, Baltimore, MD.

U'Ren, R. C. (1980) *The Practice of Psychotherapy*, Grune & Stratton, New York.

ALIENATION (*see also*: Anomie, Existential therapy)

In sociology, the condition of being an outsider; a state of isolation; estrangement from other people, society or work.

In psychology, a state of estrangement between the self and the objective world or between different parts of the personality. Alienation is one of the most serious consequences of neurotic development.

In psychiatry, alienation is a blocking or dissociation of a person's feelings, causing the individual to become less effective.

Synonyms of alienation are: deflection, variance, separation, disaffection, coolness, withdrawal, estrangement, breach, rupture, weaning away, division, diverting.

The roots of the idea of alienation are found in philosophy and religion. Karl Marx adapted Hegel's idea to produce his theory of social change. For Marx, alienation centred on people's alienation from work through the capitalist system. Some philosophers believe that alienation is inevitably produced by a shallow and depersonalized society. To Sigmund Freud, alienation was self-estrangement caused by the split between the conscious and unconscious parts of the mind.

Alienation is characterized by:

- **Powerlessness** – the feeling that one's destiny is controlled by outside agencies such as luck and fate
- **Meaninglessness** – feelings of total lack of comprehension and purpose in all aspects of life

- **Normlessness** – does not share a commitment to social behaviour
- **Cultural estrangement** – removal from the established values of society
- **Social isolation** – loneliness/exclusion in social relations
- **Self-estrangement** – where the person is out of touch with her/himself.

The roots of the idea of alienation are found in philosophy and religion. Alienation was a major perspective of 19th century thought but its antecedents date from the early Christian era. St Paul taught that man, by his innately sinful nature, alienates himself from a loving father (God); this concept assumes a particular view of human nature and of a familial relationship between God and humans.

Alienation results either from separateness from others and the world or from an inability to choose and act in a relationship.

People who feel alienated frequently turn to alternative ways of life in search of meaning; possible early symptoms of schizophrenia or an identity crisis are indications of alienation. Alienation may contribute to inner-city violence and suicide.

The central task of counselling is to enable clients who feel alienated to see themselves in a relationship to the world and to choose and act in accordance with what they see. Alienation from self results from repeated, active denial and the repression of genuine feelings and impulses. As this process continues, such people lose touch with the very core of their being, as well as the ability to determine and act on what is right for them.

People who experience alienation may be seized by weird and monstrous thoughts. The whole world seems changed. It is not a state of which one is conscious. It can only be recognized from outside the experience. Whole groups of people experience alienation. But even the individual members are remote from one another. They feel that no one is close or in touch or can meaningfully share a feeling-life. To the existentialist therapist, alienation is the patient's core problem to be overcome.

Further reading

Ivey, A. E. with Sinek-Downing, L. (1980) *Counselling and Psychotherapy Skills Theory and Practice*, Prentice-Hall, Englewood Cliffs, NJ.

Jung, Carl G. (1958) *The Collected Works – the Structure and Dynamics of the Psyche* (vol. 8), Routledge & Kegan Paul, London.

Lynch, J. (1977) *The Broken Heart*, Basic Books, New York.

ALTER EGO

A nontechnical term to describe a person so close to oneself that s/he seems to be a 'second self'; a double or counterpart. In the 'self psychology' model of Heinz Kohut, the therapist becomes the alter ego of the patient, who strives to be exactly like the therapist in order to find his/her missing parts of self. Thus transference can be viewed as an attempt to reach wholeness.

ALTRUISM

In general use, altruism means devotion to the welfare of others. In philosophy, altruism describes a theory of conduct that aspires to the good of others as the ultimate end for any moral action. The use of the term 'altruism' is due to the French philosopher, and founder of sociology, Auguste Comte (1798–1857), who adopted it to describe those dispositions, tendencies and actions that have the good of others as the ultimate concern. An altruistic act is where the donor promotes the fitness of the recipient at the donor's expense. Two basic types can be identified:

- Altruism is said to occur when one individual consciously comes to the aid of another, without expecting anything in return. Several things are believed to influence this behaviour: empathy, an emotional response that results from being aware of another's emotions; group norms, society's expectation of how people 'should' behave toward others; social learning, the personal experiences one has with others; and immediate context, the actual situation at the time an altruistic act is called for (being in a good mood, considering oneself helpful and altruistic, being with others rather than being alone).
- A rational regard for the welfare of others finds expression in what are called the cardinal virtues – courage, temperance, constancy, wisdom, justice, truth, kindness and benevolence. These virtues have their being in a person; they are not something in the air or something that has merely an abstract existence. And then, just as they belong to some individual, so they flourish only as that person finds her/himself rooted in society. The higher features of human character, which make these virtues possible in people, have emerged in human history through the social effort of humankind.

Reciprocal altruism

Where one person performs a service or makes a sacrifice for another person, to achieve some sort of balance between giver and recipient. Examples would be: helping in times of danger or distress; sharing food, tools, knowledge.

Reciprocal altruism may lead to 'cheating' if one person does not reciprocate, thus creating imbalance.

Kin altruism

This is achieved mainly through identification, coupled with some innate desire or disposition. The socializing process within the family is the one most important influence. The most potent example of kin altruism is in the upholding of the incest taboo, the breaking of which is the ultimate rejection of altruism.

Examples of altruistic behaviour:

- Blood donation
- Money donating
- Rendering assistance at an accident
- Volunteering
- Challenging shop-lifters.

The bystander effect

A variation of altruism is what has come be called 'the bystander (intervention) effect', in which individuals are less likely to help when they are in the presence of others than when they are alone. In 1964 a young woman was murdered outside her home in New York. A number of people heard her screams for help but nobody came to her aid or called the police. Research showed that it was neither apathy nor indifference that prevented bystanders taking action in emergencies but that factors like the following did represent people's responses:

- the threat of physical danger;
- 'getting involved' might mean having to give evidence in court;
- not feeling prepared to handle emergencies;
- not wishing to make a fool of one's self by misinterpreting the situation;
- waiting for someone else to take charge and do something.

The bystander response seems to be governed by:

- Age
- Sex and number of bystanders
- Characteristics of the person in need
- The help given by others
- Familiarity of the situation
- Cultural norms.

Steps in the process that leads to altruism:

- Notice that something is happening
- Interpret that help is needed
- Assume personal responsibility
- Choice of a form of assistance
- Implement the assistance.

Altruism is more than a description of behaviour, it is behaviour that springs from an underlying attitude of caring. It is doubtful if counsellors would be effective if their motives were not altruistic. At the same time, altruism may become so powerful a drive that the person is swept away by it. This could prove detrimental to the person and to other people, who become the target for 'good deeds' whether they want them or not. Such an attitude puts the recipient in an inferior position, something that goes against the philosophy of counselling.

Further reading

Badcock, C. R. (1986) *The Problem of Altruism*, Basil Blackwell, Oxford.
Latané, B. and Darley, J. M. (1970) *The Unresponsive Bystander: Why doesn't he help?* Appleton-Century-Crofts, New York.

AMBIVALENCE

A term introduced by Eugen Bleuler to describe the coexistence in one person's mind of opposing feelings, especially love and hate, in a single context. It means having simultaneous, contrasting or mixed feelings about some person, object or idea. It is often accompanied by a vacillation between the opposing feelings. It is a state in which one is pulled in two opposite directions, towards two equally attractive goals. Ambivalence is closely related to conflict.

In the normal course of development (according to psychoanalytic theory) much of the aggression is neutralized and what remains becomes a desire to win, rather than to destroy the other person. As a result, in a mature person, love for the object is dominant and aggression plays a minor role. When regression occurs, there is a return to the earlier level of functioning, in which ambivalence is a characteristic mode of feeling.

Thus, one finds obsessive-compulsive patients often consciously experiencing both love and hate toward their objects. The conflict of opposing emotions may be seen in the doing–undoing patterns of behaviour and the paralysing doubt in the face of choices that are so frequently found in persons with this emotional disorder.

Ambivalence is seen in a person's relationship to the sacred. Because the sacred contains notions both of a positive, creative power and a danger that requires stringent prohibitions, the common human reaction is both fear and fascination. Only the sacred can fulfil man's deepest needs and hopes; thus, the reverence that man shows to the sacred is composed of both trust and terror.

On the one hand, the sacred is the limit of human effort both in the sense of that which meets human frailty and that which prohibits human activity; on the other hand, it is the unlimited possibility that draws mankind beyond the limiting temporal-spatial structures that are constituents of human existence.

Further reading

Bleuler, E. (1950) *Textbook of Psychiatry*, George Allen & Unwin, London.

ANALYTICAL PSYCHOLOGY (C. G. JUNG, 1875–1961) (*see also*: Myers–Briggs type indicator, Wounded healer)

Jung, a renowned Swiss psychologist and psychiatrist, was a contemporary of Freud. Jung had already formulated some of his major ideas before he came to know Freud, and he left the psychoanalytic movement in 1913. He used the term analytical psychology to distinguish his method from psychoanalysis, even though it evolved from that source. Jung saw analytical psychology as a general concept embracing both psychoanalysis and the individual psychology of Alfred Adler. His work was influenced by religion, mysticism and parapsychology.

Psychological types

Jung's theory of psychological types has three dimensions:

- **Extraversion/introversion**: Extraversion typifies people whose interests and attention are directed outward from themselves into the world of other people and objects, who feel easy in social situations and who feel free to carry out appropriate actions in the open. Introversion describes opposite tendencies. Introverts direct their attention inward upon themselves, into the realm of images, ideas, tend to withdraw from social situations, and tend to be self-reliant. The mental or psychic energy responsible for producing both extraversion and introversion Jung called the **libido**. Everyone has tendencies to both extroversion and introversion, although one tendency will predominate.
- **Sensation/intuition**: Sensation and intuition are to do with how we perceive the world. The sensing part of us understands something by assembling the details, sees the individual trees of the wood and is more concerned with the here-and-now reality. The intuitive part of us sees the overall picture, rather than the detail – the whole forest rather than the individual trees – and prefers possibilities rather than reality.
- **Thinking/feeling**: This is how we process information and make judgements. The thinking part likes logic and things that are rational. Feeling involves making judgements through values and understanding relations.

Sensation ascertains that something exists. Thinking tells us what that something is. Feeling attaches values to it and intuition sees its possibilities.

Our individual psyche contains elements of all six types but most of us prefer some functions over the others, although this will depend on circumstances. Part of the process of individuation is to understand and integrate the functions that we least prefer.

Principal differences between Jung and Freud:

- Jung attached less importance to the role of sexuality in the neuroses.
- He believed that the analysis of patient's immediate conflicts were more important than the uncovering of the conflicts of childhood.
- He defined the unconscious as including both the individual's own unconscious and that which he inherited – the 'collective unconscious'.
- His interpretation of dreams was less rigid.
- He emphasized the use of the phenomenon of transference.
- He took a psychotherapeutic approach to the individual.

Analytical psychology does not possess a detailed personality theory. In analytical psychology, the psyche comprises several autonomous yet interdependent subsystems.

Ego

- The centre of consciousness
- The experiential being of the person
- The sum total of: thoughts, ideas, feelings, memories, sensory perceptions.

Personal unconscious

- Consists of everything that has been repressed during one's development
- Contains elements easily available to consciousness
- Contains complexes – emotionally toned ideas and behavioural impulses having an archetypal core.

Collective unconscious

- Jung's term to describe those aspects of the psyche that are common to humankind as a whole.
- It is part of everyone's unconscious and is distinct from the personal unconscious, which arises from the experience of the individual.
- Material in the collective unconscious has never existed in the conscious; it has not been repressed.
- Jung's evidence of the collective unconscious is found in myths, legends, folk tales, fairy tales and dreams.

The collective unconscious contains **archetypes**, which:

- express themselves as universal primitive images, accumulated down the ages and across cultures;
- are inherited dispositions to perceive and experience typical or nearly universal situations or patterns of behaviour;
- are transmitted in symbolic forms through myths, stories and dreams.

Persona

The persona (the Latin word for person – in classical Roman theatre it was a 'mask', worn by actors to express the role being played) is:

- The archetype of adaptation
- The mask or public face we put on to meet the world, which develops from the pressures of society
- The social archetype, something that involves compromises in order to live in a community
- The mediator between the unconscious and the conscious world.

People who identify too closely with their persona are not sufficiently self-aware and therefore run the risk of pathology.

Examples of persona:

- Gender identity
- A specific stage of development
- Social status
- Job or profession.

The animus and anima (*see also* separate entry, below)

Two complimentary parts: similar to the *yin* (feminine principle) and *yang* (masculine principle) of Chinese philosophy.

Feminine principle:

- Nature, creation and life
- Earthiness and concreteness
- Receptivity and yielding
- Dark and containing
- Collective and undifferentiated
- The unconscious.

Masculine principle:

- Driving and energetic
- Creative and initiating
- Light and heat
- Penetrating
- Stimulating and dividing
- Separation and differentiation
- Restriction and discipline
- Arousing and phallic
- Aggression and enthusiasm
- Spirit and heaven.

The self

An archetypal image of one's fullest potential and the unity of the personality as a whole. The self is our god within ourselves. The process by which we achieve the goal of realization of self is **individuation.**

Individuation describes the lifetime process by which the person becomes who s/he was meant to become, whole, indivisible and distinct from other people. It means that each one of us comes to realize that we are truly individually unique, yet we are no more than a common man or woman.

Individuation does not mean an unhealthy, narcissistic preoccupation with one's own inner world; it does mean a looking inward so that one may look outward, to the world, with clearer eyes.

Individuation is not integration, which is social adaptation and ego-bound; it is bound to self, self-experience and self-realization and emotional maturity and involves:

- Facing the dark side of ones' personality, the shadow.
- Progressing away from the constraints of the persona.
- Understanding and separation from the controlling influences of the collective unconscious.

Individuation leads to more fulfilling relationships, not to isolation of self. It does not shut other people out, it gathers them in. Individuation is uniquely individual and cannot be forced on the client by the therapist.

The shadow

- The thing a person has no wish to be
- The negative, dark, primitive side of the self
- What is inferior, worthless, uncontrollable and unacceptable.

The shadow cast by the ego is what makes us fully human. If we did not know we had a shadow (in the physical sense) we would not be fully alive. So in the psychological sense: we need the awareness of the shadow side of us to bring balance to our inner world. The shadow is kept in check by the ego and the persona. The more we attempt to live in the persona, the more potent will be the shadow's strength. Analytical therapy aims to bring more of the shadow in to the light.

The shadow involves the personal unconscious, instincts, the collective unconscious and archetypes.

The shadow is itself an archetype and as such it is impossible to eradicate.

The contents of the shadow are powerful and capable of overwhelming the most well-ordered ego.

Evidence of the shadow appears in:

- **Projections**, both negative or positive, which are powerful and potentially destructive and may be directed against individuals, groups or whole societies.
- **Dreams**, as a 'shady' character, a 'tempter', in the same sex as the dreamer, but with characteristics that the dreamer would consciously not embrace.

Jungian counselling

In Jungian counselling, the client is helped to:

- Own, accept, come to terms with, and integrate, the shadow, as something personal, and not attributable to other people.
- Develop an awareness of the images and situations most likely to produce shadow projections.
- Analyse the shadow and so break its compulsive hold.

It helpful to reflect to the client that, as in the physical world we only become aware of our shadow when the sun shines, so in the psychological sense. The more we allow the sun of individuation to shine upon us, the more of the shadow will be revealed.

The four stages of counselling:

1. **Confession:** This is not meant in a 'religious sense', but where the client tells his/her story
2. **Elucidation:** Where the therapist helps the client understand the meaning of the story
3. **Education:** The therapist helps the client to move forward, and this may include teaching her/him certain aspects of theory
4. **Transformation:** The end result of the previous three stages, although this is something ongoing rather than complete.

The goals of counselling are:

- To help the individual gain insight
- To journey toward individuation
- To facilitate greater integration of both conscious and unconscious components.

Jung, like Freud, believed that disturbance in the psyche often manifests itself in physical symptoms. He used dream analysis to understand the person's current problems as well as to uncover past conflicts. He also used interpretation and free-association, as did Freud, but advocated a more active relationship between therapist and patient.

The Jungian counsellor may:

- Teach
- Suggest
- Cajole
- Give advice
- Reflect feelings
- Give support
- Interpret dreams.

Summary

In Jungian counselling, which deals extensively with dreams and fantasies, a dialogue is set up between the conscious mind and the contents of the unconscious. Clients are made aware of both the personal and collective (archetypal) meanings inherent in their symptoms and difficulties.

Under favourable conditions they may enter into the individuation process – a lengthy series of psychological transformations culminating in the integration of opposite tendencies and functions and the achievement of personal wholeness.

The Jungian counsellor does not work to a preset plan, and the therapeutic process hinges on creating an atmosphere of trust. The approach is more passive than active, and receptive rather than directive.

Speaking of the use of chair or couch, Ann Casement points out that in her experience client regression may be aided by using the couch; however, the chair is the more usual.

Casement sums up Jungian counselling thus: 'Above all, therapy is an inner journey and the goal of this quest is the individual's true identity, which may have been hidden for a whole lifetime under a "false self".' It is in fact in the patient's symptom or wound that his/her true identity lies hidden (*see* Wounded healer).

Further reading

A word on Jung: his writings are not easy to read. There are a number of books that simplify his work, but possibly the easiest introduction is in Samuels, A., Shorter, B. and Plant, F. (1986) *A Critical Dictionary of Jungian Analysis*, Routledge & Kegan Paul, London.

Casement, A. (1996) Psychodynamic therapy: the Jungian approach. In: *Handbook of Individual Therapy*, (ed. W. Dryden), Sage Publications, London.

Von Franz, K. L. (1974) *Shadow and Evil in Fairy Tales*, Spring Publications, Jung, Zurich.

Weiner, M. F. and Mohl, P.C. (1995) Theories of personality and psychopathology: other psychodynamic schools. In: *Comprehensive Textbook of Psychiatry*, 6th edn, (eds H. J. Kaplan and B. J. Sadock), Williams & Wilkins, Baltimore, MD.

Wickes, F. G. (1988) *The Inner World of Man*, Sigo Press, Boston, MA.

ANGER

Sources of anger

- **Blocked goal**: 'I want something, and someone or some event prevents my getting it'
- **Breaking of personal expectations**: If we are not treated in the way we expect or when other people behave as we do not expect them to, anger is often the outcome.
- **As a defence**: When self-esteem is threatened, we may use anger to prevent our self-esteem being attacked. Anger may be a response to criticism.

The characteristics of anger

- Anger is a primary human emotion and needs to be experienced in order to be known.
- It has a distinct quality of its own, different from that of every other emotion; and no one could, by mere description, make it intelligible to someone who had never been angry.
- It is not derived from other emotions, it does not even presuppose experience of other emotions to give it being.

- Anger is not in itself malevolent: it is simply a protection or defence against harm or hurt and may be directed against things as well as against persons.
- It is a type of resentment, and operates instinctively and, therefore, without due regard to consequences.
- As instinctive resentment, anger is neither to be praised nor to be blamed but is to be accepted as a part of the human constitution necessary to the welfare of the individual and therefore ultimately to the good of the community.
- People are often the cause of anger and often the anger is directed at objects that had no share in arousing it; for this reason it has to be brought under the control of reason.
- The three principal reasons for anger are injustice, hurt and frustration. We become angry with others for our hurts. We blame others for our own problems, yet often anger is not directed at the appropriate source.
- When anger is voluntarily nursed it tends to magnify the offence that caused it: vanity and offended dignity come in to intensify and transform the emotion; a rankling grudge naturally exaggerates the original cause.
- Anger readily associates itself with a desire to injure others or to inflict pain on them and so is easily changed into hatred, retaliation, revenge or, keener still, vindictiveness. Vindictiveness is exclusively aimed at people and in its nature is diametrically opposed to the sympathetic and humane sentiments, the tender emotions, that bind people together; it is the very antithesis of love and, instead of attracting and cementing, alienates and repels. The feeling of 'an eye for an eye, and a tooth for a tooth' is often the feeling generated.
- When we harbour ill-will and feed our wrath, refusing to be pacified or to enter into mediation, waiting for the favourable opportunity, we are bordering on revenge. Revenge is in its very nature inequitable and relentless, bloodthirsty and cruel, satisfied with nothing less than 'the head of John the Baptist on a plate'. When revenge pursues its object spitefully with unremitting persistence and finds zest in every petty infliction of evil on the other person, it is vindictiveness.
- Anger is the first emotion we experience and often the last one we learn to manage effectively. For many people, a lifetime is spent in denying, suppressing, displacing or avoiding anger – this troublesome momentary insanity.

Recognizing anger

- Anger is a feeling of extreme displeasure, hostility, indignation or exasperation towards someone or something. These feelings are associated with the fight response and accompanied by internal and external indicators. Such feelings are often accompanied by verbal or physical attack.
- Anger is often associated with mistrust and suspicion, destruction of some valued object, and habitual overindulgence in alcohol.
- Very generally, anger is a fairly strong emotional reaction that accompanies a variety of situations such as being physically restrained, being interfered with, having one's possessions removed, being attacked or threatened, etc.

- Anger is often identified by a collection of physical reactions, including particular facial grimaces and body positions characteristic of action in the autonomic nervous system, particularly the sympathetic division. In many species anger produces overt (or implicit) attack. As with many emotions, anger is extremely difficult to define objectively.
- Angry people strive for superiority by strenuously applying all their powers. This may be a compensation for deep-seated inferiority. Any threat to their feeling of superiority will result in an angry response. Angry people generally find it difficult to tolerate equality.
- Inappropriate anger may be an indication of the feeling of lack of power, self-worth and recognition. An angry child is striving for recognition.
- A view of anger is that it is resentment, an experience that accompanies a demand or expectations that has not been made explicit. Anger seems to be a response to something outside of us, yet it is most often an **intra**personal event (within us): we **make** ourselves angry.
- Because anger is so unpleasant and we are so adept at turning it away from ourselves on to others, we usually attempt to locate the source of our anger outside ourselves with statements such as 'You make me angry', 'Your habits irritate me', 'You bother me'. We make ourselves angry and there is no one else who can honestly be blamed. Suffering the anger often seems to be the only alternative.
- Anger turned inward is experienced as **guilt**; guilt produces feelings of depression, incompetence, helplessness and, ultimately, self-destruction.
- **Displaced anger**: Anger may be directed at someone or something else that is convenient. We are angry at the traffic jam but we snap at an innocent spouse. The children consistently refuse to meet our expectations but we kick the dog. Such **displacement** of angry feeling serves to ventilate but not to resolve. The anger cycle still lacks closure. Expression of anger can lead to violence. Violence turned inward produces depression. Displacement is ultimately ineffective and can damage innocent third parties. Repeated failure to close the anger cycle can produce a hostile, cynical, negative view of reality.

Dealing with your own anger

- Recognize it
- Own it
- Gauge your response – anger is never all-or-nothing
- Diagnose the threat
- Share the perceived threat
- Letting go of the anger means: cancelling the feelings; cleaning the slate; you have forgiven.

Dealing with someone else's anger

- Define if you are the legitimate target
- Acknowledge the other's feelings – don't sidestep them – and acknowledge your own feelings

- Request feedback and give it
- Remain relaxed
- Recognize the difference between angry feelings and aggressive behaviour
- Don't invade the other person's personal space
- Encourage 'self-control' and suggest coping strategies: counting numbers, deep breathing, checking the number of joins in the wallpaper
- Above all: Listen – strategies should never be at the expense of the client's feelings
- Renegotiate the relationship.

Anger in counselling

Working with angry clients is very wearing, even when the counsellor is understanding, nonjudgemental and empathic. While counsellors may recognize that the anger is not directed at them and that it arises from within the client, it is still demanding.

Helping clients to evaluate the level of their anger may be one way of introducing them to how to exercising control. A related point is to ascertain if the anger is justified or not.

There are different views about the benefit of encouraging clients to express their anger. Some writers hold the view that not to express it is repressing it and that it is cathartic to express it; others that expressing anger only consolidates it and makes the person even more angry. The client who is encouraged to recognize angry feelings and explore them within the safety of the counselling relationship is being helped to develop useful coping skills.

Further reading

Pareek, U. (1983) Preventing and resolving conflict. In: *1983 Annual for Facilitators, Trainers, and Consultants*, University Associates, San Diego, CA.

ANIMA (THE FEELING FUNCTION) AND *ANIMUS* (THE THINKING FUNCTION)

In analytical psychology, the **anima** is the feminine principle latent in every male; the internalized female shadow image a man carries. The young man has a maternal anima, which relates to the heart rather than the head – the source of receptiveness and sensitivity.

To be fully integrated and make contact with their own unconscious (expressed in imaginative symbols) men must recognize and accept the feminine qualities within them.

Anima is one of the archetypes of the collective unconscious, which derives, in part, from the man's relationships with his mother and other significant females and from his father's attitudes towards women. In addition, he is influenced by the deeper racial archetypal images of woman.

The **animus** is the latent masculine principle that is present in every female. The anima is represented, in dreams, by a single figure; the animus by several or many figures. The animus can be negative and destructive but very positive when integrated. To be fully integrated and make contact with their own unconscious (often expressed in concrete symbols) women must recognize and accept the masculine qualities within them.

Some anima/animus archetypes that may appear in a person's dreams or imagination are: good mother, harlot, spiritual guide, temptress, vampire, virgin, witch, hero/heroine, man of authority, scholar, dark or eclipsed sun, giants, satyrs, devils. Such archetypes are also represented in mythical figures: Aphrodite, Athena, Helen of Troy, the Virgin Mary, Beatrice in Dante's *Inferno*, Hermes, Apollo, Hercules, Romeo.

Analytical psychologists propose that a person's relationship with the opposite sex, and choice of mate, are influenced by the anima and animus, whose influence may be negative or positive. The internalized images of the anima and animus are influenced by cultural patterns and expectations of what someone of the opposite sex should be.

Part of the process of analytical therapy is helping clients recognize and integrate the repressed anima or animus.

Jung, in *Psychological Types*, page 468, says this of anima (although he speaks of anima, the same applies to the animus):

> As to the character of the anima, my experience confirms the rule that it is, by and large, complementary to the character of the persona [the outward appearance of the person]. The anima usually contains all those common human qualities which the conscious attitude lacks. The tyrant tormented by bad dreams, gloomy forebodings, and inner fears is a typical figure. Outwardly ruthless, harsh, and unapproachable, he jumps inwardly at every shadow, is at the mercy of every mood, as though he were the feeblest and most impressionable of men. Thus his anima contains all those fallible human qualities his persona lacks. If the person is intellectual, the anima will quite certainly be sentimental.

One of the tasks of therapy is to achieve balance. No man is so entirely masculine that he has nothing feminine in him. No woman is so entirely feminine that she has nothing masculine in her. People who ignore their anima or animus function only on half their psyche. Ignored, the anima or animus will rule without the person's knowledge. When people understand the true nature of their anima or animus, they can express their feelings more appropriately.

Further reading

As for Analytical psychology.

ANOMIE (*see also*: Alienation, Suicide)

In the social sciences, anomie is a state of 'normlessness' created by the breakdown of commonly agreed standards of behaviour and morality; the term often refers to situations where the social order appears to have collapsed. The concept, similar to alienation, is the state of mind of a person who has no sense of continuity or obligation, where all social bonds and standards of behaviour are absent, unclear or in conflict with each other.

Anomie implies confusion, disorganization and a collective insecurity and may occur in conditions such as following some catastrophe like earthquake, war or in large-scale immigration that involves loss of social values. In such conditions, people may put self-interest before the interests of the wider community, for example by stealing and looting and general breakdown of law and order.

The concept was developed by French sociologist Émile Durkheim. Durkheim used 'anomie' to describe societies in transition during industrialization. It is also used by Durkheim in his book *Suicide* (1897) where, talking of types of suicide, the translators say, 'The third sort of suicide results from man's activity's lacking regulation and his consequent sufferings. By virtue of its origin we shall assign this last variety the name of anomic suicide.' This was a pattern of behaviour that was brought about by anomic social conditions of low cohesion and an overall weak sense of attachment of members to their community.

Thus anomie is a state where norms or standards of behaviour are unclear, absent or in conflict with each other. Where a social system is in a state of anomie, common values and common meanings are no longer understood or accepted and new values and meanings have not developed. Anomie is characterized by a sense of futility, lack of purpose and emotional emptiness and despair. Striving is considered useless, because there is no acceptable definition of what is desirable.

The term was adapted by US sociologist Robert Merton to explain deviance and crime in the USA as a result of the disparity between high goals and limited opportunities. Delinquency, crime and suicide are often quoted as being reactions to anomie.

While not everybody has been subjected to catastrophe, many people do seem to grow up feeling confused, disorganized and insecure, with no feeling of community. In the discussion on alienation, one of the points was that the person can experience self-alienation; in a similar way, I would suggest that people can feel a deep sense of anomie, even though there has not been any major catastrophe.

Durkheim linked anomie with suicide, but anomie also links with depression, for the risk of suicide is high in people who suffer from depression. One of the characteristics of depression is that the sufferer feels cut off and isolated; indeed, many of the symptoms of depression are allied to those discussed above related to anomie.

Depressed people often experience lack of social support, mainly because they cut themselves off but also because people often find themselves unable to relate to these sufferers; yet social contact and social support is vitally important to help maintain some degree of self-worth and purpose.

Social support is the provision of meaningful, appropriate and protective feedback from the social environment that enables all of us to cope with social stressors – bereavement, financial loss, interpersonal difficulties and the daily hassles of life. One of the important factors in major depressive illness is the lack of a confidant. While many confidants are not counsellors, there can be little doubt that counsellors are confidants of the highest order and, for a person who feels confused, disorganized and insecure, the counselling relationship may prove the lifeline for them to hang on to so that they can start of climb out of their particular pit of depression.

A characteristic of anomie is powerlessness, which is a psychological state in which the person feels deprived of power, control or influence over crucial events. Powerless may show in the inability to change social or political events, as well as personal circumstances.

The Alcoholics Anonymous philosophy and programme for recovery, set out in the 12 Steps to Recovery, states that the alcoholic must recognize his/her 'powerlessness over alcohol' and seek help from a 'higher power' in regaining control of his/her life.

People who migrate from one country to another often get caught up in this feeling of powerlessness, which is akin to alienation and anomie.

Further reading

Merton, R. K. (1968) *Social Theory and Social Structure*, Free Press, New York.

ANOREXIA NERVOSA (*see also*: Bulimia nervosa)

Anorexia nervosa, named about 100 years ago and existing in many countries of the world, is refusal to eat or an abnormality in eating pattern, not a loss of appetite. It occurs most commonly among adolescents but is also observed in older people.

Anorexia nervosa is commonly referred to as a 'female' problem but, although there are more female than males who suffer from it, it is not an exclusively female condition. Statistics from the Eating Disorders Association (EDA) show that around 5–10% of sufferers from this condition are males. The greater emphasis on anorexia as a female illness is possibly due to the fact that the number of men with eating disorders is not known to doctors, self-help groups and other agencies. A second reason could be ignorance or disbelief among some professionals that anorexia could be a male problem. The fact that men do suffer from what traditionally has been considered to be a female problem might indicate that the psychology of men and women is closer than we generally accept (EDA). Men who are anorexic seem more achievement-orientated and show more sexual anxiety, being athletic and placing a high value on being physically fit.

The onset of anorexia is usually between the ages of 15 and 25. The starvation regime may be pursued relentlessly, resulting in a range of health complications – involving all systems of the body – and often death. It is estimated that fatalities from anorexia run at around 13–20% per annum (EDA).

Osteoporosis, thin bones, is a major problem. One of the first complications of anorexia nervosa is a loss of fertility.

The EDA says, 'The illnesses [anorexia nervosa and bulimia nervosa] generally develop between the ages of 15 and 25 years, although they can occur at any age, even as young as 7 or 8 years. Bulimia is rare before the age of 13. Eating disorders can persist throughout life and people may fluctuate between anorexia and bulimia.'

Physical symptoms
- Malnutrition, resulting in extreme body weight loss and emaciation
- Drastic fasting, which may be interspersed with eating sprees, usually at night, after which vomiting is induced
- Cessation of menstruation and, in males, a drop in the levels of testosterone.

Emotional symptoms
- These range from a neurotic preoccupation with reducing weight to full-blown schizophrenic delusions, with an overwhelming fear of getting fat
- There is often a history of relationship difficulties and fear of meeting strangers
- Irritability and depression
- Extreme weight loss over prolonged periods results in impaired reasoning and logic.

Possible causes
- **Biological**: There is no known proven cause. A disorder of the hypothalamus in the brain is a theory. A function of the hypothalamus is the control of metabolism and intestinal activity.
- **Psychological**: The major psychological factor appears to be an inability to face womanhood, with all its changes and responsibilities. Not being able to face responsibilities may be a factor in males who suffer from anorexia. However, there is sufficient anecdotal evidence to suggest a disparity between the outward appearance and the inner body-image that the person never seems able to resolve. Stress and how it is perceived and dealt with is an important trigger for anorexia.

Characteristics of the anorexic's immediate family
- Dysfunctional communication: closed, indirect, veiled, defensive
- Parental over-protectiveness
- The anorexic person is over-concerned for and feels responsible for the wellbeing of the others
- Intense relationships with excessive togetherness and sharing
- Rigidity with resistance to change
- Anorexics often feel that if they get well their parent's marriage will fail
- There is often a family history of eating or weight problems
- Anorexics are discouraged from developing personal autonomy and their own unique identity
- Recent research shows that anorexia is more common where family members

have also suffered from it. Identical twins are more likely to have anorexia than nonidentical twins.

Characteristics of the anorexic
Anorexics have a self-esteem characterized by:
- A pathological need for approval
- Stern disapproval of themselves
- A compulsion to strive for perfection
- Considering themselves unworthy
- Fixed, almost delusional, beliefs about being unattractive
- Overestimation of their body width
- Starving themselves to achieve a still smaller body-image
- Appearing unconcerned at their undernourished state
- Self-imposed social isolation, involving eating and drinking.

Sexual relationships
- Extreme weight loss leads to reduced sexual interest and activity
- Anorexics fear taking on the sexual roles observed in their parents
- They feel that they cannot love another when they do not like themselves
- The slightly masculine look that many adopt warns males off
- The break-up of a relationship may be the result of curing anorexia
- Pregnancy is unlikely because of the extreme and prolonged weight loss.

Achievement
- Academic success is highly valued by anorexics and their families
- An extreme fear of failure pushes them on to constantly seek approval
- Anything less than a 100% pass is a failure; praise for achievement is almost impossible to accept
- Their weight is the only thing over which they feel they have control
- They must control the intake of food and every function of the body, mind and emotions.

Dieting and exercise
- Obsessive rigidity and unbalanced diets characterize the anorexic's goal of ever lower weight and slimmer figure
- So much has calorie-counting taken over that they no longer control the diet; it controls them
- Many engage in a killing schedule of exercises and sport
- There is a close parallel between anorexics and long-distance runners. Both are likely to be from fairly affluent backgrounds, introverted, with depressive tendencies and high achievers, with an obsessive interest in keeping up physical appearances.

Physical treatment

Hospital admission may be necessary to restore correct dietary intake and a balanced blood chemistry. Cooperation is vital, so undue pressure must be avoided. Weight gain alone is not necessarily a cure.

Emotional treatment

- Anorexia can be totally reversed, without lasting effects
- Anorexics must want to be cured; and this means putting on weight
- Treatment started within 1 year of the onset of anorexia has a far greater chance of quick recovery.

Treatment may be:

- Personal counselling concentrating on: adolescent conflict, interpersonal problems and personal experiences of stress and failure
- Behaviour modification
- Trance therapy and hypnotherapy
- Group therapy
- Family counselling – one particular approach includes taking meals with the family to identify the mealtime dynamics
- Self-help groups, such as Anorexic Aid, offer help in much the same way as Alcoholics Anonymous.

Recovery

Recovery rests with:

- Acceptance that there is a problem
- A sincere desire to get better
- A willingness to accept change of lifestyle and circumstances
- Exploration, understanding of the underlying issues and feelings
- Setting and striving to achieve realistic targets of attitudes to food and weight.

Early-warnings

- Becoming isolated in their room
- Missing meals or making excuses of having eaten
- Eating alone in room
- Slimming and diet magazines
- Scales in the bathroom
- Reluctance to eat in public
- Small amounts of food eaten
- Bread, potatoes and carbohydrates avoided
- Bulky, loose sweaters that disguise shape
- Food thrown away
- Ultra health-conscious
- Failure to put on weight

- Preoccupation with calorie-counting
- Excessive amounts of exercise
- Poor sleep, restlessness, hyperactivity
- Cessation of menstruation.

Prevention

- Establish effective communication
- Don't insist on increased intake
- Encourage outside help
- Don't pressure for weight gain
- Encourage self-action and responsibility
- Parents may need counselling themselves
- Remove pressure to succeed
- Encourage independence.

What happens afterwards?

- Anorexics may lapse when under pressure
- Anorexia is like alcoholism in that the person always must be on guard; joining a group of ex-anorexics may provide the support necessary to cope with living.
- Forming relationships with the opposite sex is a huge hurdle for many ex-anorexics.

Further reading

Boskind-Lodahl, M. (1981) Cinderella's stepsisters: a feminist perspective on anorexia nervosa and bulimia. In: *Women and Mental Health*, (eds E. Howell and M. Bayes), Basic Books, New York.

Eating Disorders Association Newsletter, July 1997. First Floor, Wensum House, 103 Prince of Wales Road, Norwich, NR1 1DW.

Garfinkel, P. E. (1995) Eating disorders. In: *Comprehensive Textbook of Psychiatry*, 6th edn, (eds H. J. Kaplan and B. J. Sadock), Williams & Wilkins, Baltimore, MD.

MacLeod, S. (1981) *The Art of Starvation: Anorexia Observed*, Virago, London.

Sutton, J (1999) *Healing the Hurt Within*, How To Books, Oxford.

Vaughan, E. (1979) Counselling anorexia. *Marriage Guidance Journal*, September.

ANXIETY (*see also*: Behaviour therapy, Cognitive therapy, Stress management)

Anxiety is a distressing feeling of uneasiness, apprehension or dread. The fear may be rational, based on an actual event, such as when someone has palpitations and therefore fears a heart attack or irrational, based on an anticipated event that may or may not take place, such as failing an exam that has not yet taken place. A certain amount of unrealistic and irrational anxiety is part of most people's experience; it seems to be an unavoidable part of human personality and usually takes the form of 'What if...'

Existentialists describe anxiety as a **fear of nonbeing,** which may be fear of death but may also include a sense of meaninglessness and a powerful sense of guilt.

When anxiety is chronic and not traceable to any specific cause or when it interferes with normal activity, the sufferer is in need of expert help. Anxious people are in suspense, waiting for something, they know not what. A main source of anxiety is the fear of being separated from other persons who are felt to provide security.

Anxiety is a symptom in many mental disorders, including schizophrenia, obsessive-compulsive disorders, post-traumatic stress disorders and so on, but in phobias and other anxiety disorders proper, anxiety is the primary and frequently the only symptom.

The suspense of anxious people is characterized by:

- Watchful alertness
- Over-reaction to noise or other stimuli
- Helplessness in the face of danger, whether actual or imagined
- Mood that alternates between hope and despair.

Clients often have difficulty accurately describing the feelings of anxiety. Generally the fear is directed at some undefined threat to their physical or psychological wellbeing. They use such terms as tense, panicky, terrified, jittery, wound up as tight as a clock spring.

Anxiety operates on three planes: body, mind and emotions (physiological, cognitive and psychological). The more severe the anxiety, the more these three planes will become distorted. Very often it is what is happening within the body that takes the person to the doctor.

Bodily symptoms of anxiety may include:

- Tightness in the chest and throat
- Sinking feelings in the abdomen
- Dizziness or light feelings in the head
- Skin pallor
- Sweating or, less often, flushed
- Increase in pulse rate
- Undue increase in heart rate produced by mild exertion
- Muscle tension
- Loss of sexual interest
- Twitching of the limbs.

Cognitive symptoms of anxiety may include:

- Decreased concentration
- Acute alertness
- Confusion

- Fears of losing control or of going crazy
- Everything is a catastrophe.

Behavioural symptoms of anxiety may include:

- Withdrawal
- Irritability
- Hyperventilation
- Immobility.

Perceptual symptoms of anxiety may include:

- Depersonalization (feelings of unreality or strangeness)
- Derealization (a feeling of detachment from reality)
- Hyperaesthesia (abnormally high sensitivity of the skin to heat, cold and touch).

Trait anxiety is a lifelong pattern of anxiety and is a feature of a person's temperament.

State anxiety relates to specific events – the anxiety abates when the situation is resolved.

Free-floating anxiety is a condition of persistently anxious mood in which the cause of the condition is unknown and a variety of thoughts and events can trigger the anxiety.

Anxiety frequently manifests itself as the result of opposing or conflicting wishes, desires, beliefs, life events or strain resulting from conflict between roles. An example of this would be in the newly married woman who experiences a conflict between being a wife and also maintaining a career or the new husband who has a conflict between the roles of husband and member of the rugby team.

The more desperate the feeling of helplessness and indecision, and the more difficult the decision between two opposing forces, the more severe the anxiety. Defence mechanisms do not abolish anxiety. They try to bind or keep it from awareness.

Theories of anxiety

Learning theory proposes that anxiety is both a response to learned cues and a driver or motivator of behaviour. Most learning theorists maintain that anxiety is derived from reaction to pain. Anxiety can thus be reduced by removing or avoiding the source or sources of the situations that have produced pain. Avoidance may become firmly established and lead to constricted or bizarre behaviour such as phobias.

Psychoanalytic theory: Psychoanalysis has three theories of anxiety:

- Repressed libido
- Repressed birth trauma
- A two-part theory – primary and signal:
  - **Primary anxiety** is perceived as a threat to the ego's equilibrium, which

would result in the ego being dissolved. Primary anxiety would result from a failure of the defences. Evidence of this is said to appear in nightmares.

- **Signal anxiety** serves to warn the ego of a potential threat. The function of signal anxiety is to ensure that primary anxiety is never experienced.

Jung did not deal comprehensively with the topic of anxiety and did not develop defence mechanisms to deal with it as Freud did. Jung's view of anxiety is:

- It does not always have a sexual foundation
- It may serve a useful function by drawing attention to something that is undesirable
- It may represent avoiding becoming consciously aware of suffering.

Cognitive behaviour theory postulates that anxiety is a response to perceived danger but that information has become distorted, leading to anxiety. In addition, sufferers perceive their resources as not adequate to cope with the perceived threat. One of the major threats is feeling a loss of control. Other significant threats are to self-esteem and excessive worry over how one is perceived by other people.

Some of the more florid mental disturbances, such as obsessive compulsion and panic attacks, which are characterized by a high degree of anxiety, are generally outside the scope of the average counsellor and should be referred for specialist psychiatric help.

However, it is appropriate here to draw attention to some of the more common anxiety conditions.

Panic attacks

The panic attack – a sudden, overpowering feeling of terror – is experienced by many people at some time in their lives. A panic attack typically lasts for several minutes and is one of the most distressing conditions that a person can experience. Many of the symptoms of acute anxiety are present in panic attacks. Symptoms of panic accompany certain medical conditions of thyroid, the inner ear, epilepsy, intoxication and substance withdrawal, and cardiac conditions, such as irregular heart rhythms or chest pains. People who suffer from post-traumatic stress disorder may experience panic when they are faced with situations (even on the television) that resemble the original traumatic event. It is vital to receive a thorough medical check-up and not take for granted that the symptoms are purely 'all in the mind'.

Phobias

A phobia is an extreme, irrational fear of a specific object or situation and the anxiety may vary in severity from unease to terror. A phobic disorder interferes with a person's ability to work, to socialize and go about a daily routine. A phobia that interferes with daily living can create extreme disability and the person needs medical treatment.

Phobias occur when fear produced by an original threatening situation is transferred to other similar situations, with the original fear often repressed or forgotten. All forms of phobias are disabling conditions and even mild forms can create problems of daily living. Phobias are associated with high incidence of distressing thoughts about suicide.

Fear of blood and injections may mean that the person avoids essential and urgent medical or dental care. Phobias generally respond to antidepressants and to behavioural forms of therapy. For example, cognitive restructuring therapy seeks to replace faulty thinking patterns with more constructive ones. The client says, 'I'm a complete failure.' The therapist then challenges this by getting the client to state in which areas of life s/he is successful. It is highly doubtful that someone is hopeless in everything.

Simple (specific) phobias

A simple phobia is of a specific object, animal or situation. Irrational fears of snakes, heights, enclosed places and darkness are examples. Receiving an injection or seeing blood may also assume phobic proportions.

Some common phobias are fear of:

- Mice or small animals (zoophobia)
- Spiders (arachnophobia)
- Height (acrophobia)
- Open spaces (agoraphobia)
- Enclosed spaces (claustrophobia).

In fact, almost anything can be the focus of a phobia. One medical textbook lists 33 specific situations. Phobias are quite resistant to change without treatment, although desensitization therapy has proved effective. In desensitization, the person is exposed, under relaxed conditions, to a series of stimuli that gradually come closer to the anxiety-provoking one, until the stimuli no longer produce anxiety.

Agoraphobia: People with agoraphobia avoid open spaces, crowds and travelling. Agoraphobia, which literally means 'fear of the marketplace' and indicates fear of being away from the safety of home, commonly occurs with panic disorder. Where escape is impossible the feelings of anxiety are endured with marked distress.

Social phobia: Social phobia is the irrational fear and avoidance of being in a situation in which a person's activities could be watched. Fear of public speaking or of eating in public are the most common complaints of socially phobic individuals. Social phobia sufferers are invariably loners and lonely and often fail to develop intimate relationships. Social phobias are often associated with alcohol abuse. In children, the fear may take the form of tantrums, screaming, freezing, clinging or refusing to move away from a familiar person. Young children may be excessively timid, refuse to make contact with other children in play, are often seen on the fringes of a group and prefer to stay close to familiar adult figures.

Identifying useful approaches to helping clients control anxiety

Helping people cope with anxiety through counselling is likely to make use of support and encouragement and stress-management techniques of a behavioural nature. Within an empathic relationship the client can feel able to explore the reasons for the anxiety and learn to control it. And one of the most potent, and often the easiest to learn, is deep relaxation. Learning to relax the body, then the mind, is often the first step in being able to control feelings of anxiety.

Behaviour therapy, which makes heavy demands on the person, is probably the most successful treatment but that road is not an easy one for the client to tread.

Exposure is where the person is exposed to various carefully graded situations that build up confidence. When the person copes with the anxiety of one situation, the next one is tackled, until the most feared situation is tackled.

Homework and tasks are set. The behaviour therapist will constantly challenge what the client says, so bringing various parts of the client's statement or behaviour into focus. Generalizations are turned into specifics and excuses and rationalizations are disputed. At the same time, the counsellor offers a great deal of support as the client handles what seem terrifying situations and attempts to stop doing something. The support offered by the counsellor could be staying with the client while carrying out the feared task, giving practical advice like 'Take some deep breaths', 'Focus on becoming relaxed', 'Imagine yourself doing it'. The aim of support is to give clients the skills to use when they are on their own.

One important aspect of any counselling – and this applies with particular emphasis in teaching relaxation – is that the counsellor must be a believer. If you yourself are not relaxed, if you are tense and anxious, this will show and any attempt to help the client relax will be seen as technique and not of great value. The client might well say, 'Practise what you preach.'

Further reading

Sutton, J. (1998) *Thriving on Stress: How to Manage Pressures and Transform Your Life*, How To Books, Oxford. *This book has a comprehensive chapter on 'Learning the art of relaxation'.*

Trower, P., Casey, A. and Dryden, W. (1988) *Cognitive-Behavioural Counselling in Action*, Sage Publications, London.

APATHY

Apathy, in Stoic philosophy, is the condition of being totally free from the *pathe*, which roughly are the emotions and passions, notably pain, fear, desire and pleasure.

In a psychological sense, apathy is a state where all emotion and feeling appears to be absent. It presents as coldness, and can be mistaken for indifference, but should be understood as a psychological protection against feeling, rather than as lack of feeling. As such it is a powerful psychological defence mechanism. Rather than there being no feeling within the state conveyed, there is likely to be a fear of too much feeling.

Apathy is often seen as a state of despair, an apparent indifference to possible future events or to the consequences of intended action, a sense that nothing matters, that nothing has meaning. It can lead to attempted suicide, whether intended or appearing as accidental, such as taking an overdose of drugs without caring about the result – 'It doesn't matter whether I wake up or not'.

Apathy is to be distinguished from despair, which is the loss of hope, and boredom, which is caused by blocking of expressive activity, whether for external or neurotic reasons. Apathy can be a life-saving defence in extreme situations – as it were, taking the mind out of gear – thus despair and the exhaustion following unjustified hopefulness can be avoided.

Apathy shows itself in a lack of motivation, absence of energy, inability to carry out necessary tasks and, generally, incapacity to function in an effective way. It frequently accompanies grief, is present in the worst stages of depression and is a characteristic of some chronic illnesses such as multiple sclerosis. The adjective **apathetic** is used to describe an aspect of temperament.

APPREHENSION

The word comes from **prehension**, the act of seizing or of grasping. Hence, by extension, apprehension is the mental, conscious 'grasping' of the nature of something. Apprehension is generally treated as a rather primitive, immediate act and distinguished from comprehension, which involves more in the way of reflection and interpretation.

By further extension, it is a vague fear or anxiousness about possible future occurrences. Here the notion is that one is 'seized' or 'enveloped' by a feeling of unease.

Apprehension span is the maximum number of objects or events that can be perceived in a single short exposure.

Apprehensiveness is a relatively mild sense of anxiety about an anticipated event, an uneasiness about something in the future.

Apprehension is often a distressing feature experienced by phobia sufferers. In such extreme apprehension, avoidance, anxious anticipation or distress about the feared situation often interferes with the person's daily routine and relationships. For example, a person who has a fear of flying might, for many months before a flight, suffer violent apprehension.

APPROVAL

Approval, a form of social control, relates in some ways to Carl Rogers's 'unconditional positive regard', but only in the positive sense of approval. Some people will seem to go to extraordinary lengths to gain approval from significant others.

Conditional approval creates a relationship characterized by dependency and possessiveness. Unconditional approval empowers.

The consequences of social approval:

- Recognition which confirms our identity
- Approval legitimates our existence; increases our status and affords recognition
- Approval is acceptance of what we have to offer, security of not being rejected because of inadequacy in our abilities, opinions or of what we think, feel or do
- A bond is established between approver and approved
- Approval means that we feel able to exercise a degree of control over our environment.

Approval is a crucial element in the development of a child's self-worth and self-esteem. One of the definitions of approval is, 'to pronounce to be good, to commend'. Two other words linked with approval are acceptance and affirmation.

Approval, by parents or other significant figures in the life of the child (and this includes siblings, particularly older ones, who exercise a profound influence on younger ones), is a form of control. People who as children have struggled to get approval often seem in adult life to go to extraordinary lengths to gain approval, almost as if the deficit could never be made up; as if they go through life constantly seeking someone to make up the deficiency.

The opposite of approval is rejection and one of the principal ways people use rejection is by always passing judgement, always putting the other person in the wrong. Children are particularly prone to all that goes with judgement and when this is reinforced with conditional love – 'I will love you if...' then the child has little solid ground on which to build a healthy self-esteem.

Defining what approval is:

- Recognition that confirms our unique identity and does not try to make us to be someone we are not
- Acceptance of what we have to offer, without any preconceived ideas of what we should be or ought to be
- Feeling secure
- Not being rejected because our abilities, opinions and what we think, feel or do do not match up with other people's expectations of us
- Affirmation of our uniqueness and our existence
- Something that increases our status and affords recognition
- A bond established between approver and approved
- Permission to take control of our lives and responsibility for our actions.

Any child reared in a relationship deprived of approval is likely to develop into an approval-hungry adult, for ever seeking and never finding approval; never able to trust other people's unconditional regard for them. This approval hunger may create difficulties in intimate relationships, where the person experiences a conflicting 'pull–push.' One part longs for intimacy, the other part rejects it because whatever the other person offers never satisfies and the one seeking approval pulls away.

A further characteristic of some approval-hungry people is their high drive to achieve, although seeking approval is not the only motivator for high-achievement. One of the ways a child can get approval is by pleasing the significant person (or people). Achieving high grades at school is one way the child **might** gain this approval, yet this does not always work, for whatever the child does or achieves often leaves the significant person unimpressed. Indeed, what the child most wants and needs is not recognition for achievement but unconditional acceptance for just being who s/he is, without any strings attached.

Counselling approval-hungry clients means recognizing their need. Within a relationship in which acceptance, empathy, genuineness, warmth and unconditional positive regard are lived out, the client can then feel accepted and achieve insight, then start to work toward change.

ASSERTIVENESS

Assertiveness is a clear, appropriate response to another person that is neither passive nor aggressive. It is communication in which self-respect and respect for the other person are demonstrated. Assertiveness is where one person's rights are not demanded at the expense of the rights of the other person.

Many interpersonal difficulties and difficult behaviours arise because of people's inability to express positive or negative feelings clearly.

Assertiveness training helps people to:

- Gain and maintain respect for themselves and others
- Keep lines of communication open
- Achieve goals
- Recognize and develop inner resources.

Assertiveness training uses:

- Behavioural rehearsal
- Cognitive exercises
- Modelling
- Relaxation training
- Role play
- Simulation of feared situations
- Social skills training
- Structured exercises
- Systematic desensitization.

Assertive training seeks to help people become aware of:

- **Aggressive behaviour**: Aggressive behaviour is a **fight** response. The goal is conflict.
- **Avoidance behaviour**: Avoidance behaviour is a **flight** response. The goal is to ignore conflict
- **Assertive behaviour**: The goal is direct, honest, open and appropriate verbal and nonverbal behaviour
- **Accommodating behaviour**: The goal is harmony at all costs.

Aggressive behaviour

- Competitive, motivated by results, power and control
- Offensive, because it violates the rights of other people
- Subtle, because it is often indirect
- Invasive of other people's psychological and/or physical space
- Other people are usually left feeling resentful
- Aggressive people tend to get their own way by manipulating other people's feelings
- Aggressive people spend a lot of time trying to repair hurt feelings
- Aggression often shows when they stand up for their own rights
- Aggressive people are often pushy and critical.

Avoidance behaviour

- We don't tackle intrusions on our rights, even when we feel they have been violated
- We evade and avoid any honest confrontation by emotionally running away
- We back down in the face of opposition
- Other people easily invade our space
- We may be more concerned with the image we present than being our own self.

Assertive behaviour

- It means standing up for what we believe to be our personal rights
- It means not attacking other people's rights
- It means expressing our thoughts, feelings and beliefs in direct, honest and appropriate ways
- It should nurture our esteem and the esteem of other people
- It should lead to better respect and understanding in relationships
- It should avoid the feeling of being constantly put down and frustrated.

Accommodating behaviour

- We often express our thoughts and feelings indirectly
- What we say can be disregarded because it is indirect
- We hope other people will be nice to us
- We tend to shuffle problems around instead of dealing with them

- We let problems build up, then – wow!
- Constant avoiding may mean that aggressive behaviour is just around the corner.

Obstacles to assertiveness

- Lack of awareness that we have the option of responding in an assertive manner
- Anxiety about expressing ourselves, even when we know what we want to say, in a way that expresses how we feel
- Negative self-talk inhibits self-assertion by what we tell ourselves
- **Verbal poverty**: A difficulty in finding the right words at the right time leads to self consciousness and hesitancy
- **Behavioural poverty**: A nonassertive, nonverbal manner hinders all assertive expression.

Assertive speech

Many of us fail to be assertive because of the negative labels we carry or because we feel constrained by conforming to stereotypes.

An important technique in assertiveness training is getting people to make positive self-statements instead of negative ones. Participants are encouraged to create assertive hierarchies, starting with an encounter that would be relatively easy to handle and progressing to the most difficult, then to rehearse them in the group. One of the aims in assertive behaviour is to change from being indirect to being direct and from using generalizations to being specific.

Examples:

Generalized: You don't love me.
Specific: When you come home from work, I would like you to kiss me.
Generalized: You never think about anyone but yourself.
Specific: If you know you're going to be late 'phone me. I worry about you.
Generalized: You're a male chauvinist pig.
Specific: I want you to listen to me while I'm stating my opinions, even if you don't agree.
Generalized: All you ever do is work.
Specific: I would like us to go to the beach next week.
Generalized: You never talk to me any more.
Specific: I'd like us to sit down together – with no TV – and talk for a few minutes each night.

Assertiveness is a dignified approach to human interaction that preserves the esteem of all parties while at the same time accomplishing a particular objective.

Further reading

Byrum, B. (1988) The nuts and bolts of assertive training. In: *1988 Annual: Developing Human Resources*, University Associates, San Diego, CA.

Cawood, D. (1988) *Assertiveness for Managers*, International Self-Counsel Press, Canada.
Dickson, A. (1982) *A Woman In Your Own Right*, Quartet Books, London.
Fensterheim, H. and Baer, J. (1980) *Don't Say 'Yes' When You Want To Say 'No'*, Futura, New York.
Lindenfield, G. (1989) *Super Confidence: The woman's guide to getting what you want out of life*, Thorsons, Wellingborough.
Sharpe, R. (1989) *Assert Yourself*, Cogan Page, London.
Stubbs, D. R. (1986) *Assertiveness at work*, Pan Books, London.
Sutton, J. (1998) *Thriving on Stress: How to manage pressures and transform your life.* How To Books, Oxford.

ATONEMENT (*see also*: Forgiveness)

Atonement is the process by which a person removes obstacles to being reconciled to God. It is a recurring theme in the history of religion and theology. Rituals of expiation (making amends) and satisfaction appear in most religions, as the means by which the religious person re-establishes or strengthens his/her relation to the Holy.

Atonement is attached to sacrifice, both of which often connect ritual cleanness with moral purity and religious acceptability.

Various theories of the meaning of the atonement of Christ have arisen: satisfaction for the sins of the world; redemption from the devil or from the wrath of God; a saving example of true, suffering love; the prime illustration of divine mercy; a divine victory over the forces of evil.

Other views of atonement

In Christian orthodoxy there is no remission of sin without 'the shedding of [Christ's] blood' (Heb. 9:26). In Judaism vicarious atonement has little importance. For a traditional Jew, atonement is expiation for his/her own sin in order to attain God's forgiveness. The Jew may achieve this in various ways including repentance, payment for a wrong action, good works, suffering and prayer. Repentance and changed conduct are usually stressed as the most important aspects of atonement. The 10 'days of awe', culminating in the Day of Atonement (Yom Kippur), are centred on repentance.

Taoism and Brahminism also make use of the word but it is not used in the same context as in Christianity, where forgiveness is at the root of the doctrine.

Atonement and counselling

In counselling it is possible that client and counsellor may be caught up in the whole business of the client expecting the counsellor to grant expiation of what the client considers to be 'sins'. Atonement is linked to confession and counsellors have to be aware of not entering into the role of the priest, who grants absolution. Confession is not the same as the client working through his/her feelings about whatever is causing concern.

Confession is also linked with guilt and there may be a desire on the part of the client to have that guilt taken away by confession, in order to avoid some imagined punishment. There is also a close association between confession and disclosure. The main difference is in the quality of the way in which the disclosure is made. A disclosure in which the client shows indications of being prepared to explore it and work through it is therapeutic; the client who discloses as if by doing so the guilt will be taken away is probably entering into confession and hoping for forgiveness. When the client then goes on to make promises of reparation, it is possible that the client has moved into expiation. In all of this there is likely to be a strong sense of transference, where the counsellor is seen in the role of the priest or, indeed, as God.

ATTACHMENT (*see also*: Bonding)

Attachment is a theory developed by Bowlby at the Tavistock Clinic, London. Attachment describes the relationship between an infant and its mother or mother-substitute (caregiver.) This early relationship is the foundation for all later relationships.

Attachment behaviour is evident from 6 months onwards when the infant discriminates sharply between the caregiver and other people. Early attachment influences adult behaviour, particularly during illness, in distress or when afraid. The primary attachment figure represents security. For attachment to be satisfactory, one principal caregiver needs to be identified.

Separation anxiety is anxiety at (the prospect of) being separated from someone believed to be necessary for one's survival. Separation anxiety may be objective, as in infancy or in adult invalids, or neurotic, when the presence of another person is used as a defence against some other form of anxiety. In both cases two factors are involved: dread of some unspecified danger, either from the outside or from mounting internal tension, and dread of losing the object believed capable of giving protection or offering relief.

Common manifestations are unrealistic worries about harmful things happening to the attachment figure (parent) while away, persistent fears of being lost, kidnapped or even killed if separated, social withdrawal and behaviour frequently showing protest, despair and detachment. When the caregiver returns, the child's behaviour may demonstrate avoidance, resistance and over-attachment. It is as if trust, broken by the separation, has to be re-established.

Homesickness is a lesser form of separation-anxiety disorder, although the feelings can be very powerful. It is thought that home-sickness and separation anxiety show in children who are unsure of their place within the family. The 'sickness' and anxiety are a desire to return home to make certain that the family has not disintegrated.

The work of bonding and attachment has had significant practical implications for childbirth methods and how children's hospitals are run. The understanding of grief, bereavement, mourning, loss and loneliness have all been enhanced by attachment theory.

Reactive attachment disorder

In mental health, this is a condition that is found in infancy or early childhood. It begins before the child is 5 years old, characterized by markedly disturbed pattern of social relations.

In the **inhibited** type of reactive attachment disorder, failure to respond predominates and responses are wary, avoidant or highly ambivalent and contradictory.

In the **disinhibited** type, indiscriminate sociability is characteristic, such as excessive familiarity with relative strangers or lack of selectivity in choice of attachment figures.

The majority of children who develop this disorder (either type) are from a setting in which care has been grossly pathogenic. Either the caregivers have continually disregarded the child's basic physical and emotional needs or repeated changes of primary caregiver have prevented the formation of stable attachments

In general, people who have experienced inadequate attachment are prone to experience difficulty establishing and maintaining intimate relationships as adults. Clients who have experienced 'insecure attachment' may present difficulties in counselling because their adult behaviour is a reflection of their attachment relationship. In other words, they are likely to display an **anxious-avoidance** or **anxious-ambivalent** relationship towards the counsellor.

Discussion of therapeutic techniques is outside the remit of this book; however, clients who do experience relationship difficulties of the types mentioned may respond to working with their inner child. Symbolically and through imagery, but also by using other body techniques and group work, they may find that they are able to reclaim their inner child, which feels trapped in deprivation. As in all deprivation work, the realistic aim is long- rather than short-term.

Further reading

Bowlby, J. (1969) *Attachment. Attachment and Loss*, vol. 1, Penguin, Harmondsworth.
Bowlby, J. (1973) *Separation. Attachment and Loss*, vol. 2, Penguin, Harmondsworth.
Bowlby, J. (1975) Attachment theory, separation anxiety and mourning. In: *American Handbook of Psychiatry*, vol. 6, (eds D. A. Hamburg and H. Hamburg), Basic Books, New York.
Bowlby, J. (1980) *Loss. Attachment and Loss*, vol. 3, Penguin, Harmondsworth.
Parkes, C. M. and Stevenson-Hinde, J. (eds) (1982) *The Place of Attachment in Human Behaviour*, Tavistock, London.
Zisook, S. (1995) Death, dying, and bereavement. In: *Comprehensive Textbook of Psychiatry*, 6th edn, (eds H. J. Kaplan and B. J. Sadock), Williams & Wilkins, Baltimore, MD.

ATTENDING

Attending refers to the ways in which we physically and psychologically demonstrate our availability to other people.

Attending means concentrating and involves:

- **Our body**
  - The way we sit: distance, angle of chairs
  - A naturally open posture
  - Demonstrating involvement and interest, by moving forward from time to time
  - Maintaining comfortable eye contact
  - Being aware of one's own facial expressions and body language
  - Being relaxed, without slouching
- **Our mind**
  - Thoughts uncluttered and focused
  - Open attitude
- **Our feelings**
  - To give full attention we must be secure, calm and confident. A disturbed spirit conflicts with attending. At some of the more dramatic moments of life, just having another person with us helps to prevent psychological collapse. Our face shows where our heart is.

When (though not necessarily during) counselling, we should ask ourselves:

- Was I effectively present and in emotional contact with this client?
- Did I give my whole attention or was part of it diverted?
- Did my nonverbal behaviour reinforce my internal attitudes?
- In what ways was I distracted from giving my full attention to this client?
- What can I do to handle these distractions?

ATTITUDE

An attitude is a pattern of more or less stable mental views, opinions or interests, established by experience over a period of time. Attitudes are likes and dislikes, affinities or aversion to objects, people, groups, situations and ideas. Because attitudes cannot be directly observed, they must be inferred from an individual's responses – positive or negative – toward an 'attitude object'. Thus, for example, one's negative attitude toward a certain ethnic group may be discovered through perceived responses to the group. Attitudes express feelings towards an object (affective component); influence what we do (behavioural component); influence our thoughts (cognitive component).

Many attitudes we take over lock stock and barrel, with their attached values, from other people. In the light of experience, many of our acquired attitudes become modified and tend to persist or be influential throughout life. Attitudes are determined by: the times we live in; the place we live in; the family; the education system. Attitudes do change, however. Among the most important variables in attitude change are the following: personality characteristics, the credibility of the source of different opinions or of information countering the held attitudes, group membership and personal behaviour that is inconsistent with the individual's attitudes.

While we can ask if judgements are true or false, correct or incorrect, accurate or inaccurate, we cannot ask that question of attitudes. We can only ask: Are those attitudes and the way we act logically consistent with one another, with our associated beliefs and actions? Attitudes extend into all aspects of our life. They provide us with frames of reference and mental sets that affect the way we judge and react toward the people and objects in our environment.

Not all attitudes have clear-cut and obvious behavioural consequences, although there is little doubt but that attitudes do influence our behaviour. We have a positive attitude towards certain things or people and we say we 'like' them and choose to associate with them; we feel negatively towards other things and people and so avoid them. We do not approve of certain policies and speak out against them or write to the newspapers.

Example: Mary does not approve of animals being used in circuses. If she allows that belief to influence her behaviour overtly, she may take action by organizing a campaign. Her behaviour is less obvious when she chooses not to attend circuses where animals perform. An attitude involves elements of approval or disapproval, like or dislike.

Attitudes cannot be divorced from counselling. Negative attitudes about people with mental illness may be part of a cluster of beliefs and values where sympathy is lacking for people who need help in any way.

Coupled with this the person holding such an attitude may distrust others who are different in any way from themselves. Such people are often rigid and not open to attitude change. How other people feel about counsellors might be a factor influencing a person's decision to enter counselling, particularly if the person with the negative attitude is someone powerful and important in the prospective client's life.

Even after entering counselling, the client may have to battle against negative attitudes and may not want to disclose that s/he is in counselling. This could seriously impede counselling, for it is then covered with a cloak of secrecy and fear of being discovered.

AUTHORITARIANISM (*see also*: Prejudice)

Authoritarianism, the favouring of blind submission to authority, is characteristic of certain individuals, of common belief systems shared by such individuals and, by extension, of elitist, antidemocratic governments based on such shared beliefs.

Totalitarianism is an extreme instance of authoritarianism, a political system designed to achieve complete control over people's inner and outer lives. This is, however, an extremely difficult if not impossible goal, which has rarely been achieved for very long. Even the most authoritarian societies such as Nazi Germany and the Soviet Union under Stalin failed to control most aspects of people's private lives or to stifle dissent and subversion. Since true democracy is quite rare, most governments are to some degree authoritarian and, therefore, problematic for those they govern.

Authoritarian personality

As an individual trait, authoritarianism was first systematically explored in research presented by Theodor Adorno and others in *The Authoritarian Personality* (1950). The study began as an investigation of antisemitism in the USA but led to the discovery of numerous correlations between antisemitism and other attitudes associated with stereotyped behaviour – although later work separated the attitudes toward authority from specific political views.

Adorno's hypothesis was that the origins of authoritarianism lay in childhood socialization when the parents – and especially the father – adopted a very harsh disciplinary approach towards their children. All transgressions, however minor, were severely punished.

Drawing on psychoanalytic theory, Adorno and his colleagues argued that such an upbringing would lead children to repress their aggressive feelings towards their parents but that these feelings would later be displaced on to alternative and 'safer' targets. At the same time, children would develop an anxious and deferential attitude towards authority figures, since these symbolized the parents. Further, such people would be more susceptible than others to fascist or racist ideas, especially if these emanated from prestigious authority sources.

The F-scale became widely used as a measure of prejudice. Consistent with the original hypothesis, high scores did reflect the respondents' childhood as a time of strict obedience to parental authority and they often manifested openly prejudiced views.

An example of authoritarianism in action was in an observation that, when solving mental puzzles, high authoritarians were less able or willing to change their problem-solving strategy once they had embarked on it. Low authoritarians solving the same puzzles were more adaptable. Prejudice was also reliably correlated with authoritarianism, a relationship that is still observable in more recent studies.

Characteristics of the authoritarian personality

- Respect (reverence) for power
- Uncritical submission to the authority of dominant groups
- Aggression toward subordinates
- Lack of self-insight
- Superstitiousness
- Contempt for weakness
- Closed-mindedness
- Intolerance of ambiguity
- Prejudice
- Need for strong external support systems
- Dependence on conventional values
- Sensitivity to interpersonal status
- Dominance
- Rigidity of thinking
- Cynicism

- Tendency to use projection
- Curiosity about sexual behaviour.
- Excessive concern with what is right or wrong.

Adorno's work on the authoritarian personality is best known for his **ethno-centrism scale**: a measure of the tendency to hold prejudiced attitudes toward all groups different from one's own.

High scores on this scale show a general tendency to see the world in terms of noble **in-groups** that must be supported and offensive **out-groups** that must be avoided, or rejected and attacked when they become threatening. In other words, people who are prejudiced against one group tend to be prejudiced against many groups with whom they do not agree, a hatred of Jews, for example, being associated with a hatred of Catholics.

Although controversial and the object of considerable criticism, Adorno's work is sociologically important because it seeks a connection between personality and how social systems are organized, in what it says about both how social conditions foster authoritarian personalities and how authoritarianism affects social life. The significance of more recent research findings is that it may be more appropriate to regard authoritarianism as a reaction to changes within society than as a consequence of a particular individual socialization experience.

Some authoritarian statements:

- Obedience and respect for authority are the most important values children should learn
- Young people sometimes get rebellious ideas, but as they grow up they ought to get over them and settle down´
- Businessmen and manufacturers are more important to society than artists and academics
- When a person has problem or worry, it is best for him not to think about it, but to keep busy with more cheerful things.

Authoritarianism and counselling

People with authoritarian personalities, because they see everything in 'either–or' terms and have great difficulty in tolerating ambiguity and uncertainty, do not cope well with disability. This inability to tolerate ambiguity could present a stumbling block in counselling if the person ever decides to risk this sort of relationship, for to engage in counselling would mean acknowledging that s/he is not the perfect person.

The authoritarian personality may be usefully contrasted with the opposite – open-mindedness. Open-mindedness describes how flexible and responsive we are in examining new evidence about our belief systems. It partly describes our ability to receive, evaluate and act on information from the outside on its own merits. It also relates to how we are able to free ourselves from internal pressures that would obscure or interfere with incoming information.

The open mind is relatively unencumbered by irrelevant internal or external pressures. Examples of irrelevant **internal pressures** would be unrelated habits, beliefs and perceptual cues, irrational ego motives, power needs, the need for self-praise and the need to allay anxiety. Examples of **external pressures** would be reliance on reward or punishment from external authority, such as parents, peers and other authority figures, reference groups, social and institutional norms and cultural norms. Open-minded people are more capable of discriminating between a message and its source and are less influenced by high status.

Counselling operates more in the realm of the possible, of what might be in the areas of feelings, rather than in what is factual and predetermined. It operates in the grey areas, rather than in black or white terms. Thus clients with authoritarian personalities are likely to experience difficulty in counselling, because any challenge to their preconceived ideas about themselves in relation to society could prove too threatening.

Further reading

Ruch, F. L. and Zimbardo, P. G. (1971) *Psychology of Life*, 8th edn, Scott, Foresman & Co., London.

Stubbins, J. (1977) Stress and disability. In: *Social and Psychosocial Aspects of Disability*, (ed. J. Stubbins), University Press, Baltimore, MD.

B

BEFRIENDING

A term used to describe the relationship between two people, one of whom is in need of help or care. Generally it refers to the relationship in which the befriender is not working within a professional relationship. People act as befrienders to ex-offenders or those on probation.

Counselling is not generally regarded as befriending, although befrienders may use counselling skills. For example, offering a client tea or coffee is generally associated with befriending rather than with counselling. However, even that may sometimes be part of the counselling relationship; for example, if a client is severely distressed, a cup of tea might help her/him to adjust before leaving.

Further reading

Befriending and Tracking Schemes: One to one work with children and young people in trouble or at risk (1986), National Children's Bureau, London.

BEHAVIOUR THERAPY (*see also*: Cognitive therapy, Rational emotive counselling)

This is the applied use of behavioural psychology to bring about changes in behaviour, the central principle of which is that all behaviour is learned and maintained as a result of the person's interaction with the environment. Rewarded behaviour will tend to increase in frequency, while behaviour not rewarded, or punished, will tend to decline. Behaviour therapy is a major form of therapy practised by clinical psychologists

In the treatment of phobias, behaviour therapy seeks to modify and eliminate the maladaptive response that the person uses when confronted with a phobic object or situation. Although avoiding the feared situation, responding in this way reinforces the belief that whatever it is cannot be coped with in any other way and, unless challenged, will frequently persist.

Behaviour therapy interrupts this self-reinforcing pattern of avoidance behaviour by presenting the feared situation in a controlled manner so that it eventually ceases to produce anxiety.

The behavioural therapist is concerned with what can be observed – with what is said and done – not with experiences in the past that may have caused it nor with any postulated intrapsychic conflict – what must be inferred – unconscious motives and processes and symbolic meanings.

Although the focus is on changing behaviour, the relationship is important, not in itself, but to support the client through the difficult times of change and discomfort. In distinction from, for example, person-centred counselling, the behavioural counsellor is directive and active; but a relationship without warmth and empathy will be less likely to succeed than one where these are evident.

The roots of behaviour therapy:

- Wolpe's work on experimental neuroses in cats and the clinical work which developed from that research; the most important technique is **systematic desensitization**
- Skinner's contribution of operant conditioning
- Social learning theory.

Systematic desensitization

Desensitization is the reduction or the extinction of sensitivity to something specific that causes a problem, e.g. allergies. The same behavioural principle is applied in the treatment of anxiety and phobic behaviours by counter-conditioning.

The technique:
The client is exposed, under relaxed conditions, to a series of stimuli that increasingly approximate to the anxiety-provoking one, until the stimuli no longer produce anxiety.

The stages:

1. Relaxation training, which the client is urged to practise twice daily.
2. The construction of a hierarchy of anxiety-provoking stimuli, ranked according to the level of anxiety they evoke from least to greatest.
3. Presentation of scenes during relaxation, starting with the least anxiety-provoking and working in a step-by-step progression through the hierarchy.

Some people find it very difficult to relax, to carry out visualization or to produce hierarchies that accurately reflect their problem.

Variations on the theme
Some therapists use a tape recorder for home desensitization. Some work in groups, while others carry out the process in real situations.

The main features of behaviour therapy:

- It concentrates on behaviour rather than on the underlying causes of the behaviour
- Behaviour is learned and may be unlearned
- Behaviour is susceptible to change through psychological principles, especially learning methods
- Clearly defined treatment goals are set
- Classical personality theories are rejected
- The therapist adapts methods to suit the client's needs

- The focus is on the 'here and now'
- There is a belief in obtaining research support for the methods used.

The stages of behaviour therapy:

1. A detailed analysis of the client's problems and behavioural factors.
2. Specific treatment goals.
3. Treatment plan using appropriate behavioural techniques.
4. Implementation of the plan, including full discussion with the client.
5. Evaluation.

Therapeutic techniques used:

- **Exposure**: The aim is to extinguish the anxiety, and its associated behaviour, by systematic exposure to the feared situation. This may include modelling – observing someone carrying out the desired behaviour before attempting it.
- **Contingency management**: This means reinforcing positive behaviour but **not** reinforcing negative behaviour. Rewards in the form of tokens are an example.
- **Cognitive behaviour therapy**: Concerned with thoughts and beliefs (*see also* Cognitive therapy).
- **Assertive and social skills training** (*see also* Assertiveness).
- **Self-control**: Behaviour therapy aims to teach people methods of self-control and self-help, to enable them to cope with situations they find difficult. For example, exposure to the feared situation – rehearse the difficult situation and arrange for positive reinforcement when the task has been done.
- **Role play**: Clients may be asked either to replay an actual situation or to imagine one.
- **Guided imagery**: Clients symbolically create or recreate a problematic life situation.
- **Physiological recording.**
- **Self-monitoring**: For example, recording daily calorie intake.
- **Behavioural observation**: Assessment of problem behaviour is more accurate when based on actual observation.
- **Psychological tests and questionnaires**: Behaviour therapists will not generally use tests based on psychodynamic theories. They will use tests that yield the information necessary for a functional analysis or for the development of an intervention strategy.
- **Stress management**: Particularly the use of progressive relaxation.

Behaviour therapy does not ignore the importance of the therapeutic relationship. The client who is in a trusting, supportive relationship will generally work conscientiously through the therapy.

Behaviour therapy is tailor-made to suit individual client's needs. Much of behaviour therapy is short-term – 25–50 sessions. Behaviour therapy is applicable over a full range of problems, for example:

- Anxiety disorders
- Cardiovascular disease
- Childhood disorders
- Depression
- Hypertension
- Interpersonal/marital problems
- Obesity
- Sexual disorders
- Speech difficulties
- Stress management
- Substance abuse
- Tension headaches.

While behaviour therapy is generally considered to be unsuitable in psychotic conditions, it is used in the treatment of people with chronic mental illnesses.

Further reading

Agras, W. S. (1995) Behaviour therapy. In: *Comprehensive Textbook of Psychiatry*, 6th edn, (eds H. J. Kaplan and B. J. Sadock), Williams & Wilkins, Baltimore, MD.
Goldstein, A. and Foa, E. (eds) (1980) *Handbook of Behavioural Interventions: A clinical guide*. John Wiley, New York.
O'Sullivan, G. (1996) Behaviour therapy. In: *Handbook of Individual Therapy*, (ed. W. Dryden), Sage Publications, London.
Trower, P., Casey, A. and Dryden, W. (1988) *Cognitive Behavioural Counselling in Action*, Sage Publications, London.

BIBLIOTHERAPY

The Greek meaning is 'book-healing', the aim of which is to create a psychological interplay between the reader and the material, which may be literature or audio-visual.

The therapeutic relationship so formed may then be used to promote insight, personal awareness and growth and psychological healing. It achieves this by overcoming moralization, active involvement and fostering competence.

Bibliotherapy is often used as an adjunct to other forms of therapy. It may be conducted in a one-to-one relationship or in a group. It is used with client groups of all ages.

People can be helped through a story, play, music, songs, to explore any major themes of life that are creating difficulties for them. They may create their own story.

Bibliotherapy can be helpful with people who have emotional or behavioural problems, where the objective is insight or behavioural change. The empathic or imaginative nature of the material would aim to produce catharsis. It may also be used with people who, apart from passing through a crisis, are not psychiatrically disturbed. The goal is self-actualization and growth through using both imaginative and directive, factual material. The rationale is that people are encouraged to deal with their own threatening emotions and behaviours by displacing them on to the story. Identification takes place with the characters, which promotes change (Gunzburg and Stewart, 1994, p. 130–1).

The power of the story

John Gunzburg says this of story telling:

> Martin Buber believed in the potent healing effect of story on the aching soul. He understood story to be a medium within which various existential themes of life – belonging, yearning for companionship, loss of homeland, courage in adversity, the blossoming of love – could be woven and transmitted from one group to another and from one generation to the next. The telling of story could convey the struggle to understand the mystery of life, the dilemmas encountered and the myriad ways that such challenges could be met. Above all, story could convey both the uniqueness of individual experiencing and the connectedness of all living things.

Further reading

Gunzburg, J. C. (1997) *Healing Through Meeting: Martin Buber's approach to psychotherapy*, Jessica Kingsley, London.
Gunzburg, J. C. and Stewart, W. (1994) *The Grief Counselling Casebook*, Stanley Thornes, Cheltenham (Now out of print but available on line at www.compassion-in-business.co.uk/fellowship/willstew.htm).
Howie, M. (1983) Bibliotherapy in social work. *British Journal of Social Work*, **13**, 287–319.

BLAME

The *Oxford English Dictionary* gives the following definitions of 'blame':

1. The action of censuring; expression of disapprobation; imputation of demerit on account of a fault or blemish; reproof; censure; reprehension
2. Responsibility for anything wrong, culpability
3. To find fault with; to censure (an action, a person for his action): the opposite of 'to praise'.

Thus blame is making a judgement of responsibility against someone. We can innocently blame people for how we feel – 'He makes me feel….' This is blaming the other person. Such a reaction would be better put: 'I feel … at what you have done'. 'I was startled when you jumped out on me', not 'You made me jump'.

The rationale is that nobody can make us feel anything. The fact that we **do** feel something has to be acknowledged but we also have to acknowledge the feeling as ours. Saying 'You made me…' is, in a way, blaming the other person and is guaranteed to arouse a 'fight' response.

Neither he, she, nor they ever make me feel this way.
Rather, it's the thoughts I choose that do the trick.
That makes me feel sick.

Dr Gerald Kushel

Blame is anger directed outwards at someone else. But blame may also be self-blame, whereby the person internalizes the feelings of responsibility. Self-blame is detected in such sentences as, 'I should have known better', 'Idiot!', 'I never get things right'. Such discounting language has a detrimental effect on self-esteem.

Blame is linked with guilt (*see* Guilt and shame) and guilt may be anger turned inwards. Many people spend much of their life accepting blame for what goes wrong and feeling guilty over what is clearly not their fault. This is closely allied to the Martyr attitude (*see* entry, below), where the person is weighed down by constantly feeling hard done by. Self-blame is also to do with making oneself socially acceptable. Very often such feelings border on the delusional and are not amenable to logic or reason.

Feelings of self-blame rarely respond to direct confrontation. Changing the word to 'responsibility' may be more effective.

The person who, when driving a car, kills a child who runs out in front of it would quite naturally feel guilt, blame and responsibility. Such feelings and thoughts as, 'If only I'd been driving more carefully', or 'more slowly', 'If only I'd been more observant' would be perfectly normal. They are all the sorts of self-questions that take place during grief.

The person who kills innocently is just as likely to be caught up in grief as the parents of the dead child. If such thoughts persist beyond what is normal for grieving and if, say, 10 years later, the person is still blaming her/himself for the death, then here is a case of chronic self-blame bordering on delusion.

Many people are caught up in chronic self-blame when they are the innocent victims of, for example, crimes committed by parents, the relatives of someone who has committed suicide or the survivors of some horrific accident.

It is extremely common in Western cultures for clients to view their struggles in a 'linear' or 'blaming' context. The philosophy underlying this context is that there is one underlying reason to a problem for which there is one sole cure. The problem is being created by something or someone and if only the specific cause can be uncovered, a solution will become readily apparent. Clients often regard counsellors as the experts who will discover the cause of their pain and provide the cure. One of our initial tasks, then, as counsellors is to indicate that we are facilitators rather than experts. Our job is to divert our clients' energies from searching for an underlying treatable cause towards trying to view the context of the problem from a different angle.

Gunzburg and Stewart, 1994

Even though clients may blame, attributing blame gets them nowhere. So changing the word to something like 'responsibility' may have the effect of changing something in their minds. Otherwise, if they keep on attributing blame, it may be necessary to change tack and work with the underlying anger.

Counselling is not about establishing innocence of guilt or of attributing blame, punishment or judgement. One of the tasks might be to help clients accept responsibility for their own actions and their consequences. All the while the client engages in 'passing the buck' movement forward will be stopped. Owning the problem is a crucial step in the client's progress towards healing.

Helping clients take responsibility for their thoughts, feelings and behaviours means that they stop blaming. Attributing motives, claiming that 'the devil made me do it' are sneaky, dishonest attempts to be irresponsible.

But as counselling is a two-way street, it is sometimes easy for counsellors to 'blame' clients when counselling does not go well. When counsellors own **their** thoughts and feelings, both counsellors and clients know where they are and can respond more authentically. We are all entitled to have thoughts and feelings. Being aware of them and the differences between them is one way to improve communication.

Further reading
Gunzburg, J. C. and Stewart, W. (1994) *The Grief Counselling Casebook*, Stanley Thornes, Cheltenham, pp. 57–58) (Now out of print but available on line at www.compassion-in-business.co.uk/fellowship/willstew.htm).

BODY-IMAGE (*see also*: Femininity/masculinity)

Body-image is:

- The perception, conscious or unconscious, of one's own body
- The picture we have of our own body, which we form in our mind
- The way in which the body appears to ourselves
- Our mind's eye picture of ourselves.

Body-image is the root of identity, self-esteem and self-worth, the basis from which we function.

Somewhere a part of the brain is responsible for being able to bring to our conscious awareness the total representation of our body.

The development of body-image
- The awareness of body-image begins to develop at the toddler stage
- Awareness is influenced by environment, by our attitudes, feelings, memories and experiences toward our bodies
- We register our own thoughts and opinions about our body as well the impressions we receive from other people of how they perceive us
- Self-esteem is influenced by a positive or a negative regard for our bodies (or parts thereof)
- Sociocultural environment influences body-image. People reared in one culture may experience devastating 'body-image shock' when they move into a culture where different emphases are ascribed to various body areas. For

example, in a society where strength and fitness are idealized, failing strength may produce unwelcome and unacceptable changes in our perception of ourselves because we no longer fit the ideal. These changes may be so resented that they produce emotional disturbances. That is when counselling may help.

Boundaries of body-image

- A clear awareness of our body-image separates us from other people or from our environment.
- The most obvious boundaries are height, size (slim/fat) and general appearance – how we appear to ourselves and how we think we appear to others. Part of this is the regard we have for our bodies.
- Clothes become a part of the body-image. The question could be asked: Do we use clothing to reinforce or deny certain body-image attitudes? If we wear clothes as a boundary to reinforce or deny something about ourselves, do we feel exposed and vulnerable when we remove our clothes?

Age-related changes in body-image

From babyhood to old age our body-image has to make various adjustments to what is happening in our bodies. At one end of the age-scale we are developing quite rapidly in height, weight and strength; at the other end we again experience quite marked changes. In between these two age differences there is adolescence. Its accompanying sexual maturity brings dramatic changes; some of them are welcomed, others are so disturbing as to appear doubtful blessings. Adulthood brings with it different changes as new occupational and family responsibilities are taken on board.

Motherhood brings visible body changes to which women (and their partners) have to adapt. Pregnant women incorporate the fetus into their own body-image unless there are strong feelings against the pregnancy, in which case emotional disturbance or even psychosis is likely. Women who cannot conceive are likely to experience great body-image conflict.

In any pregnancy where the foetus was successfully incorporated into the mother's body-image, the woman has to make a dramatic adjustment if an abortion takes place. She has to adjust to the missing part of her. If the pregnancy was an unwanted one or if the foetus was not incorporated into the body-image, the woman still has an adjustment to make but in the first case, I would suggest, the adjustment is greater and may take longer.

Perhaps at no other time in her life is the woman subjected to such dramatic body-image changes as during the menopause. It is at this stage of her life when it seems that she is neither young nor is she yet old. Are the women who 'grow old gracefully' those who have successfully incorporated these changes into their body-image?

Men also experience body changes to which the body-image must adjust. Sexual difficulties, especially, create problems for many men, for most men's perception of masculinity centres around virility and potency. Thus, men who are infertile not only suffer emotionally, their whole concept of body is affected. Impotence and other sexual problems that interfere with a satisfactory sex life have a strong influence on body-image.

Although men do not have a menopause, in their middle years of life body changes do occur. The man who once prided himself on his strength and endurance, now has to adjust to – if not exactly being a weakling – a body that does get tired much more quickly. Old age brings with it other changes – some welcome (like increased leisure and an increase in wisdom), others not so welcome. A man who has been the 'breadwinner' now has to adjust to being a 'pensioner' and all that means in reduced activity.

All the changes that have been mentioned – for both sexes – may seem to require nothing more or less than an emotional adjustment. But each change has very clear implications for body-image. No change can take place to or within our bodies without having some emotional impact. And, as was pointed out earlier, body-image is influenced by emotions of all kinds.

Other changes in body-image

Other changes considered normal occur during deep relaxation, when we often feel very heavy; that the body, or parts of it, becomes very large or very small. We may become aware of sensations within the body. We may hear strange sounds and see strange 'lights' and patterns. We may experience feelings almost of hallucination. We may have the sensation of floating in space and that we have become detached from our body.

All of these normal distortions may occur to any of us as we hover in the hypnagogic state between being awake and dropping into sleep. When in sleep, strange distortions may be experienced and many of these experiences are alarming and emotionally disturbing. The border between what is normal and what is pathological is a very narrow one and these feelings, experienced in dreams or near dreams, are what many mentally ill people – particularly psychotic patients – experience, only more so. The intensity and the frequency and the degree to which these experiences then start to influence a person's life is one of the characteristic differences between normal and pathological.

Pathological distortions of body-image

Distortion of body-image occurs in personality and psychiatric disorders and can be very frightening for the patient. One female schizophrenic patient, on looking in a mirror, said to a nurse, 'Where am I? I can't see myself'. The same patient said, 'Is it me talking or is it you?' Another schizophrenic patient felt that his body was 'spread over the world'. One central theme runs through many of the accounts of bizarre body-image fantasies: violation of the body boundaries – the boundaries are either obliterated or become so fluid and vague as to be worthless either as a defence against all perceived threats or as a reference point to be used in distinguishing self from the other world.

A physical example of distorted body-image is a person who has undergone an amputation of limb and still feels pain in the 'phantom' limb – the illusory feeling that the missing part of the body is still there. Although these phenomena are usually associated with limb amputations, the experience can occur when any part of the body is removed.

Distortion also occurs in eating disorders, where sufferers are convinced that they is fatter than they really are. Transsexuals who undergo surgery have to adjust to a new body-image. Acutely disturbed psychiatric patients sometimes say that they feel as if they had become diffused, like a sea mist before a wind.

When people have been the victims of crippling disease or accident or exposed to mutilating surgery, resulting in a change in the body, the body-image is forced to undergo a similar change if it is to be congruent with the 'new body'. This adjustment is often painful and emotionally disturbing.

Disturbance of body-image occurs in people who suffer from obesity. In psychiatric terms they may suffer from 'body-image disparagement', where the obese person believes that his/her body is grotesque and loathsome and that others view it with hostility. The person's preoccupation with the obesity swamps everything else and becomes the over-ruling personality factor. All other graces, talents and abilities take second place to the obesity. This disturbance is seen mostly in people whose obesity started in childhood and probably arises from the mocking and derision they received from both peers and older people.

Doubt about masculinity or femininity may make the person so ashamed of their body, either totally or parts of it, that they can only have sex in the dark or under the bedclothes.

So long as we feel certain that our body boundaries separate us from the world, we continue to feel significant and individual. If the client is able to feel a 'significant person' within the counselling relationship, this may help to maintain his/her feelings of self-esteem and self-worth and so prevent loss of body boundary.

Principal points to consider about body-image:

- The regard the person has for his/her body – is it negative or positive?
- Do specific part or parts cause concern?
- Generally satisfied or dissatisfied?
- What is the person's ideal?
- What body experiences make for pleasure or displeasure?
- What feelings are associated with size? The way we judge the size of our body or a part thereof is influenced by emotions and attitudes toward ourselves and our relationship to others.
- How aware is the person of his/her body? Some people have a high awareness while others have a minimal awareness. Most people focus more of their attention on specific sectors and less on others.
- Does the person have a clear idea of the demarcation between his/her body and the outside world, which includes other people?
- How accurately is the person able to judge body position? Spatial dimension is part of our ability to separate from our surroundings.

- Anxiety about the body – some people are very afraid of body damage while others seem unconcerned about such a possibility.
- Masculinity/femininity – does the person clearly affirm his/her gender and how does gender relate to body-image?

It is important to remind ourselves that, although some changes in body-image are pathological, what is considered pathological lies within the normal. Body changes – external and internal – are all likely to produce distortions in body-image. Some people need a great deal of emotional support in order to accommodate body changes within their body-image. Those who cannot may well wander over the border into the no-man's land of the pathological.

Further reading

Fisher, S. and Cleveland, S. E. (1985) *Body-image and Personality*, Van Nostrand, New York.

Stewart, W. (1985) *Counselling in Rehabilitation*, Croom Helm, New York.

Stewart, W. (1998) *Building Self-esteem: How to replace self-doubt with confidence and well-being*. How To Books, Oxford.

BONDING

Bonding is the relationship that one individual maintains with either an inanimate object, e.g. a bird with its nest, or with animate objects, e.g. a child with its caregiver or and adult with a mate. Behaviour is directed exclusively toward the preferred object.

Bonding partners recognize each other as individuals. Bonding occurs rapidly between adults and their young. Bonded partners tend to defend each other.

Bonding is the formation of a close personal relationship (as between a mother and child), especially through frequent or constant association. The process of bonding between mother and baby starts long before the birth. If the baby in the womb responds to noise, then how much more is it likely to respond to feelings of already being loved or the reverse, of not being wanted, or of fear on the mother's part that she will not be a good mother?

For 9 months, the environment within the womb is all-important to the developing baby; the mother's emotional and physical state plays a vital role in creating this environment. Sometimes events take over and the baby is catapulted prematurely into the world. Difficulty of delivery and premature birth add to the problems of the mother bonding with the new baby. Bonding is not just at birth; it is for life.

Babies born prematurely may induce feelings of great fear in the mother; when born with defects, the mother might not be able to accept the baby. Bonding is then fraught with difficulty. Early bonding difficulties are likely to lead to a decrease in the new mother's self-esteem. When this happens, the feelings are likely to be transmitted to the child.

Paternal bonding is said to be as important as maternal bonding and certainly, for the development of high self-esteem, the role of the father is necessary. The developing child needs to experience the feelings of being wanted and loved by both parents. When this love is deficient, the growing child is in danger of developing low self-esteem.

The effectiveness of the therapeutic relationship or alliance has characteristics of bonding. The relationship is influenced by:

- How the counsellor demonstrates the core conditions of empathy, genuineness, nonpossessive warmth, unconditional positive regard
- The client's feelings toward the counsellor, which are influenced by: trust in the counsellor, feeling safe in the relationship, having faith in the counsellor
- The style of interaction of both client and counsellor – this is influenced by the 'fit' between the counsellor's approach and the ability of the client to work within it and how far the counsellor is able to adapt to the client's particular abilities and preferences
- The way transference and counter-transference are acknowledged and worked through. In very general (though not strictly in psychoanalytic) terms, transference and counter-transference refer to the tendencies we all have to perceive, feel and act toward other people in the present, based on previous experiences with significant others in our past lives.

Bonding between counsellor and client is generally strengthened when something within the relationship is challenged (by either person) and the potential conflict is dealt with constructively.

Further reading

Bowlby, J. (1969) *Attachment. Attachment and Loss*, vol. 1, Penguin, Harmondsworth.
Dryden, W. (1989) The therapeutic alliance. In: *Key Issues for Counselling in Action*, Sage Publications, London.
Volkmar, F. (1995) Reactive attachment disorder of infancy or early childhood. In: *Comprehensive Textbook of Psychiatry*, 6th edn, (eds H. J. Kaplan and B. J. Sadock), Williams & Wilkins, Baltimore, MD.

BRAIN-STORMING

This is an established technique for creative problem-solving, usually undertaken by a small group of between two and six members. One member of the group, or an outside adviser, acts as co-ordinator. The aim is to release the mind, increase the flow of creative ideas and assist decision-making. No discussion or evaluation is permitted until all ideas have been generated. This ensures that creativity is not blocked. One person may build upon the idea of someone else. All ideas are reviewed and graded for their usefulness.

Although brainstorming is especially successful for group problem-solving, because ideas generate other ideas, its principles can be modified for use by two people. Effective brainstorming hinges on all involved being willing to listen to one another and to develop ideas. It would seem that, for brainstorming to work, group members need to feel comfortable with and to have confidence in one another. Rivalry, competitiveness, the need to score, impress or put down will all get in the way of finding a solution. or solutions, to the problem. Lack of commitment to the outcome will interfere with creativity and generating ideas.

In counselling, brainstorming is a useful technique to use, particularly when helping clients set goals for themselves or in planning action. Brainstorming puts clients in the driving seat, as it were, for as they develop ideas they realize that they can exercise control.

Further reading

Fox, W. M. (1987) *Effective Group Problem Solving*. Jossey-Bass, San Francisco, CA.
Francis, D. (1987) *50 Activities for Unblocking Organisational Communication*. Gower, Aldershot.

BRIEF COUNSELLING

The term covers a range of planned, short-term therapies. Brief counselling does not mean superficial or merely relieving symptoms. By comparison with psychoanalysis, it is short, but that does not mean lacking in quality nor any less skilled or helpful. In fact, brief counselling requires great skill, for within a few sessions the counsellor has to make sufficient impact on the client so that the client feels able to continue his or her own work of healing. Many brief therapies are based on psychodynamic, behavioural, crisis or cognitive approaches, each with its own method of working. The results of brief therapy are said to be comparable with long-term therapy.

The origins of brief counselling

In the late 1950s, Michael Balint and colleagues at the Tavistock Clinic, London, met to explore how they could reduce the length of therapy yet still be effective. They researched techniques, indications, contraindications and effectiveness. Gradually, brief counselling was born, and the concept of 'focal conflict' or 'focal therapy'. This is where the central conflict is separated from the rest of the rest of the personality. Therapy then focuses on the dynamics of that conflict, not on all aspects of the client's unconscious life.

Characteristics of brief counselling:

- Time limits, with an average of six to ten single sessions; this fits well with what is considered the norm for counselling, although in many instances the counselling relationship will continue far beyond the limit of the initial contract
- Limited goals, with the focus on specific areas
- Current problems are dealt with in the 'here and now'
- Direction – the counsellor is more active than in some other approaches
- Early assessment is needed to establish treatment rapidly; accurate assessment is essential to ascertain whether brief counselling, or something more long-term, is the most suitable option for a particular client

- Flexibility of approach is emphasized, because of the time limit
- Ventilation of feelings is considered essential
- Therapeutic relationship and contract are stressed
- Selection – brief counselling is more suitable with less disturbed clients and is not suitable for people who have chronic disturbances, which include drug or alcohol addictions, personality disorders and severe mental illnesses.

Brief counselling may benefit clients:

- Whose problem is acute, rather than chronic
- Whose previous adjustment was effective
- Whose ability to relate is adequate
- Whose motivation toward therapy is high
- Brief counselling has proved to be appropriate in stress-management.

Similar to brief counselling is single-session counselling. Counselling may be planned where it is known by both counsellor and client to involve one session only, although it may be longer than the accepted 'therapeutic hour'. Counsellors who work in 'drop-in' centres are more likely to work in one session than with long-term counselling.

Suggested principles

- Identify one salient issue
- View the client's difficulties as a stepping stone to development
- Engage the client fully
- Keep interpretations to the minimum
- Understand with empathy
- Start the client on the road toward problem-solving
- Limit the number of issues to be explored
- Make provision for follow-up at the client's request.

'Therapeutic drop out', is a term used to describe the situation where the client terminates counselling, often after only one session. Studies show that a significant percentage of those who do drop out found what they were seeking and had no real desire to enter into ongoing therapy.

Further reading

Dryden, W. and Feltham, C. (1992) *Brief Counselling*, Open University Press, Buckingham.

Mohl, Paul C. (1995) Brief psychotherapy. In: *Comprehensive Textbook of Psychiatry*, 6th edn, (eds H. J. Kaplan and B. J. Sadock), Williams & Wilkins, Baltimore, MD.

BULIMIA NERVOSA (BINGE-EATING) (*see also*: Anorexia nervosa)

Russell first used the term in 1979 to describe a group of patients who feared putting on weight yet had a compulsive urge to eat. It is most common in societies where slimness is considered desirable and attractive.

Important points about the condition

- The excessive eating, which causes distress, is not within the person's control.
- People who have also experienced anorexia are more prone to develop bulimia. This is thought to be when the iron-like control over not eating suddenly cracks and results in a binge. Guilt takes over, resulting in self-induced vomiting. The starvation and binge cycle starts all over again.
- Bulimia never comes of its own accord but follows a period of self-imposed starvation. The body revolts against this deprivation and the food gorged is what the body most needs, especially carbohydrates.
- Binge-eating is accompanied by self-induced vomiting or the abuse of purgatives, or both. Self-induced vomiting ensures a secret method of maintaining weight at a level that keeps other people satisfied.
- Bulimia may start just as the anorexic is reaching optimum body weight.
- Pressure may push the recovering anorexic into bulimia.
- Not all bulimics have been anorexic but they are just as fearful of putting on weight. They seem not to have the same iron control to do without food for such long periods.
- Bulimics are thrown into panic when they feel that their body has taken control away from them.
- Bulimics fear that if they start eating they will eat everything in sight.
- The mind of the bulimic is constantly full of thoughts about food. They dream about it. This is similar to the experiences of prisoners of war in concentration camps, whose daydreams were often about food.
- Binge eating is usually done in secret and the buying of the food is so arranged that no one could be suspicious.
- The person may resort to strenuous exercise and the use of stimulants or diuretics.
- Bulimics often feel depressed, brought on by the feeling of having lost control and self-disgust. Sustained use of stimulants often bring depression in their wake. Deterioration of relationships is also a factor in this depression.
- Constant vomiting is harmful because the body is deprived not only of food but of gastrointestinal juices essential for health. Juices that have their function in the stomach have a harmful effect on the upper parts of the alimentary tract. Continual loss of fluid often leads to dehydration.
- People who cannot make themselves vomit often resort to repeated purging, also damaging to health.
- Bulimia is but one indication of lack of control; many also overspend and get into financial difficulty. So overpowering is the desire for food that some will steal to get it. Relationships are also entered into in the same overboard way. Few succeed in a long-term lasting sexual relationship.
- Most bulimics, male and female, have low self-esteem and desperately seek for approval.
- There is some evidence to support the theory that female bulimics identify with their fathers and males with their mothers.

- The basic conflict is between their need to be admired and desired by a member of the opposite sex, on the one hand, and a fear that they are not good enough and will be rejected, on the other.
- Unlike anorexics, bulimics normally continue to menstruate. Some conceive and a few give birth. Many, however, are against the idea of becoming pregnant.
- Because bulimics normally weigh more than anorexics, their eating habits may escape notice for years. Their preoccupation with weight and size equates to that of anorexics.
- Bulimics generally feel afraid when they feel the desire to binge coming on, when they have successfully controlled it for a period.

Treatment

- A normal eating pattern must be established. This is not easy, for the patterns of eating and vomiting are firmly established.
- As bulimics are intent on keeping their weight down, co-operation is problematic, but essential if their programme is to work.
- Hospital treatment, where skilled help is available, is desirable if the pattern of binge eating and vomiting is to be interrupted. Hospital admission is essential if there are physical complications or if there is depression.
- Repeated information-giving about the effects of binge eating and persistent vomiting is a necessary part of treatment, supported by an equally forcible plugging of the physical and emotional advantages of a balanced eating programme.
- Eating small amounts slowly in the company of others encourages a normal eating pattern. Water intake is restricted; too much water gives a sensation of fullness. No eating is allowed between meals.
- Some effort is made to gradually increase the weight beyond what the client thinks to be desirable.
- Those not in hospital are trusted to keep a daily journal of all food they eat as well as times they want to, or actually do, vomit.
- Supervision is likely to continue for months or even years.

(*See* Anorexia, for related counselling.)

Further reading

Garfinkel, P. E. (1995) Eating disorders. In: *Comprehensive Textbook of Psychiatry*, 6th edn, (eds H. J. Kaplan and B. J. Sadock), Williams & Wilkins, Baltimore, MD.
Melville, J. (1983) *The ABC of Eating: Coping with anorexia, bulimia and compulsive eating*, Sheldon Press, London.

BURNOUT (*see also*: Alienation, Empathy, Stress management)

A term used in two ways: to describe the injurious effects of the stress of counselling upon counsellors; and to describe the injurious effects of stress, particularly related to work.

Counsellor burnout

In counselling, burnout, resulting in physical or psychological withdrawal, is characterized by:

- Chronic low levels of energy
- Defensive behaviour
- Distancing emotionally from people.

Counsellors often look forward to sessions where there is progress and dread sessions that don't go anywhere. Sessions that go badly have a debilitating effect on the counsellor, because prolonged client resistance depletes energy. Burnout may also be associated with the relationship in which there is a high level of empathy and with the high level of concentration that goes with giving full attention.

Counsellors who feel that they are starting to be impatient with clients or with members of the family, who are having difficulty sleeping, who feel that there are never, ever, enough hours in the day and that they simply could not face taking on another client, are probably heading for burnout.

If counsellors suggest that their clients take stock of their lives, can they do less with theirs? Finding satisfying ways to recharge the batteries is essential in order to prevent burnout.

Occupational burnout

In a more general sense, burnout is associated with stress, where people find increasingly that they feel unable to cope with the pressures at work, at home or within relationships. These factors are often compounded by feelings of failure, frustration, hopelessness and anger. These are all signs of running on under-charged batteries.

More specifically, when considering work, burnout is associated with:

- The high level of concentration that goes with giving full attention
- Situations where people have been exposed for prolonged periods to conflict in which there is little or no resolution
- Alienation from work – in this instance, burnout is more of a symptom than a cause.

The following are the main job factors linked to occupational burnout:

- **Variety of skills**: The fewer demands a job makes on our skills and talents, the more pressure we will feel
- **Conflicting activities**: Where there is conflict between different activities, we will feel more pressure
- **Influence over decisions**: The less opportunity there is to make independent decisions, and the less control we have over the outcomes, the more pressure we will feel
- **Expertise**: Where there is not a good fit between our expertise and the required skills of the job, we will feel more pressure

- **Work load**: The more we perceive our workload to be unduly heavy, the more pressure we will feel
- **Boredom**: The more monotonous, uninteresting, dull and lacking in stimulation our work, the more pressure we will feel
- **Identity**: If we are not able to clearly identify the role specifically as ours, we will feel more pressure
- **Autonomy**: The less autonomy we are allowed, the more pressure we will feel
- **Support**: If we do not feel supported in our work, we will feel more pressure
- **Accountability**: When there is a disparity between accountability and the tasks we perform, we will feel more stress
- **Significance**: The less significant our contribution, the more stress we will feel
- **Upward communication**: The greater the gap between us and those in higher positions and the less our communication is listened to, the more stress we will feel
- **Development**. The fewer opportunities our work provides for personal growth and development, to acquire work-related skills/knowledge, the more pressure we will feel
- **Income**: The less we feel our income reflects our contribution, the more pressure we will feel.

Burnout and alienation from the job

The six main components of alienation can be traced in occupational burnout.

- **Meaninglessness**: When we expect that our future will not be good in our present position or profession
- **Cultural estrangement**: Where our personal goals are not in agreement with the goals of the organization
- **Powerlessness**: Where we feel that our behaviour will have little or no effect on outcomes
- **Social isolation**: Where we feel excluded or rejected
- **Task estrangement**: Where we feel that the job we do not longer brings us satisfaction or enjoyment
- **Separation**: Where we feel dissociated from identifying with the work to which we claim membership by virtue of practice, qualification or employment.

Much of what applies to occupational burnout can be easily translated into counsellor burnout, particularly where the counsellor works in an agency or uses counselling skills in another job, such as nursing. There the 'counsellor' is part of a wider organization and may experience some of the alienation discussed above.

Further reading

Cherniss, C. (1980) *Staff Burn Out: Job stress in the human services*, Sage Publications, London.

Faber, B. and Heifetz, L. J. (1982) Process and dimensions of burn out in psychotherapists. *Professional Psychology*, **13**, 293–301.

Shearer, John M. (1983) Surviving organizational burnout. In: *1983 Annual for Facilitators, Trainers and Consultants*, University Associates, San Diego, CA.

C

CATHARSIS (*see also*: Abreaction)

This term was used metaphorically by Aristotle to describe the effects of true tragedy on the spectator. Aristotle states that the purpose of tragedy is to arouse 'terror and pity' and thereby effect catharsis – purgation or purification of these emotions.

The term catharsis was introduced into psychiatry by Freud and Joseph Breur, who used it to describe a method of treating hysterical patients under hypnosis. The patients relived, or at least remembered, the circumstances under which their symptoms originated. When the emotions accompanying those circumstances were expressed, the patient was thus relieved of the symptoms. People who block emotions may experience a great rush of feeling as the blockage is removed.

Abreaction, insight and working through are three main experiences in psychoanalysis. Catharsis is a prime treatment tool of such approaches as primal therapy, re-birthing, Z process attachment and many of the newer therapies, such as six category intervention (*see* entry, below).

CHALLENGING (ALSO REFERRED TO AS CONFRONTATION)

Counselling is more than active and empathic listening. Part of effective counselling might also mean confronting the client with certain aspects of, for example, self-defeating behaviour or thoughts and feelings that are at odds with progress.

In counselling, the aim of a challenge is to help the client face reality, as it is seen through the eyes of the counsellor. The force of the challenge depends on the type of counselling. In some instances it is offered as an observation, in others it is very strong and confronting.

There are times when it is wiser to ignore than to comment. There are times, however, when it could be valuable for the client to know how the counsellor feels about something.

The client may benefit from being confronted with the possible outcome of his/her behaviour or some contemplated course of action. Sometimes it is difficult to challenge without it being interpreted as a judgement.

Some specific points about challenging are:

- A challenge is not verbal fisticuffs!
- A challenge should be a tentative suggestion, not a declaration
- A challenge is an observation, not an accusation
- A challenge should be made only after careful deliberation
- A challenge should never be used as a retaliation, nor as a put-down
- A challenge is safest when the relationship is well-established.

The main areas of challenge:

- Discrepancies
- Distortions
- Self-defeating thought patterns
- Self-defeating behaviours
- Games, tricks and smoke-screens
- Excuses:
  - Complacency
  - Rationalization
  - Procrastination
  - Buck-passing.

Examples of challenges:

- 'You say that being rejected really hurts you, yet you smile as you talk about it.' (Discrepancy)
- 'You say you feel really depressed, yet you laugh whenever you say that, as if it was nothing at all.' (Distortion of feelings)
- 'You say your previous counsellor never really understood you. The way you said that makes me wonder if you're trying to play on my sympathy in some way.' (Manipulation)
- 'You say you don't feel up to handling this change in your life. Yet you are clearly a resourceful person. You're intelligent and persistent and have coped well with changes in the past.' (Negative thought pattern)
- 'You say you believe in taking responsibility for what you do, yet you blame your wife and daughter for everything that is wrong in your relationship with them.' (Excuse)
- 'You say you've been out of work for 6 months and it really gets you down. Yet in all that time you haven't applied for any jobs and you're quite happy to collect your money every week; "That's what I've paid in for all these years," you said.' (Complacency)
- 'A month ago you moaned because you hadn't worked for 6 months; you made a contract then to start looking for work; now you're telling me you haven't even tried. You haven't kept your contract and didn't realize how the time was flying.' (Procrastination)
- 'Last time you admitted that you kept putting off looking for a job, now you're saying you couldn't go out because the weather was wet.' (Rationalization)

A challenge should be preceded by careful consideration of:

- What is the purpose of the challenge?
- Can I handle the consequences?
- Does the challenge relate to the here and now?
- Whose needs are being met by the challenge?

Example 1

Vanessa says, 'I do wish I could do something about my weight. Look at me, 15 stones. But, I'm my own worst enemy. Stuart and I went out last night for a slap-up meal. That's the way of it. One of these days I'll win.'

Counsellor says, 'Vanessa, you say you want to lose weight and you realize that your life style probably works against that, yet the way you talk it seems as if you've a "couldn't care less" attitude. Something will turn up, you say, almost as if you're happy that it's out of your control.'

Example 2

Dan, about 40 years of age, talking about Bill, his 17-year-old son: 'I don't have any problems with my children, we have a wonderful relationship; that's because Alice and I give them responsibility. They know who's boss, though. Bill wanted a front door key. I told him, "When you're working, my lad, then you can have a key to my house." He stormed out, muttering something like, "Come into this century, old man." Cheeky young (cough).'

Counsellor says, 'Dan I want to challenge you on what you've just said. On the one hand you said you have no problems with your children and on the other you said that Bill swore at you. You also said you give them responsibility, yet you refused to respect Bill's responsibility by giving him a key. What do you think about those contradictions?'

Further reading

Ivey, A. E., Ivey, M. B. and Sinek-Downing, L. (1987) *Counselling and Psychotherapy: Integrating skills, theory and practice*, 2nd edn, Prentice Hall, Englewood Cliffs, NJ.

CHILD ABUSE (*see also*: Incest, Rape counselling)

Introduction

The spectrum of child abuse is wide. It includes not only children who have suffered physical abuse with fractures and bruises (the 'battered child') but also those who have experienced emotional abuse, sexual abuse, deliberate poisoning and the infliction of fictitious illness on them by their parents (Munchausen's syndrome by proxy).

Children under the age of 2 are most liable to suffer direct physical abuse at the hands of their parents, although it can happen to children of any age. Such abuse is more common in families who are living under stress and, in some instances, the parents themselves suffered cruelty as children.

Abused children are those of any age who have suffered repeated injuries, which may include physical, emotional and sexual abuse at the hands of a parent, parents or parent substitutes. Physical abuse often takes place as a response to minor infringements of behaviour. Child abuse also includes child neglect.

Child abuse or child maltreatment consists of different types of harmful act directed toward children. In physical abuse, children are slapped, hit, kicked or shoved or have objects thrown at them. Flesh wounds, broken bones or other injuries are common. Severe abuse may result in major injury, permanent physical or developmental impairment or even death.

Neglect, a form of child maltreatment, involves the failure to feed or care for a child's basic needs or to adequately supervise the child.

Emotional abuse involves humiliation, berating or other acts carried out over time that terrorize or frighten the child. Children are emotionally scarred when they are labelled as stupid or ugly or crazy or unwanted.

Sexual abuse consists of a wide range of sexual behaviour, including fondling, mutual masturbation, digital penetration, oral–genital contact and involvement of children in photography or filming for pornographic purposes and intercourse.

Sexual acts not involving intercourse between, for example, fathers and daughters constitute other criminal offences such as indecent assault or gross indecency with or towards a child. Sexual relationships with stepchildren count as unlawful sexual intercourse and indecent assault.

Father/son relationships come within the offences of buggery or indecent assault, not incest or unlawful sexual intercourse.

The majority of sexual assaults on children are by someone they know. The risk is higher when the child lives with a step-, foster or adoptive father. Child abusers come from every class, profession, racial and religious background.

Sexual abuse is said to be symptomatic of a family in crisis and, unless it is dealt with, the victim will be continually abused and damaged. The wounds of a victim will bleed throughout life unless properly treated.

The child victim is never responsible for the abuse. The responsibility always lies with the perpetrator. The child needs constant reassurance of this.

Children who live in families where sexual abuse has occurred between family members have frequently been the subject of previous child abuse investigations. It is a myth that the spouse must have been aware of the sexual abuse taking place, although some are. The child victim is often blamed for what has taken place. The perpetrator rarely discriminates between the sexes or the ages of the victims.

Where the mother does know, secrecy, threats and silent acceptance hold the father, child and mother in a relationship to 'stabilize' the marriage and family and prevent break-up. There is an intense relationship between the father and child that is both powerful and dependent. The father is also dependent upon his wife. The coercive and threatening web of silence is spun.

The child is also dependent and could be said to have power. In fact, the child has little power, other than to expose and destroy the father and family unit. This is a heavy responsibility and is rarely used by the abused and very vulnerable child, because of the threat from the perpetrator and enormous fear of the unknown.

When sexual abuse occurs outside the family, there is more likelihood of the child confiding in the parents. But when the perpetrator is one of the family, disclosure is difficult. There is the public shame of failure for each person involved in their own role as father, mother and child, with resulting further loss of self-esteem by all.

Violent molestation and rape generally bring condemnation down on the heads of the perpetrators. Orogenital molestation may leave no evidence except the child's story. This must be believed. Children rarely fabricate stories of detailed sexual activities unless they have witnessed them; and they have, indeed, been eyewitnesses to their own abuse.

Adult–child sex is wrong because the fundamental conditions of consent cannot prevail in the relationship between an adult and a child. Not only can the child not freely consent, s/he also cannot give informed consent. A child is not likely to be aware of the social significance of sexuality nor of the consequences. And in this, adult–child sex is morally wrong.

In the UK, a local authority can take abused children away from their parents by obtaining a care order from a juvenile court under the Children Act 1989.

Controversial methods of diagnosing sexual abuse led to a public inquiry in Cleveland, England in 1988, and several instances since, which severely criticized the handling of such cases. The standard of proof required for criminal proceedings is greater than that required for a local authority to take children into care. This has led to highly publicized cases where children have been taken into care but no prosecution has eventually been brought. In some cases innocent parents have been pilloried, so the whole area of abuse is very difficult. There is also the related point of the abused child having to give evidence and all that that means. Although there is progress towards making the giving of evidence less of an ordeal, such facilities as video links are not yet universal.

Historical

The sexual abuse of children is as old as civilization. Both the Bible and the Talmud encouraged sex between men and very young girls in marriage, concubinage and slavery. For generations we naively believed that the taboos against incest did actually operate and that, when incest did occur, it was as an isolated incident.

One of the first national laws designed to stop the mistreatment of children in their own homes was passed in 1884, when Britain's National Society for the Prevention of Cruelty to Children was organized. Earlier statutes had outlawed infant abandonment and failure to provide food, shelter, clothing and medical care for dependants. Child-labour laws regulated working conditions for underage factory workers and tried to improve the status of young apprentices, who lived almost as slaves while learning a skill from tradesmen.

Incidence

A particularly controversial aspect of the incidence problem is the number of individuals recalling memories of abuse. While repression of early traumatic memories is a concept that many psychotherapists accept, increasing concern is being raised over the alarming number of adult women in therapy who report repressed memories of abuse, particularly incest. At present, there is no way of determining whether such memories, in adults or in children, are valid or are the result of suggestive therapy or media probing.

Too often the crime goes unpunished because a child is afraid that exposing an abuser will only bring more pain. Abusive parents and caretakers may try to justify their actions as a way of punishing children for being 'bad' or of scaring them into being 'good'. A related point is the number of cases of children in care who have been abused. Much of this abuse occurred many years ago and only now have the victims had the courage to come forward.

Causes

No explanation of the cause of child abuse has emerged as conclusive but it is most likely to stem from a collection of factors, including poverty, substance abuse and societal violence. Like rape, child abuse may also have something to do with power and control over someone who is weaker and more vulnerable.

Childhood abuse is thought to lead to the person becoming an abuser in later life, although this theory does not take into consideration other moderating factors for the many people who were abused and have not become abusers. It must never be assumed at that the one follows the other and to suggest this puts abused people under a fearful cloud when they themselves become parents.

Treatment

Child abuse is a multifaceted problem best addressed through comprehensive, interdisciplinary interventions, including law-enforcement and medical, mental-health and social services. Most abused children require medical examination to detect the presence of injury or disease. Many abused children will suffer short- or long-term psychological or emotional trauma. Abusive adults require a range of mental-health and social services to help them remedy the conditions associated with their behaviour.

Jan Sutton, in her book, *Healing the Hurt Within*, draws attention to the fact that much self-harming behaviour is linked with experience of abuse as children. Thus the legacy of child abuse is a fearful one, which has brought many of its victims to the brink of despair.

Progress has been made in identifying not only effective therapeutic interventions for victims and perpetrators but also effective prevention strategies. One of the most promising of the latter is the provision of home-visitation services to new parents to promote positive parent–child interactions and ensure adequate support thereafter.

Recognizing abuse

The most important step in recognizing child sexual abuse is to be aware of the possibility of such abuse. In other words you are not going to find sexual abuse if you don't believe it exists.

On the other hand, it is impossible to give hard and fast rules for identifying abuse. Each situation is different and children will find ways of coping with the abuse and their own way of trying to tell.

Children do not always know the words to explain clearly what is happening to them. They may try to tell, e.g. by saying, 'I don't like him', 'He's ugly', 'He acts funny'. These statements are often misunderstood or ignored.

Therefore, although in many cases the child's comment will relate to something harmless, it is worth asking a few gentle questions to find out why they are saying it.

Although there are few 'conclusive' signs it is helpful for anyone involved with children and young people to be aware of the types of behaviour often found in children who have been assaulted.

The following list gives some of the signs that could possibly indicate sexual abuse:

- Repeated urinary infections/pain on urinating
- Sexually transmitted disease
- Stomach aches/cramps
- Inability to sit still (from sore bottom or genitals)
- Incontinence or bed-wetting
- Pregnancy
- Bruising, especially around genitals
- Chronic eating disorders/anorexia
- Depression
- Suicide attempts
- Self-mutilation
- Low self-esteem
- Self-neglect
- Nightmares/insomnia
- Panic attacks
- Compulsive washing/obsessive cleanliness
- Refusing to speak (elective mutism)
- Very sudden changes in behaviour
- Running away
- Truancy
- Fear of men or of one particular man
- Changes in school performance
- Regression to younger behaviour
- Falling asleep in school
- Uncharacteristic behaviour that is interpreted as sexual
- Inappropriate or detailed sexual knowledge in language or drawings.

Some of these sorts of behaviour are common to all distressed children and may not be a reaction to sexual abuse. To add to the difficulties, some abused children show none of these signs or symptoms and manage to conceal what is happening to them.

Again, the important thing when dealing with any distressed child is that we keep our minds open to the possibility of sexual abuse. Remember, however difficult it is for children to tell openly about sexual abuse, it is through these and other signs that children are asking for permission to tell and for an end to the abuse. (Taken from a paper written by the Women's Support Project, 871 Springfield Road, Parkhead, Glasgow and used with permission.)

The term 'abusing parent' is applied to a parent guilty of child abuse but is also a label for a theoretical personality type possessing a particular set of characteristics, which postulates that it is highly likely that a person of this type will become an abusing parent. However, no clear-cut personality traits that typify abusing parents have been demonstrated other than the likelihood that they were themselves abused as children – but even that is not certain.

Further reading

Bradshaw, J. (1990) *Home Coming: Reclaiming and championing your inner child*. Judy Piatkus, London.

Corby, B. (1993) *Child Abuse: Towards a knowledge base*, Open University Press, Buckingham.

Draucker, C. B. (1992) *Counselling Survivors of Childhood Sexual Abuse*, Sage Publications, London.

Saunders, P. and Myers, S. (1995) *What Do You Know About Child Abuse*, Gloucester Press, Gloucester.

Sutton J. (1999) *Healing the Hurt Within: How to relieve the suffering underlying self-destructive behaviour*. How To Books, Oxford.

CO-DEPENDENCE

Co-dependent behaviour is often related to families where there is chemical addiction, but there are other situations in which co-dependence operates. Co-dependent behaviour is learned in dysfunctional families in which certain unwritten, and in many cases unspoken, rules prevail. The behaviour is reinforced within the culture. Many rules that produce people who are not wholly functional are linked to sex roles.

Examples of dysfunctional rules:

- 'Men should be...'
- 'Women should be...'
- 'Always do...'
- 'Never do...'

The rules stem from avoidance of interpersonal issues and the need to protect oneself from others. People from dysfunctional families learn to be 'people-pleasers'.

Examples of dysfunctional family rules:

- Never talk to others about your problems – 'Don't wash your dirty linen in public'

- Never express feelings openly
- Indirect communication is best
- We have to be perfect – always; being ruled by 'shoulds' and 'oughts' creates fertile soil for shame, doubt, frustration and anger when we fail to attain perfection
- Don't be selfish, ever – other people must always come first
- Don't do as I do, do as I say
- Play and fun are irresponsible
- Whatever you do, don't rock the boat.

People who are the product of dysfunctional families tend to 'awfulize' events. Minor omissions are major transgressions. Dysfunctional behaviours become evident in people who do not know how to ask for help (asking for help implies an acceptance of vulnerability) or how to forgive themselves. Co-dependents may become dependent on other people, substances or behaviours.

Examples of dysfunctional coping:

- Compulsive, perfectionistic, approval-seeking or dependent behaviour
- May become 'doormat' co-dependents
- May suffer from physical exhaustion, depression and hopelessness
- May abuse or neglect their children
- May become suicidal
- May become self-destructive through overwork, chemical or any other form of dependency.

Development of co-dependence:

- Failure of the primary caregiver to allow the developing child to separate and establish his/her own boundaries
- Male children are more likely to be encouraged to separate than female children
- Masculinity is defined through separation from the primary caregiver while femininity is defined through attachment
- Men, generally, are threatened by attachment, while women, generally, are threatened by separation.

The two most typical behaviours of co-dependence are compulsive care-taking and attempting to control others.

Characteristics of co-dependency:

- Difficulty in identifying one's own feelings
- Difficulty in acknowledging and expressing one's feelings
- Difficulty in forming or maintaining close relationships
- Being rigid or stuck in attitudes or behaviours
- Perfectionism, with 'all-or-nothing' thinking

- Difficulty coping with change
- Feeling overly responsible for the behaviour or feelings of other people
- Becoming so absorbed in other people's problems that one is unable to identify or solve one's own
- Attempting to control the behaviour of others and feeling that one must solve other people's problems
- Continually seeking approval from others, in order to feel good and accepted – not being able to say 'No' is an example
- Difficulty making decisions, often influenced by what other people want
- Feeling powerless over one's life; an addiction to security
- A sense of shame and low self-esteem
- Weak personal boundaries – co-dependents may not know where they themselves end and other people begin
- Compulsive behaviour, excessive: working, eating, dieting, spending, gambling.

Further reading

Beattie, M. (1987) *Co-dependent No More: How to stop controlling others and start caring for yourself*, Harper & Row, New York.

Beattie, M. (1989) *Beyond Co-dependency and Getting Better at all Times*, Harper & Row, New York.

Pfeiffer, J. A. (1991) Co-dependence: learned dysfunctional behaviour. In: *1991 Annual: Developing Human Resources*, University Associates, San Diego, CA.

Mellody, P., Miller, A. W. and Miller J. K. (1989) *Facing Co-dependence: What it is, where it comes from, how it sabotages our lives*, Harper & Row, New York.

COGNITIVE DISSONANCE THEORY

This is a theory developed by the social psychologist Leon Festinger, which proposes that when a person's actions are inconsistent with his/her attitudes, the discomfort produced by this dissonance leads the person to bring the attitudes in line with the actions.

The theory also states that people will constantly strive to maintain a cognitive balance. The mental conflict that occurs when beliefs or assumption are contradicted by new information – when the new information is perceived to be incompatible or inconsistent with what is already established. Groups also strive to maintain the balance of their interpersonal relationships.

Mental conflict occurs when beliefs or assumptions are contradicted by new information or when the new information is perceived to be incompatible or inconsistent with what is already established. Groups also strive to maintain the balance of their interpersonal relationships.

People cope with dissonance by:

- Rejecting the new information
- Explaining away the new information

- Avoiding the new information
- Persuading themselves that there is no conflict
- Reconciling the difference.

Cognitive dissonance approaches have not gone unchallenged. An alternative approach, known as **self-perception theory**, suggests that we all analyse our own behaviour much as an outside observer might and, as a result of these observations, make judgements about why we are motivated to do what we do. Dissonance theory and self-perception theory are not necessarily mutually exclusive; several studies suggest that both processes can and do occur but under different conditions.

Cognitive dissonance occurs whenever we make decisions and, if the theory is correct, then we will (unconsciously) take steps to reduce the unpleasant feelings of dissonance. To summarize the theory:

1. Two thoughts, attitudes or beliefs are not in harmony
2. Disharmony creates psychological discomfort
3. Something must be done to reduce the discomfort
4. Avoidance action is taken.

Dissonance is present in both conflict resolution and decision-making. Counselling is often about helping clients make decisions and about working with them so that they can resolve conflict.

An example of cognitive dissonance in action is Mark and Gill. They had been courting for a couple of years and talked of getting married. Gill, who had a good job in the Inland Revenue, suggested that they live together, as this would be financially better for them. Mark was hesitant, because he knew his parents' views would bring them into conflict with him and Gill; his parents were very strictly religious and had brought him up to have the same values. Mark was in deep conflict: he risked either losing the love and regard of his parents or losing Gill, who had become more adamant that, while she would not rule out marriage, it would not be just yet. Mark resolved the dissonance by ending the relationship, saying, 'If money was the only reason, then it wasn't a good enough reason. I couldn't run the risk of losing my parents.' For Mark, the pull of what he would lose was stronger than what he might gain.

Further reading

Brown, R. (1985) *Social Psychology*, 2nd edn, Free Press, New York.
Festinger, L. (1957) *A Theory of Cognitive Dissonance*, Stanford University Press, Stanford, MA.

COGNITIVE THERAPY (*see also*: Behaviour therapy)

One way of defining the differences between approaches is to consider where their primary focus is – on feelings, thinking, behaviour or a combination of these. Psychodynamic and person-centred approaches concentrate on feelings.

Behaviourists believe that if the behaviour (including thinking) is adjusted, all other aspects will be put to rights. Cognitive theories (mainly concerned with thinking) put forward the view that all behaviour is primarily determined by what a person thinks. Eclectic or integrated counsellors may use any or all of these theories and approaches. What distinguishes one counselling approach from another is where the attention is focussed and the techniques and skills used.

Cognitive therapy was developed by Aaron Beck, who put forward the view that behaviour is primarily determined by what that person thinks. It is particularly relevant in treating depression, where thoughts of low self-worth and low self-esteem are a common feature. Cognitive therapy works on the premise that thoughts of low self-worth are incorrect and are due to faulty learning.

Such thoughts often centre on:

'I haven't achieved anything.'
'I have nothing to offer.'
'I deserve to be criticized.'

The aim of therapy is to get rid of faulty concepts that influence negative thinking. Karen Horney refers to the 'tyranny of the shoulds': should do this, should not do that. Cognitive therapists challenge all these assumptions, as well as all self-evaluations that constantly put the person down. Such evaluations are cumulative.

The person needs help to:

- Identify the internal rules of self-evaluation
- See how self-evaluation influence feelings and behaviours
- Decide how realistic the internal rules are
- Discover the origin of the rule
- See how the rule is maintained
- Discover ways to get rid of redundant rules
- Think through what it would mean to get rid of redundant rules.

Attributions are:

- Being told what we are, what we must do and how we must feel
- Generally approving of obedience and disapproving of disobedience.

See also Transactional analysis.

The client is helped to explore:

- Personal responsibility
- Blame and self-blame
- Whether active or passive in meeting needs
- Attributions
- Alternatives

- Am I responsible for my behaviour?
- Am I in control or am I controlled?
- If I am controlled – by whom?

The challenge the client has to face is: To change or not to change?

The person is helped to replace 'tunnel thinking' with 'lateral, flexible thinking'.

Common thinking difficulties:

- Memory lapse
- Concentration
- Incoherence
- Blocking
- Scatter
- Restrictive thinking, in 'either or' terms.

Problem-solving involves being able to work with shades of grey. The counsellor needs to question behaviour based on unproven inferences such as: 'If I blush, people will think I am...'.

Clients often need to learn decision-making and problem-solving skills as part of the process of thinking rehabilitation. Faulty self-evaluations, attributions and anticipations may lead to restricted perceptions and to restricted ability to solve problems.

Possible counselling interventions

- Giving appropriate information may clear up misinformation and facilitate movement
- Acceptance and empathic understanding
- Focused exploration
- Specificity – get away from generalizations: insist on 'I' instead of 'you' and 'my' instead of 'our'.
- Challenge:
  - The discrepancies between thoughts, feelings and behaviours within and outside of counselling
  - The discrepancies between what is said and what is left unsaid
  - Attributions
  - False logic
  - Self-evaluations
  - Responsibility
  - Irrational beliefs
- Use disputation, a form of sustained challenging: 'Why...?' 'Yes, but why...?' 'That's still not clear'.
- Interpretation from the external frame of reference: 'It seems, from my point of view...'
- Teaching: the transactional analysis Parent/Adult/Child framework, for example, or problem-solving skills.

- Information-giving: tasks; homework; questionnaires.
- Direction:
  - Persuasion
  - Exhortation
  - Advice
  - Advocating
  - Encouragement
  - Reassurance
- Modelling:
  - The counselling relationship
  - Behaviour rehearsal
  - Group counselling
  - Observing tasks being carried out
- Role play:
  - Psychodrama
  - Dramatic enactment
  - Behaviour rehearsal
  - Imagery
- Encourage performance: anticipation about tasks is often more negative than results warrant
- Skills training
- Visual aids/homework.

Techniques to help clients with thinking

See also Rational emotive counselling.

1. **Explore and list negative thoughts**:
   When do you think them?
   Is there a pattern?
   Do they occur all the time or only at specific times?
   Are they concerned with specific people or events?
   Do you always lose out? Come off worse?
2. **Use imagination**: Imagination is a powerful ally. Whenever a negative thought occurs, 'imagine the situation, then change the scene into something positive'.
3. **Use 'thought stop'**: Every time a negative thought intrudes, say (aloud, if possible), 'STOP!' If thoughts are particularly troublesome, wear a loose elastic band on the wrist and, when the thought comes, snap the elastic.
4. **Substitute a positive thought to replace the invasive negative thought**: Substitution, coupled with imagination, is a powerful way to change from negative to positive thinking. Positive thinking can become as much a habit as negative thinking has been.

Further reading

Beck, A. T. and Rush, A. J. (1995) Cognitive therapy. In: *Comprehensive Textbook of Psychiatry*, 6th edn, (eds H. J. Kaplan and B. J. Sadock), Williams & Wilkins, Baltimore, MD.

Trower, P., Casey, A. and Dryden, W. (1988) *Cognitive Behavioural Counselling in Action*, Sage Publications, London.

COLLUSION

An unconscious process whereby two or more individuals create a partnership in which they defend a common need. An example of collusion is where one parent fails to support the disciplining of a child, in order to undermine the authority of the other parent. This alliance is then used to attack the other parent.

Folie à deux is a rare functional psychosis, a form of collusion, where two people with a long-term intimate association share the same delusions. One of the two, the inductor, is usually suffering from paranoia or some other paranoid disorder. The other, the inductee, generally a woman or a passive male, seems to accept the delusional attitudes of the dominant person. When the passive person is removed from the relationship, the symptoms are likely to disappear but, for the dominant person, the psychosis remains.

Collusion between counsellor and client occurs when the counsellor unconsciously avoids confronting the deepest and most disturbed aspects of the client's condition in order to keep the relationship safe or to protect the client from pain. The collusive relationship, therefore, meets the neurotic needs of both parties.

Collusion impedes growth and the development of insight. In groups, groups members collude with one another to avoid the task of the group.

Further reading
Berne, E. (1970) *Games People Play*, Penguin, Harmondsworth.

COMMUNICATION (*see also*: Creativity, Feedback, Listening, Questions)

Communication occurs when what takes place in one person's mind so influences the mind of another person that the resultant experiences of both are reasonably alike.

Communication is a sharing of:

- Attitudes
- Facts
- Feelings
- Information.

One (linear) model of communication has the following elements:

- Source – a person on the telephone
- Encoder – the mouthpiece
- Message – the words spoken
- Channel – electrical impulses

- Decoder – the earpiece at the other end
- Receiver – the mind of the listener.

Communication is influenced by:

- **Entropy,** which is auditory or visual static that decreases the effectiveness of the communication.
- **Negative entropy,** which functions when the receiver, in spite of mixed or blurred messages, interprets enough of the message to make it intelligible.
- **Redundancy** is the repetition of parts of the message that ensure the message gets through. Redundancy works against entropy. Entropy distorts; negative entropy and redundancy clarify.
- **Feedback** corrects the default between entropy, negative entropy and redundancy. Effective communication cannot take place without feedback. The term 'feedback' derives from cybernetic theory – a cybernetic example would be a room thermostat.

Methods of communicating:

- Words (10%)
- Tones (40%)
- Visual (50%).

Styles of communicating:

- Telling
- Negotiating
- Persuading
- Listening
- Counselling.

There is more of self and less of the other person in 'telling'; more of the other person and less of self in 'counselling'.

Barriers to effective communication:

- Lack of trust
- Misinterpretation
- Stereotyped language
- Semantics – the words we use
- Emotional
- Intellectual
- Conceptual
- Cultural.

Effective communication hinges on:

- **Creating a conducive atmosphere** based on time and place, motivation and preparation

- **Being clear about why we want to communicate,** what the listener expects and how we can put the points over
- **Active reception of information, which is influenced by the skills of:**
  - Active listening
  - Attending
  - Paraphrasing
  - Reflecting
  - Open questions
  - Summarizing
  - Focusing
  - Self-disclosure
  - Challenging.

Unclear reception of information may be influenced by:

- Lack of self-awareness
- Hidden agendas
- Preconceived ideas
- Arguing
- Interrupting
- Criticizing
- Putting down
- Not being able to get into the internal frame of reference.

Feedback

The aim of giving and receiving feedback is to make someone more aware of:

- What s/he does
- How it is done
- The feelings
- The consequences.

Giving feedback requires:

- Courage
- Other-respect
- Self-awareness
- Self-respect
- Skill
- Understanding.

Feedback should focus on:

- Behaviour that can be changed
- Description
- Exploring alternatives
- Giving information

- Observation
- Sharing ideas.

Feedback should not focus on:

- Personal qualities
- Judgement
- Providing answers
- Giving advice
- Inferences
- Giving direction.

We should consider how much feedback to give and then evaluate how clear and how accurate the feedback was. Effective communication leaves people feeling OK and is therefore a basis for change.

To be effective communicators, counsellors should:

- Be clear what they want the other person to understand
- Consider their attitudes and the attitudes of the client
- Have an accurate assessment of their own communication style
- Be able to assess the communication style of the client
- Try to get on the client's thinking and feeling wavelength
- Strive for clarity of expression
- Make certain the message is understood before continuing
- Try to get into the client's frame of reference
- State ideas in simplest possible terms
- Define then develop
- Explain then clarify
- Present one idea at a time
- Take one step at a time
- Make use of appropriate repetition to ensure understanding
- Compare and contrast ideas
- Use analogies and metaphors
- Use appropriate emphasis to underline ideas
- Use language which appeals to all five senses
- Use body language, congruent with the verbal message
- Give, encourage and acknowledge verbal and nonverbal feedback
- Be sensitive to go at the client's pace
- Be aware of when they are in danger of losing the client.

Defensive and supportive communication

Communication, in addition to the foregoing, also depends on climate. Climates may be supportive or defensive.

Supportive climates promote understanding and problem-solving and are characterized by:

- Empathy (*see* Core conditions)
- Spontaneity and openness
- Agreement, co-operation and teamwork.

Defensive climates are motivated by control, recognized by persuasion, coercion and convincing. The desire to control results in:

- Evaluations – characterized by criticism and judgement
- Strategies – with the focus on winning
- Superiority. The person who feels superior views the other as unintelligent and inferior
- Certainty. Correctness with no room for negotiation.

Barriers to supportive climates

These are cultural, time/energy, risk, emotional.

- **Culture**: In some cultures competition, not co-operation, listening and understanding is emphasized
- **Time/energy**: Creating a supportive climate takes time, energy and commitment
- **Risk**: Every time we view the world through someone else's eyes, from another person's frame of reference, we run the risk of having to change something within ourselves
- **Emotional**: Hostile, angry feelings get in the way of offering support.

Facilitating supportive communication

This depends on three things:

- **Being genuinely open**: False openness will create alarm. Some people are very good at putting on a show of being open but something about their motives is not genuine.
- **Active listening** which is grasping the facts and meaning of the message; clarifying and checking.
- **Feedback**, which is sharing perspectives; moving from 'me versus you' to 'you and me together' and thinking of the goal(s), then seeking solutions to reach it (them).

Direct and indirect communication

Indirect communication is pseudocommunication, carried out with the purpose of manipulating, control, avoiding risks and self-protection.

Characteristics of indirect communication:

- **Noncommunication**: Attempting to get support which is not genuine: 'I think I speak for the whole group'.
- **Nongenuine questions**: These are generally indirect communication and seek to direct the person toward a certain response.

- **Limiting questions**:
  'Don't you think that...?'
  'Isn't it a fact that...?'
- **Punishing questions**, where the motive is to expose the other person without appearing to do so and so put the person on the spot.
- **Hypothetical questions**, which are often motivated by criticism and typically begin with 'If', 'What if', 'How about':
  'If you were making that report, wouldn't you say it differently?'
- **Demand or command questions**, where the motivation is to impress urgency or importance:
  'Have you done anything about...?'
- **Screened questions**, where the motivation is to get the other person to make a decision that fits with the speaker's hidden wish. This type of questions puts great pressure on the person being questioned, not being sure what answer is required:
  'Would you like to go to...?'
- **Leading questions**, where the motive is to manoeuvre the other person into a vulnerable position. Leading question are often used by lawyers in court to confuse the witness:
  'Is it fair to say that you...?'
  'Would you agree that...?'
- **Questions that don't need an answer**, where the motive is to forestall a response because the questioner fears it may not be a favourable one. The attempt is to secure a guaranteed agreement. No response is required:
  'You don't mind if I come for the weekend?'
- **'Now I've got you' questions**, where the motive is to dig a trap for the other person to fall into.
  'Weren't you the one who...?'
- **Clichés**: Here the motive is to appear to be communicating, without sharing anything significant. The frequent use of tired, worn-out phrases reduces the effectiveness of communication.

The effects of indirect communication:

- **Guesswork**: Without direct, open communication, people cannot get to know each other. What we do not know, we will make guesses about.
- **Inaccuracy**: Guessing means making assumptions and often we get the wrong answers.
- **Inferences**: When communication is not direct, we are forced to infer the other person's motives. Pseudoquestions and clichés hide motives.
- **Playing games**: Indirect communication encourages game-playing, leading to deception and dishonesty.
- **Defensiveness**: This is one of the surest effects of indirect communication (*see also* Defence mechanisms).

Direct communication is characterized by:

- Being two-way, in which ideas, opinions, values, beliefs and feelings flow freely
- Active listening (*see also* Listening)
- Giving and receiving feedback (*see also* Feedback)
- Not being stressful
- Being clear and relatively free from ambiguity and mixed messages.

We can foster direct communication by:

- **Making direct statements**: When we make statements, based on what we have heard, rather than ask questions, we are more likely to be communicating directly
- **Actively listening**
- **Owning** that what we say and feel do belong to us and not to someone else
- **Locating the context**: This means that in order to make a genuine response we have to understand the context in which the statement is made; we must not make assumptions
- **Sharing**. All true communication is a sharing process. For communication to be effective, we must be prepared to take risks and work toward a mutual understanding through genuine sharing of a common meaning.

Further reading

Combs, G. W. (1981) Defensive and supportive communication. In: *1981 Annual Handbook for Group Facilitators*, University Associates, San Diego, CA.

Gibb, J. R. (1961) Defensive communication. *Journal of Communication*, **11**, 141–148.

Jones, J. E. (1972) Communication modes: an experiential lecture. In: *1972 Annual Handbook for Group Facilitators*, University Associates, San Diego, CA.

COMMUNICATION MODES OF VIRGINIA SATIR (*see also*: Family therapy)

Virginia Satir – a family therapist – identifies four universal patterns of responses we use to get around the threat of rejection. We feel and react to the threat but, because we do not want to reveal 'weakness', we attempt to conceal our feelings. A fifth mode – the Leveller – is positive and genuine.

The five communication modes

Placaters:

Are frightened that people will get angry, go away and never return. However, they don't dare admit this.

Typical Placater speech:

'Oh, you know me – I don't care, really I don't.'
'Whatever anybody else wants to do is fine with me.'

'Whatever you say, darling; I don't mind, really.'
'Oh, nothing bothers me! Do whatever you like.'
'What do I want to do? Oh, well! What would you like to do?'

Two Placaters conversing cannot make decisions, however minor.

Blamers:

Feel that nobody cares about them; there is no respect or affection for them; that people are indifferent to their needs and feelings. Blamers react to this with verbal behaviour intended to demonstrate who is in charge, the boss, the one with power.

Typical Blamer speech:

'You never consider my feelings.'
'Nobody around here ever pays any attention to me.'
'Do you always have to put yourself first?'
'Why don't you ever think about what I might want?'
'I've had all I'm going to take.'
'Why do you always insist on having your own way, no matter how much it hurts other people?'

When two Blamers talk, the conversation is not a dead-end, as it is with two Placaters. It is a rapid road to a screaming match, nasty in every way.

Computers:

Are terrified that someone will find out that they have feelings. Computers work hard to give the impression that they have none. *Star Trek*'s Mr Spock – except for the troublesome human side of him that makes him so interesting – is a classic Computer type.

Typical Computer speech:

'There is undoubtedly a simple solution to the problem.'
'It's obvious that no real difficulty exists here.'
'No rational person would be alarmed by this minor event.'
'Clearly the advantages of this activity have been exaggerated.'
'Preferences of the kind you describe are rather common in this area.'

Two Computers talking is like listening to people from another planet!

Distracters:

Are tricky people to keep up with, as they shift rapidly between the other modes, yet never staying long in any one of them. The underlying feeling is of panic: 'I don't know what on earth to say, but I've to say something and the quicker the better!'

The surface behaviour is a chaotic mix.

Levellers:

Are the most contradictory type of all – either the easiest or the most difficult to handle.

Levellers do what the term implies – level with you. There's no one simpler to deal with than the Leveller – just level back. What Levellers say is what Levellers feel. The Leveller verbal message is congruent with the body language. The aim is single, straight messages.

Levelling relationships:

- Free and honest
- Few threats to self-esteem
- Potential for healing and for building bridges
- Genuine
- More likely to criticize and evaluate the behaviour not the person.

Developing Levelling attitudes will give us a good opportunity to stand on our own feet. It may not be easy; it may not be painless; but it might make the difference as to whether we grow or not.

The benefits of levelling

- Levelling is a way of responding to real people in real life situations
- Levelling permits us to agree because we really do, not because we think we should
- Levelling allows us to disagree when we really do
- Levelling allows us to use our brain freely but not to score off others
- Levelling allows us to change course, not to get someone off the hook but because we want to and there is a genuine need to do so.

Fake Levellers are more dangerous than all the other categories combined and very hard to spot. One way to spot the fake is to listen to your gut reaction. You may not unmask this person straight away, but after a time you will start to feel very uncomfortable without being able to identify the reason. When this happens, start to do a check on things that don't add up – inconsistencies, discrepancies, ambiguities.

You don't have to stay in one mode, even though the Leveller has the most to offer. To be able to switch modes has distinct advantages. When you are uncertain which mode to move into, become a Computer, who:

- Is never angry or emotional or hurried or upset
- Never uses 'I', 'me', 'my', 'mine', 'myself'
- Always talks in abstractions and generalities
- Says, 'One could...' or 'Any reasonable person would...'
- Says, 'It is ... that...' [It is obvious that there is no cause for alarm]
- Always looks calm and relaxed
- Maintains one physical position throughout the conversation

- Never commits her/himself to anything
- Deliberately creates emotional distance.

The computer mode at work

Meg was a graduate student nurse, in the last year of training, having counselling because she felt uncertain about her choice of career, coupled with panic attacks. This is part of her account.

> We weren't very close, any of us and this was something I very much regretted. I knew I was harbouring a lot of resentment against my mother. She is a very dominant, self-centred and possessive woman, toward us all, but particularly toward me, for some reason. On talking things through with William I realized that mother made very heavy demands on me. She would use words like, 'If you really loved me...' or 'Other daughters don't treat their mothers like you do'. I felt stifled by her. So strong were my feelings that I was often troubled by bad dreams in which, for example, I would be going upstairs with a knife in my hand to kill Mother. In fact, I was afraid that some day I might actually do this. The thought terrified me. I didn't know how to deal with Mother. William talked through with me a way of responding called the 'Computer'. I tried this and found I could handle my feelings better. I think Mother is jealous of me, though I can't think why she should be.

The aim was to help Meg cope with her mother's Blamer mode; the Blamer is the person who makes statements like, 'Why don't you ever think what I might want?' This seemed to be Meg's mother's mode, which usually put Meg into the Placater mode – anything for peace, even at the expense of feelings. One way to cope with the Blamer is to adopt the Computer mode. A computer has no feelings, does not react from an emotional base. Everything directed at the Computer is filtered through the impersonal screen that deflects the other person's feelings. Computers work very hard at not saying 'I', for that would be too personal. The Computer response is aimed at taking the heat off. It helps the target person by putting the question back at the sender. Meg was able to achieve some success and a little success paves the way for other successes.

Further reading

Satir, V. (1972) *Peoplemaking*, Science and Behaviour Books, Palo Alto, CA.

COMPENSATION (*see also*: Complexes, Individual psychology)

Compensation is Alfred Adler's term to describe the unconscious process we use as a reaction to our inferiority complexes and which we disguise from ourselves and other people.

As infants, because of our initial helplessness, we feel inferior and strive to overcome this feeling of incompleteness. Striving to master inferiority is a powerful motivator.

An inferiority complex arises when we cannot achieve normal development and manifests itself in ideas of personal worthlessness.

Compensation is the drive to challenge situations that will prove that the misgivings we have about ourselves are false.

If we do not achieve normal balance, there is the danger of over-compensation, where our striving for power and dominance become so exaggerated and intensified that it must be called pathological.

Overcompensation is characterized by pride, vanity and the desire to conquer everyone at any price. These attitudes bring us into contact with the dark side of life and prevent us from experiencing the joy of living.

Adlerian therapy is concerned with the personal aspirations and goals of achievement, both conscious and unconscious, as applied to our social setting and total life situation.

The man who is crippled yet becomes a mountaineer is probably compensating. He would be overcompensating if he gloated over his achievements at the expense of other disabled people.

COMPETITION VERSUS CO-OPERATION

Co-operation is a co-ordinated effort to reach mutual goals; competition is the struggle that occurs when we try to maximize our own rewards at the expense of others. Competition and co-operation can be regarded as opposite ends of a continuum of human interaction. At the one end are what could be considered positive outcomes – actions that result in gains for all. At the other end are negative outcomes, which result in one person or group gaining at the expense of other people or groups. Generally we will chose either one or the other depending on the situation and what we stand to gain from either orientation.

Many societies are intensely competitive and this is obvious throughout all sections from a very early age. This statement will be easily confirmed by studying a group of children playing at school – how they will strive for mastery over other children.

It could be argued that competition is a natural tendency, and it could quite well be, but it could equally be argued that it is a natural instinct to kill. We are encouraged in one activity and positively discouraged in the other. It is also possible that competition is a relatively harmless channelling of this primitive drive. At the same time as competition is encouraged at school, in sports, at work and in many other areas of life, attempts are made to foster co-operation. Undue competition at work may be quite a significant factor in producing intolerable levels of stress in certain individuals.

Competition has more excitement, more immediate thrill to it than co-operation; for example, the thrill of the downhill ski competition is immediately appealing, possibly because of the high level of adrenaline produced.

Whatever the outcome, physiological or psychological, the question that must be asked is: Can highly competitive people move easily into an essentially co-operative role?

The language of business, politics and education is dotted with win–lose terms. One 'wins' promotion, 'beats' the competition. Students strive to 'top the class' or 'outsmart the teacher'. Although we do recognize co-operative effort and collaboration, it seems that we tend to emphasize 'healthy' competition. Competition means an event or contest in which people compete. Generally we compete against other people who represent the opposition.

Examples of competitive behaviour:

- Interrupting when others are talking
- Getting one's own ideas across
- Not acknowledging other people's contribution or ideas
- Forming partnerships and power blocks to get one's own way.

Example of co-operative behaviour:

- A football team, even though the focus is competition
- An orchestra; every person playing his/her part to produce a whole.

We so easily drop into competing when the situation would benefit from co-operation. Win–lose contests can also develop in an organization. People strive for dominant positions. Battles rage between departments. People sabotage new ideas in order to prove that they won't work. Although there are instances where win–lose is positive, it is often destructive. Win–lose is a poison to relationships. Win–lose is a stressor that interferes with working effectiveness. Win–lose 'victories' often turn into lose–lose for both parties.

Summary of win–lose/win–win:

- **Win–lose** is characterized by each person seeking his/her own advantage, usually to the detriment of the other person – the 'win at all costs' approach.
- **Lose–win** is where one person decides in advance to yield to pressure. In the lose–win approach, one party seeks the acceptance of the other party. This is the 'peace-at-any-price' approach – appeasement.
- **Win–win** is characterized by each person seeking an agreement that provides joint gain. This is the 'everybody's-a-winner' approach.
- In a **mixed approach**, each person strives to be realistic. Both persons realize that usually one wins more than the other.

Counsellors must learn to co-operate with their clients; if we do not learn to do this, the client's needs will not be fully met. The spirit of competition, harmless on the playing-field, may spell disaster in relationships where, instead of fighting to gain possession of a ball or to score a goal, each person is constantly trying to dominate the other, to gain possession of an emotional ball.

Counsellors have to co-operate with clients and not compete with them. The counsellor who enters into a spirit of competition with the client is sure to end up in conflict with her/him. It is possible that the seeds of competition lie deeply buried in some emotion or experience that is reawakened by contact with a particular client.

On the other hand, if the counsellor is someone who always wants to win, always wants to score, always wants to get on top, then co-operating with the client may prove difficult. A client who is prepared to co-operate may very well be swamped by a competitive counsellor and be persuaded to make choices that have mental rather than emotional assent.

A highly competitive client may try very hard to engage the counsellor in a competition rather than in exploring the problem. If the counsellor does not 'play the game', conflict may be generated within the client. This could very well be the spark to kindle the desire to change.

Further reading

Hersey, P., Blanchard, K. H. and Natemeyer, W. E. (1979) *Situational Leadership, Perception, and the Impact of Power*, Leadership Studies, Escondido, CA.
Wiley, G. E. (1973) Win/lose situations. In: *Annual Handbook for Group Facilitators*. University Associates, San Diego, CA.

COMPLEXES

A complex is a group of associated ideas that are emotionally charged and have been partially or wholly repressed. These are usually outside awareness and evoke emotional forces that influence a person's behaviour.

Complexes are archetypal in character, have their origins in early relationships with parents and significant others, and have a 'magnetic' quality that attracts associated ideas and memories to them.

A complex may arise from the personal unconscious, from the collective unconscious or from both. Complexes always contain the characteristics of a conflict – shock, upheaval, mental agony, inner strife.

Complexes are the 'sore spots', the 'skeletons in the cupboard' that come unbidden to terrorize us and always contain memories, wishes, fears, duties, needs or insights that somehow we can never really grapple with.

They constantly interfere with our conscious life in disturbing and usually harmful ways. The presence of complexes act as obstacles and therefore as new possibilities of achievement of growth. They act as filters through which life is perceived.

Castration complex

In psychoanalytic theory, castration is the unconscious fear of losing the male genital organs or the feeling (in the female) that they have already been lost. Boys fear punishment by castration from their fathers because of their (unconscious) wish for a sexual relationship with their mothers, leading to castration anxiety.

Girls, so the theory goes, feel that the punishment has already been carried out; that is why they do not have a penis; they therefore have a residual penis envy. Female analysts, however, have pointed out that many males can be as envious of the reproductive power of females as females are of the male's penis.

The concept of castration complex is controversial, especially outside psychoanalysis. Not all psychoanalysts of Freud's era, or since, totally agreed with Freud. The question must also be asked: who is the castrater? Does the threat arise from without or within?

In the 19th century the threat of castration was often used as a deterrent against masturbation. Freud linked the castration complex with the incest taboo, for which it serves as a major prohibition.

People who constantly undermine the self-confidence of others are said to be castrating. It can apply to females who, because of penis envy, are constantly disparaging men and aggressively competitive toward them.

The term also applies to men who undermine their sons. An extension of the word is where men make a habit of putting women down and do their best to make them feel incompetent and second-rate.

If this and other complexes remain unresolved and persist into adult life, they can produce disturbances in the person's love relationships and ability to work productively. There is also the suggestion that castration anxiety is part of some sexual perversions.

In these days, the idea of the castration complex may seem outmoded but, although the modern term is castration anxiety, castration complex is still very much a part of psychological language and part of the wider myth.

Electra complex

In mythology, Electra was the daughter of the Greek leader Agamemnon and his wife Clytemnestra. Electra saved the life of her brother, Orestes, by sending him away when their father was murdered. Later, when he returned, she helped him avenge their father's death by slaying their mother and her lover, by whom Agamemnon had been killed.

Freud adopted the term as the female equivalent of the Oedipus complex, although it is rarely used in modern psychoanalysis. It is where a female child has an erotic attraction to her father, accompanied by hostility toward her mother.

Oedipus complex

This is a psychoanalytic concept derived from the Greek myth in which Oedipus, unknowingly, falls in love with his mother and kills the rival for his love, his father.

The oedipal triangle – father, mother and child – applies equally to male and female children during the 'phallic' stage of development, about 3–5 years. It is during this stage of development, in psychoanalytic theory, that the loving desire for the parent of the opposite sex reaches a climax. Feelings of intense rivalry are generated toward the parent of the same sex, who is the real love partner.

The rivalry resurfaces during adolescence, to be finally resolved when the young person chooses a love partner who is not the parent.

The 'Electra complex' is the female equivalent, although the resolution of the conflict is different for male and female children. The male child perceives the threat of castration by his father, so he gives up his incestuous desires toward his mother. The conflict for the female child culminates in her recognition that she has no penis – castration has already taken place. The resolution of the oedipal conflict leads to the formation of the superego and the internalization of the prohibitions and taboos of society.

Repressed oedipal wishes provide fertile ground for irrational guilt in later life. If relationships between child and parents are loving and basically nontraumatic and if parental attitudes are neither excessively prohibitive nor excessively sexually stimulating, the oedipal stage is passed through without difficulty. Children subjected to trauma are likely candidates for 'infantile neurosis', an important forerunner of similar reactions in adult life.

Melanie Klein believed that Freud interpreted the myth too literally. For her, the complex started during the first year of life and unresolved oedipal conflict did not necessarily set the scene for all future neuroses.

It is possible that the Oedipus complex is never totally resolved or overwhelmed, as Freud suggested, but that it persists in varying degrees throughout life.

Freud also applied the myth to the whole of society and in all cultures. Every social and psychological phenomenon Freud related to the Oedipus complex. However much the concept may be open to criticism, the central place of the triangle of mother, father and child is an important concept in any school of psychotherapy.

Inferiority complex

A term used in individual (Adlerian) psychology to describe exaggerated feelings of inadequacy or insecurity resulting in defensive and neurotic behaviour. Inferiority complexes are usually abnormal.

As a result of its initial helplessness, an infant feels inferior and strives to overcome this feeling of incompleteness by developing to a higher level. The feeling of inferiority and compensating for that feeling becomes the prime motivator in moving the person from one level of development to another. Adler refers to this as the 'great upward drive' toward perfection.

Constant incapability, discouragement from others, faulty self-evaluation of one's own worth, enhanced by being put down and ridiculed, all sow the seeds of inferiority.

People who view themselves against others on a vertical plane (a typical hierarchy) are bound to put themselves either higher or lower (better or worse) than someone else.

People who view relationships on a horizontal plane are more likely to adopt a view of equality, each recognizing his/her own unique attributes and contributions.

Superiority complex

In literal terms this means the conviction that one is better than or superior to, others. Adler used the term to describe the mechanism of striving for recognition and superiority as a compensation for the feelings of inferiority, inadequacy and insecurity.

Inferiority is acted upon through the processes of socialization and education. The superiority complex helps to rid the developing child of feelings of inferiority.

The striving for power and dominance may become so exaggerated and intensified that it then must be called pathological. When this happens, the ordinary relationships of life will never be satisfactory.

The pathological drive to achieve power is characterized by:

- Effort
- Haste and impatience
- Violent impulsiveness
- Lack of consideration for others
- Dominance from an early age
- Defensiveness
- Feeling of being against the world and the world being against one
- Achievements that do not benefit anyone but oneself
- Trampling on others to get to the top
- Lack of importance attached to human relationships
- Pride, vanity and the desire to conquer
- Constantly putting other people down in order to elevate oneself
- A marked distance between oneself and other people
- Joy in life is rarely experienced.

Further reading

Adler, A. (1956) *The Individual Psychology of Alfred Adler*, (eds H. L. Ansbacher and R. R. Ansbacher), Basic Books, New York.

Hamilton, V. (1982) *Narcissus and Oedipus*, Routledge & Kegan Paul, London.

Jung, C. G. (1958) *The Collected Works – Psychological Types*, vol. 6, Routledge & Kegan Paul, London.

Weiner M. F. and Mohl P. C. (1995) Theories of personality and psychopathology: other psychodynamic schools. In: *Comprehensive Textbook of Psychiatry*, 6th edn, (eds H. J. Kaplan and B. J. Sadock), Williams & Wilkins, Baltimore, MD.

COMPLIANCE

Compliance is a response to social influence in which the person towards whom the influence is directed publicly conforms to the wishes of the influencing source but does not change his/her private beliefs or attitudes. This is termed 'public compliance' and may or may not lead to private attitude change.

When a source obtains compliance by setting an example, it is called **conformity**; when a source obtains compliance by wielding authority, it is called **obedience**; e.g. the child eats tapioca pudding but continues to dislike it. In compliance the person does not need to believe in what s/he is doing.

Forced compliance (also called induced compliance), on the other hand, is when a person is induced to make a public declaration which is contrary to his/her previously held attitudes.

The term compliance has a different meaning in health care, where it refers to a patient's adherence to a treatment programme prescribed by a doctor. Faulty compliance can represent a serious problem to the patient's well-being and mental health.

Karen Horney (1885–1952), the German-born American psychoanalyst, departed from some of the basic principles of Sigmund Freud, suggesting that environmental and social conditions, rather than biological drives, determine much of individual personality and are the chief causes of neuroses and personality disorders. Horney developed a theory of neurosis that included the 'compliant character'.

According to Horney, neurosis is a disturbance in the relationship between self and others. Feelings of helplessness and despair drive us into making decisions that are not fulfilling and leave us feeling dissatisfied. Such feelings (formed early in childhood into defensive patterns) are self-perpetuating strategies against anxiety. Three strategies are available to the child in its search for safety:

- **Compliant, self-effacing:** Moving toward others, seeking affection and approval – this 'moving toward' only emphasizes helplessness
- **Aggressive, expansive:** Moving against others and in so doing accepting a hostile environment
- **Detached, resigned:** Moving away from others and in so doing accepting the difficulty of relating to people at an intimate level.

Behaviour, then, is influenced by whichever one of these strategies is found to bring the greatest rewards. Only one strategy is used, so the child does not explore the feelings and impulses of the other two. A deep sense of instability is thus created, which leads to ever greater restriction and repression of genuine feelings. Feelings are mistrusted and projected on to the outside world, where they develop into neurotic trends.

The compliant, self-effacing, moving-toward type seeks constant approval, is highly dependent, is ultra-sensitive to others' needs, constantly subordinates her/himself; is poor on assertiveness, values goodness, sympathy and ultra-unselfishness and tends to panic at the first hint of rejection.

Clients who tend towards being compliant are likely to agree with whatever the counsellor suggests, however tentatively it is put. They are also likely to be very clinging and not open to being challenged, for this would be interpreted as rejection. These two behaviours alone make progress difficult and the counsellor may be left with the feeling of treading very carefully on eggshells.

Further reading

Horney, K. (1937) *The Neurotic Personality of Our Time*, W. W. Norton, New York.

CONCILIATION

The *Oxford English Dictionary* defines conciliation as a conversion from a state of hostility or distrust; the promotion of good will by kind and considerate measures; the exhibition of a spirit of amity, practice of conciliatory measures.

Conciliation is a legal/therapeutic process whereby a counsellor mediates between a husband and wife at the point when they have begun or are considering beginning the legal process to end their marriage.

Conciliation requires close liaison with solicitors and extensive knowledge of divorce law and court procedures as well as therapeutic skills appropriate to working with couples in conflict.

The aim of conciliation is to help the parties to negotiate with each other over matters that are in dispute. These may include the divorce itself (where one party's decision to end the marriage is opposed by the other), the settlement of finances and property and the custody of children.

The aim is to make the divorce as amicable as possible so that both parties can walk away with dignity and without recrimination. Conciliation starts the grieving process and allows the couple to express their feelings openly and appropriately. Effective conciliation prepares the way for counselling.

Further reading

Howard, J. and Shepherd, G. (1987) *Conciliation, Children and Divorce: A family systems approach*, Batsford, London.

CONCRETENESS

To get clients to be concrete or specific may, at times, be quite difficult, yet it is essential if they are to come to terms fully with whatever is causing them concern. The counsellor picks up on generalizations, omissions and distortions.

The opposite of being concrete, direct and specific is making generalized, indirect and vague statements. So often, in general conversation, as well as in counselling, we confuse the issue by not being concrete, specific and direct.

A generalization does not discriminate but lumps all parts together. A generality, common in everyday speech is 'you'. Clients who say, 'You never know when people approve of what you're doing', when encouraged to rephrase it to, 'I never know when people approve of what I'm doing', will usually be able to perceive their statement in a different light. The client needs to be able to identify thoughts, feelings, behaviour and experiences in specific ways.

Personalizing a statement in this way makes it pertinent and real. In one sense it is 'owning the problem'. Being specific opens the way for a realistic acknowledgement of feelings. Owning and not merely reporting such feelings opens the door to exploring them. While this may be uncomfortable for the client, it is vital.

Sometimes thoughts, feelings and behaviours are expressed before the counselling relationship has been established firmly enough to explore them. That is why, in Egan's model, concreteness is a second-stage skill. If such thoughts, feelings and behaviours are central to the client's problem the client will return to them at some stage.

Concreteness requires clients to be prepared to examine themselves closely and not to hide behind the facade of generality. Clients may fiercely resist attempts to encourage them to be specific, particularly about feelings. They may have to be led gently into what, for many, is a new experience.

Counsellors can collude with clients by allowing them to talk about feelings second-hand, as if they belonged to other people and not to them. 'I wonder if this is how **you** feel?' or 'It sounds as if that is something like **your** situation' may be enough to bring the interview back into focus from second-hand reporting to 'This is what is happening to **me, now**'.

Counsellors who themselves speak in generalities would find it difficult to challenge a client about not being concrete.

Questions to aid concreteness

Example 1 – Mavis to Marion, the works supervisor:

Mavis (*generalized and vague*) I know I haven't been very regular at work recently, I haven't been very well. That's the truth of it.
Mavis (*concrete and specific*) I know that over the past month I've been off work six times. I've been attending the doctor for about 6 months with vague abdominal pains. They haven't yet reached a firm diagnosis but they think it's probably something to do with the gall bladder.

Example 2 – Robert to Joy, the school counsellor:

Robert (*generalized and vague*) People keep picking on me.
Robert (*concrete and specific*) My classmates pick on me because I wear glasses.

Example 3 – Trudy, student teacher, to Liz, her supervisor:

Trudy (*generalized and vague*) I know I'm dreadfully inconsistent in my work.
Trudy (*concrete and specific*) I make all sorts of teaching plans, yet when it comes to the day, I don't stick to them. I think the students run the class, not me.

Further reading
Sutton, J. and Stewart, W. (1997) *Learning to Counsel*, How To Books, Oxford.

CONFLICT

A psychological state of indecision, where the person is faced simultaneously with two opposing forces of equal strength that cannot be solved together.

Types of conflict:

- Choice between positives both of which are desirable: approach–approach. Chance factors determine the outcome, e.g. the choice between two attractive careers.
- Choice between negatives, where both are undesirable: avoidance–avoidance. For example, a man may dislike his job intensely but fears the threat of unemployment if he resigns.
- Choice between negative and positive: approach–avoidance. This creates great indecision, helplessness and anxiety, e.g. in a child, dependent on her mother, who also fears her because she is rejecting and punitive.

Conflicts are often unconscious, in the sense that the person cannot clearly identify the source of the distress. Many strong impulses, such as fear and hostility, are not approved of by society, so children soon learn not to acknowledge them, even to themselves. When such impulses are in conflict, we are anxious without knowing why.

Related concepts are cognitive dissonance and Kurt Lewin's field theory.

Conflicts may be avoided or resolved by:

- Active listening
- Appropriate disclosure.

Poorly handled, conflicts can result in negative behaviours such as:

- Aggression
- Defiance
- Forming alliances
- Gossiping
- Physical and psychological withdrawal
- Retaliation.

Conflict resolution is strongly influenced by feelings of self-worth. People with low self-worth expect to be treated badly; they expect the worst, invite it and generally get it.

People who do not feel confident generally feel small and, therefore, view others as threateningly larger.

Thinking about resolving conflict:

- Identify the rules that encourage conflict
- How much autonomy do people have and give?
- How much do we control each other?
- Identify 'musts', 'oughts' and 'shoulds'
- Examine attributions (*see* Transactional analysis)
- Who blames whom and for what?
- What are the risks and gains of resolution?

- Are there any possible compromises?
- What roles sustain the conflict?
- What 'games' do people play? (*see* Transactional analysis).

Helping people change:

- Teach assertiveness
- Use video feedback
- Teach empathic listening
- Develop open communication
- Concentrate on changeable behaviour
- Work at a time free from distractions
- Teach how to give specific and non-evaluative feedback
- Encourage the giving of written contracts
- Explore agreed areas
- Be an example of an effective, caring communicator.

Conflict: a problem-solving model

Let each person:

- Describe the situation as they see it
- Describe what they feel about the conflict and what personal meaning it has for them
- Describe a desired situation
- Identify changes necessary to achieve the desired situation
- Outline a problem-solving agenda or plan of action.

Further reading

Deutsch, M. (1973) *The Resolution of Conflict*, Yale University Press, New Haven, CT.
Main, A. P. and Roark, A. E. (1975) A consensus method to reduce conflict. *Personnel and Guidance Journal*, 53, 754–759.

CONTRACT

A formal, explicit agreement between counsellor and client. A contract helps to ensure the professional nature of the relationship and may include:

- Venue
- Frequency of sessions
- Boundaries of confidentiality
- Broad requirements of the treatment
- Duties and responsibilities of each party
- Goals of therapy
- Means by which the goals may be achieved
- The provision and completion of 'homework'
- The setting of boundaries and expectations
- The terms of the therapeutic relationship

- Time limits – of sessions and of counselling
- Provision for renegotiation of contract
- Fees, if appropriate
- How therapy will be evaluated
- Process of referral, if and when necessary
- Supervision.

The contract may be written, signed by both therapist and client or each person in a group.

In family therapy, the children need to be included in the terms of the contract – how, and at what age, needs to be considered. In group therapy, part of the contract would include a full and frank discussion on 'ground rules'.

Further reading

Sager, C. J. (1976) *Marriage Contracts and Couple Therapy*, Brunner/Mazel, New York.

CORE CONDITIONS

The core conditions are the relationship qualities embraced in most humanistic therapies and considered to be crucial in person-centred counselling.

The core conditions are:

- Empathy
- Genuineness or congruence
- Warmth
- Unconditional positive regard.

Empathy

This is the ability of one person to step into the inner world of another person and to step out of it again, without becoming that other person. An example is the singer or actor who genuinely feels the part s/he is performing.

It means trying to understand the thoughts, feelings, behaviours and personal meanings from the other's internal frame of reference.

For empathy to mean anything, we have to respond in such a way that the other person feels that understanding has been reached or is being striven for. Unless our understanding is communicated it is of no therapeutic value.

Empathy is to feel 'with'
Sympathy is to feel 'like'
Pity is to feel 'for'.

Empathy is not a state that one reaches, nor a qualification that one is awarded. It is a transient thing. We can move in to it and lose it again very quickly. Literally, it means 'getting alongside'.

Empathy is the central core condition of the person-centred approach, although therapists from a wide range of approaches rank empathy as being one of the highest qualities a therapist can demonstrate.

Levels of empathy are related to the degree to which the client is able to explore and reach self-understanding. It can be taught within an empathic climate.

Primary empathy works more with surface or stated facts and feelings; advanced empathy works more with implied facts and feelings.

The difference between empathy and identification is that in identification the 'as if' quality is absent. We have become the other person.

Some client statements about counsellor empathy:

'Helps me to learn a lot about myself'
'Understands how I see things'
'Understands me'
'Can read me like a book'
'Is able to put my feelings into words'
'Knows what it's like to feel ill'.

Genuineness or congruence

This is the degree to which we are freely and deeply ourselves and are able to relate to people in a sincere and undefensive manner. Also referred to as authenticity, congruence or truth, genuineness is the precondition for empathy and unconditional positive regard.

Effective therapy depends wholly on the degree to which the therapist is integrated and genuine. In person-centred counselling, skill and technique play a much less important role than relating to the client authentically. Genuineness encourages client self-disclosure.

Appropriate therapist disclosure enhances genuineness. The genuine therapist does not feel under any compulsion to disclose, either about events, situations or feeling aroused within the counselling relationship.

Some client statements about counsellor genuineness:

'What she says never conflicts what she feels'
'Is himself in our relationship'
'I don't think she hides anything from herself that she feels with me'
'Doesn't avoid anything that is important for our relationship'
'I feel I can trust her to be honest with me'
'Is secure in our relationship'
'Doesn't try to mislead me about his own thoughts or feelings'
'Is impatient with me at times'
'Is sometimes upset by what I say'
'Sometimes looks as worried as I feel'
'Treats me with obvious concern'.

Nonpossessive warmth

Nonpossessive warmth:

- Is genuine
- Springs from an attitude of friendliness toward others – a relationship in which friendliness is absent will not flourish
- Makes us feel comfortable
- Is liberating
- Is nondemanding
- Melts the coldness and hardness within people's hearts.

Possessive warmth, on the other hand:

- Is false
- Makes us feel uncomfortable and wary
- Is more for the needs of the giver than for the receiver
- Is smothering and cloying
- Robs us of energy.

Warmth is conveyed by:

- **Body language**: posture, proximity, personal space, facial expressions, eye contact
- **Words and the way we speak**: tone of voice, delivery, rate of speech and the use of non-words – all these are 'paralinguistics'
- All the indicators of warmth – the nonverbal parts of speech and body language – must be in agreement with the words used; any discrepancy between the words and how we deliver them will cause confusion in the other person.

Warmth, like a hot water bottle, must be used with great care. Someone who is very cold, distant, cynical, mistrustful could feel threatened by someone else's depth of warmth. A useful analogy would be to think how an iceberg would react in the presence of the sun.

Some client statements about counsellor warmth:

'Always responds to me with warmth and interest'
'Her feelings toward me do not depend on how I feel toward her'
'I can express whatever feelings I want and he remains the same toward me'
'I can be very critical of her or very appreciative without it changing her feelings toward me'.

Unconditional positive regard

This is a nonpossessive caring and acceptance of the client, irrespective of how offensive the client's behaviour might be. The counsellor who offers unconditional positive regard helps to create a climate that encourages trust within the counselling relationship. It is where we communicate a deep and genuine caring, not filtered through our own feelings, thoughts and behaviours.

Conditional regard implies enforced control and compliance with behaviour dictated by someone else.

Some client statements about counsellor unconditional positive regard:

'She always seems very concerned about me'
'Always appreciates me'
'Thinks I'm a worthwhile person'
'Still likes me even if I criticize him'
'I feel safe with her'
'I feel free to be myself'
'Makes it OK to talk about anything'
'Seems to trust my feelings about myself'
'Would never knowingly hurt me'.

When the core conditions are present and appropriately expressed, a climate is created in which a positive therapeutic outcome is likely. When clients are in a relationship in which the core conditions are demonstrated, they will learn to relate to themselves with respect and dignity.

Criticism of the core conditions centres more on their efficiency than their necessity. Some theorists argue that, while the core conditions must be present, by themselves they are insufficient. Other interventions are necessary.

There is a body of opinion that neither a 'relationship' nor a 'skills' approach is sufficient. Both are needed. This would depend on the nature of the problem and the personality of both client and counsellor. Counsellors generally choose an approach or method that suits their personality.

Further reading

Barrett-Leonard, G. T. (1981) The empathy cycle: refinement of a nuclear concept. *Journal of Counselling Psychology*, 28, 91–100.

Mearns, D. and Thorne, B. (1988) *Person-centred Counselling in Action*, Sage Publications, London.

Rogers, C. R. (1961), *On Becoming A Person: A therapist's view of psychotherapy*, Constable, London.

Rogers, C. R. (1967) *The Therapeutic Relationship and its Impact*, Greenwood Press, Westport, CT.

Rogers, C. R. (1975) Empathic: an unappreciated way of being. *Counselling Psychologist*, 3, 2–10.

Rogers, C. R. and Truax, C. B. (1967) The therapeutic conditions antecedent to change: a theoretical view. In: *The Therapeutic Relationship and its Impact*, (ed. C. R. Rogers), University of Wisconsin Press, Madison, WI.

Thorne, B. (1987) Beyond the core conditions. In: *Key Cases in Psychotherapy*, (ed. W. Dryden), Croom Helm, London.

COUNSELLING ETHICS

Counselling and psychotherapy have incurred criticism because of the lack of a common frame of reference for practitioners. The British Association for Counselling issues guidelines to its members. These have been constructed along the lines of the International Code of Medical Ethics, although this does not imply approval by any counselling body.

The therapeutic relationship

Counsellors should:
- Make clear and explicit contracts with their clients
- Ensure that the counselling relationship does not exploit clients
- Use all their skill to discourage clients from becoming dependent on the counsellor and on the relationship
- Use all their skill to encourage personal autonomy of their clients
- Ensure that they do not collude with clients against other people
- Ensure that they do not sexually exploit their clients
- Handle transference and counter-transference skilfully and to the benefit of both themselves and their clients
- Ensure that they do not enforce or impose value or attitude change on their clients
- Ensure the physical and psychological safety of their clients
- Ensure that they do not intrude, coerce or use persuasion
- Ensure that their need for regular supervision is discussed with clients
- Make explicit to clients the nature and extent of confidentiality of records, whether handwritten or computerized, to third parties, such as the Courts, other agencies or case conferences.

Competence of counsellors

Counsellors should:
- Recognize and work within limits of their competency
- Recognize their own needs
- Regularly update their knowledge, experience and technical skill
- Ensure that they seek regular supervision
- Know when to refer clients and to whom.

Responsibilities

Counsellors should:
- Exercise responsibility toward their clients by maintaining their effectiveness and ability
- Exercise responsibility to themselves to stay fresh and to protect their private and social life

- Exercise responsibility to the counselling relationship by monitoring their performance
- Exercise responsibility to their clients through personal and professional development
- Exercise responsibility to their colleagues and other professionals
- Exercise responsibility to the wider community, so as not to reduce confidence in counselling
- Exercise responsibility to know and work within the law of the land
- Exercise responsibility to be aware of the requirements of the law regarding client confidentiality.

Other issues

Counsellors should:

- Ensure the accuracy of their advertisements and announcements
- Ensure that research material and writings preserve client anonymity
- Ensure that ethical conflicts are resolved through discussion.

Further reading

Code of Ethics and Practice for Counsellors (AGM/9/90) British Association for Counselling, 1 Regent Place, Rugby, Warwickshire, CV21 2PJ, UK.
Corey, G. *et al.* (1979) *Professional and Ethical Issues In Counselling and Psychotherapy,* Brooks-Cole, Monterey, CA.

Counselling guidelines

These guidelines are offered from my own work as a teacher. When given to a group, they generate lively discussion.

Skill and art

Counselling is a balance between skill and art. Some people may be very skilled in the theory but lack the art; some may have a natural flair and would be more effective if they acquired some of the theory. Learning any job demands hard work and patience; counselling is no different.

Generate alternatives

Get agreement that there is a problem; that something is unacceptable. Then explore alternatives that are acceptable to the other person. People who are free to choose, however difficult the decision, are more likely to be committed to change.

Don't argue

We all tend to increase our resistance to match the force of an argument raised against us. Don't get into a 'win–lose' interaction.

Be prepared to listen

Being prepared to listen to people and help them explore what's bothering them does not mean we have to agree with them. Give people time and space to think, feel and talk.

Focus on behaviour

When we direct attention to specific behaviour that people are able to change, they will feel more in control and less under attack.

Give feedback

Concentrate less on what has gone wrong and more on what can be changed, how and what the benefits of that change might be. Negative feedback should be given in small doses. Small changes achieved over a long period of time have more chance of success.

People have feelings

Try to see the world through their eyes; from their frame of reference.

Be careful of advice

Advice that opens alternatives is helpful. If the other person has a weakness in a specific, clearly measurable aspect of the job, coaching may be necessary and direct advice may be appropriate. If, however, the problem lies in a clash of attitudes, values or interpersonal difficulties, direct advice in the form of 'If I were you...' is inappropriate. More will be achieved if the person's feelings are understood.

Ask skilled questions

Since the purpose is to help the person solve a problem, past facts are far less important than present feelings and attitudes. Remember! Strong, negative feelings act as stoppers to thinking or expressing positive feelings and interfere with full functioning.

Watch for signals

Become aware of verbal and nonverbal cues that signal the person's willingness to start looking at the possibility of change. Once a person assumes responsibility for overcoming his/her own shortcomings, our task is almost complete.

Impartiality

Counselling aims at objectivity. Total objectivity is seldom, if ever, achieved. Partiality interferes with objectivity – so be careful about being pulled over to the side of the client against someone else. It is easy to become partial, especially when our own feelings about the other person are involved. For instance, the client is complaining about person 'A' and you don't like 'A' very much. Unless you are very careful your dislike of 'A' may affect your judgement of the situation.

Authority and power

You have a certain authority and power by virtue of your role. Do not use that authority to persuade the client to make a decision s/he would rather not make.

Other people

Do not allow the focus of the interview to be drawn away from the client by discussing other people unless their behaviour has a direct bearing on the situation. It is far better to concentrate on the way the client's behaviour has been affected as a result of interaction with the person in question.

Personal experiences

Be careful what you say about yourself. You may be tempted to use an experience from your own life to illustrate a point. This may be interpreted as 'I can see she copes, but does she see that I can't?'

Sometimes a personal experience can be used effectively. For instance, the client may be trying desperately to get a specific point over but cannot bring himself to spell it out. If you think that you have got his message, a short personal experience will let him see that you do know what he is talking about. But remember: he is the one on whom the attention should be focussed so don't let it remain on you longer than is necessary (*see* Self-disclosure).

Interpretations

Psychological interpretations are more appropriate to in-depth psychotherapy and psychoanalysis, which deal with personality change, and must be left to those qualified to make them.

Credibility

The perceived ability of the counsellor to possess the knowledge and skill required by the client together with the willingness to use them on behalf of the client.

The essential elements of credibility:

- Effective communication
- Empathy and warmth
- Expertness – qualifications and experience
- Reliability
- Reputation
- Trustworthiness.

COUNSELLING PROCESS (*see also*: Relationship principles)

The main aspects are:

- Getting on the client's wavelength and staying there
- Active listening and appropriate responding
- Remaining impartial and suspending judgement
- Using the skills of:
  - Attending
  - Paraphrasing the content
  - Reflecting feelings
  - Open questions
  - Summarizing
  - Focusing
  - Challenging
  - Self-disclosure
  - Immediacy
  - Concreteness
- Waiting for a reply
- The constructive use of silences
- Keeping pace with the client
- Reading between the lines
- Demonstrating the principles of the counselling relationship:
  - Individualization
  - Feelings
  - Involvement
  - Self-determination
  - Confidentiality
  - Acceptance
  - Nonjudgement
- Expressing understanding of the client's feelings
- Being able to enter the client's frame of reference
- Demonstrating empathy
- Expressing support
- Keeping the interview moving forward
- Keeping objective when planning action
- Dealing with transference and counter-transference
- Saying goodbye constructively.

CREATIVITY

Most people are born with the ability to be creative yet not everyone makes use of that potential. Conformity thwarts expression of creativity in the developing child. The spark of creativity will be extinguished if it is not given expression. Increasing personal effectiveness requires creativity, plus unlearning nonproductive and self-defeating behaviours. Helping clients tap into their creative potential, particularly through the use of imagination and intuition, may help to restore an essential part they may have lost.

Creative people are generally:

- Open to experience
- Flexible in thinking
- Able to deal with conflicting information
- Not unduly swayed by criticism or praise.

Creativity develops within a psychologically safe environment in which there is acceptance, a nonjudgemental attitude and freedom to think and feel.

Barriers to developing creativity

Barriers are mental fogs that prevent us from perceiving a problem correctly or conceiving possible solutions.

- **Perceptual – how we see things**: These barriers are recognized by:
  - Failure to use all the senses in observing
  - Failure to investigate the obvious
  - Inability to define terms
  - Difficulty in seeing abstract relationships
  - Failure to distinguish between cause and effect
  - Failure to use the unconscious, such as not using visualization or fantasy
  - Inability to use the conscious mind, such as inability to organize data.
- **Cultural – how we ought to do things**: These barriers are recognized by:
  - A need to conform
  - An overemphasis on competition or on co-operation
  - A drive to be practical and economical at all costs
  - Belief that fantasy is time-wasting
  - Too much faith in reason and logic
  - A deep-seated need to find the proper setting and to give oneself every advantage
  - A work-orientated need to keep trying and to be always prepared and ready.
- **Emotional – how we feel about things**: These barriers are recognized by:
  - Fear of making mistakes
  - Fear and distrust of others
  - Grabbing the first idea that presents itself
  - Personal feelings of insecurity, such as low self-esteem
  - Feelings of anxiety, fear of criticism, fear of failure or lack of curiosity
  - Need for security, such as lack of risk-taking or of not trying new things.

Further reading

Martin, L. P. (1990) Inventory of barriers to creative thought and innovative action. In: *1990 Annual: Developing Human Resources*, University Associates, San Diego, CA.

CRISIS COUNSELLING (*see also*: Post-traumatic stress disorder)

A crisis is a limited period of acute psychological and emotional disorganization brought about by a challenging or hazardous event.

Crisis counselling is a brief form of social and/or psychological treatment offered to people who are experiencing a personal crisis, whose usual methods of coping have proved ineffective. Their thinking, emotions and behaviours are all affected and not coping adds one more factor to the stress they are experiencing.

Types of crisis intervention:

- Appropriate social and material assistance
- Emotional 'first aid' – supportive therapy, containment of the crisis and care, particularly during the early days following the event
- Crises, such as bereavement, have a similar meaning and effect upon individuals, regardless of their personalities and can usually be approached in the same way
- A dynamic approach that helps the client understand current reactions to previous crises.

Examples of crises:

- Death of a relative or friend
- Hearing bad news about self or a close relative
- Witnessing a horrific event
- Family break-up
- Divorce
- Loss of part of the body.

The objective of all crisis intervention is the restoration of psychological balance to at least what it was prior to the crisis. The aim is not insight or exploration of feelings or of working toward change but of coping with the immediate difficulty.

Dealing with crises usually means, initially, that a more directive approach is often appropriate, because the person's inner resources have been paralysed. When someone needs to take control, the authoritarian person often turns up trumps. They are not afraid of action and are often excellent in emergencies.

Another plus for an authoritarian approach is when we recognize that the person is immobilized by some trauma, e.g. at a road accident or some other traumatic experience. Very often people in deep shock need others to take temporary control.

After the acute stage has passed, therapy should be directed towards:

- Helping the person to talk about the crisis
- Catharsis and ventilation of feelings and to understand what it means from the client's frame of reference.
- Nurturing self-esteem and positive self-image.

- Developing problem-solving behaviour and coping skills.

Crisis counselling means just that; it does not mean that the person takes on a commitment to long-term counselling. In fact, when a person is in crisis, the counsellor might be well advised to discourage the client from undertaking long-term counselling. People who are in crisis are already vulnerable and may take decisions that are not founded on reality. Just as in post-traumatic stress disorder counselling is not mixed up with debriefing, so crisis counselling should not be mixed up with long-term counselling. A related point is possibly to help the person find support from friends and relatives, for this is part of what is normal.

One of the basic principles of counselling is that the client is helped to help her/himself. Thus in crisis, the object is to do no more for the client than will aid the client to do whatever is necessary for get her/himself back to normal.

Further reading

Everstine, D. S. and Everstine, L. (1983) *People in Crisis*, Brunner/Mazel, New York.
Langsley, D. G. (1981) Crisis intervention: an update. In: *Current Psychiatric Therapies*, vol. 20, (ed. J. H. Masserman), Grune & Stratton, New York.

D

DEFENCE MECHANISMS

Introduction

Defence mechanisms (also called mental mechanisms) are unconscious mental processes that enable us to reach compromise solutions to problems that we are unable to resolve in any other way. These internal drives or feelings, which threaten to lower our self-esteem or to provoke anxiety, are concealed from our conscious mind. Thus they function to help us cope.

In Freudian theory, these unconscious drives are in conflict with one another and are the cause of mental disorders. Defence mechanisms are developed unconsciously to ward off internal and external dangers and to protect the individual from being annihilated. Their purpose is thus to protect the ego and maintain the status quo by diverting anxiety away from consciousness. The functioning of the adult should be controlled by the perceptive and intelligent ego and action by the ego ideally should satisfy the demands of id, superego and reality.

Defences are not necessarily pathological, even although the ego may not function adequately. They become pathological when they fail to ward off anxiety and when more defences have to be used to control the ego. Neurotic symptoms are then formed that interfere with pursuing a satisfactory way of living. Psychosis is where there is a complete breakdown of the defence system.

Although defence mechanisms derive from psychoanalytic theory, they have become widely used in psychology, even although some of the basic tenets may not apply other than in psychoanalysis. There is lack of agreement as to the number of defence mechanisms but there is agreement on the following characteristics:

- They manage instincts, drives and affect
- They are unconscious
- They are singular and distinct
- They are dynamic and reversible
- They can be adaptive (working for the individual) or pathological.

Defences do not remove the cause of the anxiety, they change the way we perceive, or think about, a situation. All defence mechanisms hide the truth and are therefore self-deceptive. We all use defence mechanism at some time or other. They help us over rough patches until we are more able to deal with the stressful situation. They become pathological when a particular way of coping becomes so ingrained that we are oblivious to any other way of responding.

The defence mechanisms outlined

Acting out

Acting out is where the individual expresses an unconscious wish or impulse through action to avoid being conscious of the accompanying feeling. Acting-out behaviour is impulsive and gratifying, whereas control or inhibiting the impulse would provoke tension and anxiety. Freud applied the term to transference and also to all breaking-through behaviour within and outside of the therapeutic relationship, although the concept is applied much more broadly than that.

In counselling, acting out may take the form of aggressive behaviour or sexual responses directed toward the therapist. In psychoanalytic terms, as acting out is a substitute for words, it is regarded as a resistance and a hindrance to therapy. It may be regarded as an inability to grieve appropriately for the past and since the feelings cannot be expressed in **healthy** grieving, they are expressed in **abnormal** behaviour. However, acting out must not be regarded as 'bad behaviour', for it is related to emotional conflict, which is not always the case with bad behaviour.

Examples of acting out:

- Re-enactment of violence on others
- Taking it out on our own children
- Spontaneous age regression – temper tantrums
- Inappropriate rebellion
- Carrying on the rules of idealized parents
- Child abuse
- Promiscuity without pleasure.

Very often acting out is not accompanied by apparent guilt. Severe acting out invariably engenders fear in the observer. It seriously threatens the therapeutic relationship.

Acting in

The term is used in contrast to acting out; a midway stage between acting out and verbalization. 'Acting in' means directing inward the behaviours associated with acting out. – punishing ourselves in the way we were punished as children. Unresolved emotions from the past are often turned against the self.

The child who is taught to be perfectly obedient and that anger is 'sinful' may well turn that anger inward, to be expressed behaviourally as depression, apathy, ineptness and powerlessness. Physical problems – affecting any of the bodily systems – may also result from acting in. Accident proneness, for example, where one punishes oneself by accident, is another form of acting in.

Altruism

Through this defence mechanism (similar to reaction formation) the individual experiences inner satisfaction through unselfish service to others. It is different from **altruistic surrender,** where serving others is to the detriment of oneself and arises from an almost pathological feeling of self-worthlessness.

Anticipation
Though this may apply to many of us **at times,** other people deal with conflict and stressors by living in the future and experiencing the full gamut of feelings associated with an event that has not yet taken place. This includes anticipating the consequences and results. Very often they live in dread of the future, because they more often than not anticipate what is negative.

Asceticism
In this defence, any pleasure resulting from experiences is eliminated. To experience pleasure from some act or experience has a moral value attached to it that some people need to deny. Indirect gratification is derived from the renunciation of the pleasure that would be normal to enjoy from that experience.

Avoidance
Avoidance is thinking and acting in ways that evade dealing with reality. A wish to dwell on the past may be a way of avoiding working in the present. Avoidance acts powerfully against the implementation of programmes. Avoidance will take place if the rewards for **not doing** something are stronger than the rewards for **doing** it. Avoidance means we take a certain course of action because that is preferable. For example, we avoid thunder storms by staying in the house. We avoid meeting a certain person when we cross the street.

Avoidance is manifested in:

- Procrastination
- **Trading down**: choosing an alternative that is more psychologically acceptable and attractive
- **Devaluing alternatives.**
- **Delegating the decision** to someone – fate horoscope, dice, obeying rules.

Avoidance as a defence in therapy is characterized by:

- **Externalization**: The fault is outside of me
- **Blind spots**: If I don't look, it will go away
- **Excessive self-control**: I won't let anything upset me
- **Being right**: My mind is made up, don't confuse me with facts
- **Elusiveness and confusion**: Don't pin me down
- **Self-disparagement**: I'm always wrong
- **Playing the martyr role**: My suffering controls other people.

In mental health **avoidant personality disorder** is where the individual shows extreme shyness and fear of being negatively evaluated by others. This condition, which usually begins in early adult life (although there is also a childhood version) pervades many areas of the person's life. Commonest features are:

- Social inhibition
- Feelings of inadequacy
- Low self-esteem
- Avoids occupations that involve close contact with others, because of fear of criticism, disapproval or rejection
- Will generally steer clear of relationships unless there is a guarantee of being liked and accepted
- Avoids any social situation where there is the slightest risk of being embarrassed.

From a counselling perspective, working with such clients might prove difficult, partly because they will generally not voluntarily seek counselling and partly because, if they do, they may be so hungry for approval and eager to please that they are ultrasensitive to any sense of challenge, fearing rejection. Refusal on the part of the counsellor to extend the relationship into friendship might be interpreted as rejection.

The counselling relationship might founder on the rocks of what makes for effective counselling. The client might not be able to handle empathy and understanding, for it is this very intimacy which the person avoids. However, while the client has the desire to persist, there is hope of making progress toward less avoidant behaviour.

Blocking (*see also* Resistance)

This is a temporary or fleeting restraint of thinking, feelings or action that resembles repression but differs in that tension results from the inhibition. Blocking may manifest itself at any time during counselling. It may become apparent in the way the client refuses to consider what is being said or argues against it without consideration.

Blocking may be an indication of transference or counter-transference. The counsellor may have used words that trigger some half-forgotten memory to which the client feels unable to respond at that moment. Feelings generated by interaction may also have their roots in past relationships that the client now cannot relate to and to which s/he blocks the response.

Compensation

This is the tendency to cover up a weakness or defect by exaggerating a more desirable characteristic: 'I'm the greatest'. An example would be someone who feels inferior because of lack of height and compensates by becoming overbearing and bossy. Material repressed into the unconscious by the conscious develops so much energy that it eventually breaks through as dreams, spontaneous images or neurotic symptoms. Compensation, then, acts as a link between the conscious and the unconscious. Jung's view is that compensation is an unconscious attempt to achieve psychological homeostasis of the contents of the conscious. Compensation means balancing, adjusting and supplementing.

Conversion
In psychoanalytic terms, conversion is where repressed material, ideas, wishes, feelings are converted into physical manifestations, such as hysterical paralysis of a limb. The physical symptom symbolizes the original conflict. Paralysis of a limb (properly, **conversion hysteria**), for example, would remove the person from a conflict at work, where work depended on using the arm. The person who uses conversion hysteria often adopts a curiously indifferent or theatrical attitude toward the paralysis, which invariably does not stand up to neurological analysis.

Denial
'It hasn't happened.' 'It's not really happening'. A mechanism employed to avoid becoming consciously aware of some painful thought, feeling or experience or event or part of self. The existence of facts can not be tolerated in the conscious mind. It is not deliberate lying: the person fails to perceive the facts.

Freud maintained that denial of painful experiences is governed by the **pleasure principle** and that the denial is part of wish-fulfilment, which borders on hallucination. There may be massive denial of a particular idea, experience, the event itself, its memory or only the associated affect. Complete denial is seldom encountered.

Denial is a frequently used defence mechanism in personality disorders. It is commonly employed in crises and serves to protect the ego. It is the scar of the psychic traumas experienced by the individual but it does not make the traumatic experiences disappear. The excessive use of denial may precipitate a psychosis and the denied reality may be replaced by a fantasy or delusion. An example would be the man who refuses to accept that his leg has been amputated. Psychotic denial is a term used when the person is grossly out of touch with reality.

However, it is incorrect to talk of denial in, for example, a person whose husband has recently died but who still hears his voice, expects him to walk through the door and believes that he is still around. If the widow was still saying and experiencing this 2 years after the death, then maybe denial would be in operation. It is essential to distinguish disbelief from denial. Disbelief is conscious; denial, by its very nature, is unconscious.

Devaluation
A mechanism whereby the individual deals with emotional conflict and stressors (internal or external) by attributing exaggerated or excessively negative qualities to self or to others. Devaluation is often present in people with narcissistic tendencies. Freud used the Narcissus myth to describe a morbid condition in which sexual energy, which naturally focuses firstly on self and then upon the parent and then onto others, remains focused on self.

The person can rarely achieve satisfactory sexual relationships, because of mistrust of other people.

Displacement
'She's to blame, not me'. Displacement is the shifting of affect (feeling) from one mental image to another (normally less threatening) to which it does not belong, in order to avoid anxiety. It can be used to protect a valued object by channelling negative feelings on to a substitute that closely resembles the original. An example would be the man who comes home in a temper because of a row with his boss and verbally attacks his wife.

Dissociation
A temporary but extreme change in a person's character or personal identity in order to avoid emotional distress. It is the separating off of thoughts, feelings and fantasies from conscious awareness. The term was used by Freud but he later dropped it in favour of 'repression'. Although the mental contents are disowned and separated from the rest of the personality, they are not repressed or projected on to someone else. The term is often associated with aggressive and sexual impulses, fantasies and theatrical behaviour. In amnesia, the memory is dissociated.

A **fugue state** is a psychiatric condition in which the characteristic feature is that the person suddenly and unexpectedly leaves home and assumes a new identity elsewhere. During the fugue state the person has no recollection of the former life or identity. After recovery, there is no recollection of the assumed identity or events.

Distortion
This is where external reality is grossly restructured to preserve the person's inner world. Its function in dreams is to make acceptable the content that otherwise would be unacceptable.

Examples of distortion:

- Hallucinations
- Wish-fulfilling delusions
  Fantasies of power
  Delusions of superiority.

Fantasy
Also known as autistic or schizoid fantasy. People who are most likely to make use of this as a defence are those who are lonely and frightened; eccentric people and those labelled schizoid; aloof and unsociable people and those who fear intimacy. They seek comfort in their own inner world by creating an imaginary life, especially imaginary friends. Acceptance of them, just as they are, is essential, without pressure to change. Fantasy thinking allows the person to escape from or to deny reality; it can be seen in normal and pathological

thinking. Slips of the tongue may also be construed as a form of fantasy in which, for a moment, the speaker denies the unpleasant reality and substitutes a different image.

Hypochondriasis

This is a mechanism that emphasizes excessive preoccupation with bodily symptoms (especially pain) and is often accompanied by fears of serious physical illness, such as cancer or heart disease. Hypochondriac people are typically concerned with the 'vital functions' – head, heart, lungs, bowel and bladder functions and reproduction. The appearance of the occasional pimple or spot is interpreted as heralding a more serious and often life-threatening complaint. These are the people who shop around for sympathetic doctors: reassurances are futile. Hypochondriasis is linked with borderline, dependent or passive-aggressive traits.

Hypochondriasis often conceals a help-rejecting personality, characterized by complaining or continually making requests for help; such requests often disguise feelings of hostility towards others. Hypochondriacs gain control over people by asking and then rejecting the help offered. The complaints (or requests for help) may involve physical or psychological symptoms or life problems. Hypochondriasis often conceals bereavement, loneliness and unacceptable aggressive impulses.

Three useful therapeutic guides in dealing with hypochondriac clients:

- **Amplification**: Overstating the severity often leads the client to minimize the complaint
- **Dependency**: Make some symbolic effort to meet the client's overall need for dependency, rather than attacking the presenting symptom
- **Respond, don't react**: A careful history-taking, accompanied by active listening and trying to work within the client's frame of reference, is more reassuring than any attempt to argue against the symptoms.

Idealization

This is where the person, as a defence against guilt, attributes exaggerated positive qualities to self or others in order to deal with emotional conflicts and internal or external stressors.

Idealization views external objects as 'all good' or 'all bad' and endows them with great power. Most commonly, the 'all good' object, the 'ideal', is seen as possessing god-like power, while the badness in the 'all bad' object is greatly exaggerated. In psychoanalytic psychology, idealization refers to the overvaluing of the sexual drive.

Clients might idealize the counsellor and attribute wonderful powers to her/him; this may be part of transference and in this instance projection is also involved. Idealization, as distinct from admiration, denies or fails to see any weakness in, for example, the counsellor, thus maintaining the fantasy of perfection. Such a feeling is in danger of creating a relationship of dependency, where everything the counsellor says is received with the same reverence and awe as if it came from God. Failure on the part of the client and collusion on the part of the counsellor to recognize and deal with this will inevitably mean that the client will stop making progress. An essential factor of the counselling relationship is helping the client to face reality and that invariably means accepting that the counsellor is human.

Identification (*see also* Projective identification, below)
This is the process by which we model aspects of ourselves upon other people. We behave, or imagine ourselves behaving, as if we were the person with whom we have a strong emotional tie and take on the attitudes, patterns of behaviour and emotions of that person.

The psychoanalytic view is that it is an important means by which the ego and superego are developed. Empathy depends, to some extent, upon the therapist's ability to identify with the client's feelings.

Freud's theory was that a child's conscience is formed by incorporating parental standards of conduct. The child acts in accordance with these standards even when the parent is absent and experiences guilt when those standards are violated.

For Jung, identification is an alienation of people from themselves, for the sake of some object in which they are, so to speak, disguised.

Adler goes so far to say that it is impossible to understand people if at the same time we do not identify with them. Therapists need to be aware of the danger of 'over-identification'.

An inability to identify with another person is as much a defence mechanism as identification is. Imitation and modelling depend on the extent of identification achieved. Identification is unconscious; imitation is conscious.

Identification is useful until it gets in the way of becoming a separate person.

It is important in the development of the child; maturity, conversely, is marked by separateness.

For the behavioural therapists, identification is continuous throughout life.

Identification is a major link between the psychoanalytic and social learning theories of development and it is a powerful influence in the socialization process.

Intellectualization
This is a mechanism where the ego deals with threats by using the mind rather than dealing with feelings. The person excessively analyses problems in remote, intellectual terms, while emotions and feelings are ignored or discounted. The process is closely allied to **rationalization.**

The person concentrates on the inanimate at the expense of dealing with people. Detail is concentrated on to avoid looking at the whole. Intellectualization can act as a severe block in therapy, preventing feeling work and working through. It can be used constructively, however, to temporarily bypass affect in order to deal with a crisis.

Introjection

Introjection is a major influence in the development of both ego and superego. The term was introduced by Ferenczi to describe the way in which aspects of the outside world are internalized into the ego as fantasies or mental representations. Introjection is similar to internalization and identification and the opposite of projection. Jung viewed Introjection as a defence against separation or threatened separation.

Feelings may also be introjected – blame, for example. Introjection helps to keep the person in touch with 'good' objects when separated from them and so prevents or minimizes anxiety. Introjection of 'bad' objects permits control over them.

Isolation

Isolation protects an individual from anxiety-provoking feelings and impulses. When isolation occurs, the associated feeling and impulse are pushed out of consciousness.

When isolation is total, the feeling and impulse will be totally repressed. The person is then able to view the idea (memory or fantasy) without the feelings attached to it.

If isolation is incomplete, partial awareness of impulses may break through in the form of disturbing compulsions to perform some violent action. Sufferers may be puzzled and disturbed at their compulsions.

Isolated people may be obsessed with images and thoughts of violence or destruction. In psychodynamic terms, isolation is viewed as a conflict between impulses and controlling defensive forces.

The personality of the person who uses isolation tends to be orderly and obsessively compulsive. They keep their feelings very controlled and remember events in fine detail. They often respond well to rational explanations. The urgent need in therapy is to get such clients to tap into their feelings.

Isolation of affect

This is a mechanism whereby we deal with emotional conflict or internal or external stressors by separating ideas from the feelings originally associated with them, thus protecting us from anxiety. When isolation occurs, the associated feeling and impulse are pushed out of consciousness. When isolation is total, the feeling and impulse will be totally repressed. The person is then able to view the idea (memory or fantasy) without the feelings attached to it.

If isolation is incomplete, partial awareness of impulses may break through in the form of disturbing compulsions to perform some violent action. Sufferers may be puzzled and disturbed by their compulsions.

Isolated people may be obsessed with images and thoughts of violence or destruction. In psychodynamic terms, isolation is viewed as a conflict between impulses and controlling defensive forces. The personality of the person who uses isolation tends to be orderly and obsessively compulsive. They keep their feelings very controlled and remember events in fine detail. They often respond well to rational explanations. The urgent need in therapy is to get such clients to tap into their feelings.

Projection

'It's happening to you, not to me.' In psychoanalysis, projection is the process by which one's own traits, emotions, dispositions, ideas, wishes and failings are attributed to others, who are then perceived as an external threat. Projection of aspects of oneself is preceded by a denial that one feels such an emotion, has such a desire or wish, but a belief that someone else does possess these feelings and tendencies. In the process some conflict is repressed; threatened by our own angry feelings, we accuse someone else of harbouring hostile thoughts. In psychoses, projection takes the form of delusions of persecution.

People who consistently use projection tend to be excessively fault-finding, very sensitive to criticism, openly prejudiced and apparently sensitive to real or imagined injustices. An example of projection would be where a student cheats in an exam, then justifies his action by claiming that all students cheat.

In a professional relationship, openness and concern for the client's rights and maintaining a professional formality are helpful. Confrontation is likely to lead to the relationship being terminated. Being able to work within the client's frame of reference is essential, without necessarily lending support to what is often an underlying paranoid feeling.

Projective identification

This is similar to projection, where the individual copes with stressors and conflicts by attributing unacceptable parts of self – feelings, thoughts and impulses – and putting them on to another. Unlike projection, the person remains aware of the feelings, but considers them justified. It serves to protect the ego against the anxieties of being persecuted by others and being separated from them.

Projective identification allows one to distance oneself from others, while at the same time to make oneself understood by applying pressure on others to experience feelings similar to one's own. It has a nonpathological function; it is an early form of empathy and of symbol formation, both of which are essential in therapy. It is also a feature in the process of scapegoating.

Rationalization

'I would be different if. . ..' In general, rationalization means the process one uses to make clear something that is confused, irrational and unclear. In psychoanalytic terms it means, in addition, giving an intellectual, rational explanation in an attempt to conceal or justify attitudes, beliefs or behaviour that might otherwise be unacceptable. An example would be where the person who fails a driving test blames the failure on 'a migraine'. To that person the rationalized reason is more acceptable than the truth.

Reaction formation

'I've never wanted to hit anyone in my life.' In psychoanalytic terms, this is a mechanism that is used to defend the ego against the anxiety of expressing a repressed wish, whereby we believe as though the opposite were true. It is where one's anxieties about unacceptable impulses are kept at bay by developing behaviour patterns that are directly opposed, as a means of controlling the impulses. To the observer, these reactions seem highly exaggerated and/or inappropriate. Reaction formation is closely associated with obsessive-compulsive disorder. An example would be the heavy drinker who gives up alcohol and becomes an ardent 'ban the drink' campaigner.

Regression
'I hate you, hate you!' (with foot stamping, metaphoric, if not actual) is a return to an earlier (fixated) level of functioning, with the feelings and behaviours attached to it. Regression is prompted by an unconscious desire to avoid anxiety, tensions and conflicts evoked at the present level of development.

The psychoanalytic theory of regression is that remnants of the stages of development remain and are activated when under threat, so that we repeat the behaviour appropriate to that stage of development. This return, however, does not remove anxiety. The current anxiety is replaced by a re-experiencing of the anxiety encountered at the regressed stage. In cognitive therapy regression is referred to as a temporary falling back upon an earlier form of thinking. Or beginning to learn how to deal with something new. An example of regression would be the young husband, who, following the first quarrel with his new wife, 'runs back to mother'.

Repression
'It never happened.' The basic meaning of the word 'repress' is put down, suppress, control, censor, exclude. In all depth psychology it is where an idea or feeling is banished or not allowed to enter consciousness. It is the cornerstone concept of psychoanalytic theory.

- **Primal repression** is where primitive, forbidden id impulses are blocked and prevented from ever reaching consciousness
- **Primary repression** is where anxiety-producing mental content is forcefully removed from consciousness and prevented from re-emerging and where ideas and feelings are acted upon before they can become conscious
- **Secondary repression** is where ideas and feelings once conscious are now excluded from consciousness – repressed material makes its presence known through symbolic behaviour, dreams, neuroses and parapraxes.

Repression prevents ideas, wishes, anxieties, impulses and images from becoming conscious and rejects to the unconscious mind ideas, wishes, anxieties, impulses and images that have become conscious. If they did come into the conscious, the person would experience anxiety, apprehension or guilt. The effects of repression can be seen in someone who has performed a shameful act then develops total amnesia about the act and all the surrounding circumstances.

Somatization

This is where psychic disturbances are converted into physical symptoms that preoccupy the individual. The physical symptoms are not in keeping with any actual physical disturbance. Somatization is a way of dealing with emotional conflicts or internal or external stressors.

In **desomatization**, infantile somatic responses are replaced by thoughts and feelings.

In **resomatization**, there is regression to earlier somatic forms when the person cannot face unresolved conflicts.

Splitting

A psychoanalytic term to describe a division within the psyche. Splitting is commonly seen in clients with behavioural and antisocial problems. People who use splitting tend to:

- See others in black or white terms
- Think in 'all or nothing' terms
- Categorize people as all good or all bad
- Idealize or disparage others
- Draw wrath upon themselves by turning people against them.

In Kleinian terms, splitting characterizes the very young. It is the active separation into good or bad of experiences, perceptions and emotions linked to objects. Splitting interferes with the accurate perception of reality and nurtures denial. The opposite of splitting is **synthesis**. This takes place when the infant is able to distinguish part from whole objects.

Sublimation

'I'm dedicating my life to prayer, instead of crime.' In psychoanalysis, sublimation is the channelling of what would be instinctual gratification into new, learned behaviour; something that is more conforming to social values and behaviours. It is usually referred to in a sexual context and classical psychoanalytic theory regarded creative and artistic tendencies as manifestations of sublimation. In the same way, intellectual curiosity is said to be a sublimation of **scophilia** (the desire to look; voyeurism, Peeping Tom). Anna Freud maintained that sublimation indicated a healthy progression, in that it produces an acceptable solution to infantile conflicts that otherwise might lead to neurosis. In a more general sense, sublimation is the redirection of energy from social unacceptable behaviour into something more acceptable. An example would be the person who finds an outlet for aggression through competitive sports.

Suppression

In a broad sense, suppression is the voluntary and conscious elimination of some behaviour, such as a bad habit or suppression of unacceptable ideas. In psychoanalytic terms, suppression refers to conscious, voluntary inhibition of activity, in contrast to repression, which is unconscious, automatic and prompted by anxiety, not by an act of will. Disturbing ideas, feelings, memories are banished from the conscious to the preconscious. Suppression is less total than repression and, because it resides in the preconscious, is more accessible to the conscious. While issues are deliberately cut off, they are not avoided; discomfort is present but is minimized.

DEFINITION OF COUNSELLING

The British Association for Counselling (previous) definition was:

People become engaged in counselling when a person, occupying regularly or temporarily the role of counsellor, offers or agrees to offer time, attention and respect to another person temporarily in the role of client. The task of counselling is to give the client an opportunity to explore, discover and clarify ways of living more resourcefully and towards greater well-being.

The newer (1989) BAC definition reads:

Counselling is the skilled and principled use of relationship to facilitate self-knowledge, emotional acceptance and growth and the optimal development of personal resources. The overall aim is to provide an opportunity to work towards living more satisfyingly and resourcefully. Counselling relationships will vary according to need but may be concerned with developmental issues, addressing and resolving specific problems, making decisions, coping with crisis, developing personal insights and knowledge, working through feelings of inner conflict or improving relationships with others. The counsellor's role is to facilitate the client's work in ways that respect the client's values, personal resources and capacity for self determination.

Points about the two definitions:

- Not every person who uses counselling skills is designated 'counsellor'. We can distinguish two broad groups of people who use counselling skills: people who are called 'counsellors', who engage in counselling as a distinct occupation; and 'others' who use counselling skills as part of their other skills. They would be 'temporarily in the role'.
- Most people enter into counselling of their own volition and it is something agreed between client and counsellor. Sometimes, particularly where counselling is part of another job, the need for counselling may be perceived and suggested. In any case, counselling should not be entered into without agreement from both parties. The relationship should be made explicit and the roles clearly defined.
- People who engage in counselling make a contract where one of the boundaries is time – number and length of sessions. Giving total, undivided attention means being able to free oneself from external and internal distractions.
- One of the aspects of respect is that we recognize and accept the uniqueness

of each and every person while at the same time taking account of shared similarities. Many people who have difficulties – in whatever area of life, be it work or at a personal level – suffer from damaged self esteem. The counselling relationship encourages people to repair their damaged self-esteem, for it is here that, free from judgement and criticism, they are able to start to respect themselves. It is almost as if the damaged self-esteem devalues all they are and all they do. Respect should be total – for the person and for what transpires during counselling.

- People are not clients for life. The counselling relationship is only one of many and takes place for one hour out of the 168 hours in the week.
- Counselling helps clients to make some sense out of confusion, choice from conflict and sense out of nonsense. Counselling helps clients to discover resources not hitherto recognized and to put those resources to work on their behalf.
- Counselling makes use of relationship skills (*see* Relationship principles) for the benefit of the client.
- Counselling harnesses the client's own resources.
- Counselling makes a different in the client's overall well-being, in that the client is more able to take control of the direction of his/her life.
- Whatever the focus in counselling, it must always be on the client's needs and the action taken must always be the client's decision.

Further reading

British Association for Counselling (1989) *Definition of Counselling*, British Association for Counselling, 1 Regent Place, Rugby, Warwickshire, CV21 2PJ, UK.

Woolfe, R. (1989) *Counselling Skills: A training manual*, Scottish Health Education Group, Edinburgh.

DEPRESSION (*see also*: Sadness)

This article is only a very brief introduction to a vast topic. Depression may refer to a transitory change in mood, a definite and sustained change in mood, a symptom or a psychiatric illness.

In psychology, depression is a mood or emotional state that is marked by sadness, inactivity and a reduced ability to enjoy life.

A person who is depressed usually experiences one or more of the following symptoms, although this will depend on the basic personality and the severity of the depression:

- Feelings of sadness, hopelessness or pessimism
- Guilt and worthlessness
- Lowered self-esteem and heightened self-depreciation
- A decrease or loss of ability to enjoy daily life
- Reduced energy and vitality
- A lowering of thought or action

- Paranoid ideas and deep suspicion
- Disturbed sense of time
- Suicidal thoughts, preoccupations and tendencies. Depression is a major contributory factor to suicide. The future seems grey, then black. Sufferers see no future and only exist from day to day, with no joy or pleasure. They wish never to have been born and that they could fall asleep and not wake up. Existence seems so bleak that the only remedy is to end it all
- Anxiety and obsession
- Loss of appetite; and disturbed sleep or insomnia
- Physical, such as loss of weight
- Loss of sexual function
- Retardation and agitation (retardation refers to a general slowing down of bodily functions; agitation comprises severe anxiety together with overactivity of the limbs)
- Pain is a common manifestation of depression, and may show as backache, rheumatic pains or facial neuralgia, against which normal pain-killers are ineffective.

Depression differs from simple grief, which is an appropriate emotional response to the loss of loved persons or objects. Where there are clear grounds for a person's unhappiness, depression is considered to be present if the depressed mood is disproportionately long or severe in relation to the precipitating event. Severity can range from feeling low to crippling and incapacitating.

Abnormal depression can be an accompaniment of a physical illness or to any emotional illness or disturbance. It frequently accompanies anxiety and may occur following the birth of a baby, as **postnatal (postpartum) depression**.

Bipolar disorder (formerly manic depression – some sufferers still prefer this term to the more modern one) is when a person experiences alternating states of depression and mania (extreme elation of mood). Many people never experience full-blown manic phases but there is a swing of mood. The term **unipolar** describes single phase depression, with repeated attacks, rather than the swings of mood of the bipolar type.

The whole subject of depression is fraught with difficulties of terminology. The DSM-IV (page 317) describes several variants, under the heading 'Mood disorders' and the ICD-10 (page 112) describes similar mood states under the heading 'Mood (affective) disorders'. Mania and severe depression are at the opposite ends of the affective spectrum.

Where depression accompanies suicidal thoughts, the person is best treated in hospital.

Depression is probably the most common psychiatric complaint and has been described by physicians from at least the time of Hippocrates, who called it melancholia. The course of the disorder is extremely variable from person to person; it may be fleeting or permanent, mild or severe, acute or chronic.

Depression is more common in women than in men. The rates of incidence of the disorder increase with age in men, while the peak for women is between the ages of 35 and 45.

Depression can have many causes. When there is substantial reason for suspecting a definite cause, it is called **reactive depression**. Frequently, no direct 'cause' can be demonstrated. The loss of one's parents or other childhood traumas and privations can increase a person's vulnerability to depression later in life. Stressful life events in general are potent precipitating contributors to depression, although why some people develop a severe mood depression is still not certain. Depression often occurs in members of the same family, although it is not clear if the illness is genetic or if it results from being exposed to someone with the illness.

Treatment

There are three main treatments for depression. The two most important are psychotherapy and drug therapy. Psychotherapy aims to resolve any underlying psychic conflicts that may be causing the depressed state while also giving emotional support to the patient.

Antidepressant drugs, by contrast, directly affect the chemistry of the brain and presumably achieve their therapeutic effects by correcting the chemical imbalance that is causing the depression.

In cases of severe depression in which therapeutic results are needed quickly, electroconvulsive therapy is a third treatment that has proved helpful. In this procedure, a convulsion is produced by passing an electric current through the person's brain. In many cases, the best therapeutic results are obtained by using a combination of psychotherapy with drug therapy or electric shock treatment.

The one theme that repeats itself is the isolation felt by depressed people, cut off as they are from emotional contact. In a sense, depressed people pre-empt and pre-experience their own death – the final isolation. The relationship between counsellor and client is crucial in maintaining contact and thereby reducing the risk of isolation. Human contact has a calming effect on the cardio-vascular system of a person under stress. Thus it is quite feasible that our very presence achieves as much, or more, than our words of counsel, however profound.

What we do when we counsel is to offer ourselves in a relationship that makes no demands for itself. When we reach out to make emotional contact with depressed people we break through the invisible barrier that keeps them isolated. This emotional contact builds a bridge. Across this bridge they may walk away from their isolation.

Further reading

Gilbert, P. (1992) *Counselling for Depression*, Sage Publications, London.

DILEMMA

In popular use, a dilemma is a choice between two (or, loosely, several) alternatives that are or appear to be equally unfavourable; a position of doubt or perplexity, a 'fix'. The alternatives are commonly spoken of as the 'horns' of the dilemma.

An example of a dilemma would be: 'If I don't go on holiday with my in-laws, my wife will make my life a misery; if I do on holiday, my in-laws will make my life a misery. So I am stuck with being miserable, whichever way I jump – a double bind.'

The dying patient who asks his doctor to give him a lethal dose of pain-killing drugs places the doctor on the horns of an ethical and moral dilemma.

Social dilemmas exist; for example, there is a need for transport yet the increasing number of vehicles on the roads produces health hazards.

Another example of a moral dilemma would be if my son, whom I knew to be addicted to drugs, came home covered in blood. I hear on the radio that a shop has been robbed and the owner seriously wounded by a man answering the description of my son. If I obey my conscience I will report my son; if I don't, I don't know that I could live with my guilt.

Resolution of a moral dilemma means the over-riding of one of the obligations by the strength of the other. Once over-ridden, it is no longer obligatory. However, it also appears that what influences us in making the choice is the sense of duty, although deciding which course of action evokes the stronger sense of duty is not always easy.

Choosing means making a decision and for some people making decisions is very painful and tortuous. And whatever decision is made, we have to live with the consequences. In deciding to 'shop' my son, I have to live with the consequences of him, and possibly my other children, rejecting me for being an uncaring father and not putting family interests first. If my family's opinion means more to me than law and order and of justice, then I might decide to turn a blind eye and then I would have to live with the consequences of not being a citizen of integrity.

The choice of action might be influenced by the fact that I don't have a very high regard for my son anyway, and that the shopkeeper is a friend. Here I have conformed to what I believe is the 'highest intrinsic good'.

People often feel caught on the horns of a dilemma, feeling that whichever way they move they will lose out or the solution is too difficult. For example, the child whose father is sexually abusing her feels she cannot tell anyone, for if she does, she knows he will be taken away and the family will be split up. The mother of the child who knows about the abuse, yet fears she would not be able to handle the scandal, is also trapped.

Not all moral dilemmas are as dramatic as have been quoted, yet so often clients do feel hopelessly stuck; being able to sort the 'problem' into two opposing forces, On the one hand it seems that ... and on the other it seems that ... is often the first step towards helping sort out the two forces. When the client can give some value to the opposing obligations, s/he is well on the way towards resolving the moral dilemma.

DOUBLE BIND

Double bind is Gregory Bateson and Donald Jackson's description of the contradiction experienced by people who receive contradictory messages from someone more powerful. It means that the person is placed in a situation in which there is no winning, no matter what is said or done.

The term evolved from the study of the nature of schizophrenic communication. Now it is applied to a wide range of interpersonal communications. Only repeated exposure within a survival relationship produces severe pathology.

It is likely to arise in a family where one or both parents, who cannot express affection, responds coldly to the advances of the child. When the child withdraws, confused, they respond in simulated love, coupled with accusations such as, 'You don't love your mother, after all she's done for you!'

As relationships are mutual, both parties become 'victims' of the double bind. It is experienced by people suffering from schizophrenia who, whatever they do, will be labelled either 'mad' or 'bad'.

The essential elements:

- Two or more people involved
- The 'victim' repeatedly experiences the double bind
- Threat of punishment or withdrawal of approval
- Statements that conflict with the threat – 'I only want what is good for you'
- Escape is impossible; the relationship has survival value for the 'victim'.

Further reading

Bateson, G. *et al.* (1956) Toward a theory of schizophrenia. *Behavioral Science*, 1, 251–264.

Berger, M. M. (1981) *Beyond the Double Bind: Communication and family systems*, Brunner/Mazel, New York.

Sluzki, C. E. and Ransom, D. C. (eds) (1976) *Double Bind: The foundation of the communication approach to the family*, Grune & Stratton, New York.

DRAMA TRIANGLE (ALSO KNOWN AS THE RESCUE TRIANGLE) (*see also*: Transactional analysis)

A significant part of transactional analysis (see entry) is identifying the games people play. One of these games is the rescue triangle of Rescuer, Persecutor and Victim.

- We adopt the role of Rescuer by helping and keeping others dependent on us
- We adopt the role of Persecutor when we set unnecessarily strict limits on behaviour or are charged with enforcing the rules, but do so with brutality
- We adopt the role of Victim when (without cause) we feel we are being unjustly treated.

All three roles are interchangeable and we may play them all in turn.

The Rescuer

There are many situations in life where one person is in need of help and another person is capable of offering it. In a fire, the firefighter is in a legitimate role of 'rescuer'. This does not qualify as a 'game'. True helping is based on the life position of 'I'm OK, You're OK'.

We drop into the game when we see the person as helpless and hopeless and not able to manage without our help. In such a situation, we assume the complete burden of caring and helping, thus relieving the other person of any responsibility for helping themselves.

The Persecutor

In the Rescue Game, the Victim poses a question from a position of power-lessness; the Rescuer attempts to give answers. Every suggestion is rejected; a new one is suggested, until eventually the Rescuer becomes angry, switches roles and persecutes the Victim.

When we rescue people who don't need it, we put them down, emphasize their helplessness and exalt our own superiority and they will become angry with the Rescuer.

Every Rescuer–Victim transaction will result in a Persecutor–Victim trans-action.

The Victim

In a Rescue situation, the person helping is the Rescuer and the person being helped (often without asking for it) is called the Victim.

There are situations in life when a person is truly a victim, e.g. someone who has been burgled. However, the Victim in the Rescue Game generally contributes to the situation.

When the Victim is being overpowered or oppressed by a person or situation, s/he colludes with the Persecutor, to the extent that s/he discounts feelings of being persecuted. In addition, the Victim doesn't use all of his/her own power to overcome the oppression.

The firefighter rescuer would be thanked by his victim; a Rescuer would normally be persecuted by his/her Victim.

How it begins

The family is the training ground for the three basic roles of the Rescue triangle, which is, in effect, training for powerlessness. Children are forced into the Victim role while the roles of Rescuer and Persecutor are taught by example, as provided by the parents. We train children into the Victim role of powerlessness by attacking all the areas in which they have potential power

Areas of power attacked by the 'game':

- The power to love; to successfully relate to other human beings
- The power to think; the capacity to understand the world

- The power to enjoy ourselves; the capacity to experience and make full use of our bodies and emotions.

The degree to which children are not allowed to love, to understand the world and themselves, forces them into a Victim position. The parents (and others in authority) are either Persecutors who oppress their children in their abilities or Rescuers who then do what they have actually prevented the children from doing for themselves.

Training children in powerlessness

- In relationships, by not allowing children to make their own social contacts and their own decisions about who they want to be with and when (all such decisions must be appropriate to age)
- In knowledge of the world, by not allowing children to come up against situations in which they have to understand the world well enough to make decisions and to think in it
- To learn about themselves, what gives them pleasure, how they feel and how to act upon those feelings
- Many parents treat males differently from females, so that male children are trained to be powerless in the capacity to know themselves; female children are trained to be powerless in their capacity to think and to know the world
- Powerlessness is a requirement of an oppressive family, community or society. In the typical authoritarian family, father is the Persecutor, mother is the Rescuer and the children are Victims.

As the children grow up, they often take over the Persecutor role, while the parents become the Victims, which may appear as poor school records, refusing to work, drug-taking, violence or lawlessness.

Children raised in the shadow of the Rescue triangle are excellent candidates for accepting the vertical relationships of hierarchies, although they often carry their rebellion over and become misfits.

Caught in the trap

Selflessness, doing for others, generosity and co-operation are encouraged, even when people are selfish, stingy and do not co-operate with us. This is exploitation and characteristic of the Rescuer role.

Being one-down in a relationship is the experience of many women, while the reverse is true of many men. Women are more likely to be trained into the playing of the Rescuer role, to always be available.

Don't rescue me! If we don't want to be a Victim, we must demand not to be Rescued. We may have to repeat our demand many times, because people who are confirmed Rescuers experience tremendous feelings of guilt if deprived of the Rescuing role.

Counsellors, too, can get caught up in the game. The client who ends a long recital of what is wrong in her life by saying, 'I really don't know what to do. I feel so helpless. It's not my fault, is it?' is casting herself in the Victim role. The unwary counsellor, intent on action rather than on exploring and challenging, who agrees that life is cruel and that the client is entirely innocent, is falling into the role of Rescuer. A simple, 'You feel as if you are an innocent victim in all this. Perhaps it would be productive to look at your part in the break-up of your marriage,' would be enough to convey to the client that she has the resources within her to challenge herself and the counsellor would not become the Rescuer and run the risk of the client becoming the Persecutor.

Further reading

Karpman, S. B. (1968) Fairy tales and script drama analysis. *Transactional Analysis Bulletin*, 7(26), 39–43.

DYING – STAGES OF (KUBLER-ROSS)

The science of the study of death is called **thanatology**, a term invented by Russian biologist Elie Metchnikoff. The field includes not only the biological changes associated with death but also the social, psychological, emotional, legal and ethical factors that may be involved.

In 1969 the Swiss-born psychiatrist Elisabeth Kubler-Ross conceptualized five stages in facing one's terminal illness: denial, anger, bargaining, depression and acceptance. Although most thanatologists accept the Kubler-Ross stages, they also recognize that these stages occur neither with predictable regularity nor in any set order.

Further, the five Kubler-Ross stages are simply general reactions to many situations involving loss, not necessarily dying. Seldom does a dying person follow a regular, clearly identifiable series of responses. With some, acceptance may come first, then denial; others may cross over constantly from acceptance to denial. Some may never go through denial.

Thanatology also examines attitudes toward death, the meaning and behaviours of bereavement and grief and the moral and ethical questions of euthanasia, organ transplants and life support.

Kubler-Ross found that many dying patients are comforted if someone sits and listens to their openly expressed fears and thoughts. Patients may be assisted in reaching acceptance by the hospital staff's and family's openly talking about death when the patient so desires.

The stages:
1. Shock and denial
   - Shocked
   - Dazed
   - Disbelieving
   - Seek confirmation.
2. Anger
   - Frustrated, irritated, angry
   - 'Why me?'

- Anger may be displaced
- May alienate friends and carers.

3. Bargaining
  - Attempt to negotiate with God, friends, doctor, for a cure or more time
  - 'I promise ...'

4. Depression
  - May be due to the illness itself or its effects or to work, economic hardship, isolation
  - Anticipation of the loss of life shortly to occur
  - Withdrawal
  - Psychomotor retardation
  - Sleep disturbances
  - Hopelessness
  - Possible thoughts of suicide.

5. Acceptance
  - Death is inevitable
  - Ideally, able to talk about facing the unknown

'Fear not death; remember those who have gone before and those who will follow after.' (William Stewart)

Further reading

Kubler-Ross, E. (1970) *On Death and Dying*, Tavistock, London.

Poss, S. (1981) *Towards Death with Dignity*, National Institute Social Services Library No. 41, George Allen & Unwin, London.

Zisook, S. (1985) Death, dying and bereavement. In: *Comprehensive Textbook of Psychiatry*, 6th edn, (eds H. J. Kaplan and B. J. Sadock), Williams & Wilkins, Baltimore, MD.

E

ECLECTIC COUNSELLING

The word 'eclectic' means deriving ideas, tastes, style, etc. from various sources; generally, not following any one system but selecting and using whatever is considered best in all systems.

Some practitioners regard eclecticism as being healthy; others think that a more formal and structured approach is more appropriate. Eclecticism is usually put at one pole of a dimension that runs from the eclectic to the formal.

Those who favour eclecticism feel that such an approach suits their personality and that they can offer variety, rather than expecting the client to fit some theoretical model which suits the counsellor.

While many counsellors work to one model of counselling, probably an equal number are eclectic counsellors, using a variety of approaches. They are most likely to have one core framework but borrow from other models and apply them to suit their particular needs.

Purists might not approve of this varied use of theories or models but eclectic counsellors would possibly counter this with, 'If it will help, use it'. Eclectics would also believe that, instead of trying to fit the client into one framework or model, the counsellors should be adaptable and find what works for you, rather than the other way round. Every person is unique and has needs and goals specific to his/her own life stage, particular problem(s) or degree of self-awareness.

Thus a counsellor using an eclectic or integrated approach may use a psycho-dynamic approach to bring unconscious drives/and or defences into conscious awareness. Behavioural therapy may be appropriate if a particular behaviour pattern is inhibiting, e.g. if the client has a specific sexual difficulty. Cognitive therapy could help if the messages from the client's earlier life are leading to self-defeating or self-destructive thought patterns or behaviours. Most counsellors using an eclectic approach work with the person-centred core principles.

Norcross and Tomcho point to the difference between eclectic and syncretic counselling, which is an attempt to unify or reconcile differing schools of thought. Syncretic counsellors 'fly by the seat of their pants'. They operate in a muddle.

Eclectic counselling is systematic, based on the counsellor being trained and skilled in several therapeutic systems and using them appropriately. Eclectic counselling is backed by research and experience.

The authors quoted above end their article by saying (speaking to would-be therapists seeking therapy for themselves) that competence, clinical experience, professional reputation, warmth and caring rank much higher than theoretical orientation.

Sue Wheeler highlights a difference between eclectic and integrated. The one fits with the general view of being eclectic; the integrated approach is a hybrid, made up of difference theories, models, approaches. This corresponds with what Norcross and Tomcho call syncretic.

Wheeler points out that for a counsellor to be fully trained in at least two models, the counsellor would have to be in training (part-time) for at least 5–6 years. She also says that offering 'modules' is not a satisfactory substitute for true eclectic training, mainly because there is no true integration of the theory and practice.

Further, 'if there is no core theoretical model that is studied in depth, students have no secure frame of reference in which to conceptualize their clients' concerns or on which to rely when the going gets tough'. Whatever the core model, that does not preclude the counsellor from exploring other models.

At a practical level, and this is perhaps where the counsellor might experience great conflict, is the therapeutic relationship. For example, in person-centred counselling, the counsellor works with being warm, accepting, genuine and real; in psychodynamic counselling the counsellor interprets unconscious motivation from a theoretical base, not from what something means to the client, as in person-centred counselling. In transpersonal counselling, working with the body, through touch and movement, may be totally acceptable.

Further reading

Norcross, J. C. and Tomcho, T. J. (1993) Beyond specific orientations. In: *Questions and Answers on Counselling in Action*, (ed. W. Dryden), Sage Publications, London.
Wheeler, S. (1993) Reservations about eclectic and integrative approaches to counselling. In: *Questions and Answers on Counselling in Action*, (ed. W. Dryden), Sage Publications, London.

ENCOURAGEMENT

Encouragement, in counselling, should not be equated with reassurance. Encouragement is positive; reassurance is often negative, for it stops the client from exploring important issues. As with reassurance, encouragement is not used deliberately – not by 'well done' or 'that's good' but by how the counsellor reflects the client's feelings and helps the client to move forward.

Encouragement communicates trust, respect and belief. Many psychologists contend that there are only two basic human emotions: love and fear. Encouragement communicates caring and movement toward others – love, whereas discouragement results in lowered self-esteem and alienation from others – fear. Yet, despite the intention to be encouraging, all too often we discourage communication. An example is the manager or parent who 'lets things go' as long as they are going well and who comments only when things go wrong.

Encouragement means that we should:

- Value clients as they are, not as their reputations indicate or as we hope they will be
- Believe clients to be good and worthwhile and act toward them accordingly

- Have faith in clients' abilities – this enables you to win confidence while building their self-respect
- Show faith in your clients – this will help them to believe in themselves
- Recognize honest effort as well as honest achievement
- Plan for success and assist in the development of skill
- Focus on strengths and assets rather than on mistakes
- Use the client's interests in order to motivate learning and instruction.

Many people's feelings of inadequacy can be overcome by substituting negative self-talk with positive affirmation. Encouragement can assist us to rediscover our values and joys, to identify strengths instead of dwelling on mistakes, to challenge and change old patterns and to have the courage to be imperfect!

ENVY (*see also*: Jealousy)

In general, envy is classified as a special form of anxiety, based on an overpowering desire to possess what someone else has.

Kleinian theory relates envy to the conflict between love and hate. The developing infant may experience hate toward the good objects. This love–hate relationship may be seen in adult life where something is hated because of its goodness.

Schizophrenic states have been attributed to prolonged and early envy, with continued confusion between love and hate.

For Adler, envy is present wherever there is a striving for power and domination. The person who is consumed by envy has a low self-evaluation and is constantly dissatisfied with life.

Envious people act as if they wanted to have everything. The universality of the feeling of envy causes a universal dislike of it.

People who envy someone else's achievements tend to blame others for their own lack of success.

Envious people tend to be aggressive, obstructive and officious, with no great love for relationships and with little understanding of human nature.

Envy may go so far as to lead a person to feel pleasure in a someone else's suffering and pain. Working to raise self-esteem may help to reduce envy.

Further reading
Adler, A. (1937) *Understanding Human Nature*, George Allen & Unwin, London.
Klein, M. (1957) Envy and gratitude. In: *The Writings of Melanie Klein*, vol. 3, Basic Books, New York.

EVALUATION

Individual counselling sessions

By evaluating or analysing counselling sessions, counsellors will continue to make progress. Evaluation encourages the growth of both client and counsellor.

If counsellor and client are active partners in the evaluation process, they can learn from each other.

Ongoing evaluation gives both partners an opportunity to explore their feelings about what is happening and also to appraise, constructively, what should next be done.

What happened within the counsellor?
Was the counsellor:

- Fully attentive
- Listening actively
- Asking too many questions
- Leading the client
- Open or closed
- Afraid to challenge
- Insensitively challenging
- Able to empathize
- Relaxed or tense
- Friendly or aloof
- Anxious or at ease
- Quiet or talkative
- Interested or bored?

What happened within the client?
Was the client:

- Fully present
- Responding to the counsellor
- Showing evidence of blocking
- Open with feelings
- Prepared to explore
- Waiting for answers
- An active partner?

What happened between counsellor and client?
Was there:

- Participation
- Involvement or over-involvement
- Argument
- Persuasion
- Feeling versus intellect
- Reassurance versus exploration
- Tolerance
- Achievement of insight?

Was the following behaviour exhibited: if so, by whom?

- Tension release
- Support
- Caring
- Aggression
- Hostility
- Manipulation
- Rejection?

Body language and its significance (*see* Nonverbal communication)
Was there:

- Physical contact
- Proximity and position
- Gestures
- Facial expressions
- Eye contact?

Atmosphere:
Was the atmosphere:

- Formal/informal
- Competitive/co-operative
- Hostile
- Supportive
- Inhibited/permissive
- Harmonious/destructive?

On termination of counselling

A terminal evaluation gives both client and counsellor a feeling of completeness. It gives the counsellor an opportunity to look at some of those things that did not go according to plan, as well as those that did.

A well-carried-out evaluation not only looks backward, it also looks forward. A final evaluation provides the client with something positive to carry into the future.

Termination should be well planned and worked through. Abrupt termination can be very traumatic to both client and counsellor. It should be approached with as much sensitivity and caring as any stage in the counselling.

When counselling has taken place over a long period, the original reason(s) may have faded into insignificance. Counselling is like taking a journey: we know from where we have come and roughly the route taken, but looking back, the starting point has become obscured, partly through distance but also through time.

Unlike a journey, it is necessary for both counsellor and client to look back in order to firmly establish the final position.

Looking back to where and why the journey began may prove difficult; feelings, as well as memories, fade with time. Looking back is not always comfortable. It may reveal obstacles not previously recognized.

Evaluation should identify:

- The different problems and how these were tackled
- The goals and how they have been achieved.
- Areas of growth and insights.

The relationship between counsellor and client is not an end in itself. Evaluation helps to establish just how the client has been able to transfer the learning into relationships outside of counselling.

Evaluation helps the client to realize and acknowledge personal gains. The counsellor, in return, receives something from every counselling relationship.

Success in counselling is not easily measured, however:

- Clients who have succeeded in climbing a few hills are more likely to want to tackle mountains and, emotionally, are more equipped to
- Counsellors who have helped create an atmosphere of trust and respect and have helped a client travel a little way along the road of self-discovery are entitled to share the success the client feels.

The feeling of failure in counselling is difficult to handle. Blame should not be attributed to either counsellor or client. Both (if possible, if not, the counsellor alone) should examine what did happen rather than what did not happen.

If counselling goes full term, it is unlikely to be a failure. The feeling of failure and consequent blame is more likely when the client terminates prematurely.

If counsellors have created a conducive climate and clients are unable to travel their own road toward self-discovery, then the responsibility for not travelling that road must rest with them. We can only take people along the road of self-discovery who are willing to travel with us. We can only travel at their pace. Unless two (or a group) are in agreement, the journey toward self-discovery will be fraught with impossibilities.

Some possible indicators of impending termination:

- Abandonment
- Acting out
- Apathy
- Decrease in intensity
- Denial
- Expressions of anger
- Feelings of separation and loss
- Futility
- Impotence
- Inadequacy

- Intellectualizing
- Joking
- Lateness
- Missed appointments
- Mourning
- Regression
- Withdrawal.

Further reading

Cormier, W. H. and Cormier, L. S. (1979) *Interviewing Strategies for Helpers: A guide to assessment, treatment and evaluation*, Brooks/Cole, Monterey, CA.

Ivey, A. (1983) *Intentional Interviewing and Counselling*, Brooks/Cole, Monterey, CA.

Ward, D. E. (1989) Termination of individual counselling: concepts and strategies. In: *Key Issues for Counselling in Action*, (ed. W. Dryden), Sage Publications, London.

EXISTENTIAL THERAPY

Existential therapy is a psychodynamic approach within psychotherapy influenced by existentialism. Enshrined in this approach is a belief in the individual's capacity to become healthy and fully functional; to rise above self through self-consciousness and self-reflection. This is achieved as the client concentrates on what is happening in the present; accepting that what happens in life is partly his/her personal responsibility and influenced by decisions.

Existentially oriented psychotherapists concern themselves with how the client experiences life rather than with diagnosis and cause. Psychoanalysis, conversely, concentrates on cause and effect and on trying to reduce complicated patterns to individual parts.

Important principles:

- The immediate moment of experience
- Conscious, personal identity
- Unity of the person
- The search for the meaning of life
- Pathology arises from the need to defend against alienation from self and others and the anxiety generated by the threat of the immediate experience
- Alienation from self leads to rigid, restrictive behaviour, a clinging to the past and a desire to impose a false order on the present and future
- Existential therapists engage in a dialogue within an authentic and equal relationship, in which the therapist is totally present.

The aims of therapy are to help clients:

- To take responsibility for their own being in the world
- To become independent and self-governing
- To move beyond self into full fellowship with others

- To exercise conscious intention
- To make ethical choices
- To accept high ideals
- To engage in loving relationships
- To confront normal anxiety, an unavoidable part of being human
- To confront and reduce anxiety that is related to fear – anxiety is more basic than fear
- To live without neurotic anxiety but to be able to tolerate normal, existential anxiety.

The cost of change may mean having to deal with anxiety and inner crises. The person's only authentic response to the contribution of the family and other social institutions may be to choose madness.

Existentialism is similar to humanistic therapies, although it may be more confronting. It is the opposite of the more technical, behavioural and strategy-dominated therapies. It is an attempt to grapple with the meaninglessness and extinction that threaten present-day societies.

Basic concepts

The 'I am' experience
- The 'I am' experience is known as an 'ontological' experience, which translated from the Greek means 'the science of being'
- It is the realization of one's being and the choice one has of saying, 'I am the one living, experiencing. I choose my own being'
- Being is not tied to status or what one does, occupation or the life one leads
- When everything else is stripped away, one can still say, 'I am'
- The experience of being also points to the experience of nonbeing or nothingness
- Examples of nonbeing would be the threat of death, destruction, severe and crippling anxiety or sickness
- The threat of nonbeing is ever present, e.g. in the remark by someone that puts us down.

Normal and neurotic anxiety
- In existential terms anxiety arises from our personal need to survive, to preserve and to assert our being; it is the threat to our existence or to values we identify with our existence
- The characteristics of normal existential anxiety are:
  - It is proportionate to the situation
  - It does not require to be repressed
  - It can be used constructively, e.g. to discover the underlying dilemma that created the anxiety
- The characteristics of neurotic anxiety are:
  - It is not appropriate to the situation

- It is repressed
- It is destructive and paralysing, not constructive and stimulating.

Guilt feelings

- Neurotic guilt feelings usually arise out of fantasized transgressions
- Normal guilt feelings make us sensitive to social and ethical aspects of behaviour
- Existential guilt feelings arise from locking up our potentialities.

The world

- The world includes all past events and influences that condition our existence
- The way one relates to these events and influences is what holds meaning
- The three forms of world:
  - **The 'world around'** (environment): the world of objects, the natural world, biological drives
  - **'Own world'** (relationship to self): self-awareness, self-relatedness, grasping the meaning of something in the world
  - **'With-world'** (fellow humans): interpersonal relationships and love. To truly love, one must have become truly individual and sufficient unto oneself. The 'with-world' is empty of vitality if 'own world' is lacking.

The significance of time
Time is considered to be the heart of existence.

- Experiences such as anxiety, depression and joy are usually related to time
- People who cannot relate to time, who cannot hope for the future, who view each day as an island with no past and no future, are seriously disturbed
- The ability to relate to time is one of the characteristics of being human
- Time fixes us in the here and now and prevents us from being lost in space
- Some experiences, such as the development of life, cannot be measured by time
- Experiencing in the 'now' breaks through time
- Insight is not time-controlled; it comes complete
- When one's past does not come alive, it is probably because one's future has no attraction
- Being able to change something, however small, in the present, gives hope to work toward a future.

The capacity to transcend the immediate

- Existing means a continual going beyond the past and present to reach out to the future
- Transcendence means being able to think in terms of 'the possible'
- People who are unable to think in terms of the possible feel threatened by the lack of specific boundaries – it is as if they already perceive themselves as 'lost in space'

- People who are unable to think of the possible experience a world that has shrunk around them, with consequent loss of freedom
- The existential model of personality postulates that the basic conflict is between the individual and the 'givens' (or 'ultimate concerns') of existence.

Death

A core conflict exists between one's awareness of death and the concurrent wish to continue living. It is an emotional disturbance that is often the result of inadequate death transcendence, which then leads to terror of death.

Freedom

In existential terms, freedom is bound to dread. Inherent in freedom is self-responsibility, for life design and its consequences. Responsibility for one's situation is bound to the principle of 'willing', which consists of wishing and then deciding.

Many people cannot wish, because they cannot feel. When we fully experience a wish, we are then faced with a decision. Some people experience 'decisional panic' and try to pass the decision-making on to others.

Isolation

- **Interpersonal isolation** is the separation of oneself from others, which results from either a deficiency in social skill or a pathological fear of intimacy
- **Intrapersonal isolation** is where we have dissociated parts of ourselves – experiences, desires, feelings – out of awareness
- **Existential isolation** is a fundamental isolation from people and from the world. People who suffer from depression may also experience existential depression, where they can no longer find meaning in their activity and can find no sense of purpose.

There is always a gap that cannot be bridged. The personal dilemma is that, no matter how intimate the relationship, there is always a part that we will never be able to share. This has been referred to as 'the fundamental loneliness'. The most poignant example of the fundamental loneliness is the experience of death.

The fear of death and of isolation keeps many people from entering relationships of any depth and intimacy. Some people doubt their own existence so much that they only feel they exist in the presence of another. Many undergo a 'fusion' with others, so that 'I' becomes 'we', resulting in the safety of conformity. Compulsive sexuality is a common antidote to the terrifying prospect of isolation. The sexually compulsive person relates only to part of the other, not to the whole.

Meaninglessness

This often revolves around questions such as:

- What possible meaning can life have?

- Why do we live?
- How shall we live?
- Is my self-created meaning of life strong enough to bear my life?

In the same way as we need to organize random events into something we can understand, so we deal with the existential situation. Were we not able to find some meaning, we would be desperately unsettled. From a sense of the meaning of life, we generate values that provide a master- plan for life conduct. Values not only tell us why we live, but how to live.

The dilemma of existential meaninglessness, then, is: How do I find meaning in a universe that has no meaning?

Defence mechanisms

To an existentialist therapist, anxiety results from confrontation with death, freedom, isolation and meaninglessness. Two defence mechanisms ensue.

Specialness

- This involves a deep, powerful belief that one cannot be destroyed, is totally invulnerable and will never die
- The person believes that the laws of biology do not apply
- These beliefs (of delusional quality) give rise to narcissism, search for glory, search for power, suspicious behaviour
- Such people often seek therapy when their defence of specialness no longer holds up and they are hit by anxiety.

An ultimate rescuer

- This is the belief in an omnipotent protector who will always snatch us from the deepest hell
- These beliefs (of delusional quality) give rise to passivity, dependency and servile behaviour
- Such people often dedicate themselves to living for the 'dominant other', which is fertile ground for depression
- Existential therapy is not a system of psychotherapy, it is a frame of reference, a pattern for understanding a client's suffering in a distinctive manner.

Further reading

Binswanger, L. (1967) *Being-in-the-World*, Harper & Row, New York.
Deurzen-Smith, E. van (1988), *Existential Counselling in Practice*, Sage Publications, London.
Frankl, V. (1973) *Psychotherapy and Existentialism*, Penguin, Harmondsworth.
Macquarrie, J. (1972) *Existentialism*, Penguin, Harmondsworth.
Yalom, I. D. (1981) *Existential Psychotherapy*, Basic Books, New York.

F

FAMILY THERAPY

Family therapy brings all the members of one family into a therapy group, on the assumption that families operate as an interacting system and that one member's problems are only symptomatic of problems in the system. Thus the focus of therapy is on the whole family (the system) as the client. A family is more than the sum of its members.

The family as a focus for treatment usually comprises the members who live under the same roof, sometimes supplemented by relatives who live elsewhere or by other people who share the family home. Family therapy may be appropriate when the person referred for treatment has symptoms clearly related to such disturbances in family function as marital discord, distorted family roles and parent–child conflict or when the family as a unit asks for help. It is not appropriate when the patient has a severe disorder needing specific treatment in its own right.

The approach may be psychoanalytical, systems or behavioural. The psychodynamic approaches will concentrate on interpreting behaviour and increasing insight. The systems therapist concentrates on the present and on changing how the family functions, by helping the family look at its rules and assumptions. The behaviourist will help the family look at what reinforces certain behaviours that the family regard as undesirable.

The aim of family therapy is fourfold:

- Understanding the dynamics of the specific family
- Mobilizing the psychological resources of the family
- Working to so change relationships between family members that dysfunctional behavioural symptoms disappear
- Developing problem-solving and coping skills.

The family as a system

A system has in common:

- Interconnected and interdependent parts
- Every part is consistently related to the other over a period of time. Systems may be closed (house heating) or open (the family).

Properties of an open system

- Wholeness
  - Wholeness is the sum of the parts plus the interaction
  - One part cannot be understood unless its relationship to the other parts is also understood
  - Wholeness is a *Gestalten* – the interdependence between parts
  - The family consists of the members and the relationships between them

- Relationship
  - Relationship concerns the what rather than the why of what is happening
  - The shift is from what is happening **within** the members to what is happening **between** them
- Equifinality (self-perpetuation)
  - When interventions are made in the 'here and now', changes are produced in the family open system
  - Concentrating on the here and now and not becoming involved in blaming the past is valid, because a system has no memory.

The building blocks of the family system are a series of interlocking triangles, the function of which is to reduce or increase the emotional intensity within the family.

The man in a partnership that is shaky who becomes a workaholic could be seen as creating a triangle to reduce tension.

The prime therapeutic task is to analyse the various triangles in a family and make interventions to change the system.

The family systems school of thought considers triangles over three generations. The structuralist school of thought is more concerned with triangles within the nuclear family.

Feedback, the mechanism by which the system is constantly being adjusted and equilibrium restored, is an important concept and function in systems theory. Positive feedback forces change on the system by not allowing it to return to its former state.

Main schools

1. Object relations family therapy
Here the identified 'patient' is often seen as the one who carries the split-off, and therefore unacceptable, impulses of the other family members; the 'sick' one; the one on whom the family focuses their dysfunctional behaviour.

2. Family systems therapy
This works with eight concepts:

- Triangles
- Differentiation of self; which measures the amount of fusion between members
- The emotional system of the family
- Family projection process; how a family selects the identified patient
- Emotional cut-off; the extent to which one member relates to the others
- Transmission; the mechanism by which pathology is passed through generations
- Sibling position – determines one's existential view of the world
- Societal regression; patterns that occur in the family are also found in society.

Families are taught not to react but to respond. Reacting means acting only on the basis of feeling and ignoring the needs of other people. Responding is making a rational, not a purely emotional, choice and taking into account the needs of others. Family members learn to be both 'self' and a member of the system.

3. Structural family therapy
This views pathology as either 'enmeshed' or 'disengaged'. In an enmeshed structure, the therapist works on loosening the boundaries. In a disengaged structure, the therapist works toward establishing or strengthening the boundaries.

4. Strategic intervention family therapy
This views therapy as a power struggle between client and therapist. In family therapy, the identified 'patient' is the controller who makes the others feel helpless. The role of the therapist is to restructure the system by re-establishing family boundaries and changing the balance of power.

Family therapy seeks to answer three questions:

- **What is a family?** A family has physical and emotional needs and the basic emotional needs are intimacy, self-expression and meaning.
- **What is a 'dysfunctional family'?** This is a family where there is an inability of the family to meet basic emotional needs. In family systems therapy, all members are an essential part of the therapeutic process. The functional family will work to solve conflicts, while the dysfunctional family will not.
- **Why must a family change?** In order to be functional, families must become 'we' as well as retaining their individual 'I'. Feedback, possible with adults, is entirely different with children and is not immediate. The birth of subsequent siblings changes the system. Entry to school admits others into the system, so forcing further change. Children with school phobia may be responding to the family's inability to widen the boundaries. Adolescence, with its need for greater freedom, is a potential for dysfunction, as parents experience loss of meaning. The 'empty nest syndrome' is often experienced by parents when children leave home. Dramatic change may allow martial differences to surface.

Three family dimensions

Marital subsystem

- Two people become a couple
- 'Fusion' or 'enmeshment' is where one or both are unable to separate from their family of origin – the boundaries of the new relationship are thus blurred
- The ability to close a door and shut out others (symbolically) is important in the development of a functional family system
- In functional families, it is spouse first and others next

- Children-oriented marriages are invariably dysfunctional, because the children are needed to give meaning to the marriage
- A firm alliance between parents prevents a child from forming an alliance with one or other of the parents.

Sibling subsystem

- The alliance between parents forces children into forming their own subsystems with brother and sisters or others of their own generation
- The sibling subsystem has its own boundaries.

Questions to ask:
- Are parents clearly separated from children?
- Is the difference between children clear?
- Are older children treated differently from younger ones?
- What are the levels of responsibility?
- What are the levels of respect for their uniqueness, privacy, common courtesies, freedom?
- What is the influence of the neighbourhood culture? The school culture? Peer group pressure?

Homeostasis

This is the balance between marital and sibling subsystems. If disrupted limits cannot be corrected, homeostasis is upset and the system will eventually disintegrate. Homeostasis is threatened, for example, when a family moves to a new neighbourhood or culture. 'Destructive behaviour' may be an attempt to restore homeostasis.

Goals of therapy

A primary goal in family therapy is to produce visible change in behaviour, even though family members may not be totally aware of what is happening. Insight, helpful for the therapist, is not considered important for the family; getting them to be aware of the interactions **is**.

The history of the family is important for object relations and family systems therapists, less important for structural and strategic intervention therapists, for whom the present is what is relevant. Family therapists are less concerned than are traditional therapists with arriving at a correct diagnosis.

Feelings, which are thought to arise from behaviours, are not given first place; possibly because of the emphasis on the 'system'.

Learning and teaching form an essential part of the therapies of schools 1 and 2, but less so in 3 and 4.

Transference and working through it do not form an explicit part of family therapy; the concentration is on the family interaction not on the relationship between individual and therapist.

The therapist is viewed as a model, a change agent or teacher, who helps the family develop problem-solving skills.

Therapists are active; they are not 'blank screens'.

Techniques

- **Re-enactment**: Instead of 'talking about', the family are encouraged to 'talk' and interact; sometimes called 'psychodrama *in situ*
- **Homework**: To build bridges between the sessions and interaction in the home
- **Family sculpting** (*see* Psychodrama)
- **Genogram**: This is a multigenerational diagram that graphically illustrates family relationships
- **Behaviour modification** (*see* Behaviour therapy)
- **Multiple family therapy**: Some of the advantages of involving several families at the same time are that it:
  - Points up similarities and differences in interactions
  - Permits the family members to act in a co-counselling role
  - Loosens the authority of the therapist
  - Helps to hasten the formation of the therapeutic alliance.

A phenomenon of family dynamics has been referred to above: the 'sick role' – a label attached to a person that affords that person certain privileges and obligations as 'the sick one'. The sick role may perform a function for the person but it also does so for the rest of the family: the sick one becomes the focus of attention and, often, the scapegoat (see entry) for all that goes wrong within the family.

The family may show great unity, as distinct from a 'delinquent' family, which is often fragmented. However, the person filling the sick role feels a weight of responsibility for keeping the family together and when the sick person is removed the family often disintegrates. This places the person in a double bind – s/he may want to get well, yet if s/he recovers, blame for family break-up is likely to follow.

Family therapy does produce change, although it is not clear how that is accomplished or why one approach works with one family and not with another.

Further reading

Gurman, A. S. and Kniskern, D. (1981) *Handbook of Family Therapy*, Brunner/Mazel, New York.

Hoffman, L. (1981) *Foundations of Family Therapy*, Basic Books, New York.

Steinglass, P. (1995) Family therapy. In: *Comprehensive Textbook of Psychiatry*, 6th edn, (eds H. J. Kaplan and B. J. Sadock), Williams & Wilkins, Baltimore, MD.

FEEDBACK (*see also*: Communication, Johari window)

Feedback is a term borrowed from rocket engineering by Kurt Lewin and gives one person the opportunity to be open to the perceptions of others.

Feedback is an essential mechanism in any interpersonal communication, particularly in group work. An example of social feedback is returning a smile.

Giving feedback is both a verbal and a nonverbal process where people let others know their perception of and feelings about the other people's behaviour.

Soliciting feedback is asking for other people's perceptions of our behaviour.

Guidelines for giving feedback

- Your intention must be to help
- If the person has not asked for feedback, check whether s/he is open to it
- Deal only with observable behaviour
- Deal only with modifiable behaviour
- Describe specifics, not generalities
- Describe behaviours
- Do not judge the person
- Do not make assumptions or interpret
- Let the person know the impact the behaviour has on you
- Check that the message has been received and understood
- Suggest, rather than prescribe means for improvement
- Should be directed toward meeting the need of the other person, not designed to punish
- Encourage the person to check out your feedback with other people
- Feedback, if well-timed and accurate, enhances the relationship.

Guidelines for receiving feedback

- When you ask for feedback, be specific in describing the behaviour about which you want feedback
- Try not to act defensively
- Try not to rationalize the behaviour
- Summarize your understanding
- Share your thoughts and feelings
- Accept the responsibility for the behaviour
- Try to see things through the other's eyes
- Explore the feedback, don't use it as an excuse to attack
- Don't brush it off with misplaced humour or sarcasm
- Don't put yourself down, assuming that everyone else is correct
- Plan how you could use the feedback
- If it is hard to take, remember, you did ask!

Examples of feedback

- **Direct expression of feelings:** 'I like you'
- **Descriptive feedback:** 'Your fists are clenched'
- **Non-evaluative feedback:** 'You are angry and that's OK'
- **Specific feedback:** 'When you shouted, I felt anxious'
- **Freedom of choice to change:** 'When you called me "son", I felt put down and small'

- **Immediate feedback**: 'I'm feeling angry at what I consider to be a sexist remark'
- **Group-shared feedback**: 'Does this group see me as being supportive?'

Further reading

Hanson, P. C. (1975) Giving feedback: an interpersonal skill. In: *1975 Annual Handbook for Group Facilitators*, University Associates, San Diego, CA.

Rogers, C. R. (1970) *Encounter Groups*, Harper & Row, New York.

FEMININITY/MASCULINITY (*see also*: Anima and Animus, Myers–Briggs type indicator, Self)

Femininity/masculinity generally refers to gender, those personal characteristics that are believed to differentiate one sex from another. Gender is more than the manifest biological differences between the sexes.

Family patterns and wider cultural behaviours exert a powerful influence on the development and acceptance of what is 'feminine' or 'masculine'. It can be said (in Freudian terms) that men adopt the masculine role and women accept the feminine role and only do so when they have renounced the penis. This view has been seriously criticized by female psychoanalysts.

Gender difficulties occur when people feel pressured into denying attributes that they feel are vital to their identity and other people feel are inappropriate.

Feminist issues

The feminist issue has to be addressed in counselling, for there is a whole ideology – assumptions, ways of thinking, attitudes, values and beliefs – that needs to be examined.

The word 'different' is important in counselling. The words 'superior' and 'inferior' carry connotations of competition, win–lose, hierarchy, strong–weak, capable–incapable.

Alfred Adler (*see* Individual psychology) speaks of the difference between 'horizontal' and 'vertical' relationships. A hierarchy is a vertical relationship that does not respect differences but places people in superior/inferior positions. Many of the differences will disappear and true equality (not uniformity) will be established when we relate to men and women in horizontal, not vertical relationships.

In order for men to truly accept women and women to accept men as equals they must accept the male or female within themselves, which is so often our 'shadow' side. An acceptance of our shadow brings a wholeness and richness hitherto seen only through darkened glass.

Much of the difference between men and women is learned rather than genetic. There is tremendous variation within the two groups. Many women behave more aggressively than some men. Many men are involved at a higher level of caring than some women. Many men never resort to physical violence; some women are violently aggressive.

We can make a conscious choice to incorporate traits or values associated with either men or women if they are appropriate for us. Rigid sex roles restrict behaviour. Sex-typed feminine women attend to babies and people in need but do not exhibit appropriate independent and assertive behaviours. Sex-typed masculine men are the opposite of this.

When we integrate characteristics of both sexes, we incorporate independent-assertive behaviours and responsible-helping behaviours. Integration helps us to be more spontaneous. We are able to respond appropriately to situations calling for both assertiveness and caring.

Counselling, of whomsoever, is about wholeness and integration. Counsellors who ignore the fact that for centuries women have been put down and made second-class citizens (and in some respects, still are), will never be able to make effective contact with female clients, which is essential if integration and wholeness is to take place.

Likewise, we need to recognize when the feminine side of male clients is being repressed and help them work toward liberation, integration and wholeness so that they, too, can become wholly alive. Women and men have to believe that they are both equal and different from the other sex and that their unique differences are valuable to each other.

However much women tell other women this, the greatest change will come when men start valuing women for themselves. It is not what men say but what they do that will convince women that their uniqueness is respected for what it is.

Cross-gender counselling

Many cultures in the world are still very male-dominated; this is reflected in the way women relate to men and is demonstrated in the way power is shared.

Men have assumed, and women for centuries have colluded with them, that their role is to provide and the role of women is to do. Male counsellors (the archetypal 'doctors') may (unconsciously) reinforce this power difference.

The female client who is compliant and submissive and does not argue openly may well be caught in this power trap. The reverse may be true. A male client with a female counsellor may feel uncomfortable with what he (consciously or unconsciously) perceives as a reversal of roles, and attempt to dominate the session.

Cross-gender counselling may also create difficulties where the subject is a delicate one. Just as some female patients prefer male doctors and some prefer same-sex doctors, so with counselling. However, there are many issues where same-sex counselling is more appealing than dealing with someone of the opposite sex.

Some women may prefer to talk with a female counsellor about, for example, the problems associated with premenstrual tension, rape or abortion. Likewise, some men would probably find it easier to talk with another man about sexual impotence.

Another area of potential difficulty in cross-gender counselling is sexual attraction and, in some instances, sexual harassment. While there are many jokes about clients 'falling in love' with therapists (of either gender) the reality of it is far from humorous. The possibility should always be hovering in the wings of the counselling room. Apart from any overt involvement, these transference feelings (*see* Transference and counter-transference) may cause the relationship to flounder unless they are recognized and dealt with.

A potential difficulty lies in expressing an opinion. Between two people of the same sex an opinion can be expressed and both parties will generally be able to discuss and argue it through. When the same statement is made by a person of one gender to someone of the other, the statement is filtered through gender values. What is said by a man to a woman may be interpreted as a pronouncement rather than a suggestion or a possibility. What was acceptable in one situation could be perceived as patronizing or domineering in another.

Counsellors, of whichever gender and of whatever professional persuasion, will never fully understand femininity or masculinity unless they are willing to enter the other's frame of reference. Only as we risk leaving our own frame of reference will any of us be able to understand anyone else's personal meanings. The more one person can work with and understand someone's personal meanings, the more that person will understand her/himself and will achieve new insights into themselves.

Entering the client's frame of reference in cross-gender counselling will mean confronting our own hidden Anima or Animus. When we accept the challenge of integrating our Shadow, our personality will be more complete and our counselling will be richer.

Further reading

Brown, L. and Liss-Levinson, N. (1981) Feminist therapy. In: *Handbook of Innovative Psychotherapies*, (ed. R. Corsini), John Wiley, New York.
Chaplin, J. (1988) *Feminist Counselling in Action*, Sage Publications, London.
Chaplin, J. (1989) Counselling and gender. In: Dryden, W., Charles-Edwards, D. and Woolfe, R. (eds) *Handbook of Counselling in Britain*, Tavistock/Routledge, London.
Dickson, A. (1982) *A Woman In Your Own Right*, Quartet Books, London.
Orbach, S. and Eichenbaum, L. (1985) *Understanding Women*, Pelican, London.

FIGHT/FLIGHT RESPONSE (*see also*: Stress management)

The effect of a stressor is to mobilize the body's fight/flight system to combat a perceived enemy. Stress stimulates chemical, physical and psychological changes to prepare the body to cope with a potentially life-threatening situation. The process is controlled by the autonomic nervous system and the endocrine system. The process is:

- The liver releases extra sugar to fuel the muscles
- Hormones are released that stimulate the conversion of fats and proteins to sugar
- The body's metabolism increases in preparation for increased activity

- Certain unessential activities, such as digestion, are slowed up
- Saliva and mucus dry up, so increasing the size of the air passages to the lungs and giving rise to the early sign of stress, a dry mouth
- Endorphins, the body's natural painkillers, are secreted
- The surface blood vessels constrict to reduce bleeding in case of injury
- The spleen releases more red blood cells to help carry oxygen and the bone marrow produces more white cells to help fight infection.

The autonomic nervous system, regulated by the hypothalamus (the stress centre) with the pituitary, is responsible for releasing more than 30 hormones that control these physiological responses to an emergency.

When neither response – to fight or to run away – is appropriate, the biochemical changes have already been aroused and the body takes time to return to normal. It is the continued presence of the stress hormones that gives rise to the prolongation of bodily symptoms described above. When appropriate action is taken, the chemicals are used up and the body returns to normal functioning. People who experience stress live in a state of constant readiness to respond to fight or flight.

Fight/flight defences in counselling (*see* Competition versus co-operation)

In addition to the listed defence mechanisms, various manoeuvres by the client (and sometimes by the counsellor) may be included in this section on the fight/flight response.

Fight manoeuvres

These are based on the premise that the best defence is a good attack.

- **Competing with the counsellor**: The client who struggles to control the counsellor is very probably doing so to avoid dealing with some hidden agenda
- **Cynicism**: This is characterized by frequent challenging of the counsellor's role and method of working, questioning genuine behaviour in a sceptical way
- **Interrogation**: Here the client cross-examines the counsellor 'to gain helpful information and understanding'.

Flight manoeuvres

- **Intellectualization**: This is a deliberate avoidance of dealing with feelings by filtering and analysing everything through head logic
- **Generalization**: This is a refusal to get to grips with specifics, applying to someone else what we ourselves are experiencing
- **Rationalization**: This is an attempt to justify certain behaviour by substituting 'good' behaviour for the real one; an example would be: 'I would be able to look at my feelings if I had a different counsellor'
- **Projection**: Here the client attributes to other people the traits of his/her own personality

- **Withdrawal**: This may vary from boredom to actual physical removal from the session – the tendency to avoid dealing with the 'here-and-now' is also a flight response.

FOCUSING

Focusing is:

- A body-centred therapy technique
- A counselling skill.

Gendlin's body-centred therapy

- Focusing helps the client get to grips with a complex problem, with its feelings, by examining the problem in stages
- Specific instructions concentrate attention on what is happening in the body.

Examples of focusing:

1. How does the body feel inside?
2. What feelings are being experienced?
3. Allow a problem to emerge and gain a sense of it as a whole
4. Pay attention to the most powerful feeling
5. Allow the feeling to change
6. Put an image to the feeling
7. Watch the image change
8. Relax and reflect on the changes.

Focusing tries to address the client's problems directly rather than just talking about them. It is also used in existential and humanistic therapies.

Focusing in counselling

- Focusing helps the client get to grips with a complex situation by teasing out details and exploring specific parts in depth
- Focusing helps the client look beyond the problem to possible solutions or alternatives
- Focusing helps both client and counsellor not to get lost
- Focusing involves a certain degree of direction and control by the counsellor, which has to be carefully used.

Principles of focusing:

- Help the client deal with the immediate crisis
- Focus on issues important to the client
- Begin with a problem that causes pain
- Deal with issues the client is willing to work on
- Work on manageable parts of a larger problem

- Work for something with quick success
- Work from the simple to the complex.

Underlying focusing is the clients' need to feel some reward and some hope. Focusing implies a certain degree of direction and guidance of the exploration and not everything can be worked out at once.

Focusing uses specific questions to tease out detail and to explore particular topics in depth. There needs to be a focus in the helping process, around which the resources of the client can be mobilized. Focusing helps client and counsellor to find out where to start or, having started, in which direction to continue.

Points to bear in mind

- If there is a crisis, first help the client to manage the crisis
- Focus on issues that the client sees as important
- Begin with a problem that seems to be causing the client pain
- Focus on an issue that the client is willing to work on, even if it does not seem important to you
- Begin with some manageable part of the problem
- Begin with a problem that can be managed relatively easily
- When possible, move from less severe to more severe problems
- Focus on a problem where the benefits will outweigh the costs
- Make the initial experience of counselling rewarding as an incentive to continue.

Example

Mr Davies, aged 80, is dying of cancer. As the pastoral counsellor, Mrs Phillips, listens to him, she picks up Mr Davies's concern for his wife. At the same time, she detects underlying fears about his own death, fear he is not admitting to.

Mrs Phillips says: 'Mr Davies, I hear a number of issues you would probably like to talk about, not necessarily right now. My hunch is that the one you would like to spend time talking over is your concern for your wife and how she is managing.'

Some useful focusing guidelines:

- Does the problem use a lot of energy?
- Is the problem of high, moderate or low significance?
- What priority would the client give to this problem?
- Could it be managed if it was broken down?
- If it is resolved, would it influence other issues?
- Small issues resolved give a boost
- Is it within the client's direct control?
- In cost terms, how important is it? In other words, would the client be spending 80% of time to get 20% result?
- Is the client open to explore this issue?
- Does it need more time than is available now?

Three responses help the client to focus

The contrast response
'Contrast' describes a marked awareness of the differences between two conditions or events that results from bringing them together.
    Example: 'If you think about (for example) staying in your present job or moving to another job, what would it be like then?'

The choice-point response
'Choice-point' describes any set of circumstances in which a choice among several alternatives is required.
    Example: 'From what you've said, it looks as if these are the major issues (itemizing them); which of these would you feel most comfortable working with first?'

The figure-ground response
'Figure-ground' describes how a person perceives the relationship between the object of the attention or focus – the figure – and the rest of what is around – the perceptual field, the ground. The figure generally has form or structure and appears to be in front of the ground. The figure is given shape or form and the background is left unshaped and lacking in form.
    Thus, figure-ground focusing helps to give one part of the problem shape and form and so helps the client to more readily grasp hold of something and work with it.
    Example: 'These are the various points of the problem; it seems to me that the most worthwhile to address first could be the need for you to get a job. How do you feel about that?'
    When working on any of the above techniques, the choice is best put last, otherwise it becomes lost. There should be no further exploration after you have invited the client to consider a particular response. The specific response should be the last thing the client hears, and so responds to.

FORCE FIELD ANALYSIS (*see also*: Goals and goal setting)

Force field analysis (FFA) is a decision-making technique, developed from Lewin's field theory, designed to help people understand the various internal and external forces that influence the way they make decisions. For most of the time these forces are in relative balance; but when something disturbs the balance, decisions are more difficult to make.
    When the forces are identified, counsellor and client work on strategies to help the client reach the desired goal.

Stages:

1. What is the goal to be achieved?
2. Identify restraining forces

3. Identify facilitating forces
4. Work out how either the strength of some of the restraining forces can be reduced or how the strength of some of the facilitating forces can be increased
5. Use imagery to picture moving toward the desired goal and achieving it.

Forces may be external or internal.

Examples of internal forces:

- Type of personality
- Age
- Health
- Previous experiences
- Motivation
- Attitudes
- Beliefs.

Examples of external forces:

- Family and friends
- Locality
- Job and career
- Finance
- Mobility
- Commitments
- Hobbies.

The underlying principle is that, by strengthening the facilitating forces and diminishing the restraining forces, a decision will be easier to make because energy, trapped by the restraining forces, has been released.

The hindering forces are the obstacles that are, or seem to be, restraining us from implementing our plan of action. Once the hindering forces have been identified, ways of coping with them are explored. We must ensure that we do not dwell on these forces and become demoralized.

Our resources are the positive, facilitating forces. These forces can be persons, places or things. Any factor that facilitates or assists us to attain our goal is to be utilized. This part of the process of searching for facilitating forces actually pushes us to look at our positive attributes.

The plan of action is born out of using the facilitating forces to reach the defined goal. The plan needs to be simple and easily understood.

The model expanded

Goal
What is the goal to be achieved?

'I want to do well in my grades' is not a goal; it is a wish. 'I will get my next assignment done by next Tuesday' is a goal – something that can be measured and we will know when we have achieved it.

Everything in FFA should be specific. Imagine you were telling someone how to get from London to Glasgow; you would be as specific as you possibly could be. FFA is a bit like that. You would know you were in Glasgow when you arrived there. FFA helps you to be specific. Work out how to weaken some of the restraining forces or how to strengthen some of the facilitating forces or both.

Use imagery to picture moving toward and achieving the desired goal by using the action plan. You should be stating precisely what you must do in order to reach the goal.

I have run into debt:

- I will ask for an interview with the bank manager
- I will sit down and work out a balance of accounts
- I will discuss with the family how we can...
- I will try to get some overtime
- I will have done all this by ....

Discussion
The discussion should centre on the interplay between the forces and the possible difficulties there might be in achieving the goal.

Example 1. John had lost his job through redundancy. The counsellor to whom John was talking had a hunch that John no longer wanted to remain in the same line of work. Had John been pushed into looking for work he could very well have failed. As it was, he was young enough to undergo retraining in a totally different field. So his restraining force was turned into a facilitating force.

Example 2. John's wife, Lesley, wanted to get a job but had no experience of job-hunting. She had left work 15 years before to bring up the family. She, John and the counsellor had a brainstorming session and came up the following list of possibilities:

- Place an ad. in the local newspaper
- Go the Jobcentre
- Cold-canvass by telephone
- Register with a private work agency
- Look for part-time work
- Start own business as dressmaker
- Get friends and relatives to spread the word
- Undertake a training course.

Force field analysis in action
Marjory's doctor has told her she is about 15 kilos overweight and that her blood pressure is too high. The doctor recommends that Marjory lose some weight.

Goal
To lose 7 kilos within 3 months. This goal is both realistic and specific.

Restraining forces

- Marjory likes cooking
- Marjory's husband, Peter, likes 'three good meals a day and none of this nonsense about dieting for me, thank you'
- Marjory doesn't like doing exercises
- Marjory is not convinced that her blood pressure is related to her weight
- Marjory's grown-up children say, 'We like you as you are, mum'.

Facilitating forces

- Marjory is a very determined lady
- Marjory wants to wear dresses a size smaller
- Marjory has a friend who is enthusiastic that she, too, wants to lose weight
- Marjory wants to look presentable again in a swimsuit.

Action plan

- Get a well-balanced diet plan from the dietitian at the Health Centre
- Buy a new pair of reliable bathroom scales
- Borrow from the library a book on healthy eating
- Buy a dress one size smaller and keep it visible.

Discussion
Marjory's determination was her major strength, plus the thought that, if she didn't lose weight, the doctor would insist on medication for the blood pressure. She spent as much time as possible with her like-minded friend and they drew up diet plans together.

Marjory became very calorie conscious, without becoming phobic about it. She regularly carried out 'dream sessions', as she called them, in which she imagined herself lounging on a sunny beach wearing a fashionable swimsuit. This visualization carried her through some of the grey days when it seemed she wasn't winning the battle.

Peter pooh-poohed the idea at first but, when Marjory showed that he could eat what he wanted and she would still prepare it for him but she would eat what she wanted, he gradually dropped his cynicism and even started munching some of her whole-grain foods. Marjory felt that Peter's opposition was the major restraint. When that force diminished, she felt as if a great weight had been taken from her and it released a great surge of mental energy.

Further reading

Egan, G. (1988) *Change-Agent Skills B : Managing innovation and change*, University Associates, San Diego, CA.

FORGIVENESS (*see also*: Guilt and shame)

In Christian thought, forgiveness is one of the constituent parts of justification. In pardoning sin, God absolves the sinner from the condemnation of holy law because of the work of Christ, i.e. he removes the guilt of sin or the sinner's actual liability to eternal wrath on account of it.

Justification is a legal term opposed to **condemnation**. As regards its nature, it is the legal act of God by which he pardons all the sins of those who believe in Christ and accounts, accepts and treats them as righteous in the eyes of the law, i.e. as conformant with all its demands.

In addition to the pardon of sin, justification declares that all the claims of the law are satisfied in respect of the justified. Justification is the act of a judge and not of a sovereign. The law is not relaxed or set aside but is declared to be fulfilled in the strictest sense; and so the person justified is declared to be entitled to all the advantages and rewards arising from perfect obedience to the law (Rom. 5:1–10).

In counselling, as with atonement, the client may be looking for absolution for some wrongdoing – real or imagined. Part of forgiveness is being able to accept forgiveness from God and from other people. Just as relevant is clients being able to forgive themselves – to act as their own God, to mete out absolution and justification, particularly where the forgiveness is not related to some religious omission or commission.

The desire (and note that this is a conscious act of will) to hold on to bitterness and resentment against someone who has injured us lies deep in the human heart. Unforgiveness, however, has serious spiritual and psychological consequences.

The longer a person holds on to bitterness and resentment, the harder it is for her/him to forgive. Listing the hurts and offences that need to be forgiven is useful and brings things into the open and stops them coming up at another time.

The next step is to get the person to view these hurts and offences from the other person's point of view. A useful technique is to get people to post each point on a board, then to get them to read each one out aloud as if it were a notice, or for the counsellor to read it out. Looking at it dispassionately in this way may bring the degree of objectivity necessary – for the client to stand back from the problem.

When working with self-forgiveness, help the client to find a part of self that can act as a forgiving, all-loving God, who will offer absolution. In the article on psychosynthesis there is a section on subpersonalities; a study of this, and of using imagery, may well show a way in which the client can create a subpersonality who can act as internal priest.

Finally, show the client that forgiveness is an act of the will. If we wait until we feel like forgiving, we may never do it.

FRAMES OF REFERENCE (*see also*: Person-centred counselling)

This is a two-part concept that is emphasized in person-centred counselling.

Internal frame of reference (the inner world of the client)
Examples:

- Behaviours
- Cultural influences
- Experiences
- Feelings
- Meanings
- Memories
- Perceptions
- Sensations
- Thoughts
- Values and beliefs.

External frame of reference (the inner world of the counsellor)
The contents of the counsellor's frame are similar to that of the client's frame and therein lies a danger. When the experiences of one person are similar to those of someone else, it is tempting to 'know' how the other person feels. This knowing cannot come from our experience. It can only resonate within us as we listen to what it means to the other person.

The external frame of reference is when we perceive only from our own subjective frame of reference and when there is no accurate, empathic understanding of the subjective world of the other person.

Evaluating another person through the values of our external frame of reference will ensure lack of understanding.

When we view another person within the internal frame of reference, that person's behaviour makes more sense.

The principal limitation is that we can then deal only with what is within the consciousness of the other person. That which is unconscious lies outside the frame of reference.

For person A to understand the frame of reference of person B, person A needs to:

- Build a bridge of empathy, in order to enter the other person's world
- Help the other person to communicate
- Understand the personal meanings of B
- Communicate that understanding to B.

The bridge of empathy is built upon the foundations of self-awareness. Lack of self-awareness acts as an obstruction to being able to enter someone else's frame of reference. The more we feel able to express ourselves freely to another person, without feeling on trial, the more the contents of our frame of reference will be communicated. Indeed, it is impossible to understand what something means to another person unless you are able to engage that person's frame of reference.

Communicating with another person's frame of reference depends on:

- Careful listening to the other person's total communication – words, nonverbal messages, voice-related cues
- Trying to identify the feelings that are being expressed and the experiences and behaviours that give rise to those feelings
- Trying to communicate an understanding of what the person seems to be feeling and of the sources of those feelings
- Responding by showing understanding, not by evaluating what has been said.

Example of engaging a client's frame of reference
Jane says, 'My mother died and I feel devastated.'
Person A says, 'That sounds really awful.'
Person B says, 'It sounds as if your whole world has collapsed.'

Further reading

Rogers, C. R. (1961) *On Becoming a Person: A therapist's view of psychotherapy*, Constable, London.

FREE ASSOCIATION

Free association is the psychoanalytic technique whereby the patient reports spontaneous thoughts ideas or words. The 'golden rule' in psychoanalysis is that the patient reports everything that comes to mind, without any attempt to control or censor it; the unconscious mind is thus tapped. The analyst refrains from any prompt that might influence the patient's selection of material.

The rationale for free association is that all lines of thought tend to lead to what is significant; that the patient's unconscious will lead the associations towards what is significant; resistance will influence this process but that resistance is minimized by relaxation and concentration.

Free association is similar to Jung's word association test, where the person responds to a stimulus word with the first word that comes to mind. Conclusions are drawn about the associated words. Jung, building upon the work of Bleuler, Galton and Wundt, perfected the technique for tapping the personal complexes.

Where Freud and Jung differed is that Freud continued to use free association, while Jung developed his work with the archetypes to overcome complexes.

Further reading

Samuels, A. (1985) *Jung and the Post-Jungians*, Routledge and Kegan Paul, London.
Stewart, W. (1998) *Self-counselling: How to develop the skills to positively manage your life.* How To Books, Oxford.
Zdenek, M. (1983) *The Right-Brain Experience*, Corgi, London.

G

GENETIC COUNSELLING

Genetics is the scientific study of how physical, biochemical and behavioural traits are transmitted from parents to their offspring. The word itself was coined in 1906 by the British biologist William Bateson. Geneticists are able to determine the mechanisms of inheritance because the offspring of sexually reproducing organisms do not exactly resemble their parents and because some of the differences and similarities between parents and offspring recur from generation to generation in repeated patterns. The investigation of these patterns has led to some of the most exciting discoveries in modern biology.

Genetic counselling advises and counsels prospective parents on any genetic disorder that they may pass to their offspring. This is a highly specialized field of counselling in which the counsellor needs a high level of knowledge of various conditions that could have a genetic base, such as Down's syndrome (mongolism) and muscular dystrophy.

Counsellors not in the field of genetics may well become involved when a person, a couple or a family, long after the more specific aspects of counselling on the genetic difficulties have been dealt with, find that they are left with a legacy of bitterness, confusion and despair, which only time has brought to the surface.

Further reading

Berg, K. and Kirch, D.G. (1995) Genetic counselling. In: *Comprehensive Textbook of Psychiatry*, 6th edn, (eds H. J. Kaplan and B. J. Sadock), Williams & Wilkins, Baltimore, MD.

Clarke, A. (ed.) (1994) *Genetic Counselling: Practice and Principles*, Routledge, London.

GESTALT COUNSELLING

Gestalt is a German word that, when translated loosely, means 'pattern' or 'form'. When the pattern or *Gestalten*, is incomplete, we talk of 'unfinished business'.

The chief tenet of Gestalt psychology is that analysis of parts, however thorough, cannot provide an understanding of the whole. An analogy is the human body, each part of which has its distinct function yet all are integrated to make up the body. Parts are not understood when analysed in isolation. Mental processes and behaviours come complete. An example is that we hear a melody as a whole and not merely as a collection of individual notes.

Gestalt psychology sprang out of dissatisfaction over the inability of both psychoanalysis and behaviourism to deal with the whole person. Gestalt therapy, developed by Fritz Perls (1893–1970) aims to help the person to be self-supportive and self-responsible, through awareness of what is going on within the self at any given moment, the 'here-and-now'. Gestalt therapy is heavily influenced by existentialism, psychodrama and body therapies.

The emphasis of Gestalt counselling is on:

- Change through activity
- The central meaning of present experience
- The importance of fantasy and creative experimentation, particularly using the right, creative hemisphere, though not ignoring the contribution of the left, structured hemisphere
- The significance of language.

The counsellor draws attention to:

- What the client says
- How it is said
- The client's behaviour
- Nonverbal communication
- Breathing pattern
- Tensions within the session.

Clients are encouraged to act out various roles in life that they and others, have played or are currently playing and to take responsibility for their own conflicts.

Gestalt counsellors believe:

- That human beings are responsible for themselves, for their lives and for living; therefore counsellors do not foster dependency
- That the important question about human experience and behaviour is not 'why' but 'how'
- That each person functions as a whole, not as separate parts
- In the philosophy of holism
- In the principles of homeostasis – a state of equilibrium produced by a balance of functions within an organism
- That the past exists only within a faulty memory. The future exists only in present expectations and anticipations. The past affects the individual and persists as unfinished business.

Counselling goals

- To re-establish contact and normal interaction; restore ego function and restore the whole
- To foster:
  - Maturation and growth
  - Independence
  - Self-support
  - Awareness

- To help the client:
  - Deal with unfinished business
  - Learn to live in the 'here and now'.

The counselling process

Clients are asked, and sometimes actively encouraged, to experience as much of themselves as possible – gestures, breathing, voice, and so on. In so doing they become aware of the relationship between feelings and behaviours and are thus able to:

- Integrate their dissociated parts
- Establish an adequate balance and appropriate boundaries between self and the environment.

Unfinished business must be concentrated on and re-experienced, not just talked about, in order to be resolved in the here and now. Unfinished business is something that acts as a block or interruption to the flow of energy, the task of which is to form a Gestalten. When there is completion we can move on because we are able to build only on what is completed. As each piece of unfinished business is resolved, a Gestalten is completed and the way is thus prepared for the client to move on to the next unfinished business. When a prior need was left unsatisfied, that particular Gestalten could not be completed. Part of the counselling task is to help the client to close off and complete what was previously unfinished – similar to closing the chapter of a book.

Clients are constantly required to repeat and complete the basic sentence, 'Now I am aware...' and its variations:

- 'What are you aware of now?'
- 'Where are you now?'
- 'What are you seeing? ... Feeling?'
- 'What is your hand, foot doing?'
- 'What do you want?'
- 'What do you expect?

Therapists make clients take responsibility by getting them to use 'I' not 'it' when referring to their body. Any statement or behaviour that does not represent self is challenged.

Integration means:

- Owning disowned parts of oneself
- Being responsible for one's own life goals
- Expressing everything that is felt in the body
- Expressing the vague feelings associated with shame and embarrassment at expressing certain thoughts and feelings. Shame and embarrassment are the prime tools of the defence mechanism of repression. Endurance of embarrassment brings repressed material to the surface.

Techniques

- **The 'chair'**: Clients move forward and backward from one chair to another and engage in dialogue between parts of themselves, between other people or between dream objects
- **Skilful frustration**: In this the therapist:
  - Repeatedly frustrates clients' avoidance of uncomfortable situations, until they show willingness to try and cope
  - Helps clients to identify the characteristics they project on to others that are most missing in themselves
  - Helps clients express and understand resentment, in the belief that the expression of resentment is one of the most important ways of helping people make life a little easier; Gestalt theory proposes that behind every resentment there is a demand and that expressing the demand is essential for real change
- **Monotherapy**, where the client creates and acts every part of the production
- **Fantasy**: through the use of symbols – fantasy can be verbalized, written or acted
- **Shuttle**: Directing the client's attention back and forth from one activity or experience to another
- **Topdog–underdog**
  - **Topdog** represents the 'shoulds' that the person has introjected; Topdog is righteous, perfectionist, authoritarian, bullying and punishing
  - **Underdog** is primitive, evasive, 'yes, but', excusing, passively sabotaging the demands of Topdog
    The client enters into a dialogue and alternately takes the part of Topdog and Underdog.

Disowned parts of the personality are integrated into the whole to complete that person's Gestalten. When a need is satisfied, the situation is changed and the need fades into the background. If a need is not fulfilled – if a Gestalten is not completed – it may produce a conflict that is distracting and draining of psychic energy.

The awareness of, and the ability to endure, unwanted emotions is the precondition of a successful outcome. It is this process and not the process of remembering that is the royal road to health.

Critics of Gestalt therapy say that it may help clients get in touch with their needs but does not necessarily teach them the skills or wisdom to deal with those needs.

Further reading

Clarkson, P. (1989) *Gestalt Counselling in Action*, Sage Publications, London.
Van de Riet, V., Korb, K. and Gorrell. J. J. (1980) *Gestalt Therapy*, Pergamon, Oxford.

GOALS AND GOAL-SETTING (*see also*: Action plans)

Many people become counselling clients because they feel stuck in situations from which they can see no way out. Counselling can help them to develop a sense of direction, which often accompanies hope.

Direction
In order to move from Point A (the now) to Point B (the desired outcome), counsellor and client need to explore:

- Feelings
- Thoughts
- Behaviours

in order to develop a new perspective and work through hindrances.

Example
Point A: Tom is dissatisfied with work.
Point B: Tom to look for satisfying job.

Perspective
There is no reason why Tom should stay in an unsatisfying job.

Hindrances

- Tom's self-defeating beliefs and attitudes
- Tom's misplaced loyalty
- Tom prefers the comfort zone.

Problem-solving counselling is successful only if it results in problem-handling action. Listening, as part of problem-solving, is effective only if it helps clients to become more intentional and leads to realistic goal-setting.

Intentional people:

- Are in charge of their own lives
- Do not waste time and energy blaming other people or circumstances for their problems
- Refuse to capitulate to unfavourable odds
- Have a sense of direction in their lives, characterized by:
  - Having a purpose
  - Feeling they are going somewhere
  - Engaging in self-enhancing activities
  - Focusing on outcomes and accomplishments
  - Not mistaking aimless actions for accomplishments
  - Setting goals and objectives
  - Having a defined lifestyle
  - Not indulging in wishful thinking

- Are versatile – thinking about and creating options
- Become involved in:
  - The world of other people
  - Social settings
- Evaluate their goals against the needs and wants of others
- Are ready to work for win–win rather than win–lose situations.

Advantages of goal-setting

- Focuses attention and action
- Mobilizes energy and effort
- Increases persistence
- Is strategy oriented.

The goal-setting model of Gerard Egan

Dr Gerard Egan is professor of psychology and organizational studies at Loyola University in Chicago. He has written many books, including *The Skilled Helper*. He currently writes and teaches in the area of counselling, counsellor education and management and organization development.

Stage 1 – The present scenario

The aim of stage one is to help clients:

- Understand themselves
- Understand the problem
- Set goals
- Take action.

The client's goal is self-exploration: The counsellor's goal is responding.
  The counsellor helps clients to:

- Tell their story
- Focus
- Develop insight and new perspectives.

Stage 2 – Creating new scenarios and setting goals

The aim of stage two is to help clients:

- Examine their problem
- Think how it could be handled differently
- Develop their powers of imagination.

The client's goal is self-understanding: The counsellor's goal is to integrate understanding.
  The counsellor helps clients to:

- Create new scenarios
- Evaluate possible scenarios
- Develop choice and commitment to change.

Stage 3 – Helping clients act

The client's goal is action: The counsellor's goal is to facilitate action.
  The counsellor helps clients to:

- Identify and assess action strategies
- Formulate plans
- Implement plans.

Some useful questions for clients to ask:

- What would this situation look like if I managed it better?
- What changes would there be in my life style?
- What would I do differently with the people in my life?
- What behaviours would I get rid of?
- What new behaviours would there be?
- What would exist that doesn't exist now?
- What would be happening that isn't happening now?
- What would I have that I don't have now?
- What decisions would I have made?
- What would I have accomplished?

GRIEF AND BEREAVEMENT COUNSELLING (*see also*: Dying – stages of)

Grief is a normal reaction of intense sorrow, following:

- The loss of an emotionally significant person
- The loss of a material object or objects
- The loss of a part of the self
- The end of a stage of the life cycle
- An event such as divorce or separation
- The loss of a limb or a faculty, e.g. blindness or deafness
- The scarring of one's body, possibly through drastic surgery such as mastectomy.

The psychoanalytic view is that grief allows ties with the lost object to be broken through the withdrawal of libido. Freud identified a period of between 1 and 2 years as the normal period for accomplishing 'grief work', with improvement after about 6 months.

  Bowlby's view is that grief is an attempt to re-establish ties rather than withdrawing them. Grief can also be viewed as the working out of conflicting impulses. Grief is the price we pay for loving; we would not know grief if there were no attachment to what we have lost.

Some definitions

- **Bereavement**: loss through death
- **Bereavement reactions**: Psychological, physiological or behavioural responses to bereavement

- **Bereavement process:** The term that covers bereavement reactions over time
- **Grief:** The feelings and associated behaviours, such as crying, that accompany bereavement
- **Mourning:** The social expressions of grief – funerals and rituals.

Types of grief

Anticipatory grief
Anticipatory grief ends when the actual loss takes place. A variation of this is where there is slow dying of a loved one. Anticipatory grief may help to soften the blow of the eventual death. On the other hand, if separation occurs too long before the death, there may be a secondary reaction when death does occur and the feelings of loss may be intensified.

Acute grief
Acute grief has several sub-stages:

- **Shock,** where the focus is on the past, is characterized by alarm and denial
- **Realization,** where the focus is on the present, is characterized by:
  - Intermittent denial
  - Searching behaviour
  - Preoccupation and identification with the lost object
  - Idealization
  - Regression
  - Crying
  - Bodily symptoms
  - Depression/helplessness
  - Guilt, anger, shame
- **Integration,** where the focus is on the future, is characterized by acceptance and a return to physical, social and psychological wellbeing.

Morbid or pathological grief
This may be:

- **Inhibited,** where reactions are absent or distorted
- **Chronic,** where severe reactions are prolonged
- **Delayed,** where severe reactions occur later.

Pathological grief is more likely to occur following:

- Experience of loss or separation in childhood
- Lack of effective support
- Sudden or violent death
- The loss of a child.

Normal grief reactions
Grief is considered normal following any bereavement. Indeed, not to experience

grief could be considered inappropriate and even pathological. However, it has to be pointed out that feeling grief and showing it openly are two different things. Freud considered that grief work was complete when the person was able to invest energy elsewhere other than in what had caused the grief reaction.

John Bowlby's work on attachment and loss draws attention to grief as an expression of separation anxiety and the intense desire to recapture the lost relationship (*see* separation anxiety, in Attachment). The following stages of separation from an attached object (not necessarily a person) related to bereavement can be identified:

- Protest, a great deal of crying
- Searching behaviour, characterized by restlessness and inability to tolerate any attempt to hinder the search – anything, everything must be done to keep the memory of the person alive
- Despair and detachment: As the searching and hope of re-establishing the relationship diminishes, despair sets in
- Reorganization and acceptance that the 'lost' person is not going to return. Now the person has an opportunity to redefine the relationship with the deceased and move forward alone. At the same time, it is important to forge realistic ties to the deceased. Accepting the loss is likely to generate anguish; establishing realistic ties is likely to bring comfort.

Influences on grief reactions

Grief reaction is influenced by:

- Coping strategies
- Relationship support
- How a person normally functions
- Psychological strength
- Self-esteem
- Previous life experiences
- The significance of the loss
- State of health.

Phases of grief

The work of Kubler-Ross on death and dying gives insights into similar phases of grieving, principally:

1. Initial shock, disbelief and denial, where numbness prevails. The period of mourning, with the meeting of friends at the funeral, is often accompanied by severe separation pangs and searching behaviour.
2. Immediate period of acute discomfort and social withdrawal, where acute anguish prevails. Acute anguish may last weeks or months, gradually moving into wellbeing and the ability to get on with life.
3. Resolution and reorganization. Grieving has been accomplished, although the person may be surprised by how small things can again trigger tears.

As with the Kubler-Ross model, these are not discrete phases but overlapping and fluid.

Bereavement

Bereavement is the process that includes grief and mourning, over the loss of a significant person or object. Ideally, counselling is commenced before the loss.

Mourning

Mourning is the period of time that follows a bereavement, which allows the expression of grief through accepted rituals. Mourning follows bereavement, is accompanied by grief and may or may not be followed by attachment to a new object.

Mourning is distinguished from grief in that it involves physiological and psychological processes. Mourning is more to do with the customs and traditions of a particular culture or society.

Grief and mourning do not necessarily occur at the same time but, for some, a period of ritualized mourning aids the grieving process. The mourning for a spouse is the loss most frequently ritualized in most societies. Mourning rituals are frequently linked with religious observance and practice.

Mourning and burial customs

Mourning customs are influenced by beliefs about life and death that are passed down through the generations. Religion is concerned with questions of mortality and immortality. All the major religions have a belief system that influences the way the rituals of burial and subsequent mourning is carried out.

Central to the Christian belief is the hope of resurrection. At the same time, there must be an acknowledgement of the reality of the grief of parting. The funeral will usually take place at a church or chapel, followed by a short committal at the graveside or the crematorium. The choice of flowers, procession and headstone is a matter of family choice, in contrast with several generations ago when the ritual was more predictable. Mourning clothes are also a matter of choice. Normally there is some sort of social gathering as farewell. The role of the funeral director has become more prominent in recent years.

The basic belief of the Hindu religion is that the cremated body returns to its elements of fire, water, air and earth and is thus reunited with God. The eldest son lights the funeral pyre, while mantras and sacred texts are recited by the priest. Then follows a period of ritual where gifts of food are left for the soul of the departed. When this period is over, the bones of the deceased may be buried. Hindus believe in reincarnation (transmigration), which is the rebirth of the soul in one or more successive existences, which may be human, animal or, in some instances, vegetable.

The basis of Judaism is the first five books of the Old Testament (the Torah). Death and mourning are highly ritualized. The funeral must take place within 3 days of death, but not on the Sabbath or on a festival day. The body is dressed in a simple white garment and is never left unattended. Burial is the norm but some non-orthodox Jews living in other countries than Israel will permit cremation. A 7-day period of formal mourning (Shivah) is observed after the death of a close relative. Prayers are said, candles are lit, family and friends will visit and bring gifts of food. Though normal life will be resumed after Shivah, certain social activities are not resumed until 30 days have passed.

The followers of Islam believe that the one God was revealed through the prophet Muhammad. When a Muslim dies, the body is turned to face Mecca. Death for the Muslim is but a parting for a short space of time, so prolonged grief is not encouraged. The body is washed, wrapped in clean white sheets and buried shortly after death. Prayers are said before the burial.

Sikhs believe in one God and the equality of humankind. They also believe in reincarnation. The body is dressed in white by the family, prayers are said, then cremation takes place. Prayers and the reading of sacred scriptures continue for a further 10 days. The death of an elderly person is not a time of sadness and is usually followed by feasting and rejoicing.

Buddha is seen not so much as a god, rather as a model for life. For the Buddhist, belief is demonstrated by good behaviour. Buddhists believe that the qualities of the deceased are reincarnated to become the 'germ of consciousness' in the womb of a mother. A monk leads the cremation service.

People of other world religions, living in an alien society, may observe compromised rituals instead of orthodox observances.

Rituals help the grieving person to make some sense of the experience; within a socially accepted framework, they allow for a sharing of the experience and for eventual reintegration. All of this may not be so easily achieved where traditions have been eroded, as in many Western societies.

Mourning is an essential part of grief and whatever the religious belief (or none at all) understanding what mourning means to that person is of utmost importance in grief counselling. Of equal importance is the fact that, for some people, where the ritual has been interrupted or has not been observed, it may not be emotionally possible to close the grief chapter, e.g. where the eldest son of a Hindu has not been able to light the funeral pyre or where the body has never been found, as in loss at sea or some other tragedy.

Counselling guidelines following a death

- Support is necessary to help deal with the many practical issues surrounding the death
- Work with feelings and encourage catharsis, but do not push the person too far, too fast, too soon
- Helpers need to be able to accept the bereaved person's feelings, whatever they are
- Feelings, however negative, are valid
- Support by repeated telling of the story, with the associated feelings
- Encourage the acceptance of the finality of the loss
- Facilitate disengagement and establish separateness from the deceased

- Help the bereaved person to gain a positive but realistic memory of the deceased through repeated discussion
- Help the deceased to accept the changes in role, social situation and self-image in becoming a widow/widower, fatherless, childless, no longer pregnant, disabled
- Encourage the bereaved person to think about new relationships, activities, self-help groups.

Depression is a common feature of many bereaved people, particularly after the death of the lifetime partner, often occurring after about a month. In severe cases, psychiatric illness may be precipitated by bereavement.

Some helpful counselling aids

- **Journals and diaries**: Writing down what is happening, including feelings and thoughts, can be very therapeutic. Some people feel able to burn the writings at some stage, thus signifying a letting go.
- **Pictures**: These need not be 'artistic'. What is important is what the person includes, as well as what is left out. The picture can then be used as a talking point, not as something to be 'interpreted'. This method is superb when dealing with children. Children's drawings may take the form of fantasy, with monsters and other frightening figures.
- **Photographs**: Family 'snaps' provide a focus for communication. The person in a photograph always has a certain substance. The viewer often has to contain the 'then' within the reality and pain of the 'now'.
- **Scrapbooks**: As with photographs, collecting material to paste into a scrapbook may be painful. The therapeutic benefit of having put together a memorial in this way, as something to look back on, is of inestimable value.
- **A family tree**: A family tree is a visual record of one's heritage and should include those dead as well as those still alive. It is an ideal medium for the grieving person to talk about the interaction between various people on the tree. A related techniques is **family sculpting**, where shapes can be used to represent members of the family.
- **Bibliotherapy** (*see* main entry, above)
- **Relaxation therapy**.

Some things to avoid

Being afraid to confront the client's pain often makes people resort to euphemisms, like, 'I'm sorry you have lost your husband', or 'I hear he has passed over/gone to his great sleep/passed away/departed this life', or simply 'I hear he has gone'. We use euphemisms to protect the other person and ourselves from reality. Using 'death' or 'has died' helps the client to face reality.

There is a difference between 'You have lost your wife' and 'You are suffering the feelings of loss'. The one is an avoidance; the other highlights the feelings of loss.

Part of the process of healing is accepting that the loved one is dead, not lost.

Certainly the person feels great loss, but that is a different meaning. When we speak of 'the loss of a person' we confuse the issue, particularly when we then try to help the person explore feelings of loss. It is true that many people who are bereaved seek for their loved one as if s/he was lost. We can add to that confusion by not helping them acknowledge the finality of death. No one can come out of the experience of loss and be the same as before.

Another pointer is the difference between 'You are grieving' and 'You are going through the grieving process'. The first phrase is more immediate and accepts the uniqueness of the client. Drawing attention to a 'process' makes it sound detached and predictable. And, as we know from all the literature, while models are useful, they are only guidelines and bereaved people dip in and out of the various stages or phases rather than progress neatly from one to the other.

Helping adults to confront the reality of death is often a difficult enough task; helping children may be doubly difficult, yet surprisingly simple. Children often have a clearer grasp of reality than adults give them credit for. We all hate being told untruths and children are very quick to detect what is not true. 'Dad's gone away and he won't be coming back' is cruel and deceptive. Adults often say they only said what they did to protect the child. While this might be true, the whole truth is that they needed to protect themselves.

One of the counselling tasks in bereavement, where children are involved, is to help the survivor to realize that any disturbance within the child is likely to be an expression of the survivor's inability to accept the loss and know how to deal with it.

Nothing can protect the child from the fact and it is proved to be healthier that the child knows the truth, although not every detail, rather than fobbing the child off with lies or evasions. For example, I grew up with the clear knowledge that at the age of 10 months a brother of mine had died in a fire in Australia before I was born. This was no secret to be hidden away but neither did my parents dwell on the horrors of the event. It was enough that I knew that John was a part of my family tree, even though his life had been cut off.

Further reading (see also references under Dying – stages of)

Ainsworth-Smith, I. and Speck, P. (1982) Letting Go: Caring for the dying and bereaved, SPCK, London.

Backer, B. et al. (1982) Death and Dying, John Wiley, New York.

Cook, B. and Phillips, S. G. (1988) Loss and Bereavement, Lisa Sainsbury Foundation, London.

Cruse – Bereavement Care (Spring 1993) Supporting Bereaved Children and their Families: A Training Manual. Cruse, Richmond, Surrey.

Glick, I. et al. (1974) The First Year of Bereavement, John Wiley, New York.

Lewis, C. S. (1961) A Grief Observed. Faber & Faber, London.

Machin, L. (1990) Looking at Loss: bereavement counselling pack, Longman, Harlow.

Parkes, C. M. (1972) Bereavement: Studies of grief in adult life, Tavistock, London.

Poss, S. (1981) Towards Death with Dignity, National Institute Social Services Library No. 41, Allen & Unwin, London.

Schoenberg, B. (ed.) (1980) Bereavement Counselling, Greenwood Press, London.

Zisook, S. (1995) Death, dying and bereavement. In: *Comprehensive Textbook of Psychiatry*, 6th edn, (eds H. J. Kaplan and B. J. Sadock), Williams & Wilkins, Baltimore, MD.

GROUPS (*see also*: Tavistock method)

A group is a social system involving regular interaction among members and a common group identity. This means that groups have a sense of togetherness that enables members to identify themselves as belonging to a distinct entity and usually distinguished from other groups.

Some social systems have intense involvement and strong group identity, such as families, a neighbourhood association or a close-knit 'circle' of friends (all of which can be thought of as a group). Groups also vary in how often and how extensively members interact, how long the group survives and the reasons that people join and participate.

The group is an important sociological concept because groups play such a complex and important part in social life. Group membership, for example, is an important part of an individual's social identity. The group is a key agent of social control over individuals, for it is in groups that social pressures toward conformity can be most directly applied, especially when those who deviate risk being alienated from other members.

Groups are also important because it is in groups that many of the most important social activities take place, e.g. the socialization and care of children in families, the production of goods, religious worship, formal education, social movements, scientific research, politics and the making of war. Attention to how groups work is thus essential for a full understanding of social life.

The study of groups is an important topic, because most of us work in groups of one kind or another. Some groups we choose to be in, although there are some, such as work groups, in which we have little choice. The very nature of being present with a number of people has the potential for producing stress. Therefore, learning what makes groups tick is an important factor in reducing stress levels.

Kinds of group

- **Simple groups**: The dyad, or two-person group, and the triad
- **Formal groups**, where each person has a specific role allocated.
- **Informal groups**: A group of people who join together
- **Primary groups** (also called small groups): Usually bound by ties of affection and personal loyalty; involve many different aspects of people's lives and endure over long periods of time; involve a great deal of face-to-face interaction where the focus is on people's feelings and welfare more than accomplishing specific tasks or goals. The family is an example of a primary group.
- **Secondary groups**: Organized around secondary relationships and are usually

task-oriented. The services one receives from the bank is an example of a secondary relationship.

Group dynamics

Group dynamics refer to the psychological and social forces arising from the interaction of people in such groups as families, committees and athletic teams and in work, educational, therapeutic, religious, racial and ethnic groups. The study of group dynamics is concerned with such processes as power and shifts of power, leadership, how the group is formed and how the group interacts with other groups, how cohesive the group is and how decisions are made within it.

As group size increases, a smaller proportion of the group's members take part in group discussion and decision making, interaction becomes more impersonal, satisfaction declines, group cohesiveness is reduced and the group tends to become divided into factions. Most groups, especially those that include seven or more people, begin to develop role specialists, such as task leaders, who try to get people to do the work of the group, and the best-liked group members, who generally are not the task leaders.

Group-think

Group-think, a concept developed by Irving Janis, is a process through which the desire for consensus in groups can lead to poor decisions. Rather than object to poor decisions and risk losing a sense of group solidarity, members may remain silent and thereby lend their support. The presence of a directive leader strengthens the desire to be with everyone else. Defective decision-making is characterized by:

- Limited discussion on only a few alternatives
- Failure to re-evaluate previous solutions
- Failure to seek the advice of experts
- Options presented are strongly biased
- Objectives are not scrupulously examined
- Little or no account taken of the views of other groups
- No contingency plans developed.

Group-think can be minimized by every person:

- Identifying the problem
- Writing down the solutions
- Privately ranking each solution.

The group then selects the highest ranking solution as the group decision.

Group psychotherapy

Group psychotherapy or group therapy is a form of psychotherapy carried out with groups of patients, of both sexes, who come together regularly with the therapist as group leader. They are encouraged to talk freely about themselves, their problems and their feelings towards each other and the therapist.

There are many kinds of group psychotherapy; some are based on psychoanalysis, others involve or are derived from psychodrama. A group usually consists of six to eight patients who meet for treatment once or twice a week. A closed group keeps its membership for the duration of the treatment, about 2 years, whereas membership of an open group changes when patients leave or are discharged and new patients join the group.

While the majority of counselling is carried out on a one to one basis, counsellors may become involved in group counselling. They may also be involved in teaching. In both situations, a knowledge of how groups work is an advantage. It must not be assumed that knowledge of groups applies only to groups that we join willingly; knowledge of group interaction can be of enormous benefit wherever people gather. Being aware of what is happening is one sure way of relieving stress. The more intimate the group, the more possible it is for stress to develop.

Among the strategies for survival are **fight or flight responses**. We can observe both of these reactions to situations that are perceived as threats. Part of the skill of handling groups is to intervene in such a way that people don't feel put down. The aim is for the interaction to help people feel OK.

We all may experience stress when we meet in a new group or when a new leader takes over, as in a work group. A knowledge of group dynamics would help us realize that even though 'The king is dead, long live the king', the old leader still has to be mourned and we may demonstrate our suspicion of the new leader, even though we are too polite to say it verbally.

The role of the group facilitator is important – not that the facilitator is infallible but the role carries with it certain responsibilities and duties that reflect the facilitator's training, competence and experience. Of equal importance are the personal qualities of the facilitator; one may have a great deal of experience yet, if there is no integrity, the group will flounder and be unproductive.

It is important to identify the different roles we adopt within groups: roles that focus on the task, that build the group or that work against the group. How these roles are played and held in balance determines how productive the group is.

Groups are born, live, work and then die. The death of a group has echoes of all death; something that is not easy to come to terms with or accept.

Further reading

Brown, R. (1988) *Group Processes: Dynamics within and between groups*, Blackwell, Oxford.

Janis, I. L. (1982) *Victims of Group-think*. Houghton-Mifflin, Boston.

GUILT AND SHAME (*see also:* Blame)

Guilt

Objectively, guilt is a fact or state attributed to a person who violates the will of God and/or some moral or penal code. Subjectively, guilt is awareness of having violated personal norms or the norms of family, religion or society. The offence may be real or imaginary. Normally the reason for the guilt is known only to the person concerned.

The feeling of guilt may nor may not be proportionate to the nature of the offence. Guilt is often experienced as an alienation from relationship with God, others or self. The act that causes shame is often inconsequential, but the self feels attacked.

'False guilt' is usually associated with sexuality, self-assertion, self-love and putting oneself first, sometimes. A distinction needs to be made about having desires to do 'wrong' and acting upon such desires.

Pathological guilt is present when a person not only feels the guilt but also considers her/himself to be a bad person deserving of punishment. This is linked with self-blame and might, in the case of a person suffering from depression, lead to self-harm.

Guilt about having wrong desires often wreaks havoc with the psyche, producing severe neuroses and sometimes psychoses. Guilt and shame are both concerned with internalized standards of conduct. Guilt is more abstract and judgemental than shame.

It is possible to say one feels guilty without experiencing it; one cannot be ashamed without feeling it. Shame is more tied to threat of exposure than is guilt. Shame is the more fundamental of the two feelings.

Psychoanalytic theory regards guilt as internalization of prohibitions and is not so concerned with the fact of guilt as with the sense of guilt. Psychoanalysis distinguishes 'normal' guilt (remorse), which would respond to 'confession', from 'pathological' guilt for which therapy would be more appropriate. Behaviourists regard guilt as a conditioned response to past actions that have involved punishment.

One view of guilt is that it is anger turned inward. A total absence of guilt is one of the features of 'character disorder'. Dealing with guilt is difficult. Working at it indirectly by tackling the underlying feelings that support the guilt may be more productive.

Jung makes a distinction between 'collective guilt' and 'personal guilt'; a sense of guilt may arise from either. Collective guilt may be compared to fate or to a curse or to a form of pollution. An example of collective guilt would be where a nation feels guilty about the crimes of a previous generation, such as the Holocaust.

A sense of guilt may be necessary to avoid the projection on to other people of those parts of the personality called the Shadow, the dark side of us which, was it known, would invoke moral condemnation. The sense of guilt inspires reflection on what is evil – which is as important as reflection on what is good.

Guilt differs from **anxiety** in the following ways:

- Anxiety is experienced in relation to a feared future occurrence, while guilt is experienced in relation to an act already committed

- The capacity to experience guilt is related to the capacity to internalize objects whereas the capacity to experience anxiety is not.

While animals and infants seem to feel anxious, so far as we know only human beings with some awareness of time and of others feel guilt. Neurotic guilt and anxiety may, however, be indistinguishable owing to the fact that the neurotic sense of guilt is associated with dread of punishment and retribution.

All defences used to reduce anxiety can also be used to reduce the sense of guilt but one defence – reparation, the making good of damage imagined to have already been done – is used specifically to reduce the sense of guilt.

Some expressions of guilt

'I feel I've let someone down so badly, I deserve to be punished'
'I've done something wrong against someone'
'I've not done anything wrong, but I feel I've left something undone I should have done'
'I feel caught between what's realistic and the selfish desires of other people'
'I've made a mistake and can't live with it'
'I can't forgive myself and I'm being punished'
'I can't help people making me feel guilty'
'I need to get a balance between guilt and what I've done or feel I've done'
'I feel guilty because other people make demands on me that can't meet and I feel I should'
'My burden of guilt robs me of any self-esteem and makes me feel so unworthy'.

Points to remember about guilt:

- Guilt may be anger turned inward. Work, therefore, with the anger.
- Guilt often has delusional qualities, in that it cannot be shaken by reason or logic. Sometimes there is the feeling of being excommunicated, even though the person may not be 'religious'.
- Guilt is a common symptom of depression.
- No one can make us feel guilty (or feel anything else) if we do not want to. When we say 'That person makes me feel...', we pass on to that person the responsibility for how we feel. We have chosen to take on board something someone else wants to off-load on to us.
- In all work with guilt, there is an urgent need to help the person balance conscience with responsibility.

Authentic awareness of guilt seems to be a necessary aspect of healthy human beings. Religious guilt is a warning system that we are at odds with God or with the structures, values and truths to which we subscribe, although this would depend on whether the person had a religious belief.

Shame

Shame is a complex, painful feeling resulting from a strong sense of guilt, unworthiness or disgrace. We feel shame when we are faced with something that draws attention to a discrepancy between what we are and what, ideally, we would like to be. The act that causes shame is often inconsequential, but the self feels attacked.

Shame is an emotion of self-abasement experienced when we are conscious of acting contrary to, or below, the standards of which we approve and by which we know (or feel) others judge us. This sense of self-abasement is stronger than in the related states with which it is often confused – modesty, bashfulness, shyness and coyness, which are marked rather by hesitation, caution and inhibition. They arise through consciousness of being under the gaze of others whose attitude is that of curiosity or superiority or searching criticism. But shame involves a sense of unworthiness and demerit. Like its kindred states, it may arise in connection with matters of sex, but it is also found in a great variety of situations not concerned with sex. The sense of shame consists in the consciousness of failure and exposure before other persons in connection with a point of honour or of strong self-esteem.

Blushing is often an expression of shame and is frequently accompanied by other signs, such as drooping of the body, lowering of the head and averted gaze. We tend to hide or want to hide, to escape notice and, in extreme cases, to inflict injury upon ourselves as a kind of self-imposed punishment for some imagined wrong committed. Shame may also arise from a conflict between impulses or resulting from comparison with someone with whom we consider ourselves to be inferior in some way. We then act in a way that draws attention to the powers and attributes in which we consider ourselves deficient. So the self-fulfilling prophecy is completed.

We are more likely to feel shame when we feel in competition with someone, e.g. when there is one rival who can excel us, as in athletics. On the other hand, if we have no athletic prowess or ambition we will not be depressed by the fact that every one can surpass us. When we have great expectations of success, our self-esteem might result in shame when lack of success reinforces our inadequacies, particularly if those expectations were unrealistic and boosted by unrealistic claims.

Social psychology emphasizes the fact that one's social group furnishes the determining influences in forming one's standards of taste and conduct. Infringement of social conventions, or *mores*, is likely to be accompanied by shame. Some sociologists speak of 'shame cultures', e.g. the traditional Japanese culture, and 'guilt cultures', e.g. Judaeo-Christian cultures.

In psychology shame has received less attention than guilt, anxiety and depression. Freud interpreted shame as fear of ridicule. Guilt occurs when we fail to meet a standard imposed from outside; shame, when we fail to meet self-imposed standards or when we are aware of being tactless or of behaving in bad taste.

We feel shame when we are faced with something that draws attention to a discrepancy between what we are and what, ideally, we would like to be. The act that causes shame is often inconsequential, but the self feels attacked. This extract from the above text highlights what could be a difficult area for the client; for if the client is to be true to her/himself, then certain things need to be explored, yet it is possible that it is these very things that bring a sense of shame. The fact that I feel I should be generous and forgiving expresses what I would like to be, what I feel I 'should' be, yet the reality is that I am vindictive and unforgiving; hence there is a discrepancy between the two parts of self.

As a client I might find it relatively easy to disclose that I am not always kind, and not feel ashamed, yet the knowledge that I secretly harbour murderous thoughts and feelings towards someone might create so much shame in me that I cannot disclose that. The deeper the feelings of shame, the more the client will feel resistant to disclose them; yet the more trust the client has in the counsellor, the more able the client will feel able to disclose and then explore. Movement and growth depend so much on the strength of the counselling relationship but also on the client's willingness to move towards healing.

Challenging the feelings of guilt or shame is one way of working with these feelings; on the other hand, working with the underlying anger, in the case of guilt, or the feelings of self-devaluation, in the case of shame, could be productive. A second approach, with guilt, is to help the client clarify whether it is justified or false. But in either case, the feelings are just as real and not easily dealt with.

Further reading

Coleman, V. (1982) *Guilt: Why It Happens and How to Overcome It*, Sheldon Press, London.

Lewis, H. (1971) *Shame and Guilt in Neurosis*, International Universities Press, New York.

H

HATRED

Hatred is a deep, enduring, intense-emotion-expressing animosity, anger and hostility toward a person, group or object. Hatred is usually assumed to be characterized by the desire to harm, destroy or cause pain to the object of the emotion and the deriving of pleasure from the object's misfortunes.

Hate is often confused with anger, despite the fact that the latter is a passing not an enduring emotion, which can be felt in relation to someone one loves. According to McDougall (the early 20th-century psychologist) hate is a sentiment and anger a simple, primary emotion.

According to Freud's earlier writings, hate is the response to threats to the Ego, but later he viewed it as a manifestation of the death instinct.

Analysts, influenced by these later ideas, tend to regard love and hate as opposites and to see the psyche as a battleground between these two opposing principles. Love is the great antithesis of hatred, for love conserves while hatred destroys; love engenders feelings of pleasure or satisfaction with the person loved and the desire to do her/him good, while hatred engenders dissatisfaction with the object, mixed with pain and a desire to inflect harm. Love sees no fault; hatred only sees detestable qualities. Love extends outwards towards other people with feelings of generosity and well-being, while hatred produces the opposite effects. Love is one means of turning an enemy into a friend; hatred invariably makes enemies. Love begets love; hatred begets hate. There is no hatred so strong as that which was once love, a state brought about by love that has been spurned. Conversely, previously hated objects now loved will be loved with stronger passion.

Alfred Adler (*see* Individual psychology) says some interesting things about hate. Hate is often a characteristic found in belligerent people. He says that a tendency to hate frequently appears early in childhood as in temper tantrums, while at the same time it appears in a milder form as nagging and maliciousness. The degree to which people are capable of hating and nagging is a good index of their personality.

Hate directs itself in various ways. It may be pointed towards various tasks that one must perform, against single individuals, against a nation or a class, against a race or against the other sex.

From the ethical point of view, hatred is condemned, for, although it brings pleasure to the person who hates, that pleasure is dearly purchased and the consequences far-reaching and disastrous. It seems that hatred unleashes such malignant passions as retaliation and revenge and the person is often described in such terms as 'cruel', 'deadly', 'fierce' and 'vindictive'. People who hate end up with blunted feelings and warped judgement and alienate themselves from other people unless they are of a like mind.

Hate may expand itself in breaking all contact possibilities which an individual may have. Sometimes the degree to which an individual may hate is suddenly disclosed, as by a stroke of lightning.

HIERARCHY OF HUMAN NEEDS (ABRAHAM MASLOW, 1908–70)

Maslow, an American psychologist who became an influential figure in humanistic psychology and humanistic psychotherapy, is probably most known for his hierarchy of human needs related to motivation and problem-solving and his work on self-actualization and peak experiences. Maslow was active in the development of the human potential movement and the founding of the Esalen Institute in California.

His self-actualization theory of psychology proposed that the primary goal of psychotherapy should be the integration of the self and that integration is achieved as needs are experienced and met. Our behaviour motivations, priorities and actions are determined by these needs. Motivated behaviour thus results from tension when a need presents itself, whether the tension is pleasant or unpleasant. The goal of behaviour is the reduction of tension.

Maslow identified five levels of human needs. In order to progress upward, the person must have experienced secure footing on the first rung in order to proceed to the next. Inability to fulfil a lower-order need may create locked-in, immature behaviour patterns.

The theory is that it is only as each need is satisfied that we are motivated to reach for the next higher level; thus, people who lack food or shelter or who do not feel themselves to be in a safe environment are unable to concentrate on higher needs such as self-actualization. Our drive for self-actualization may conflict with our rights and duties and responsibilities to other people who are involved. Maslow did not say that all needs of a certain level must be fulfilled before progress upward was possible. It is a question of how much energy is being used up at a lower level.

While people might be high on self-actualization today, tomorrow something could happen that would change that and thrust them back into satisfying their basic needs. For example, if I lost my job, then, however much I might want to continue the upward climb towards reaching my potential, my prime concern would probably be trying to find another job, trying to meet the security needs. If I were flying over the desert and the plane crashed, my immediate need would be very basic – food and water, not self-actualization.

Another way of looking at Maslow's model is that, rather than moving on from stage to stage, as in climbing a ladder, all five needs are being met simultaneously, to some degree.

The hierarchy

1. **Basic:** Physiological and survival needs – met by food, shelter, clothing, sex
2. **Safety:** Security, orderliness, protective rules and risk avoidance – met by salary, insurance policies, alarm systems

3. **Belongingness:** The need of relationship with others, to be appreciated and accepted – met through family ties and membership of groups
4. **Ego-status:** Related to status within a group, ambition and a desire to excel – the ego-status needs will motivate the person to display competence in an effort to gain social and professional rewards; meeting status needs depends on the willingness and ability of other people to respond appropriately
5. **Self-actualization:** The capacity of human beings to grow and develop toward emotional and psychological maturity and self-fulfilment. This level of personal growth may be met through the challenge of creativity or demanding greater achievement. Self-actualizing behaviours include risk-taking, seeking autonomy and freedom to act.

The term is used by most humanistic therapies to describe the dominating, motivating life force that drives the individual toward ever-developing, ever-perfecting his/her capacities to the highest heights and deepest depths. Therapies that emphasize minimal direction or person-centred philosophy also embrace the principle of self-actualization.

Self-actualization is the road; to be self-actualized is the goal, striven for but never absolutely attained. Self-actualization involves the successful mastery of conflicts, which always involve anxiety. It is closely linked with 'peak experiences', although not synonymous with them. Our drive for self-actualization may conflict with our rights and duties and responsibilities to other people who are involved.

The characteristics of self-actualization

- Psychological growth and maturation
- The awakening and manifestation of latent potentialities
- Ethical, aesthetic and spiritual experiences and activities.

For Maslow self-actualization is:

- A liberating of the person from factors that stunt personal growth
- Freeing of the person from the neurotic problems of life – infantile, fantasy or otherwise 'unreal'
- Something that enables the person to face, endure and grapple with the real problems of life; a moving from unreal toward real issues.

Self-actualization is not:

- A state of no conflict
- A state of once-and-for-ever full unity
- An absence of problems.

Further reading

Maslow, A. H. (1970) *Motivation and Personality*, Harper & Row, New York.
Stewart, W. (1998) *Self-counselling: How to develop the skills to positively manage your life*, How To Books, Oxford.

HONESTY AND OPENNESS

Honesty or the quality of being honest is a virtue that belongs to the ethic of justice. In common speech it usually means being honourable or having integrity. Honesty involves regard for the rights of other people, whatever those rights are. Breaches of the law of justice often involve dishonesty, untruthfulness or covetousness and are judged to be bad because they inflict harm on others.

In Christian theology, we are urged not to distinguish the welfare of other people from our own wellbeing, so one cannot be dishonest without harming one's self. Honesty, then, is not just about obeying the laws of the land; honesty is a moral code of practice.

Honesty means that there are no contradictions or discrepancies in thoughts, words or actions. To be honest to one's real self and task earns trust and inspires faith in others. Honesty is never to misuse that which is given in trust. Inner honesty needs to be examined to provide wisdom and support and ensure strength and stability, giving confidence to be grounded in one's self-esteem.

An honest person is one who aspires to follow the highest codes of conduct, who is loyal to the benevolent and universal principles of life and whose decisions are based clearly on what is right and wrong. Such an individual maintains standards that provide guidance and courage to understand and respect the subtle connections of the world in relation to his/her life. An honest person does not take for granted his/her own resources such as mind, body, wealth, time, talents or knowledge.

When applied to counselling, honesty, although similar to openness, should not be confused with it. Counsellors talk of 'genuineness' and 'congruence' and openness is about those, but it is more. Some people enjoy relationships where they talk about their feelings, their secrets and their innermost thoughts. They enjoy having one person or at most a few people in whom they confide. Other people avoid being open. They prefer to keep things impersonal and have acquaintances rather than close friends.

Some people are very high on openness, as if they can't get close enough to people. As a consequence they tend to treat everyone in a close, personal way. They have a strong desire to be liked and for intimacy. They fear rejection and being unloved by all. They may be possessive and they may punish people who do not respond with intimacy.

On the other hand, some people are very low on openness, as if they don't want to get emotionally involved with people at any level. As a consequence, they tend to avoid close personal ties. They have a fear of being 'discovered', which results in superficial relationships. They fear not being loved and being rejected and they feel unlovable. Distrust of others often shows in antagonism. By keeping everyone at a distance they avoid having to show affection to one person.

Between these two extremes there are many gradations and the ideal is to achieve a balance between the two extremes. But at all times, openness has to be appropriate. Behaviour appropriate in the bedroom is inappropriate in the high street. What is appropriate between close friends is inappropriate between strangers. Counsellors who have no problem with being open with clients always have to remember that they are who they are and the clients have travelled to counselling by a very different life journey. They may have to be led very gently into honesty and openness.

HOPE

To hope is to entertain a wish for something with confidence and expectation of fulfilment. Although the future cannot be known, we imagine the outcome. Sometimes the imagined prospect is terrifying. When we are convinced that the future is totally empty or bleak, we may lose our will to endure even the present.

In Christian thought, hope is one of the three theological virtues, the others being faith and charity (love). Hope is distinct from faith because it is directed exclusively toward the future, as fervent desire and confident expectation. According to St Augustine, 'hope deals only with good things and only with those which lie in the future and which pertain to the man who cherishes the hope'. When hope has attained its object, it ceases to be hope and becomes possession. Consequently, whereas 'love never ends', hope is confined to a person's life on earth.

Hope is essential for perseverance

Pain and suffering are often endured in the present in the hope that the future will be better and it is therefore worth struggling through. Hope therefore generates the ability to rise above the limitations of the present and be open to new possibilities.

While hope is essential for effective living, living in false hope – which resembles wishful thinking – is symptomatic of a dysfunctional psyche that functions in the realm of illusion. Authentic hope is founded on being realistic about the way things are.

Some people attempt to counsel with the hard face of reality, believing in the 'short, sharp shock'. This, in the early stages, is likely to lead to despair and hopelessness. Hope founded on evasion does nothing to reassure, but coating reality with hope does not mean living in a world of unreality. Acceptance does not mean banishing hope.

In counselling, hope comes not from trying to reassure the client but from the relationship itself, which engenders hope. Where clients are encouraged to explore their feelings, always with the implication that they **can** do it, hope grows. As clients make progress, they are encouraged to press on with hope. The fact that the counsellor believes in them is a related source of hope.

Further reading

Christensen. B. and De Blaissie, R. R. (1980) Counselling with parents of handicapped adolescents. *Adolescence*, 15, 58.

HUMANISTIC PSYCHOLOGY

The roots of humanistic psychology are in humanism, a philosophy that attaches importance to humankind and human values. It is often described as the 'third force' in modern psychology. It derives much of its impact from the 'growth movement' of the 1960s, involving such people as Abraham Maslow, Carl Rogers, Rollo May and others.

Within the broad framework of working in a partnership, in which the client becomes a conscious partner with the therapist in determining the course of treatment, many different approaches have developed – Carl Rogers's person-centred approach, Roberto Assagioli's psychosynthesis, Abraham Maslow's theory of self-actualization, Albert Ellis's rational emotive therapy, Eric Berne's transactional analysis, Jacob Moreno's psychodrama.

From their work sensitivity-training sessions or T groups developed, in which facilitators group activities and observe interactions between members as they actually occur. Such groups are designed to help groups of people develop sensitivity, awareness of self and others, interpersonal skills and personal effectiveness and are said to reduce authoritarianism, prejudice and the need for structure and control.

The focus of humanistic counsellors is on:

- Working with clients to achieve their goal of a healthy personality
- Helping clients to become aware of and communicate their feelings
- Focusing on what the client's life is like from the client's own frame of reference
- Affirming the client's freedom of choice and emphasizing the striving for the highest potential for each individual
- Helping clients to develop and recognize inner resources, identify choices and formulate goals.

Although fundamentally eclectic, there are common themes in humanistic psychology:

- Personal growth, human potential, responsibility and self-direction
- Lifelong education
- Full emotional functioning
- The need to learn, or to relearn, what play and joy are about
- Recognition of a person's spirituality, with an acknowledgement of human capacity for altered states of consciousness.

Humanistic psychology is a way of dealing with problems related to the following beliefs:

- Intense personal experiences radically alter attitudes to self and others.
- Unity of the human and natural worlds are achieved through 'peak experiences'. Peak experiences describe life-events that are ecstatic,

overwhelmingly intense, positively valued by those who experience them and have long-term effects. The experience can be neither earned nor manufactured, nor even worked up. Maslow used art, music, dance and sex in the search for the paths to peak experiences. For Maslow such an experience is where the person feels in harmony with all things, is clear, spontaneous, independent and alert and often with little awareness of time or space.

- Existential experiences lead to being completely independent and totally responsible for one's thoughts and actions.

Further reading

Assagioli, R. (1980) *Psychosynthesis*, Turnstone Books, Wellingborough.
Ferrucci, P. (1982) *What We May Be*, Turnstone Press, Wellingborough.
Maslow, A. H. (1969) *Motivation and Personality*, Harper & Row, New York.
Maslow, A. H. (1971) *The Farther Reaches of Human Nature*, Penguin, Harmondsworth.
Ornstein, R. E. (1975) *The Psychology of Consciousness*, Pelican, Harmondsworth.
Rowan, J. (1983) *The Reality Game*, Routledge & Kegan Paul, London.

HUMILIATION

Before considering humiliation, it is necessary to examine the word 'humility'. Humility is usually looked down upon in the world, being too often confused with 'ever-so-humbleness', and wilful self-disparagement. In Christian tradition, humility ranked high. Augustine said, 'if you ask me what is the first precept of the Christian religion I will answer, first, second and third, humility'.

St Thomas à Kempis and St Bernard held humility necessary for the imitation of Christ. Martin Luther condemned 'instead of being humble, seeking to excel in humility'.

For Calvin, humility alone exalts God as sovereign; it is part of self-denial, with the abandonment of self-confidence that constitutes faith, and of self-will. (Calvin insisted on being buried in an unmarked grave.) Puritans cultivated humility as an antidote to self-righteousness, by constant self-examination. Jonathan Edwards thought humility an essential test of religious emotionalism.

The example was set by Jesus in washing the disciples' feet as the servant who humbled himself. So, whoever would be first must be servant of all (Mark 10:43).

Thus, humility is something to be cherished and cultivated. Humility is uplifting – if it is genuine, if it is not it is false and pretentious – humiliation is totally degrading; it does nothing for the self-esteem of the person who feels humiliated.

To humiliate a person is to injure the dignity or self-respect of that person. Synonyms are often a useful way to get at the depth of a word. Synonyms for humiliation are: abasement, belittlement, degradation, depreciation, derogation, detraction, discredit, disgrace, dishonour, disparagement, embarrassment, humbling, ignominy, indignity, loss of face, mortification, obloquy, shame, shaming.

People feel humiliated by certain things that happen to them; often associated with abuse, and humiliation is a feature of masochism and sadism. The counselling relationship is one way in which the person can start to climb out of the pit from humiliation to self-respect.

Humility in counselling comes from the realization that, in spite of our weaknesses, limitations and foibles, we have something to offer our clients. We do not work from a position of superiority but from equality; not from a position of flawlessness but from one of vulnerability. It is the recognition of our own woundedness and the journey we have travelled to where we are that keeps us on the pathway of humility.

Humour

Humour is defined simply as a type of stimulation that tends to elicit the laughter reflex. The co-ordinated contraction of 15 facial muscles, accompanied by altered breathing, combine to produce a conventional pattern we call smiling or laughter.

The only biological function of laughter is to provide relief from tension. It is the only form of communication in which a complex stimulus produces a predicable, physiological response. Humour, then, can be applied to a stimulus, a response or a disposition.

Humour is also regarded as a form of play involving symbols, images and ideas. Through laughter and smiling, it serves a variety of social functions:

- Assisting interaction
- Revealing attitudes
- Engendering fellow feeling
- Aiding understanding
- Raising esteem
- Confirming the standing of relationships.

Humour is different from wit, which involves distraction from the feelings associated with the issue. The emotion discharged in laughter often, though not always, contains an element of aggression. Malice may be combined with affection in friendly teasing and the aggressive component in civilized humour may no longer be conscious. There is often a relationship between laughter and ugliness, deformity and cruelty, delight in suffering and contempt for the unfamiliar.

Humour as a defence mechanism:

- Is an antidote to sympathy
- Is a protection from the shortcomings of others
- Is a defence against showing true feelings
- Allows the individual to focus on something in a way that makes bearable what, in reality, is too terrible to be borne.

Humour in counselling requires a distinction between that which is used to attack and humour as a shared response. Appropriate humour may aid therapy: it lowers anxiety, reduces distance, focuses attention on the material being discussed, assists in building the relationship and promotes catharsis

Freud regarded jokes and parapraxes as revelations of the unconscious. The *Oxford English Dictionary* defines parapraxis as 'the faulty performance of an intended act; in psychoanalysis, a minor error said to reveal a subconscious motive'.

Parapraxis is a general term that includes momentary amnesias, slips of the tongue and pen, errors in action and forgetting.

In psychoanalytic thought, parapraxis is caused by the intrusion of unconscious processes on the conscious, causing the 'mistake', the 'Freudian slip' that somehow betrays the truth.

Examples of parapraxes

'I'm glad you're better' was the intention, which turned into 'I'm sad you're better'

'My husband can eat what he wants' was the intention, which turned into 'My husband can eat what I want'

Man entering a restaurant with a woman: 'Do you have a table?' was the intention, which turned into 'Do you have a bedroom?'

King Henry VIII greeting Anne Boleyn: 'Good morning, beloved' was the intention, which turned into 'Good morning, beheaded'.

Humour is as essential to healthy interaction, to healthy people and to any productive relationship, as oil is to smooth-running machinery.

Humour is a tool which helps to:

- Prevent the build-up of stress
- Improve communication
- Enhance motivation and morale
- Build relationships
- Encourage creative problem-solving
- Smooth the way for change
- Make learning fun
- Decrease problems with discipline
- Focus listening and attention
- Decrease the pressure to be perfect
- Increase retention, by freeing attention through laughter
- Increase the comfort level
- Build interest and energy through laughter
- Contribute to achievement and productivity
- Enhance self-confidence
- Build empathy

- Hear feedback and new information
- Develop a new perspective on problems.

Sharing humour with your client, when based on caring and empathy:

- Builds confidence
- Involves your client in the fun
- Amuses and encourages your client to laugh
- Is supportive
- Brings you both closer
- Encourages positive exchange
- Demonstrates that counselling is not always deadly serious.

Further reading

Cade, B. W. (1982) Humour and creativity. *Journal of Family Therapy*, 4, 35–42.

McGhee, P. E. (1976) *Humour: Its origins and development*, W. H. Freeman, San Francisco, CA.

McGhee, P. E. and Goldestein, J. H. (1983) *Handbook of Humour Research*, Springer-Verlag, New York.

I

IMAGERY (*see also*: Creativity, Psychosynthesis)

This article draws together imagination, guided fantasy, directed daydream and guided affective imagery (GAI).

- **Imagery**: The inner representation of objects and events created at will by the conscious mind
- **Fantasy**: Imaginary activities that are produced spontaneously (as in daydreams) or as a requested response to stimuli such as inkblots or ambiguous pictures
- **Imagination**: Expresses repressed parts of personality.

Imagery has an obvious and a hidden meaning:

- The obvious is conscious and concrete
- The hidden is unconscious and implied and takes the form of symbols. Understanding the fantasy means working with the symbols.

Guided imagery (also referred to as 'symboldrama')

This is a form of creative imagination facilitated by the therapist, who prompts, encourages, develops and brings the fantasy experience to a close. The material may then be analysed in terms of its meaning and symbolism – similar to dream analysis. Symbols, which may conceal or reveal, always derive from archetypes. Symbols have four meanings:

- Literal
- Allegorical
- Moral
- Mystical.

Kinds of symbol:

- Nature
- Animal
- Human
- Man-made
- Religious
- Mythological
- Abstract
- Individual/spontaneous.

Guided imagery is used in one form or another in many different therapies. It may also be used in groups, either for individuals or for the whole group. The fundamental truth of therapeutic imagery is that the psyche always strives to represent itself in fantasy using images.

Principles of guided imagery therapy

- **The principle of symbol confrontation**: The client is encouraged to be courageous and to confront images (usually a part of self) that cause anxiety. Successful confrontation causes transformation and removal of anxiety.
- **The principle of feeding**: Where confrontation is inappropriate or unacceptable – the challenge may be too great – the therapist may suggest that the client feeds the frightening figure, to make it lazy and sleepy.
- **The principle of transformation**: While transformation may take place in confrontation, sometimes the transformation has to be more clearly directed if it doesn't occur spontaneously. Changing the feared object into something more acceptable is not just a way of coping; the new object often reveals significant psychological growth.
- **The principle of reconciliation**: This is where the client makes friends with hostile symbolic figure, by addressing it, touching it, making friends with it.
- **The principle of the magic fluid**: The brook or stream represent the flow of psychic energy and the potential for emotional development. Bathing in the stream or drinking from it may prove therapeutic. Bathing in the sea can be very revealing, from what is felt and from what one discovers in the depths.
- **The principle of exhausting and killing**: Should only be used by an experienced therapist, because it is very often an attack against the client's self.

Principal motifs

- Meadow
- Brook
- Mountain
- House
- Edge of woods
- Animals
- Rosebush and automobile
- Lion/dragon
- Significant person
- Cave
- Swamp
- Volcano
- Book
- Sword
- Container
- Witch/sorceress/wizard/magician
- Sleeping Beauty
- Wise person – guide.

Principal groups of symbols

- **Introversion or interiorization**: The external life must be counterbalanced by an adequate inner life. The task is to discover our Centre.

- **Deepening – descent**: The exploration of the unconscious. To become aware of and incorporate one's Shadow, the lower parts of one's personality.
- **Elevation – ascent**: The mountain-top, sky or heaven. The levels of the inner worlds are:
  1. Emotions and feelings
  2. Mind/intellect – concrete, analytical, philosophical reason
  3. Imagination
  4. Will
  5. Transcendence.
- **Broadening – expansion**: Consciousness can be enlarged or broadened to include increasingly larger zones of impressions and contents. This happens spherically, in all directions, not just in one direction.
- **Awakening**: The natural conscious state is that of being asleep. In this dreamlike state we see everything and everyone through a thick veil of colouring and distortions, which derives from our emotional reactions, the effect of past psychic traumas and from external influences. To awaken from this state requires courage.
- **Light – illumination**: Illumination is the means by which we move from consciousness to intuitive awareness.
- **Fire**: The function of fire is essentially one of purification.
- **Development and evolution**: The principal symbols are:
  – The seed
  – Flower (lotus, rose).
- **Strengthening – intensification**: The reinforcement of all our latent, underdeveloped energies and functions. This may include transpersonal or peak experiences.
- **Love**: Human love is an attempt to come out of oneself and to enter communion with another.
- **The way, path, pilgrimage**: The 'mystic way', e.g. Bunyan's *Pilgrim's Progress*, Dante's passing through Hell, Purgatory and Paradise.
- **Transformation**: Transformation, or transmutation, is the theme of psychospiritual alchemy, which Jung explores in relation to dreams and symbols. Transformation occurs through the combined actions of elevation and descent.
- **Rebirth – regeneration**: Transformation paves the way for regeneration, which, in its most profound meaning, constitutes a 'new birth'.
- **Liberation**: Elimination of encumbrances, a process of liberation from our complexes, from our illusions and from identification with the various roles we play in life, from the masks we assume and from our idols. Freedom from fear is a goal to be won and safeguarded every single day.

What imagery does is to cut through the control of the mind, which so often blocks tapping into the feelings. This does not mean that the client is out of control; that would be too frightening to contemplate and would certainly not be therapeutic. At all times clients are totally aware of what is happening, of where their imagination is taking them, although why and the outcome are obscured. Using imagery is a rewarding experience for both counsellor and client, for it takes them both beyond the realms of normal dialogue into the client's inner world in ways that normal dialogue cannot.

Further reading

Gallegos S. E. and Rennick, T. (1984) *Inner Journeys*, Turnstone Press, Wellingborough.
Leuner. H. (1984) *Guided Affective Imagery: Mental imagery in short-term psychotherapy*, Thieme-Stratton, New York.
Ornstein, R. E. (1975) *The Psychology of Consciousness*, Pelican, Harmondsworth.
Stewart W. (1996) *Imagery and Symbolism in Counselling*, Jessica Kingsley, London
Stewart W. (1998) *A Dictionary of Images and Symbols in Counselling*, Jessica Kingsley. London
Zdenek, M. (1983) *The Right-Brain Experience*, Corgi, London.

IMMEDIACY (HERE AND NOW)

Immediacy is also referred to as 'here and now' or 'you–me' talk. It is where the counsellor helps the client to look at the interaction within the relationship, as it is happening. There is often a natural tendency to talk about feelings in the past (the 'then and there'), rather than in the 'now'. People who rarely talk in the present often dilute the interaction by the use of 'you' instead of 'I'. They may be helped to feel the immediacy of the statement when 'I' is used. As with challenging, immediacy is more appropriate when the counselling relationship is firmly established.

As concreteness contrasts with generality, so 'here and now' immediacy contrasts with 'then and there'. The principal difference is that, in the one, clients are encouraged to own their feelings and not to generalize; in the other, they are encouraged to own their feelings as they exist at that moment.

Immediacy involves:

- Being open with the client about how you feel about something within the relationship
- Disclosing a hunch about the client's behaviour toward you, by drawing attention to discrepancies, distortions, avoidances, games
- Inviting the client to explore what is happening, with a view to developing a more productive working relationship.

Immediacy in action

Situation 1
Sue is a facilitator of a counselling training group of 12 people. One of the group, Andy, is very vocal and always seems to have an answer to any point that Sue or anyone else raises. In the third session, Sue started to feel irritated. The source of her irritation is that, whenever silences occur, Andy invariably jumps

in with a comment that does not always facilitate what has gone before. Sue also notices that other members of the group start to fidget and cast knowing glances at one another when Andy starts speaking. The immediate issue is that Andy cuts across what one of the women in the group is saying.

The response

Sue says, 'Andy, I feel a bit uncomfortable in what I'm going to say, as I'm not sure how you'll take it. Over the past few weeks I've become increasingly frustrated and irritated. You are obviously very knowledgeable and have lot of insight into counselling and what you say is often to the point. There are times, however, when you've cut across me, as if what you have to say is more important than what I am saying. There are times when the group lapses into silence, as if we're all struggling with some deep issue and you break the silence with a comment that doesn't seem to be relevant to what is happening. I just need you to know how I feel right now, for it's possible that this is the affect you have on other people. I wonder how you feel about what I've just said?'

Situation 2

Steve is Andrea's client and this is the sixth session. When he started counselling, he said, 'Oh, I'm fairly well off, so the fee isn't a problem'. Andrea, personally, has difficulty talking about charging a fee, she would much rather leave that to someone else to handle, but there is no one else. At least three times during their time together, Steve has said things like, 'I hadn't realized just how expensive this business would be'. Andrea finds that this issue is unresolved. She also wonders if Steve thinks that the length of the counselling relationship is more to do with her needs than with his.

The response

Andrea says, 'Steve, I feel embarrassed talking about money, you probably remember that from our first session, so right now I'm really uncomfortable about saying what I've wanted to for a few weeks. Although you said at the start that the level of fee was OK, several times you've dropped hints that I'm charging too much and I feel some sort of a heel when you say that. Linked to that is another issue, which is that you say that therapy is taking longer than you thought. I'm wondering if you think I'm holding on to you to increase my bank balance at your expense. What are your feelings about what I've said?'

Further reading

Sutton, J. and Stewart, W. (1997) *Learning to Counsel*, How To Books, Oxford.

INCEST (*see also*: Child abuse, Rape counselling)

Definition

Any overtly sexual contact between people who are either closely related or perceive themselves to be ... if that special trust that exists between a child and parent figure or sibling is violated by a sexual act, that act becomes incestuous.

Forward, S. and Buck C. (1981) *Betrayal of Innocence*, Pelican Books, London.

Incest is universally condemned and usually greeted with horror. (Punishment for incest may be very severe.) It has been countenanced in exceptional circumstances, usually associated with the marriage of royal children.

Initiation ceremonies at puberty reinforce the idea that the mother and sister are forbidden to the young male as sexual partners.

Freud and Émile Durkheim, the French sociologist, both contributed to understanding the incest taboo. Freud sees the Oedipus complex – son–mother love – as a fundamental psychological conflict.

Jung interpreted incest fantasies as symbolic of wanting close emotional contact, although acknowledging the sexual feelings to be real.

To act upon the sexual urges and not acknowledge the taboo leads to abuse. To acknowledge the taboo and deny the sexual urges leads to repression, with all its consequent pathology.

Adult–child incest strikes at the very core of civilization. It disturbs both the social order and the developing child. Although sibling incest does exist, unless it happens by force, it does not generally constitute abuse in the same sense as does adult–child incest.

Within the category of sexual abuse, the most prevalent examples are incestuous.

Child abuse may take the form of:

- Fondling a child
- Talking dirty
- Pornography
- Masturbating a child
- Forcing a child to masturbate an adult
- Oral, anal or vaginal intercourse.

Social, cultural, physiological and psychological factors all contribute to the breakdown of the incest taboo. There is a higher incidence of incest among families where remarriage has occurred. Incest, because it usually involves a stronger male, is a variation of child abuse and rape. Children are cajoled or intimidated into incestuous relationships. Bribes and threats are used to keep children silent. Children are further damaged and confused because they are told by the abusing relative that there is nothing wrong with the incestuous behaviour.

Father–daughter incest is reported to be more common than either sibling or mother–son incest. Families at risk of father–daughter incest include those with violent fathers, as well as those with mothers who have been disabled because of depression, alcoholism, psychosis, frequent involuntary childbearing or chronic illness.

Incestuous daughters tend to develop character disorders such as promiscuity, antisocial behaviour, frigidity, homosexuality, learning difficulties and depression.

There is role confusion: is the father paternal or sexual? The incestuous father, fearful of exposure, is jealously possessive of the victim and this has adverse influence on her relationships with siblings, other children and other adults.

In father–son incest, the taboos against incestuous behaviour and against homosexuality are both violated. The son is frequently the eldest child and, if he has sisters, they are likely to be sexually abused by the father as well.

Authoritarian fathers with poor impulse control who were abused as children, abuse alcohol, view children as property and are sexually attracted to children place their children at risk of incest abuse unless mitigating factors intervene.

Mitigating factors

Mitigating factors are conditions that serve to decrease the likelihood of incest:

- Adherence to proscription ('I want to, I could, but I shouldn't')
- Social support groups often help to reinforce society's norms
- Close family ties outside the nuclear family
- Official intervention and/or the threat of it
- Sex education is potentially the single most effective mitigating factor
- Media reporting.

Rape and other sexual attacks by strangers, however traumatic, are usually single events, but incest may continue for years with intercourse taking place daily or several times a week. Survivors sacrifice a part of their childhood to exploitation, pain, fear and secrecy.

Some of the consequences for child victims:

- Pregnancy
- Physical injury
- Secrecy
- Helplessness
- Entrapment and accommodation
- Disclosure brings shame
- Retraction of accusation.

Many women presenting severe psychological or behavioural difficulties admit a history of incest. Many prostitutes claim that their first sexual experience was with their fathers.

Incest survivors persistently describe how they tried to cut themselves off mentally from the act, freeze up or pretend it wasn't happening. This can spread into other areas of life beside sex, causing feelings of social isolation, inability to communicate or to get close to other people. Self-disgust is compounded by intense shame and guilt, particularly when the act is exposed, with publicity and family break up. There is no escape from the 'Catch-22' – the emotional burden of silence; the trauma of disclosure.

Myths of incest

The victims

- It preserves the family
- It didn't happen
- They must have asked for it
- Children are very sexy, encourage and invite sex with adults
- Incest is an accepted part of some subcultures; they enjoy it
- Incest is a caring relationship
- They are that sort of children anyway

The mothers

- She colluded. What could be her 'Catch-22'?
- The marriage is faulty – her fault
- She is the 'silent partner'
- She must be an inadequate or flawed personality.

The perpetrators
Which view do you subscribe to?

- Most incest aggressors are criminals and need to be locked up
- The offender can be helped and should be kept close to his family
- He is a deviant – 'There's got to be something wrong or ill about a father who does that sort of thing to his child'
- He is a product of his family history – the sins of the father ... Is incest carried around in the genes like a genetic illness?
- A normal man has to have sex – 'The poor fellow must have been driven to it'
- Incest is a sign of a dysfunctional family.

Further reading

Carter-Lourensz, J. H. and Johnson-Powell, G. (1995) Physical abuse, sexual abuse, and neglect of child. In: *Comprehensive Textbook of Psychiatry*, 6th edn, (eds H. J. Kaplan and B. J. Sadock), Williams & Wilkins, Baltimore, MD.

Nin, A. (1993) *From a Journal of Love: the unexpurgated diary of Anais Nin*, Peter Owen, London.

INDIVIDUAL PSYCHOLOGY (ALFRED ADLER, 1870–1937)

Alfred Adler was one of the neo-Freudians and the first to break with Freud. He resigned as president of the Vienna Psychoanalytic Society in 1911 and formed a society that later became the Society for Individual Psychology.

Adler established many child guidance centres in schools in Vienna and is credited with being the pioneer psychiatrist of group counselling. He disagreed with Freud over the libido theory, the sexual origin of neurosis and the importance of infantile wishes.

Individual psychology is a broad, socially-orientated, humanistic and holistic personality theory of psychology and psychotherapy. Adler's system is invested with a great deal of common sense, for it makes sense to the average reader.

According to this theory, people are guided by values and goals of which they may be aware, not driven by unconscious instincts. Adler believed that the main motives of human thought and behaviour lie in the individual's striving for superiority and power, partly in compensation for feelings of inferiority. The individual moves from a sense of inferior to a sense of mastery.

Every individual is unique and our personality structure, including our unique goal and ways of striving for it, is our style of life, a product of our own creativity. The individual cannot be considered apart from society, for all human problems – relationships, occupation and love – are social. Adler coined the term 'inferiority complex'.

The neurotically disposed person is characterized by increased inferiority feelings, underdeveloped social interest and an exaggerated, unco-operative goal of superiority. These characteristics express themselves as anxiety and aggression.

Individual psychology emphasizes:

- Social relationships, rather than biological factors
- Self, rather than the id and the superego
- Striving for self-actualization, rather than the sex instinct
- The present, rather than early experiences
- Equality and co-operation between the sexes
- The person moves away from situations that make her/him feel inferior and toward goals of success and superiority.

Basic assumptions

All behaviour has social meaning

- Social interest creates an attitude toward one's own place within society and one's relationship to others. The tasks of living are to love and to be loved; to experience friendship; to work; to develop a satisfactory self-concept and to search for meaning. Thus the person has to be viewed within his/her social environment.
- People choose their own goals.
- A person with high self-esteem and high social interest will move toward others in an encouraging manner.
- A person suffering from self-doubts or inadequacies or who has few concerns for the rights and needs of others will move away from others in swamping dependency or in an independent manner that cuts other people off.

The human personality is a unity
'Unity' means synthesizing our physical, emotional, intellectual and spiritual aspects. Adler used the term 'style of life', a key term that describes variously:

- Self
- Personality
- A personal problem-solving method
- An attitude toward life
- A line of movement
- A pattern
- A technique.

The unique life style is developed from an early age and is as characteristic as a theme in a piece of music.

Behaviour is subjectively determined
Personal reality is determined through subjective experience, perceiving and learning. Every person develops a 'private logic'.

All behaviour is goal-directed
By seeking to discover the payoff or purpose of behaviour, therapists can more readily understand dysfunctional behaviour. Goals are not always conscious.

Motivation explains striving for significance
Each of us moves from a feeling of relative inferiority to a feeling of superiority. This striving for success and superiority is the upward drive toward perfection.

Neurosis and psychosis force people to impose their (often unfounded) achievements on to others in order to boost a weakened self-esteem. This weakened self-esteem frequently leads to overcompensation, which takes the form of deprecating others, a tendency that is at the root of sadism, hatred, quarrelsomeness and intolerance.

Behaviour
This changes throughout life, to meet current demands and long-term goals.

People are not pushed by causes
We are determined neither by our heredity nor by our environment.

Self-realization is other-directed
Self-realization, if it does not help to make the world a better place, is sterile.

Every person has the freedom of choice
Some choose to remain neurotic; others choose to strive toward the goal of wholeness.

The concept of mental health
Mental health is the sum total of the individual's:

- Social interest
- Contribution to society
- Degree of self-respect and self-confidence
- Degree of belongingness as social equals in the family, groups and the wider society.

Adler's 'masculine protest' describes the drive for superiority or completeness, arising out of a felt inferiority or incompleteness, femininity being regarded as incomplete and inferior.

The myth of masculine superiority
Society has been so structured that in the division of labour, males assume dominance and superiority over women. In Adlerian psychology, the differences between males and females is very slight, so assumed dominance by males creates tension between the sexes.

From a very early age, boys and girls are conditioned into an acceptance of dominance or submission. Adler insists that this masculine superiority is a myth that creates many psychological problems.

The thought of such superiority scares male children and imposes on them an obligation they can never expect to fulfil. At the same time it compels female children to rebel against enforced inferiority.

Individual psychology emphasizes horizontal relationships between the sexes, a position of difference but of equality, rather than vertical relationships, in which, for ever, we compare ourselves favourably or unfavourably with someone else who happens to be of a different sex. The idea is also applied to relationships in general. A hierarchy is an example of vertical relationships.

The concept of organ inferiority (*see also*: Complexes)
Adler uses the term to describe the perceived or actual congenital defects in organs of the body or their functions. For example, children compare themselves in stature with adults and adult abilities and this sense of inferiority is reinforced by adults, who draw attention to the failings of the child **as compared with adult standards.** The move toward mastery and high self-esteem is often blocked by such organ deficits as poor eyesight, speech difficulties, physical disability or poor health.

Adler referred to children who suffered from organ inferiorities as 'stepchildren of nature'. They are engaged at an early age in a bitter struggle for existence where social feelings become strangled. A consequence of this is that there is morbid preoccupation with self and in trying to make an impression on others. This may lead to intense approval-seeking.

Adler also believed that a child's educational potential may be shattered by exaggerated, intensified and unresolved feelings of inferiority and a goal that demands security and peace fuelled by a striving to express dominance over others. Such children, Adler says, are easily recognized. They are 'problem children' who interpret every experience as a defeat and consider themselves to be always neglected and discriminated against, both by nature and by people.

Adults who demand of the child more that the child can do reinforce the child's helplessness and pave the way for the realization that there are but two things over which the child has power: the pleasure and displeasure of adults.

Adler also believed that organ inferiority resulted in compensation, a striving to overcome the weakness.

Birth-order theory

Another factor contributing to personality development is birth order. Adler, along with Jung and others, disputed the importance of sexual motives. Adler assigned a prominent place to family dynamics in personality development. Children's position in their family – their birth order – was seen as determining significant character traits.

Oldest child: reported characteristics

- Parents' undivided attention
- Afraid of losing parents' favour, conforms to standards
- Often becomes quite responsible
- May feel 'dethroned' initially by other arrivals and may refuse to share
- When a male firstborn child is only slightly older than a female, permanent dethronement can occur because of the girl's accelerated rate of growth and development
- Frequently ambitious and anxious to achieve
- Often serve as pacesetters for the other children in their families
- Dislike change and may develop conservative viewpoints
- Likely to be authority-oriented
- Tend to relate better to adults than to peers
- Tend toward being conservative.

Middle child: reported characteristics

- May feel an intruder between the oldest child and the parents
- Often becomes proficient in areas in which the oldest child is not
- Often more sociable than oldest children
- Often sensitive to injustices, unfairness and feelings of being slighted or abused or of having no place in a group
- Tend to favour change and become interested in social change
- May feel dethroned by the competition from any new arrival.

Youngest child: reported characteristics

- The youngest child is never dethroned
- Adept at inducing others to do things for her/him

- Often 'spoiled', usually the most powerful person in the family
- Often not taken seriously.

Single child: reported characteristics

- Similarity to the youngest child
- May become very demanding
- Often expects a 'special place' in life without having earned it
- They may try to reach their parents' adult level of competence
- They may remain helpless and irresponsible as long as possible
- Usually establish better relationships with people much older or much younger than with peers
- Often experience difficulty with sharing and often become loners.

Adopted child: reported characteristics

- Reaps the benefits of having been planned and wanted by the parents and of the adoption agency's investigation of the home environment prior to placement
- When adopted by parents who are unable to bear their own, the adopted child may be overprotected or pampered
- A child adopted into a family where there are already children may be in an 'in' or 'out' situation with the siblings.

Theories are given for guidance, not to be interpreted as infallible or predicable. In some instances the above structure does not apply; for others it may apply in part. However, birth order is one more factor to consider in counselling.

Life tasks

The basic challenges of life are:

- Love
- Living in society
- Working
- Sex
- Spiritual growth
- Self-identity.

Lifestyle mistakes:

- Tendency to overgeneralize
- False, or impossible goals of security
- Misperceptions
- Minimization or denial of one's worth
- Faulty values.

Adlerian counselling goals

- To establish and maintain a therapeutic relationship in which there is equality, trust and acceptance and which does not reflect differences but sameness
- To uncover the uniqueness of the client
- To give insight
- To encourage redirection and reorientation.

The stages of Adlerian counselling

1. The therapeutic relationship
This encompasses the qualities of unconditional positive regard, genuineness, empathy, nonpossessive warmth, self-disclosure and concreteness

2. Psychological investigation
This is in four parts.

- **The subjective situation** – what is happening within the client
- **The objective situation** – what is happening in the client's external world
- **Getting the answer to 'the fundamental question', 'What would be different if all these problems or concerns were solved?** – gives clues as to possible payoffs or reasons why the person persists in a specific behaviour
- **Life-style investigation** – may involve psychometric testing, an examination of the family atmosphere and an exploration of the client's early recollections.

3. Interpretation
Interpretation is not counsellor-centred, it is a mutual sharing of basic attitudes about life, self and others, where the emphasis is on goals and purposes, not on causes.

An interpretation identifies:

- Problems and feelings of deficiency
- Directions taken to overcome the perceived deficiencies
- The relationship between direction and other significant areas in the client's life
- Specific life-task difficulties
- Strategies used to avoid resolution
- Feelings of superiority about avoidances
- Contribution of past influences.

Adler disapproved of the 'red pen' approach, where only weaknesses are examined. We can build only on strengths, not on weaknesses.

4. Reorientation
Counsellor and client work together to consider what changes could be made in the client's life style. Two basic techniques are:

- **'Stroking'**, which is synonymous with encouragement and caring
- **'Spitting in the soup'**, which is a discouraging response, based on the idea that a bowl of soup would no longer be appetizing if spat in. When clients have insight into faulty thinking and self-defeating behaviours they become contaminated and no longer appealing.

Confronting illogical, faulty thinking is also an important part in therapy. Illogical thinking may be:

- Causal inference – false logic
- Blowup – exaggeration
- All-or-nothing – thinking in extremes
- Responsibility projection – failing to own
- Perfectionism – idealistic demands on self
- Value-tainted – 'shoulds', 'oughts', 'bad'
- Self-depreciation – punitive statements.

Faulty thinking may be corrected by:

- Factual description
- Generating alternative explanations
- Designing positive course of action.

Adlerian general counselling skills

- Active listening
- Reflection of feelings
- Empathic understanding
- Challenging
- Interpretation
- Encouragement.

Specific therapeutic techniques

Paradoxical intention
(Adler originally called this 'prescribing the symptom'.) The client is encouraged to emphasize the symptoms or develop them even more. When people discover that they cannot intentionally do what they feared would happen, they are often able to laugh at the situation.

Frankl, the originator of logotherapy, said that such an intervention 'takes the wind out of the sails of fear'.

Acting 'as if'
To 'If only I could…', the counsellor replies, 'Pretend – act as if you could do it that way'. Acting 'as if' is like wearing a different suit. Feeling different is important.

Catching oneself
When clients become aware of engaging in behaviour they want to change, they are encouraged to say, 'There I go again'.

Creating movement
The element of surprise may encourage the client to change behaviour. Agreeing with the faulty logic and 'going over the top', provided it is not an attack, nor sarcastic, may jolt the client into action.

Goal-setting and commitment
Homework, assignments and change cards related to some change in behaviour. An example of a 'change card' might be:

'This week I will...' (something specific)
'I know I could sabotage my task by...'
'I will evaluate my achievement on...'

Adler's social relations, interpersonal behaviour, ego development, self-direction and group work have influenced many other approaches to therapy.

Child-guidance

> *Whenever a child lies you will always find a severe parent. A lie would have no sense unless the truth were felt to be dangerous.*
>
> Alfred Adler, *New York Times* 1949.

Child-guidance clinics – staffed by psychiatrists, psychologists and social workers specializing in child development – work on parent–child relationship problems through individual and group counselling; the guidance clinics also give help to parents with emotionally disturbed children.

The traditionally accepted working relationship is that the psychiatrist works directly with the child while the social worker works with the parent(s). The premise is that, while it would be inaccurate and mistaken to imply that the parents are to blame for the child's behaviour, it is certainly true to say that when there is a problem child the whole family is disturbed. If the child is to change, then the whole family also needs to change; hence the focus of the social worker.

Further reading

Eckstein, D. (1981) An Adlerian primer. In: *1981 Annual Handbook for Group Facilitators*, University Associates, San Diego, CA.
Kern, A. *et al.* (1978) *A Case of Adlerian Counselling*, Alfred Adler Institute, Chicago, IL.
Mosak, H. and Dreikurs, R. (1973) Adlerian psychotherapy. In: *Current Psychotherapies*, (ed. R. Corsini), F. E. Peacock, Itasca, IL.

INSIGHT

Insight is mental discernment, direct understanding of the meaning or implication of something. It is the illumination or comprehension of one's mental condition that had previously escaped awareness. It is where immediate and clear learning or understanding takes place without apparent trial-and-error testing behaviour.

The term derives from the work on animal behaviour by Gestalt psychologist Wolfgang Kohler.

In psychopathology it is the awareness of one's own mental condition and is considered an essential in most forms of psychotherapy. A person achieves insight when s/he understands what is causing a conflict. Insight is often accompanied by catharsis.

Insight in counselling refers to the extent to which clients are aware of their problems, origins and influences. It may be sudden – like the flash of inspiration; the 'eureka experience'. More usually it develops stage by stage as the client develops psychological strength to deal with what is revealed.

Insight cannot be given by one person to another. We all must arrive at it by ourselves. A function of the counselling relationship is to help the client see how to put the new-found insight into practice.

Insight operates on three levels. Level 1 is a superficial awareness of one's situation – where the person is aware of a problem. Level 2 is deeper and involves an intellectual appreciation of what the problem is. Level 3 is deeper still and combines an intellectual and emotional appreciation of the problem. It is at this level that the client feels and understands the significance of what is happening and achieves awareness and the impetus to change. Intellectual insight by itself is insufficient: unless there is emotional accord, the results will be minimal.

In psychodynamic counselling, clients defend themselves against insight by resistance. When clients are willing to accept the counsellor's interpretations, insight occurs; the client is empowered to face reality. Many other counsellors do not work directly with unconscious material, yet the client who is able to work at level 3, who can get in touch with the unconscious, has a greater capacity for achieving insight.

Further reading

Jager, J. and Gitlin, M. J. (1995) Clinical manifestations of psychiatric disorders. In: *Comprehensive Textbook of Psychiatry*, 6th edn, (eds H. J. Kaplan and B. J. Sadock), Williams & Wilkins, Baltimore, MD.

INTERNALIZATION

Internalization is a term that describes the process whereby one incorporates beliefs, values, attitudes, practices, standards, norms and morals into one's inner world as one's own. As children develop, they become able to give themselves the instructions that were previously given by significant others. Full internalization is achieved when the behaviour takes place not in response to reward or fear of punishment but because it is perceived to be correct or appropriate.

When children learn to value hard work or financial success or a belief in God, they tend to acquire a sense of vested interest in such ideas and feelings as these become their own. Internalization maintains social systems through voluntary means rather than requiring them to be monitored and corrected by external authorities. In contrast, coercion is a far less effective means of social control.

The goal of parents, educators and, indeed, counsellors, is not compliance but internalization. Internalization is generally obtained by an influence source who has credibility, whose message is persuasive and believable.

In the psychoanalytic theory, the superego is the last of three agencies (with the id and ego) of the human personality to develop. The superego is the ethical component of the personality and provides the moral standards by which the ego operates. The superego's criticisms, prohibitions and inhibitions form a person's conscience, and its positive aspirations and ideals represent one's idealized self-image or 'ego ideal'.

The superego is assumed to develop through the process of internalization of the standards and values of the parents, a process greatly aided by a tendency to identify with the parents. The superego continues to develop into young adulthood as a person encounters other admired role models and copes with the rules and regulations of the larger society. Within traditional approaches to social psychology and the study of personality, an important issue is the degree to which a person attributes his/her behaviour to such internalized motives. Identification is a major link between the psychoanalytic and social learning theories of development and it is a powerful influence in the socialization process.

Identification, by which we model aspects of ourselves upon other people, is an essential part of internalization. Most of our important beliefs and attitudes are probably initially based on identification. Whenever we start to identify with, for example, a new reference group, we start 'trying on' the new set of beliefs and attitudes. From the moment we engage in this process our belief system is in a state of flux; the more so if the new beliefs contrast sharply with previously held ones. The test of whether identification has led to internalization is whether the induced beliefs, values and attitudes stay the test of time.

Counselling is neither persuasion not compliance, yet in a sense it is a process of internalization. Clients are challenged to face up to the fact that something in their life has to change if they are to move forward. While it is not the aim that the client internalizes the counsellor's beliefs, values and attitudes, as someone to be admired, there is the sense that the counsellor holds up to the client alternative beliefs, values and attitudes, as together they engage in the process of reframing. Neither is it that the client looks upon the counsellor as the 'ideal'; the counsellor holds up the mirror so that the client can identify with his/her own ideal self. When the client has done this, internalization takes place and the client can then begin to separate from the counsellor.

Further reading

Meissner, W. W. (1981) *Internalization in Psychoanalysis*, International Universities Press, New York.

INTERPERSONAL TECHNIQUES

Therapeutic

- Acceptance
- Challenging
- Encouraging action
- Encouraging comparison
- Encouraging descriptions and perceptions
- Exploring
- Focusing
- Giving broad openings
- Offering nonspecific leads
- Offering observations
- Placing the event in time or sequence
- Reflecting
- Restating
- Seeking clarification
- Silences
- Suggesting collaboration
- Summarizing
- Translating into feelings
- Verbalizing what is implied.

Nontherapeutic

- Apportioning responsibility/blame
- Closed advice
- Defending
- Directing, leading, taking control
- Disagreeing
- Feigned attention, interest, involvement
- Giving literal responses
- Inappropriate explaining/lecturing
- Inappropriate interpreting
- Inappropriate self-talk
- Inappropriate use of humour
- Insensitive probing

- Interrogating, threatening
- Introducing irrelevancies
- Labelling and diagnosing
- Making aggressive statements
- Making judgemental statements
- Moralizing, preaching, patronizing
- Prying
- Rejection
- Using denial
- Using stereotyped language
- Verbal reassurances.

INTERPRETATION (*see also*: Insight, Psychodynamic counselling, Transference and counter-transference)

Interpretation is the act of making clear in one language what has been expressed in another; the process of clarifying and elaborating something that is obscure.

The aim of therapeutic interpretation is to bring repressed material, by way of dream-work and free association, from the unconscious into the conscious and so facilitate insight.

Psychological interpretation, which is influenced by the counsellor's model or method, involves verbal communication, dreams, visions, fantasy and metaphors, and involves the therapist in:

- Understanding the material
- Communicating the understanding of the material in such a way that the client not only understands it but takes it on board (interpretations are taken on board when the client accepts their relevance and begins to see how to apply them)
- Delivering the interpretation sensitively so as not to attack defence mechanisms brutally or prematurely.

Psychoanalytic therapists place great emphasis on the interpretation of transference. Freud maintained that interpretation of dream symbols was a model for all interpretation. Other models are less rigid.

In Jung's opinion, interpretations, particularly of dreams, should bring something new to consciousness, should not moralize, should take account of the personal context of the client. The dream belongs exclusively to the dreamer. Interpretations relate only to the personal unconscious.

The dividing line between reflecting feelings and interpretation is very fine. But generally, in interpretation, the counsellor offers an explanation of behaviour. Jacobs makes this point about interpretation:

An interpretative response is aimed more at elucidating unconscious feelings or ideas, of which the client is unaware. A skilful interpretation observes feelings which are close enough to the surface, and allows them to enter into consciousness. A badly timed interpretation, however accurate it seems, is often resisted, because the client is not ready to hear it.

Further reading

Cheshire, N. M. (1975) *The Nature of Psychodynamic Interpretation*, John Wiley, Chichester.

French. T. (1970) *Psychoanalytic Interpretations*, Quadrangle Books, Chicago, IL.

Jacobs, M. (1988) *Psychodynamic Counselling in Action*, Sage Publications, London.

INTIMACY (*see also*: Loneliness)

Intimacy is like a harp. The music it produces comes from all its strings. Intimacy means discovering the particular harmony and melody that is enjoyed by the people involved. Sometimes the melodies will vary. Sometimes a minor key will be more appreciated than a major one.

Source unknown.

Intimacy has been used to describe the process of revealing one's inner self to others; to refer to relatively intense nonverbal engagement; or to describe the stage of life in which the primary developmental task is to establish an emotionally close, trusting and sexual relationship with another person. It is also used as a synonym for closeness, sexuality or marriage. In a more general sense, intimacy is the state of being closely familiar with another person, not necessarily of the opposite sex and not necessarily sexual. Intimacy with at least one other person is generally regarded as an essential ingredient of a healthy and satisfying life. It is thought that intimate relationships are an essential component of human well-being and that their absence causes distress.

Self-disclosure seems to be essential in the development of an intimate relationship; however, too little or too much disclosure, in comparison to personal standards and situational norms, tends to hamper the development of a relationship. We also convey feelings related to intimacy by body language, such as distance, through facial expressions, eye contact and nonvocal cues.

Erik Erikson, in his Lifespan model of development, proposes that young adults must resolve the crisis of intimacy versus isolation. Intimacy is achieved if a primary relationship has several characteristics: mutual trust and openness; co-ordination of work, procreation, and recreation; mutually satisfying sexuality; feelings of love; mutual support and understanding; and trust, openness, and shared experiences.

The absence of an intimate relationship, the inability to share emotions, to trust others or make a commitment to a stable, lasting relationship, is often a significant cause of mental and/or physical distress and an indication of an intimacy disorder. The capacity for intimacy fosters self-worth and a feeling of belonging. Many people, of either sex, have difficulty talking about intimate matters.

Applied to counselling

Erikson defined the major task of the young adult as resolving the ambivalence between intimacy and isolation. The ability to be intimate has its origins in the early parent–child relationship and the successful resolution of any parent–child power struggles (in psychoanalytic terms, the Oedipus complex).

The loneliness of Erikson's theory is that the adolescent feels isolated from the love once experienced from the parents; the intimacy of the young child is no longer felt to be appropriate for the new stage of life. Whatever sexual experiences the adolescent has had do not fill the void and no longer boost his/her self-esteem. Mere repetition of the sexual act no longer satisfies. There is a deep hunger for intimacy, which can only be found in a relationship of commitment. The young adult who fails to develop the capacity for intimate relationships runs the risk of living in isolation and self-absorption in later life.

By implication, people who have been deprived of parental love and a family to act as a role model – children brought up in care, for example – are likely to have difficulty in establishing and maintaining intimate relationships.

The counselling relationship is one of depth and intimacy, unlike any other relationship. For within the security of this unique relationship clients have the freedom to express their feelings knowing that the relationship exists primarily for them. The counsellor makes no demands for self, and the clients can be exactly themselves. This freedom to be themselves within a warm and trusting, and at times challenging, relationship, can be scary for some clients.

The person who finds intimacy difficult may be so terrified of allowing the counsellor into his/her inner world that dialogue is stilted and sterile. In just talking about feelings, the client is forced to come out from behind the safety-barrier that s/he has erected to protect the vulnerable self. If the inability to be intimate has its origins in the parent–child relationship, then it would seem obvious that, in counselling, the remedy lies in the client experiencing intimacy, albeit not from a parent, but delivered with as much love and caring **as if** the counsellor were a parent. As the client begins to experience intimacy, so s/he is able to redraw the boundaries and gradually begin to feel safe with intimacy.

The role of confidant – spouse or someone else – is significant in depression and in working through the sadness of loneliness and isolation and lack of intimacy. If it is important to share intimacies within a caring relationship, then the lack of such a relationship could be conducive to developing depression. Everything must be done to foster an atmosphere in which intimate feelings may be shared. There is no doubt that having an opportunity to talk with someone, to express one's feelings, is a safeguard not only against loneliness and isolation but against weaving, out of one's defensive mechanisms, a blanket to suffocate all feelings. Counselling offers the sort of support that avoids smothering feelings.

In human intimacy there is a secret boundary; neither the experience of being in love nor passion can cross it, though lips be joined together in awful silence, and the heart break asunder with love.

Anna Akhmatova, Russian poet (1889–1966), In Human Intimacy (1915), translated by Dmitri Obolensky.

Further reading

Hinde, R. A. (1979) *Towards Understanding Relationships*, Academic Press, New York.
McAdams, D. P. (1989) *Intimacy: The need to be close*, Doubleday, New York.

J

Jealousy (*see also*: Envy)

Jealousy is a close relative of envy. They have much in common, although they are distinct emotions. They are selfish and malevolent, they are both concerned with persons, and both imply hatred of, and a desire to harm, their object. But there is a deeper malevolence in jealousy than in envy, and jealousy is the stronger and more demanding passion.

Jealousy differs from envy in that it involves three parties: the subject, an object whom the subject loves and a third party who arouses anxiety in the subject about the continuing security of the second party's affections. Envy involves only two parties: the subject and an object whose good fortune or possessions the subject covets. Jealousy is related to possessiveness of the other, envy to comparison of the self with the other. Jealousy is a complex emotion implying the existence of the sentiment of love.

Jealousy is grounded on some estimate of what is due to self rather than a consciousness of inferiority, as in envy. Secondly, there is irritation and displeasure to the jealous person arising from the circumstance that there is a rival to contend (individuals or group). When I am jealous of a person it is because s/he has gained possession of the regard of another whose attachment I claim. This means that I hate the usurping person, but also that I am annoyed with the other who has allowed the rival to intrude. When I feel jealous of an individual's popularity with one person or a group of people, my meaning is that I hate this person for taking away a popularity that I myself claim or aspire to, which I feel is rightly mine. I also resent the person or group who have allowed themselves to come under this person's influence.

It is characteristic of jealousy that it distorts the nature of the person who harbours it. It deprives the person of the power to see things as they really are, rendering the person's judgements unjust. It makes the person suspicious, leading her/him to catch at straws and make much of trifles, and driving us on to acts of cruelty.

Jealousy or something like it seems to be present to some degree in animals, as well as in humans. An example is the response of one's favourite dog when petting another dog or a neighbour's cat. S/he will sometimes slink away and hide and appear to be sulking or will keep pushing her/himself forward to be patted, with sidelong glances at the cat. Some very young children behave in a similar way when their mother pays attention to another child. In both cases the jealous creature is apt to exhibit anger towards the intruder.

The psychoanalytic view

In psychoanalytic terms, jealousy typically forms part of the Oedipus complex. Pathological jealousy, i.e. persistent, unfounded, delusional jealousy, appears to have some fundamental connection with paranoia. According to Freud, jealousy and paranoia are defences against latent homosexuality, but the contemporary psychoanalytic view is to regard the paranoia as the primary member of the triad of jealousy, paranoia and homosexuality.

Pathological jealousy

Marked jealousy is a symptom (usually termed pathological or morbid jealousy) of many psychiatric disorders, including schizophrenia, epilepsy, mood disorders, drug abuse and alcoholism. When jealousy occurs in delusional disorder or as part of another condition it can be a potentially dangerous feature and has been associated with violence in both suicide and murder.

One form of jealousy expresses itself in self-destruction, another expresses itself in energetic obstinacy. Spoiling the sport of others, senseless opposition, the restriction of another's freedom and that person's consequent domination are some of the protean shapes of this character trait.

Jealousy can also be put to the purpose of degrading and reproaching people in order to rob them of their freedom of will, to set them in a rut or to chain them down. Jealousy is an especially well-marked form of the striving for power.

Delusional jealousy, also called 'Othello syndrome' afflicts men, often with no prior psychiatric history, and is the false belief that one's sexual partner is unfaithful.

Alfred Adler's view

On a wider front, jealousy is a character trait, interesting because of its frequency. Jealousy is found in children who want to be superior to one another. Adler says that jealousy is the sister of ambition and that the trait, which may last a lifetime, arises from the feeling of being neglected and a sense of being discriminated against.

Jealousy occurs almost universally among children with the advent of a younger brother or sister who demands more attention from his/her parents and gives an older child occasion to feel like a dethroned monarch. Those children become especially jealous who basked in the warm sunshine of their parents' love prior to the advent of the younger child. Jealousy may be recognized in mistrust and the preparation of ambushes for others, in the critical measurement of others and in the constant fear of being neglected. Just which of these manifestations comes to the fore is dependent entirely upon the previous preparation for social life. Jealousy is an especially well-marked form of the striving for power.

Adler quotes the case of a little girl who had committed three murders by the time she was 8 years of age, to show to what lengths this feeling may go. This little girl was considered 'backward' and was prevented from doing any work because she was 'delicate'. Life for her was relatively pleasant, a situation that changed suddenly when she was 6 years old and a sister was born. A total transformation took place and she persecuted her younger sister with a ruthless hate. The parents, who could not understand her behaviour, became strict, and attempted to show this child her responsibility for every misdeed. It happened that one day a little girl was found dead in the village stream. Some time later another girl was found drowned, and finally the little girl was caught in the act of throwing a third young child into the water. She admitted her murders, was put into an 'insane asylum' for observation and was finally placed in a 'sanatorium' for further education.

In this case, the little girl's jealousy of her own sister was transferred to other young children. It was noticed that she had no hostile sentiments toward boys, and it seemed as though she saw the picture of her younger sister in these murdered children and had attempted to satisfy her feeling of vengeance for her neglect in her murderous deeds.

Jealousy also invariably involves the spirit of competition and, as the above text suggests, a client who has strong jealous feelings (although not necessarily directed at the counsellor) may also harbour feelings of suspicion, and these may well be directed at the counsellor. Such a client may also experience great difficulty in the intimacy of the counselling relationship.

JOHARI WINDOW (*see also*: Insight, Feedback, Self-disclosure)

This is a name coined from the names of the psychologists Joseph Luft and Harry Ingham. It describes a model of four 'windows' to represent personality and is used to gain insight through feedback and self-disclosure (Figure 1).

	Known to self	Hidden from self
Known to others	**Arena**	**Blind spot**
Hidden from others	**Façade**	**Unknown**

Figure I

The Johari Window

Arena: Known to self and others

- Free and open exchange of information
- Behaviour is public and freely available
- The arena increases in size as trust grows.

Blind spot: Perceived by others, hidden from self

- Self-awareness is lacking
- Motives, feelings and behaviours perceived by others
- Communicated by what is said and how
- Communicated nonverbally.

Façade: Hidden from others, known to self

- Private and secret
- Rarely disclosed
- Fear of hurt, rejection, judgement.

Unknown: Hidden from self and from others

This is the realm of the unconscious and subconscious. Unconscious material is often hinted at through nonverbal language. The unconscious is made up of early childhood memories and feelings, latent potentialities and unrecognized conflicts and complexes. It is possible to look – delicately – at subconscious material. Exploring truly unconscious material is rarely appropriate except in specialized settings.

The internal boundaries of the windows are movable: up, down or across. The extent to which the Blind spot and Façade are reduced, and the Arena enlarged, is entirely dependent upon the willingness to give and ask for feedback and to disclose. The size and shape of the Arena is determined by the balance between giving and soliciting feedback.

A large arena suggests:

- Behaviour that is open, above board and not liable to be misinterpreted
- That other people do not have to make guesses
- A fairly even balance between giving and soliciting feedback.

Large Arenas are not necessary nor appropriate for every situation. Too large an Arena may threaten casual relationships.

A large blind spot suggests:

- Someone who gives feedback and solicits very little
- A 'telling' style of communication
- Someone who may be highly critical – 'I speak my mind'
- Usually, insensitivity to feedback
- Rarely an effective listener
- Disclosures that are out of touch, evasive or distorted

A large façade suggests:

- Someone who asks questions, asks for opinions but gives little information or feedback
- Someone who uses intellectualization as a defence
- Someone who withholds feelings
- Someone who solicits feedback but gives little.

A large unknown suggests:

- Someone who knows little about the deeper personal life

- Perhaps the silent member of a group; the 'observer'; the 'mystery man'
- Someone surrounded by a shell
- Someone who says 'I learn more by listening'
- Someone not actively involved in a group.
- Someone who gives little feedback and solicits little
- A small Arena maintained at the expense of self-exploration and personal growth.

As data are moved from the Blind spot and the Façade, the Arena is enlarged, so new material becomes available from the Unknown and the person experiences insight.

The model expanded

While the model is useful to use by oneself or with a partner, it is more powerful when working with a group, because feedback is multiplied.

The left hand side represents 'Things I know about myself'
The right-hand side represents 'Things I don't know about myself'
The top row represents 'Things they know about me'
The bottom row represents 'Things they don't know about me'.

The process

When a group comes into being, the individual Arenas are quite small. This is natural and to be expected. Disclosure is generally best given and accepted in small doses.

Arenas increase in size as the level of trust increases between individuals or between the individual and the group, as information and feelings are shared. There should be no forcing of the boundaries. To do so would cause alarm.

Blind spots contain information that we ourselves do not know about but that the group share, although they may not be conscious that they do. As people begin to participate in the group they communicate all kinds of information; verbal cues, mannerisms, and the way they says things or the style in which they relate to one another. We may not always like to know what we communicate, so feedback can be challenging.

The Façade is the front we put up to protect ourselves from other people, to keep ourselves safe and to keep others at a distance. The fear, if articulated, would be something like, 'If the group knew my feelings, perceptions, opinions about other people in the group, they would attack, reject or hurt me in some way'. So, we hold back, thinking that they won't perceive what is going on behind the façade. However, that is a fallacy; in some way we portray what we wish to keep hidden.

Feedback and self-disclosure involve taking risks. We try out a small risk then, when we see that we are not demoralized or annihilated, we take heart and can then risk something greater. If we never take risks, we will never learn the reality or unreality of our assumptions. Another reason why we withhold feedback is that it gives us power and we can then manipulate others.

The Unknown is the part that neither the group nor the individual knows. If we know something, it is not unconscious. The model suggests that material will pop through from the unconscious as and when it is ready. Some people play the game of 'I'm a psychoanalyst' and probe other people's unconscious motives and behaviours. This can cause trauma and should be vigorously resisted in groups that are not specifically set up for such purposes. At the same time, the amateur, self-appointed, analyst will generally resist any probing of his/her unconscious.

However aware we become, there will always be other depths of the unconscious to plumb.

Increasing the arena

We can increase the Arena by reducing the Blind spot. Since the Blind spot contains information that the group members know about us but of which we are unaware, we can increase our awareness by soliciting feedback. However willing we are to receive feedback, sometimes it hurts. Sometimes it is accurate and at other times the feedback may not be accurate, but we must be prepared to examine it openly and honestly.

We can increase the Arena by decreasing the Façade. This area includes information that we have not given to the group – about them and about us. When we give feedback in this way, we disclose our feelings, reactions and thoughts about ourselves and others. Because we are open, the group does not need to guess where we stand or what we are thinking or feeling.

Further reading

Hanson, P. C. (1973) The Johari Window: a model for soliciting and giving feedback. In: *1973 Annual Handbook for Group Facilitators*. University Associates, San Diego, CA.

K

KLEIN, MELANIE (1881–1960)

Born in Vienna, Klein lived most of her life in England and is linked with the Objects Relations school. Her interest in psychoanalysis arose from her time as a patient of Ferenczi, although she never trained in psychiatry.

Encouraged by Abraham, she developed her own system of child analysis and it is her contribution to child psychiatry for which she is mostly remembered. Play, she believed, is the child's symbolic way of controlling anxiety. She used free play with toys to gain insight into the fantasies, anxieties and defences associated with the early years of life.

Klein's personality theory agrees with Freud's about the life and death instincts, and that inborn aggression is an extension of the death instinct. Oral sadism is where the death instinct is directed outward, giving rise to fantasies of the bad, devouring breast. These unconscious fantasies, from birth onward, become the origins of love and hate.

Other powerful, negative emotions, include:

- Envy, which is derived from the fantasy of the wilfully withholding breast and finds expression in greed, penis envy, envy of the creativity of others and guilt over one's own creativity
- Jealousy, which develops from the Oedipus triangle. A third person is hated because that person takes the love and libidinal energy from the desired object. In oedipal terms, the son directs hate at the father for stealing the mother's love, love that is rightfully his.

The 'good breast' is responsible for all positive, gratifying feelings associated with the life instinct, feelings that reinforce trust and balance the life and death instincts.

Gratitude, the predominant emotion, allows the expression of trust and decreases greed. It is the origin of authentic generosity.

The term **part object** refers to parts of the person that are perceived by the infant and related to as the 'whole'.

Some major Kleinian concepts

Anxiety
Anxiety, the ego's expression of the death instinct, becomes fear of persecutory objects, which in turn leads to fear of internalized persecutors. The major fears are **oral**, the fear of being devoured; **anal**, the fear of being controlled and poisoned, and **oedipal**, the fear of castration.

Introjection and projection
Both contribute to the growth of the ego through trust and to ego defence

through paranoid feelings. Which one is dominant depends on whether what is introjected or projected is perceived as good or bad.

Splitting

Splitting characterizes the very young. It is the active separation into good or bad of experiences, perceptions and emotions linked to objects. Splitting interferes with the accurate perception of reality and nurtures denial. The opposite of splitting is synthesis. This takes place when the infant is able to distinguish part from whole objects.

Internalization

Internalization of the good object is a prerequisite for the development of a healthy ego firmly rooted in reality. A predominance of aggressive feelings works against a healthy ego. An ego that is based on unhealthy internalization leads to excessive idealization and excessive splitting.

Paranoid-schizoid position

The paranoid-schizoid position, which occurs during the first 6 months of life, is characterized by:

- Splitting
- Idealization
- Denial
- Projective identification
- Part object relationships
- Persecutory fears about self-preservation.

Depressive position

The depressive position, adopted during the second 6 months of life, is characterized by idealization of the good object, to avoid destroying the object. Depressive idealization creates an over-dependence on others in later stages of development.

Superego

Klein believed that the superego starts to develop within the second 6 months of life. A return to the paranoid-schizoid position may occur when excessive pressure from the superego prevents working through the depressive position.

Split-off, and projected, bad objects are later introjected and form the basis of the superego. Sadism, once projected, is then re-introjected, resulting in guilt.

The internalization of mainly bad objects is normally outweighed by internalization of good objects, although there is always some contamination by the bad objects. A perfectionist superego imposes the harsh demands of infantile virtues. A balanced superego responds realistically to demands for improvement on the one hand and sublimation on the other.

The Oedipus complex

In Kleinian theory, the early stages of the complex develop from the first year of life. The desire in both sexes for the good breast becomes a desire for the father's penis. Likewise, the bad breast is displaced on to the bad penis. When a boy perceives his father's penis to be bad, it makes a healthy father–son relationship difficult.

When the oedipal relationship is not resolved, the boy is likely to develop sexual inhibitions and a fear of women. Castration fears arise from an oral-sadistic desire to destroy the penis.

For a girl, the good breast prepares the way for expecting a good penis. Intense oral aggression prepares the way for rejecting a positive oedipal relationship with the mother. An Oedipus complex in a girl develops when the mother is perceived as possessing the father's penis. Penis envy arises from oral sadism, not from an envy of the male genitals.

Envy of the opposite sex occurs in both sexes.

Working through (*see also* main entry)
Working-through of the depressive position consists of:

- **Reparation** (the origin of sublimation) is the mechanism of trying to repair damage done to a good object by expressing love and gratitude, and by so doing, preserve it
- **Reality testing** increases as splitting decreases; love from the mother accelerates reality testing
- **Ambivalence** is the infant's awareness and acceptance of both love and hate toward the same object, with the eventual triumph of love over hate
- Mourning in adult life reactivates the depressive position and guilt of infancy. In the latter, however, the mother is present to help the infant to work through toward wholeness.

Fixation at the paranoid-schizoid position
This may result in either a paranoid or a schizoid personality.

- The **paranoid personality** combines:
  - Denial of reality
  - Excessive projective identification
  - Pathological splitting
  - Confusional states
  - Development of paranoia (fear of external persecutors)
  - Hypochondriasis.
- The **schizoid personality** combines:
  - Shallow emotions
  - Limited capacity to tolerate guilt feelings
  - Tendency to experience objects as hostile
  - Withdrawal from object relations
  - Artificiality and superficiality in social adaptation.

Fixation at the depressive position
This may result in pathological mourning or the development of manic defences.

- **Pathological mourning** may lead to the development of a sadistic superego, which evokes extreme guilt and feelings that the whole world is empty of love. Pathological mourning is characterized by:
  - Cruelty
  - Demands for perfection
  - Hatred of anything instinctual
  - Despair
  - Self-reproach
  - Suicide, which may be an attempt to protect the good object by destroying the bad self
  - Hypochondriacal delusions
  - Fantasies of world destruction.
- **Manic defences** include:
  - Omnipotence, based on identification with an idealized good object, accompanied by
    - Denial of reality
    - Identification with the sadistic superego
    - Introjection – object hunger that can never be satisfied
    - An exalted state of power
    - Manic idealization; the merging of one's exalted self with idealized objects.

Therapy

Klein believed that analysis of children could protect them from serious guilt-producing impulses. She favoured:

- Direct, immediate interpretations of the child's unconscious motivations
- The analysis of the child's feelings, displaced from the parents and transferred to the analyst
- The analyst, from the very commencement, interpreting the unconscious paranoid-schizoid and depressive fantasies within the transference.

In interpreting play as the symbolic expression of conflicts and anxieties, the analyst does not offer the child reassurance but works exclusively with the transference, in language the child can understand.

Counselling from a Kleinian perspective, as with almost every other approach, is based on the development of the relationship between counsellor and client. Within this relationship clients are encouraged to face whatever it is that is causing their immediate anxiety and to achieve a healthy balance between the feelings of love and hate. The hoped-for outcome of counselling is that clients:

- Will achieve insight into the causes of their anxiety
- Will be able to establish and maintain more satisfactory relationships because they feel released from their fixations and repressions
- Will experience freedom to live their lives with increased wellbeing
- Will enjoy more ego strength to cope with the stresses of life
- Will feel that they want to survive rather than feel they are always losers.

Cooper identifies five criteria in selecting clients for counselling:

- Their problems can be clearly defined in psychodynamic terms
- They are motivated enough to change
- They have insight into their previous behaviour
- They have enough internal strength to cope with the counselling process
- There is evidence that they are able to accept and sustain a long-standing therapeutic relationship and a relationship with significant others in their immediate surroundings.

The Kleinian style is formal, with the client being offered a chair or a couch. The number of sessions is five or six a week for analysis, but in counselling this would not be the norm. Free association and interpretation are used within a relaxed and facilitative atmosphere.

Whatever the client's needs, however caring and compassionate the counsellor, s/he must never become a surrogate parent. However close counsellor and client become, the counsellor must remain detached and separate; this helps the client face reality. The boundary between counsellor and client must remain firmly established. Client and counsellor are two separate and distinct people.

Further reading

Cooper, C. (1996) Psychodynamic therapy: the Kleinian approach. In: *Handbook of Individual Therapy*, (ed. W. Dryden), Sage Publications, London.

L

LABELLING (*see also*: Stigma)

In its broad sense, to label is to describe, classify, categorize and designate objects, and labelling helps us make sense and order of the world around. It is also used to describe the process by which people are designated by some behaviour that society has called 'deviant'.

Labelling is a two-way process: the person so labelled has one set of responses; the person labelling has another set. Clusters of behaviours are attached to specific labels or stereotypes; the role and its behaviours have to be learned and internalized. People so labelled then tend to behave in a way that reinforces the negative feeling attached to the labels.

People and society may derive gains from the labels and roles people are given and have accepted, i.e. 'the sick one'. Society may feel freed from a burden. Removing the label may itself be therapeutic but new behaviours also have to be learned, as well as changing attitudes of others. The stigmatizing and dehumanizing effect of labelling was one of the processes that the antipsychiatry movement brought to notice, leading to a more humane and personalized approach to psychiatry.

At a different level, clients may carry around invisible labels put upon them by other people, often at an age too young to refuse to accept them. Some examples of labels are: 'You're stupid', 'You'll never do anything with your life', 'You're too delicate', 'You need looking after'. Such labels seriously affect the person's self-esteem. Getting the client to identify the labels is the first step toward change. When the label has been identified, getting the client to substitute a positive label is often a major step in building self-esteem.

Labelling and antipsychiatry

One of the things that Szasz and Laing and the antipsychiatry school loudly condemned was diagnosing someone as mentally ill. The *Oxford English Dictionary* defines diagnosis as 'determination of the nature of a diseased condition; identification of a disease by careful investigation of its symptoms and history; also, the opinion (formally stated) resulting from such investigation'. A medical definition is 'the process of determining, through examination and analysis, the nature of a patient's illness'. Both of these definitions are straightforward and logical, so why should diagnosis create problems?

Stage 1 – diagnosis

Diagnosis is the first stage in the process of what has become known as 'labelling'. A person is diagnosed, but then a curious thing happens: the person becomes the illness. John is not referred to as 'John, who is suffering from schizophrenia' (or depression, or any other illness) but 'John, who **is** a schizophrenic'. John's character has thus changed – he has been labelled. The same thing applies to all sorts of conditions – 'He is a geriatric', 'She is a Down's syndrome', 'He is an amputee'. The list is endless.

It is so easy to drop into the trap of referring to 'the mentally ill' or 'the mentally handicapped' or 'the disabled'. Labelling dehumanizes the person and in so doing emphasizes difference, implying that those who are so labelled are deviant – not normal – in some way. It was precisely this dehumanizing that sparked off the antipsychiatry movement.

A related aspect is that, once a diagnosis is made, the person becomes a 'patient' and enters into a different sort of relationship; s/he assumes a new identity, a labelled identity. Once the diagnosis has been made, the person (now called 'the patient') becomes one of a vast number of people – past and present – who all carry the same label.

Stage 2 – treatment and prognosis

The next stage after diagnosis and labelling is treatment and prognosis. Doctors (in almost all branches of medicine) are expected to have certain god-like qualities mixed with the divination when it comes to declaring a prognosis – the duration and direction of a particular illness or condition. That is something society has come to expect, and this in turn puts the psychiatrist into a strait-jacket, for the psychiatrist can only work on assumptions and experience, and in order to do this s/he may resort to treating all patients with a certain diagnosis in very much the same way. Again, this is what the antipsychiatrists call 'dehumanizing the individual' – lumping all such people together without regard for their individuality. Medication is prescribed according to what works for the majority – again, without account being taken of the real person.

The antipsychiatry lobby tried very hard to remove the label of mental illness from people and to introduce a more humane regime. To some extent they have succeeded, and counselling, where the individual is respected, is one way of redressing the balance. Perhaps the growth of counselling skills for people working with people with mental illness will – over the next few decades – prove to be another quiet revolution, as they somehow strive to perform a delicate balancing act between dehumanizing and humanizing regimes.

Further reading

Horowitz, A. V. (1982) *The Social Control of Mental Illness*, Academic Press, New York.
Szasz, T. (1962) *The Myth of Mental Illness*, Secker & Warburg: London.
Szasz, T. (1973) *Ideology and Insanity*, Calder & Boyars, New York.
Wing, J. K. (1978) *Reasoning About Madness*, Oxford University Press, Oxford.

LEARNED HELPLESSNESS

A term, introduced by Seligman, derived from the response of dogs to inescapable stress and related to depression in humans. After prolonged stress, dogs became inactive and submissive, lost appetite and failed to escape from electric shocks, from which they had previously known how to escape.

The learned helplessness model has been applied to depression and proposes that, when people are faced with situations – often in childhood – and have no control over the outcome and cannot initiate an escape, they learn the futility of trying to respond. The inference is that such people become victims of circumstance and as such cannot be held responsible for what happens to them. The theory states that they learn to exploit their weaknesses and complaints in order to force others to do something for them. This behaviour drives them deeper into the darkness of depression and isolates them still further from others. Every manipulation that results in increased isolation reinforces the negative view they hold of themselves.

However, the learned helplessness model can be applied to other mental dispositions and life situations, e.g. social powerlessness. It can also be applied to victims of sexual and physical abuse, where there seems no escape. For example, women who are battered by their men often say they feel trapped and unable to take what seems obvious action.

Further reading

Seligman, M. E. P. (1973) Fall into helplessness. *Psychology Today*, 7, 43–48.
Seligman, M. E. P. (1975) *Helplessness*, Freeman, San Francisco, CA.

LEFT/RIGHT BRAIN

The left and right hemispheres of the brain specialize in different activities.

Left brain

The 'left, logical, systematic brain':

- Controls movements on the right side of the body
- Is more concerned with 'active doing'.

Left brain cognitive style is predominantly concerned with:

- Analysis and deduction
- Convergent thinking
- Facts, data, figures
- The end product
- Structure
- Logical, sequential, linear thought
- The mathematics mode
- Order
- Processing
- Rationality
- Reducing problems to workable segments
- Science and technology
- Step-by-step precision

- Using a highly sequential approach
- Verbal, literal, concrete language
- Working to well-defined plans.

'Left brain' language patterns

- 'Why don't we look at the facts?'
- 'These data show us that...'
- 'We must work to specific objectives'
- 'Here is what I think – A, B, C'
- 'You haven't explained yourself'
- 'Where's the logic in that?'
- 'This is what you do – 1, 2, 3.'
- 'I'll have to work it out carefully'.

'Left brain' nonverbal patterns

- Creates endless lists
- Puts everything down in strict time order
- Spends much time on detail
- Must get one point clear before moving on.

Some typical 'left brain' occupations

- Accountant
- Administrator
- Computer programmer
- Engineer
- Personnel specialist
- Production manager
- Purchasing agent
- Systems analyst.

Right brain

The 'right, intuitive brain':

- Controls movements on the left side of the body
- Is more concerned with the whole, not parts.

'Right brain' cognitive style is predominantly concerned with:

- Abstract topics
- Artistic expression
- Body image
- Concentrating on ideas and feelings
- Constructive tasks
- Crafts

- Creativity
- Divergent, global thinking
- Emotions
- Focusing on the process, not the outcome
- Using experience
- Nonverbal knowledge through images
- Perception
- Prayer, meditation, mysticism
- Problem-solving
- Perceiving
- Remembering faces
- Spontaneity
- What is visual
- Working with symbols and fantasy, dreams
- Working with metaphors and imagery
- Working with opposites
- Working with the unknown.

'Right brain' language patterns

- 'My gut feeling is ...'
- 'I sense that ...'
- 'Can't we look at the whole picture?'
- 'Let's look at things on global terms'
- 'The solution is really quite simple'
- 'Common sense tells me ...'
- 'I know the answer, but I'm not sure how'.

'Right brain' nonverbal patterns

- Uses a lot of visual aids
- Becomes agitated over data
- Often appears to be disorganized
- 'Thinks' with the eyes
- Displays the problem graphically

Some typical 'right brain' occupations

- Advertising agent
- Counsellor/therapist
- Graphic artist
- Marketing manager.

In Jungian typology

Left-handed (right brain) activities are also associated with the feminine principle. The left brain is more associated with extraversion, sensing, thinking and judgement. The right brain is more associated with introversion, intuition, feeling and perception. For left-handed people the specialization is not so consistent. Even in right-handed people it is not an 'either/or'.

Damage to the left hemisphere often interferes with language ability. Damage to the right hemisphere is likely to cause disturbance to spatial awareness of one's own body. Damage to the left brain may prove disastrous to an author, scientist or mathematician but may not prove so damaging to a musician, craftsman or artist. The hemispheres have a partnership function. A poet using deep feelings, imagery and metaphor draws on the right brain, and then the left for the words to express what the right side creates. The hemispheres may also be antagonistic: when, for example, the left hemisphere becomes too aggressive, trying to solve everything with logic and analysis, intuition and feelings are subdued.

Some clients experience difficulty moving between left and right hemisphere activities, but this does not mean that they should not be encouraged to do so. A person who is more left- than right-brain orientated, might chose to work with intuition or imagery, thus tapping into parts that normal activity leaves untouched. A person who is more right- than left-brain orientated might chose to work with a cognitive approach, thus developing sharper thinking ability.

Further reading

Buzan, T. (1983) *Use Both Sides of Your Brain*, E. P. Dutton, New York.
Edwards, B. (1982) *Drawing on the Right Side of the Brain*, Collins, London.
Ornstein, R. E. (1975) *The Psychology of Consciousness*, Pelican, Harmondsworth.
Wonder, J. and Donvan, P. (1984) *Whole-Brain Thinking*, William Morrow, New York.
Zdenek, M. (1983) *The Right-Brain Experience*, Corgi, London.

LIBIDO

A psychoanalytic concept originally applied to sexual desires. Later it became associated with 'vital impulse' or 'vital (mental) energy'. Freud regarded the ego as a reservoir that supplies objects with libido and reabsorbs it from them, although its source is the id.

In psychoanalytic theory, two drives – one for sexual pleasure, called libido, the other called aggression – motivate and propel most behaviour. In the infant the libido first manifests itself by making sucking an activity with pleasurable sensations in the mouth. Later, similar pleasure is experienced in the anus during bowel movements, and finally these erotically tinged pleasures are experienced when the sexual organ is manipulated. Thus psychosexual development progresses from the oral through the anal to the phallic stage. (Phallic, in psychoanalytic theory, refers to both male and female sexual organs.)

For Jung, libido is 'psychic energy', the intensity or value of a psychic process. It has no moral, aesthetic or intellectual value. Energy can never disappear: it is dynamic, it always produces something. Jung linked libido to introversion, or inward into the realm of images, ideas and the unconscious; and extroversion or outward into the world of other people and objects.

Psychological conflict can be thought of as a disturbance in the flow of psychical energy, a natural process, if one thinks of conflict in relation to nature. In nature there is a continuous cycle of death and rebirth. When the life and death instincts are thought of in this way, the conflict becomes more understandable.

Transformations of libido from one sphere of expression to another, e.g. from sexuality to religion, if it is unconscious, makes up the defence mechanism of sublimation. If it is at a conscious level, then strictly speaking it is substitution.

LIFESPAN PSYCHOLOGY

Erik Homburger Erikson (1902–94) was a German-American psychoanalyst who had a major influence on the behavioural and social sciences.

In his classic study, *Childhood and Society* (1950; 2nd edn 1963), Erikson introduced his theories on identity, identity crisis (which term he popularized) and psychosexual development. Erikson proposed that people grow through experiencing a series of crises. They must achieve trust, autonomy, initiative, competence, their own identity, generativity (or productivity), integrity and acceptance.

Lifespan psychology is the study of people throughout life. Erikson, building on the work of earlier theorists, is the name most associated with lifespan psychology. Erikson's view of personality development has widely influenced the views of educators.

Psychological development does not necessarily parallel physical maturity. Physical maturation is predictable within reasonable time limits, within specific societies and cultures. The eight stages represent points along a continuum of development and each stages is accompanied by physical, cognitive, instinctual and sexual changes. How these changes are resolved results either in regression or in growth and the development of specific virtues, defined by Erikson as inherent strengths. With every stage the individual acquires a specific 'virtue' or quality but only if that stage has been worked through and all the conflicts resolved.

Erikson's stages ('nuclear crises') of the psychosocial development model

Stage of development – Basic trust versus mistrust
Approximate age – Infancy: birth to about 18 months
Virtue – Hope

If the caretaker provides for the infant's needs, hope develops. Severe disturbance of this early relationship that does not result in the development of a sense of trust or the virtue of hope is likely to lead to severe emotional disturbance in later life.

Stage of development – Autonomy versus shame and doubt
Approximate age – Toddler: about 18 months to about 3 years
Virtue – Will.

Parental control that is too strict or rigid, or control exercised too early, may interfere with the child's developing need for autonomy. Lack of appropriate control exposes the child to dangers from his/her own desires. Judicious control helps the child to develop a healthy balance between loving good will and hateful self-insistence; between co-operation and wilfulness; and between appropriate self-expression on the one hand and compulsive self-expression on the other. Too rigid a control can result in compliance. Problems with control in early life may manifest later as being suspicious of other people. According to Erikson, the obsessive-compulsive personality is rooted in the earlier conflicting tendencies to hold on or let go.

Stage of development – Initiative versus guilt
Approximate age – Pre-school: about 3 years to about 5 years
Virtue – Purpose.

A stage characterized by inquisitiveness, competitiveness and physical aggression, jealousy and rivalry. The stage in which the Oedipus complex is manifested. The development of conscience, as 'forbidden' impulses, thoughts and desires are repressed. The virtue of purpose grows as the child develops ambition. Inability to resolve the conflict between initiative and guilt, says Erikson, is the foundation for the personality of the person who creates stress by driving himself or herself too hard.

Stage of development – Industry versus inferiority
Approximate age – School age: about 5 years to about 13 years
Virtue – Competence.

This is the stage where the young person discovers the value and rewards of the 'work principle' through diligence and persistence. In order to move through this stage, conflict from previous stages has to be resolved. Interference with the development of this stage can lead to despair of ever achieving anything, coupled with feelings of inferiority and inadequacy. The ability to work with and get on with people has its beginnings in this stage of development.

Stage of development – Identity versus role confusion
Approximate age – Adolescence and young adulthood: about 13 years to about 21 years
Virtue – Fidelity.

The burning issue is identity – who am I? young people in this stage are more concerned with appearing right in the eyes of others than with knowing how and who they feel they are. This is the stage of cliques, of alliances, coupled with an intolerance of individual differences. The young person complies with the group, rather than with his/her own self-identity. The group gives identity. This is the stage of falling in love and a developing concept of faithfulness. Failure to form a clear sense of identity can lead to gender-identity confusion and delinquency.

Stage of development – Intimacy versus isolation
Approximate age – Young adulthood: about 21 years to about 40 years
Virtue – Love.

The main issue of a balanced identity is that the person develops an ability to both love and work. Love is to be interpreted as the ability to be intimate and not to be limited to genital love. People who do not have a clear identity might find difficulty in establishing and maintaining intimate relationships, because intimacy demands mutual giving and receiving. Both loving and work have to be held in balance; obsession with either can be destructive and indicate unresolved conflicts over identity.

Stage of development – Productivity versus stagnation
Approximate age – Middle adulthood: about 40 years to about 60 years
Virtue – Care.

Erikson refers to 'generativity', the concern for the next generation. It implies the passing on of knowledge and skills, having concern for all the generations as well as for social institutions. The person has usually achieved a satisfying role in life. Failure to develop generativity may lead to excesses at work or in personal life, including infidelity; mid-life crises or premature physical or psychological old age may occur.

Stage of development – Ego integrity versus despair
Approximate age – Later adulthood: about 60 years to death
Virtue – Wisdom.

Integrity, according to Erikson, is acceptance; acceptance of self, of the significant people in one's life. One of the crucial elements of this stage is the realization (and that is acceptance) that the significant people (parents, for example) were as they were and that no amount of wishful thinking will change that. That is, accepting responsibility for one's own life story. Integrity helps a person face the reality of death. One the other hand, failure to attain integrity leads to a deep contempt for the whole, coupled with resentment, bitterness and regret that there is not enough time left to start again.

Lifespan psychology in counselling

Life-span psychology has produced major contributions in the fields of:

- Relationships between generations
- Cognitive development
- Age and the social system
- Social policy
- Occupational choice.

One of the implications of the above model for counsellors is that development is lifelong. Secondly, to view a client from a psychosocial development perspective adds another dimension to one's understanding of the client's frame of reference. It is highly doubtful that every last conflict of one stage could ever be resolved in order to make sense of the next stage, but what Erikson's model does imply is that serious disturbance in one stage of development might give the counsellor a focus to work on and enable her/him to grow.

Further reading

Newton, P. M. and Newton, D. S. (1995) Erik H. Erikson. In: *Comprehensive Textbook of Psychiatry*, 6th edn, (eds H. J. Kaplan and B. J. Sadock), Williams & Wilkins, Baltimore, MD.

LISTENING (*see also*: Interpersonal techniques)

Sensitive, active listening is an important way to bring about personality changes in attitudes and the way we behave toward ourselves and others. When we listen, people tend to become:

- More emotionally mature
- More open to experiences
- Less defensive
- More democratic
- Less authoritarian.

When we are listened to, we listen to ourselves with more care and are able to express thoughts and feelings more clearly.

Self-esteem is enhanced through active listening, because the threat of having one's ideas and feelings criticized is greatly reduced. Because we do not have to defend, we are able to see ourselves for what we truly are, and are then in a better position to change.

Listening, and responding to what we hear, is influenced by our own frame of reference. Therapeutic listening is also influenced by one's theoretical model.

Poor listening habits identified

- Not paying attention
- Pretend-listening
- Listening but not hearing the meaning
- Rehearsing what to say
- Interrupting the speaker in mid-sentence
- Hearing what is expected
- Feeling defensive, expecting an attack
- Listening for something to disagree with.

Things to avoid

- **Trying to get people to see themselves as we see them or would like to see**

them: This is control and direction and is more for our needs than for theirs. The less we need to evaluate, influence, control and direct, the more we enable ourselves to listen with understanding.

- **Responding to a demand for decisions, action, judgement and evaluation or agreeing with someone against someone else**: We are in danger of losing our objectivity. The surface question is usually the vehicle with a deeper need as its passenger.
- **Shouldering responsibility for other people**: We remove from them the right to be active participants in the problem-solving process. Active involvement releases energy, it does not drain it from the other person. Active participation is a process of thinking with people instead of thinking for or about them.
- **Passing judgements – critical or favourable**: Judgement is generally patronizing.
- **Using platitudes and clichés**: These demonstrate either lack of interest or verbal poverty.
- **Giving verbal reassurances**: This is insulting, for they demean the problem.

Things to do

- **Get into the person's frame of reference**: Listen for total meaning, which is content and feelings. Both require hearing and responding to. In some instances the content is far less important than the feeling for which the words are but vehicles. We must try to remain sensitive to the total meaning the message has to the speaker:
  - What is s/he trying to tell me?
  - What does this mean to this person?
  - How does this person see this situation?
- Note all cues. Not all communication is verbal. Truly sensitive listening notes:
  - Body posture
  - Breathing changes
  - Eye movements
  - Facial expression
  - Hand movements
  - Hesitancies
  - Inflection
  - Mumbled words
  - Stressed words.

What we communicate by listening

We communicate interest in the importance of the speaker, respect for the speaker's thoughts (not necessarily agreement) and non-evaluation, and we validate the person's worth.

Listening demonstrates, it does not tell. Listening catches on. Just as anger is normally met with anger, so listening encourages others to listen. Listening is a constructive behaviour and the person who consistently listens with under-standing is the person who is most likely to be listened to.

Responding as a part of listening

Passive listening, without responding, is deadening and is demeaning. We should never assume that we have really understood until we can communicate that understanding to the full satisfaction of the other person. Effective listening hinges on constant clarification to establish true understanding.

Effective listeners

- Put the talker at ease
- Limit their own talking
- Are attentive
- Remove distractions
- Get inside the talker's frame of reference
- Are patient and don't interrupt
- Watch for feeling words
- Are aware of their own biases
- Listen to the paralinguistics
- Are aware of body language.

Listening with the 'third ear'

The phrase 'listening with the third ear' was coined by Theodor Reik to point up the quality of psychotherapy where active listening goes beyond the five senses. The 'third ear' hears what is said between sentences and without words, what is expressed soundlessly, what the speaker feels and thinks.

Principles for third ear listening

- Have a reason or purpose for listening
- Suspend judgement
- Resist distractions
- Wait before responding
- Repeat verbatim
- Rephrase the message accurately
- Identify important themes
- Reflect content and search for meaning
- Be ready to respond.

We convey nonacceptance by:

- Advising, giving solutions: 'Why don't you...?'
- Evaluating, blaming: 'You are definitely wrong'
- Interpreting, analysing: 'What you need is...'
- Lecturing, informing: 'Here are the facts...'
- Name-calling, shaming: 'You are stupid'

- Ordering, directing: 'You have to ...'
- Praising, agreeing: 'You are definitely right'
- Preaching, moralizing: 'You ought to ...'
- Questioning, probing: 'Why did you ...?'
- Sympathizing, supporting: 'You'll be OK'
- Warning, threatening: 'You had better not ...'
- Withdrawing, avoiding: 'Let's forget it'.

Further reading

Reik, T. (1972) *Listening With the Third Ear*, Pyramid Publications, New York.

Wismer, J. N. (1978) Communication effectiveness: active listening and sending feeling messages. In: *1978 Annual Handbook for Group Facilitators*, University Associates, San Diego, CA.

LISTENING, BELIEFS ABOUT

These 22 points about listening are adapted from Nelson-Jones, R. (1986) *Human Relationship Skills*, Holt Rinehart & Winston, London, and used with permission. I have altered and developed this questionnaire to include the results of several years work with it. People are asked to score each question as True or False.

1. **Most people are brought up to be good listeners**
   False. Many people answer this as True, possibly because as children we were very often told to 'listen' or 'pay attention'. And very often if the child does not, there is some punishment. But this is not the listening we mean in counselling.

2. **Listening to others means also listening to ourselves**
   True. 'Listening to myself' often causes confusion. Many confuse listening to the words and how they are expressed with the inner listening to attitudes and one's own judgements.

3. **It is always up to other people to communicate precisely what they want to say**
   False. This often results in heated discussion in training groups. In normal conversation, yes, each one of us does have an obligation to say clearly what we want to. But do we always? In counselling, however, many clients do not have the facility of clear speaking. Part of counselling skill is to help the person to clarify constantly.

4. **We sometimes listen because we are afraid of revealing something about ourselves**
   True. This is getting at the fact that, here, 'listening' has moved from being active and has become passive, and that if we respond we may reveal something we would rather keep safe.

5. **Talking is more important than listening**
   False. Only a few people believe that talking is more important than listening in counselling.

6. **What people reveal about themselves is likely to influence what others tell them**

   True. Some people find this difficult. They confuse 'reveal' with verbal disclosure. After discussion they usually agree that we reveal many things about ourselves, indirectly, through speech and nonverbal behaviour. This question is also to do with openness in communication.

7. **To be a good listener, one has to feel emotional about issues**

   False. When we are impassioned about something, there is a danger of getting so 'hot' over it that we cease to listen.

8. **When we repeatedly do not listen to and understand someone, we could be accused of a form of psychological violence**

   True. The phrase 'psychological violence' generally pulls people up with a jolt. Some modify their views, others react strongly against it; others reserve judgement. Most people agree, whatever the word used, that repeated nonlistening is psychologically damaging.

9. **We are more likely to hear messages that agree with the views we hold of ourselves than messages that challenge our views**

   True. Some people argue quite strongly against this, putting forward the view that they often look for views that are contrary to their own. In counselling, we need constantly to be aware that this is a possibility.

10. **We listen well when we have something to say on a subject**

    False. This is similar to question 7. However, the difference is that it focuses on the fact that so often we cease to listen effectively because we have something to say. When we start formulating a reply, we have stopped listening.

11. **Our thoughts may interfere with how we listen**

    True. Very few people have difficulty with this question.

12. **Listening is a natural ability for most people**

    False. As with question 1, many people believe they have a natural ability, until they explore exactly what listening (in the counselling sense) means.

13. **We may resist listening to people when we blame them**

    True. Most people accept this statement, for blame is passing judgement and it is also related to point 7.

14. **Being a good listener does not require self-discipline**

    False. Many people get this wrong because they miss the word 'not'. This is a useful demonstration that even in reading sometimes we 'skip', so, in listening, we may not hear everything the other person says.

15. **People will feel able to talk with us if they feel safe and accepted**

    True. Most people would agree with this.

16. **Keeping confidences is important in developing trust**

    True. This generally does not present any difficulty.

17. **Fatigue never affects the quality of listening**

    False. Most people do not agree with this statement. As with 14, some miss the 'never'. Some people just have difficulty with double negatives.

18. **Effective listening entails making a series of correct choices in receiving what is being said**

    True. Many people score this as False, possibly because they think that they should remain completely open to what the client is saying and not make judgements. This is true, of course, and I normally get them to consider the possibility that it is only in retrospect that we can determine if the choices were the 'correct' ones or not. The question would probably cause less difficulty if 'accurate' were substituted for 'correct'.

19. **Observing body language and voice quality plays no part in effective listening**

    False. Few people get it wrong, though some dispute the degree to which it plays a part.

20. **When we are angry we are not very good listeners**

    True. As with 7 and 10, listening is affected by emotions.

21. **Our listening is not affected by our previous experiences**

    False. This is another question where the 'not' is often missed. When this little word is pointed out, it makes all the difference.

22. **We sometimes send mixed messages that are difficult for the other person to understand**

    True. Few people argue with this, although some want to know more about 'mixed messages'.

This is a useful training aid, but also forms a valid way of getting clients to think about how they listen, particularly if they are in a relationship that is fraught with difficulties, one of which may be ineffective listening.

LONELINESS (*see also*: Intimacy, Existential therapy)

Loneliness is an unpleasant experience that occurs when a person's network of social relationships is deficient in some important way. Loneliness exists when there is a discrepancy between the needs of a person and the social contacts available to meet those needs. Loneliness is something felt by the person and relates to the degree of emotional contact one person has with others. So being with a crowd of people does not mean that one stops feeling lonely.

Emotional loneliness stems from the lack or absence of a close attachment. This form of loneliness results in intense and unpleasant feelings of anxiety and apprehension. Social loneliness stems from the absence of adequate or effective social networks. The feelings associated with this type of loneliness – boredom and exclusion – are not so intense as emotional loneliness.

It would appear that it is not the number of relationships that ward off loneliness but the depth of the relationships we do have – in other words, intimacy. It also seems that loneliness is linked to low self-esteem, anxiety, depression, shyness, self-consciousness and the lack of social skills that help in forming new relationships.

Loneliness is characterized by:

- Apathy
- Distress
- Emptiness 'as vast as a frozen wilderness'
- Feeling of drifting, without rudder or line
- Futility
- Helplessness
- Lack of concentration
- Lack of motivation
- Over-sensitivity
- Restlessness
- Suspicion
- Withdrawal
- A worn-out feeling.

Loneliness is often precipitated by:

- Age
- Disability
- Extreme introversion
- Infirmity
- Isolation through environment
- Isolation through loss of partner
- Low self-esteem
- Over-dependence
- Poor social skills
- Rigidity of personality
- Self-deprecating trait
- Shyness
- Being a single parent.

Loneliness may be coped with through denial. Social contact may be devalued and a refuge sought in work, social activities or addiction.

The link between loneliness and depression is an important consideration. Feeling lonely may result from knowing that one has fewer friends than other people. People who attribute being lonely to some personality deficit are likely to experience depression and pessimism. When relationships end, other than by mutual consent, the person ending the relationship is reported to experience less loneliness than the other person. The one who was 'dumped' is very likely to feel a victim.

People who have a schizoid personality disorder have great difficulty with intimate relationships and are characteristically loners. They are often to be found in occupations where they can work in isolation. People with a paranoid personality, likewise, often experience difficulty with intimate relationships. People with social phobia are invariably loners, and lonely, and as such often fail to develop intimate relationships. People with a histrionic personality often consider relationships to be more intimate than they actually are.

The aim of counselling is to help the client live with the deep loneliness that lies at the heart of existence. Counselling should not propel the client into establishing relationships that may simply be perpetuating the denial.

Further reading

Bowlby, J. (1979) *The Making and Breaking of Affectional Bonds*, Tavistock, London.
Hobson, R. F. (1974) Loneliness. *Journal of Analytical Psychology*, **19**, 71–89.
Peplau, L. A. and Perlman, D. (1982) *Loneliness*, John Wiley, New York.

M

MANIPULATION

Counselling is not manipulation. There are some definitions of manipulation that could be loosely thought of as guidance, but what counselling definitely is not is 'unfair influence'. Manipulation in this sense means something underhand, a plot, deception.

When people are persuaded by others to do or attempt something (even though it may be against their better judgement or wishes), they usually realize what is happening. People who manipulate others to do what they want do so subversively, not in the open, and (this is the essential difference) usually for some personal gain and not in the best interests of the other person.

The dividing line between manipulation and seeking ways and means to resolve a problem may not always be easily seen but the deciding factor must be 'who benefits?'

Some students of counselling think, initially, that the counsellor manoeuvres clients so adroitly that they agree with what the counsellor proposes as if they themselves had thought of it. This can be done and it is a very subtle means of ensuring that the client takes the direction that the counsellor feels is right. This can be done by loading the exploration in favour of the direction you have chosen, by limiting the exploration to one avenue or by putting forward all the difficulties against any other choice.

The counsellor can make suggestions that manipulate the client's feelings. For example, Joe is passing through a difficult time with his girlfriend. The counsellor, in the belief that it would be best for him to end the relationship, introduces a whole gamut of moral issues that make Joe feel so guilty that he severs the relationship in an inappropriate manner, which leaves both him and the girl feeling resentful.

Sometimes people who counsel will manipulate the client's feelings to satisfy their own emotional needs. It is probably true to say that we all counsel to get something out of it, but the majority of us have enough awareness of our own emotional needs not to let them overshadow our counselling. When referring to 'the counsellor', I mean anyone doing counselling; I would not want to imply that counsellors who have undergone training would be guilty of this sort of manipulation but neither would I want to suggest that those who have not received such a training would be any more guilty. Manipulation of any kind is caused by underlying, and often well-hidden, motives.

Counsellors must also be watchful that their own emotional needs do not intrude to the extent that they could be accused of manipulation. It is not always easy to detect when we have moved from exploration to manipulation but, as I have already said, a great deal depends on motives. If you are not clear when you are manipulating, the clients will be, although they may not use that word. They may not realize at the time what is happening but, when the session has ended and they have time to reflect, their feelings are likely to be something like: 'The cunning ——' (with a suitable expletive), 'so that's what s/he was after. I won't trust her/him again!'

THE MARTYR ATTITUDE

The martyr attitude is based on the belief that sorrows and troubles are evil machinations heaped upon the defenceless heads of suffering saints. Martyrs will invariably use the concepts of religious duty and spiritual living as flights from reality.

Behaviourally, they shoulder other people's burdens and then complain to make sure that everyone around commiserates with them. The burdens of others weigh them down and they experience little joy or peace.

Martyrs are subservient and humble and create an impression of everlasting goodness, sweetness and light. Were the Inquisition to return, they would be the first to be burned at the stake. They often need to enjoy poor health; in a curious way it makes them feel 'good'.

Counselling, even of the most intense sort, is difficult. What martyrs gain from being ill is more than they would gain from being well. So, identifying the gains and losses is a positive step along the road.

Further reading

Rowe, D. (1971) Poor prognosis in a case of depression as predicted by the repertory grid. *British Journal of Psychiatry*, **118**, 297–300.

MOMENTUM, MAINTAINING

During the early stages of counselling, as counsellor and client are getting to know each other, as clients spend time telling their story, there may not be any pressing need for you to find ways to keep the interview on the move. Later, however, when the tale has been told and the problem has been identified, or partially so, and as counselling enters the exploratory stage, it may happen that the process slows up or comes to a halt. There are a number of possible reasons for this. Sometimes you may get the impression of 'having been here before' – a sense of repetition. A moment's reflection may be enough to reveal that the wheel has come full circle. Then is the time either to move on or to terminate the session. Perhaps the client has had enough, or perhaps you have.

To move the interview on, it may be sufficient to say something like, 'We seem to have come full circle. Maybe I missed something important before.' If this approach is not used, you may refer to something that emerged earlier in the session or you may ask at which point the person would like to restart. This may provide an opportunity to explore why the session has come back to the beginning.

The point may have been dealt with inadequately at a previous time, and it has now reappeared. But it is also possible that only by going back can the person speak about something that caused difficulty before. It could also mean that you are trying to direct the person into an avenue that the client felt could have been explored before but was not.

Comments such as 'And then?', 'What happened?', 'What was the outcome?', 'Tell me about...', 'What were your feelings at the time?' are all aimed at moving the interview forward – gently, not pushing it. But there is usually a natural time for a session to end. If momentum slows down, that may be the appropriate time to stop, by summarizing what has taken place.

On the other hand, momentum may slow down because the client is thinking deeply about some comment you have made or something that has been triggered off as part of a chain reaction. The client may be hesitating to mention something, not certain of its relevance, its importance or possibly its controversial nature. You may have become preoccupied, allowing your attention to waver. When this happens, the client will feel uneasy; conversation most likely will falter. A simple, 'Sorry, I've lost track' will be enough to get you both back on track.

MULTICULTURAL ISSUES

Cross-cultural counselling is similar in many ways to cross-gender counselling. Counselling has its roots in white cultures and it is possible that this way of relating is not readily accepted by people from different cultures. However well-versed and aware we are, our counselling could benefit from a study of three important factors.

Firstly, we could learn from our clients how the history of their own culture influences them now. We also need to have explored our own cultural influences and recognized how our attitudes, beliefs, prejudices, stereotypes and judgements influence our interactions.

Secondly, we must be prepared to take on board what our clients say of their experiences of discrimination, exploitation, stereotyping and those indefinable but palpable phenomena, 'awkwardness' and 'joking', and how these affect them. Discrimination applies not only to people of different colour; many other groups of people are also subjected to as much prejudice and discrimination as people of African origin.

Thirdly, however self-aware, it is only as we become involved in cross-cultural counselling that we will truly be able to explore our own values and attitudes toward people from different cultures.

For centuries white nations conquered, then dominated, other races and considered them ignorant and of lower intelligence. These beliefs still lurk in our cultural unconscious. For an example of how insidious the process of cultural superiority is, one only has to look at picture books, adverts and comics, to pick out how discrimination is still being thrust at the reader or viewer. Cross-cultural counselling, then, may be as fraught with difficulty as cross-gender counselling.

The major influences that make for cross-cultural difficulties in counselling are language, education, religion, gender, values, beliefs and attitudes.

Language

Language unites people on the one hand and separates them on the other in a more powerful way than even skin colour does. Language conveys thoughts. Thinking is any cognitive or mental manipulation of ideas, images, symbols, words, propositions, memories, concepts, precepts, beliefs or intentions. Concepts are structured in hierarchies, with increasing complexity the more the original idea is broken down into properties. Conceptual thought often creates difficulty in cross-cultural counselling.

People with English as their second language often have to translate what they have heard into their own language and then retranslate into English before replying. They understand the meanings of broad concepts but not every property in the hierarchy. This difficulty is similar to two people listening to a piece of music. The one may hear only the melody; the other hears all the notes of both melody and harmony.

The way people from other cultures respond in counselling is moderated by the length of time they have spent in new culture. Skin colour or, indeed, accent (although accent is more open to moderation) are not reliable guides to how a person will respond. Many people with different skin colours are in fact second-, third- or fourth-generation residents of this country. In every respect they would respond as anyone else.

Education

Methods of education vary from culture to culture. People who have come through an education system where discussion is the norm are generally more able to deal with sophisticated concepts, while a person (of no matter what culture) who has learned mainly by rote usually experiences difficulty handling them. So it is necessary for the counsellor to be sensitively alert to the cues given out that something has not been understood.

'Talk and chalk' and rote learning are the methods of an authoritarian, obedience-dominated, system of education. An outcome of the authoritarian approach is that experiential learning is difficult. People who have been educated under a heavily authoritarian system expect to be told what to do and what to learn. Many such people cannot see the relevance of experiential work; they have little by which to measure their learning. When they can leave a session with pages of notes or dictation, they feel satisfied that the session has been productive.

This has implications in counselling. Apart from the restriction of conceptual thinking, a relationship of equality, in which the client works toward finding solutions, is to many an alien concept, unproductive and time-wasting. At the same time, the fundamentals of accepted counselling practice conflict with the client's value system.

Religion

Religion has a profound bearing on the values and beliefs of both client and counsellor, on the style of education they have received and on their relationships with the opposite sex. Many people have been saddled with a double authority: an authoritarian style of teaching within a religious system of education. This atmosphere of traditionalism supports the belief that women are inferior to men. Males and females from such a culture develop a deep and unhealthy fear for and of authority which shows itself in compliance and submission. It also perpetuates the male–female dominance and submission system.

The male counsellor may then be related to with the same awe and reverence as the priest, as possessing the same god-like function and qualities. Clients from such a background would find a relationship of equality difficult to accept. As most religions are male-centred, clients with a religious-based culture may find it difficult to accept the credibility of female counsellors.

On the one hand, the client (of whichever gender) may not be able to enter into a relationship of active equality and will expect the counsellor to be directive and prescriptive. On the other hand, the female counsellor could be rejected because a woman in a position of perceived authority creates too much ambiguity in the client's belief system.

Aids to cross cultural counselling

- We should always aim for clarity of expression in the language we use
- We should be aware of our use of jargon and unfamiliar figures of speech
- Constant checking for understanding, essential in any counselling, is crucial in cross-cultural counselling; to be aware that something said is being agreed with and not fully understood demonstrates empathy
- If possible, allotting extra time may be an advantage, in order to facilitate exploration
- We should be alert to how our personal experiences can colour our judgement; we should also be careful to separate our experiences from other people's prejudices and from myths and legends
- We should be aware that such moral concepts as truth, honesty, loyalty, politeness and respect may not mean the same in the client's culture as they do in ours
- In some cultures, showing feelings to a comparative stranger is taboo
- The client's verbal and nonverbal language should not be filtered through the screen of our own standards. What we might consider 'rude' may be perfectly acceptable in the client's culture. The more we are able to suspend judgement, the more we shall be able to stay on the client's wavelength.

Finally, it has to said that not all people within our own culture accept counselling, preferring to work things through for themselves. People from other cultures might find great difficulty in speaking to a stranger about their innermost feelings, preferring to talk with some wise person of their own culture. However, this article paves the way by highlighting some important areas of potential difficulty when counselling someone from a different culture.

Further reading

Dummett, A. (1980) Nationality and citizenship. In *Conference Report of Further Education in Ethnic Minorities*, National Association for Teachers in Higher Education, London.

Jones, E. E. (1985) Psychotherapy and counselling with black clients. In: *Handbook of Cross-cultural Counselling and Therapy*, (ed. P. Pederon), Praeger, London.

Katz, J. H. (1978) *White Awareness: Handbook for* Anti-racism Training, University of Oklahoma Press, Norman, OK.

Lago, C. and Thompson, J. (1989) Counselling and race. In: *Handbook of Counselling in Britain*, (eds W. Dryden, D. Charles-Edwards and R. Woolfe), Tavistock/Routledge, London.

Sue, D. W. (1981) *Counselling the Culturally Different*, John Wiley, New York.

Myers–Briggs type indicator

The Myers–Briggs Type Indicator (MBTI) is a widely used psychometric test, based on the work of Carl Jung and developed by Isabel Myers and her mother Katherine Briggs. It measures eight personality preferences along four dimensions:

Extraversion (E) $\rightarrow$ Introversion (I)
Sensing (S) $\rightarrow$ Intuition (N)
Thinking (T) $\rightarrow$ Feeling (F)
Judgement (J) $\rightarrow$ Perception (P)

Generalizations

- People who have similar strengths in the dimensions will seem to 'click', to arrive at decisions more quickly, to be on the same wavelength. Their decisions, however, may suffer because of their similar blind spots.
- People with dissimilar strengths in the dimensions will not be on the same wavelength and may have difficulty accepting the views, opinions and actions of the other person. Decisions arrived at through their interaction will, however, generally be more sound and therefore more acceptable.
- The parts of our dimensions we don't use much – the 'Shadow' side – we are more sensitive about and are more prone to react negatively when they are criticized. As a result, conflict may occur when we must work with our Shadow sides or when our deficiencies are pointed out by others.
- We are generally attracted to people who display similar preferences. On the other hand, we are often drawn to others because of the strengths we observe in them – the flip side of our own preferences.
- Our values, beliefs, decisions and actions are all influenced by the four stronger dimensions of our typology.

- Although our preferences are fixed, we can work with our Shadow sides and strengthen them in order to overcome problems that result from the weaknesses.

Extraversion/introversion

Extraversion/introversion describes the way we relate to the world around us.

Extraversion
People who are more extraverted than introverted (Es):

- Are generally sociable and outgoing
- Relate to people and things around them
- Endeavour to make their decisions in agreement with the demands and expectations of others
- Are interested in variety and in working with people
- May become impatient with long, slow tasks
- Do not mind being interrupted by people.

Introversion
People who are more introverted than extraverted (Is):

- Prefer making decisions independently of other people
- Tend to be quiet, diligent at working alone
- Tend to be socially reserved
- Dislike being interrupted while working
- Are liable to forget names and faces.

Sensing/intuition

Sensing/intuition describes the way we perceive the world.

Sensing
People who are more sensing than intuitive (Ss):

- Prefer what is concrete, real, factual, structured, tangible, here-and-now
- Tend to mistrust their intuition
- Think in careful, detail-by detail accuracy
- Remember real facts
- Make few errors of fact
- May possibly miss a grasp of the overall.

Intuition
People who have more intuition than sensing (Ns):

- Prefer possibilities, theories, patterns, the overall, inventions and the new
- Become bored with the nitty-gritty details, the concrete and actual
- Feel that facts must relate to concepts
- Think and discuss in spontaneous leaps of intuition

- May leave out or neglect details
- Find that problem-solving comes easily
- May show a tendency to make errors of fact.

Thinking/feeling
Thinking/feeling describes the way we make judgements.

Thinking
People with more thinking than feeling (head types, Ts):

- Make judgements about life, people, occurrences and things based on logic, analysis and hard evidence
- Avoid irrationality and decisions based on feelings and values
- Are interested in logic, analysis, and verifiable conclusions
- Are less comfortable with empathy, values and personal warmth
- May step on others' feeling and needs without realizing it
- Often neglect to take into consideration the values of others.

Feeling
People with more feeling than thinking (heart types, Fs):

- Make judgements about life, people, occurrences and things based on empathy, warmth and personal values
- Are more interested in people and feelings than in impersonal logic, analysis and things
- Feel that conciliation and harmony are more important than in being on top or achieving impersonal goals
- Get along with people in general.

Judgement/perception
Judgement/perception describes the way we make decisions.

Judgement
People with more judgement than perception (Js):

- Are decisive, firm, and sure
- Like setting goals and sticking to them
- Want to make decisions and get on to the next project
- Will leave an unfinished project behind and go on to new tasks and not look back, if that's what has to be done
- Give priority to work over play
- Are good at meeting deadlines
- Tend to be judgemental of themselves and other people.

Perception
People who have more perception than judgement (Ps):

- Always want to know more before making decisions and judgements
- Are open, flexible, adaptive, nonjudgemental
- Are able to appreciate all sides of an issue
- Always welcome new perspectives and new information about issues
- Are difficult to pin down
- Hate working to deadlines
- Are often so indecisive and noncommittal that they frustrate themselves and other people
- Are often involved in many tasks
- Give priority to play rather than work.

A person's type is made up of the four dominant functions. Helping a client to understand his/her personality preferences is just one more way in which the client will gain insight into how to mange his/her life with less stress.

Preferences and communication

- **Es** may feel under pressure in a group to do all the talking for themselves and for **Is**. **Is** may feel ignored by **Es**, who are often more willing to enter a conversation and keep it going.
- **Ss** may feel irritated by **Ns**, who jump to conclusions (sometimes correctly) without working through obvious stages. **Ns** may feel irritated by the caution of **Ss**, who, to them, often take a long time to arrive at conclusions.
- **Ts** may feel irritated by **Fs**, who do not approach a problem logically and want to talk about how they feel. **Fs** may feel irritated by **Ts**, who want to analyse everything with cold logic before making a judgement
- **Js** may feel irritated by **Ps**, who never seem to be able to make a decision, always want to put things off and always want to put play first. **Ps** may feel irritated by **Js**, who insist on having everything planned, won't let things just happen and insist upon work first.

Temperament and intimate relationships

Differences in type between people may give rise to friction, although this can often be diminished or eliminated when the origins are understood. Opposites have much to offer each other, **provided we accept each other's differences as being valid and worthwhile.**

E/I differences

The major differences appear to be sociability versus privacy.

- When the work of the **I** is socially demanding, time and space is needed at home to recharge the emotional batteries – some silence and a chance to think quietly is essential
- On the other hand, **E** requires an opportunity to talk, especially if that has been denied during the day
- The **E** partner is more likely to reach decisions by talking them out and getting feedback

- The **I** partner is more likely to work things out then give a conclusion. When this happens the **E** partner feels excluded from mutual sharing – something of great importance to the **E**.

S/N differences
Of the preferences, **S** or **N** appear to be most crucial.

- Sharing the same way of perceiving an issue is important for understanding
- If partners are opposites, clarification is clearly essential
- The **S** partner may feel intellectually slow by comparison with the **N** partner. The **N** partner may feel impractical and unobservant by comparison with the **S** partner.

T/F differences
Thinking and feeling both influence the way we make judgements.

- Feeling is more subjective than objective; thinking is more objective than subjective
- The **T** partner may become irritated by the **F** partner's lack of logic
- The **F** partner may become irritated by the **T** partner's lack of feeling
- **T**s can improve relationships by paying attention to their tendency to criticize and learning to show appreciation
- **F**s can improve relationships by learning to express themselves clearly, so that the **T** partner knows precisely what is being said without having to guess. Feeling types are sensitive to any comment that sounds like a personal criticism.

J/P differences
J and **P** are to do with control or spontaneity.

- The **P** partner may be irritated by the **J**'s need for ordered surroundings and territorial lifestyle
- The **J** partner may be irritated by the **P**'s need for spontaneity, freedom and, oftentimes, indecision
- When one partner realizes that the other is not being deliberately awkward, that it is something within the personality makeup of both of them that causes differences, they are much more likely to work together to resolve the differences. If the counsellor can point out that one person's strength is often the other's weakness, and *vice versa*, then by putting the two together they have much to offer each other.

How preferences might influence counselling
- People who are too extroverted often get on people's nerves; someone who is too introverted often has difficulty making contact with people at all
- People who are high on sensing can get so caught up in counting the trees that they miss the beauty of the wood; people who are too intuitive often seem 'away with the fairies'

- People who are too high on thinking often intellectualize everything; people who are too high on feeling often swamp others by their warmth
- People who are too high on judgement often become judge, jury and executioner; people who are too high on perception often give the impression of being grown up children.

These are generalizations, however, how client and counsellor interact, and an understanding of what is going on could be significantly enhanced by knowing why you, the counsellor, prefer certain ways of working above others.

Counselling is almost always linked to change. What follows demonstrates how each of the eight preferences may help or hinder change in counselling.

Extraverts/introverts

The E part will tend to accept change with enthusiasm, mainly because change brings with it the possibility of new relationships. If anything, the E may rush into change with open arms before counting the cost. The E part of us likes to talk, to hold the floor, but might have trouble listening.

The I part proceeds with caution. Change for the introvert brings more questions than answers, and that is unsettling. The I part likes to take things in, digest them, then – and only then – speak, and the response is given with caution. The E part would be less comfortable with silence than the I part, which might prompt you to say anything just to keep things moving. The E part tends not to like reflection, which is one of the strengths of the I.

Sensing/intuition

The S part tends to resist change, because it disturbs the status quo. When the S part cannot find the next logical piece in the plan, there is anxiety. S needs to know what is, to have hands on. The S is cautious, rarely jumps to conclusions and often needs careful explanation and to work through logical stages.

The N part enjoys possibilities and revels in the unknown and new beginnings. N is creative. Change energizes. Because the N sees things with the intuition, it often jumps ahead to make what might seem illogical conclusions but are often correct. The S prefers to work with the obvious; the N is comfortable working with the imagination.

Thinking/feeling

T asks if it is 'true or false'. Analysis requires time, so if change is hurried, before the logic is fully accepted, it will produce stress and will be rejected. Thus if something is not logical it is likely that the client will feel irritated. The thinking part would prefer to debate than to discuss feelings and will generally want to make judgements based on logic and reason.

F asks if it is · 'agreeable or disagreeable'. Change would be acceptable provided there was sufficient attention paid to the 'human' aspect and ample time for discussion. The F tends to become irritated if asked to be too logical and reasoning. Feelings are what make the world go round, not cold logic.

Judgement/perception

The **J** part excels in plans, decisions and conclusions. If change is protracted by people who can't make up their minds, stress is likely to occur. The **J** part will plan an event well in advance and expect other people to comply. The **J** part puts work first and is often judgemental of people.

The **P** part puts off making decisions. Open-mindedness is a **P** strength. Putting perceptive people under pressure, such as deadlines, will create stress. The **J** part would be comfortable working toward set goals, whereas the **P** part would find it difficult to look that far ahead, as they prefer to live in the moment.

Although the eight preferences have been presented as if they were separate entities, each is modified by all the other preferences. However, having an idea of basic preferences is one way of making sense of what is happening in counselling.

When counsellors are aware of their own and their client's personality preferences, even though they may not work specifically with the Myers–Briggs type indicator, they will certainly add another dimension to the counselling interaction.

Further reading

Bayne R. (1990) A new direction for the Myers–Briggs Type Indicator. *Personnel Management*, **March**.

Briggs Myers, I. (1980) *Gifts Differing*, Consulting Psychologists Press, Palo Alto, CA.

Briggs Myers, I. (1980) *Introduction to Type*, Consulting Psychologists Press, Palo Alto, CA.

Briggs Myers, I. and McCaulley, M. H. (1985) *Manual: A guide to the development and use of the Myers–Briggs Type Indicator*, Consulting Psychologists Press, Palo Alto, CA.

Kiersey, D. and Bates, M. (1998) *Please understand me II*, Prometheus Nemesis, Del Mar, CA.

Stewart, W. and Martin, A. (1999) *Going for Counselling: How to work with your counsellor to develop awareness and essential life skills*, How To Books, Oxford.

N

NARCISSISM

In Greek mythology, Narcissus was the son of the river god, Cephissus, and the nymph Leiriope. Narcissus was beautiful and his mother was told that he would have a long life provided he never looked upon his own features. He fell in love with his own reflection in the waters of a spring and pined away and died. The narcissus flower sprang up where he died. The myth possibly arose from the Greek superstition that it was unlucky to see one's own reflection.

Freud used the myth to describe a morbid condition in which sexual energy, which naturally focuses firstly on self and then upon the parent and then on others, remains focused on self. The person can rarely achieve satisfactory sexual relationships because of mistrust of other people.

A narcissistic personality disorder is characterized by:
- An exaggerated sense of self-importance
- A tendency to overvalue one's actual accomplishments
- A need for attention and admiration that is exhibitionistic in character
- A preoccupation with fantasies of success, wealth, power, esteem or ideal love
- Inappropriate emotional reactions to the criticisms of others
- The narcissistic adult person is cut off from others, self-absorbed, vain and somewhat superior in manner.

It is suggested that narcissism develops when a child's fears, failures and vulnerabilities are responded to with disdain, criticism or neglect. However, no hard and fast evidence exists on why some people develop a narcissistic personality.

Counselling a person who is strongly narcissistic is a long-term process involving a relationship in which the client's self-involvement is slowly changed to involvement with others, confronting the client's defences of devaluation and idealization to avoid acknowledging weaknesses and interpreting what some consider are the basic issues of anger and envy. Other therapists allow an idealizing transference to develop, constantly reflecting what is taking place, until disillusionment sets in and then the work is to establish a positive transference and a more satisfying relationship. Group therapy is often useful alongside individual therapy.

Further reading

Jacoby, M. (1981) Reflections on H. Kohut's concept of narcissism. *Journal of Analytical Psychology*, **26**(1): 19–32.

NONVERBAL COMMUNICATION (BODY LANGUAGE)

Verbal language is mainly conscious; body language, the language of signals, is mainly unconscious. Approximately 50% of information on the character, impact and credibility of the person is conveyed by body language. Any interpretation of body language, therefore, must be offered with the same tentativeness as one would interpret any unconscious exploration.

Nonverbal communication takes place by means of facial expressions, head movements, body positions and gestures, tones of voice, clothing and even odour. People such as actors and politicians are conscious of the importance of body language and use it deliberately. Nonverbal messages, being mainly unconscious, may betray discrepancies between the spoken words and our true feelings.

Personal space

An intrusion into our personal space is threatening and disturbing and is likely to meet with a defensive reception. Invasion of space can be both physical and psychological. For example, we may even feel that a character on the TV screen has invaded our personal space.

- **The intimate distance zone** – up to 60 cm maximum (strongly influenced by culture). The more our intimate space is violated, the more we will use these defence tactics of crossed arms and legs, nervous shifting in chair, playing with fingers, avoiding eye contact, shrugging of shoulder, lowering the chin.
- **The personal distance zone** – 40–150 cm. The space reserved for family members and people we like. The most common defence tactic is to ignore, characterized by no eye contact, stiff body, preferably no talking. The more the space available, the more we seem to need.
- **The social distance zone** – 1.5–3.5 m. This is the zone for daily contacts, superficial, acquaintances, colleagues, the 'boss'. This is usually the most comfortable distance for counselling.
- **Public distance zone** – 3.5–7 m. This is the distance preferred by speakers, teachers and actors.

In working with people within the intimate counselling relationship, observing the client's personal space is not only essential, it conveys empathy. Being able to get close to people is not just about physical space; emotional space is of equal importance and keeping the counsellor at a physical distance might also mean a difficulty with emotional distance and intimacy that goes beyond the counselling relationship.

Counselling uses all the senses: if all we listen to are the words we shall have heard only half of the message. Having a heightened ability to notice changes in body language helps the counsellor to recognize how the client is responding to the interaction. Accurate perception aids rapport and empathy.

However, observing body language is not an exact science and we can easily get it wrong. I was leading a group in which one of the women kept pointing her toes and moving her foot around. Taking a deep breath, I said, 'The books say that your foot is telling you it's time to go.' She laughed and said, 'No, William, I've had my varicose veins done and I'm doing my leg exercises.'

While some readers may not agree about the validity of body language and while it is dangerous to make interpretations (as my anecdote shows), the various people who have made a serious study of the subject show it is a form of communication we cannot ignore, but too much emphasis on it may be equally misplaced.

Further reading

Argyle, M. (1969) *Social Interaction*, Methuen, London.

Argyle, M. (1975) *Bodily Communication*, Methuen, London.

Argyle, M. (1978) *The Psychology of Interpersonal Behaviour*, 3rd edn, Penguin, Harmondsworth.

Morris, D. (1977) *Manwatching*, Jonathan Cape, London.

Morris, D., Collett, P., Marsh, P. and O'Shaughnessy, M. (1979) *Gestures: Their origins and distribution*, Jonathan Cape, London.

Pease, A. (1981) *Body Language*, Sheldon Press, London.

OBSERVING COUNSELLING (*see also*: Feedback)

Sometimes it is possible to observe a counsellor at work. More often, observing is associated with counselling training, where students observe each other.

Observing means listening to:

- What is said
- How it is said
- What is not said

and watching the unconscious communication of body language.

Some guidelines:

- Did the counsellor seem certain/uncertain in the counselling role?
- How was the client put at ease?
- What evidence was there of rapport?
- What evidence was there of empathy?
- What evidence was there of acceptance of the client by the counsellor?
- What evidence was there of genuine concern?
- Did the counsellor concentrate on facts at the expense of feelings?
- How would you rate the counsellor's listening with the 'third ear' and responding skills?
- Was there any evidence of argument?
- How did you feel as the observer?
- How would you describe the pace of the interview?
- The particular comments by the counsellor that seemed most helpful were...
- What evidence was there of the counsellor 'reading between the lines'?
- What body language was there?
  - Eye contact
  - Personal spacing and distance
  - Gestures
  - Body posture
  - Facial expressions
  - Tone of voice
  - Timing of speech
  - Evidence of being relaxed/tense.

The above questions are a useful self-appraisal.

OWNING THE PROBLEM

'It's all her fault,' said Mr Taciturn, as he faced the counsellor. 'She leads me a dog's life. I can't think why. I've done nothing to upset her.'

As the counsellor listened, she was thinking, 'If he talks like that about her to me, what's he like at home? How does he talk to her in front of the children?'

To him she said, 'You say you have no idea why she is like she is?'

'None at all. If the marriage breaks up it's all her fault. I can't reason with her. She's the one who should be here, not me.'

Mr Taciturn had difficulty owning the problem – owning the possibility that perhaps he had some part to play in the difficult marriage. Many people, when under stress because their emotions are in turmoil, cannot see that they have contributed to the problem – they try to push it away on to someone else.

Jack Fairweather, a trainee fitter in the railway works, was dismissed for unsatisfactory conduct. His sickness record was appalling, made up mainly of single days. His record reflected that he was absent a great deal without having made contact with the chargehand. His excuses were: 'The alarm clock broke (or didn't go off)', 'The bus went without me', 'I overslept', and so on. It was never his fault. Misadventure was always thrust upon him by some malevolent super-being who had a grudge against him. The problem was not his, or so he thought.

In both these instances, the problem was being pushed aside. Mr Taciturn needed help to realize that his attitude towards his wife and children was a very powerful factor in the strained relationship. Jack Fairweather was never able to accept that his attitude towards life contributed to his downfall. Unless both of them – and all people who seek counselling – own the problem as theirs, counselling will be a sterile waste of time. Owning the problem 'as mine' is a vital stage to be reached before effective counselling can really get going, just as alcoholics must reach this stage before they can start to climb out of the pit into which they have dropped.

Owning that the problem is mine is only part of what could be a difficulty in counselling: owning feelings may be equally important. Owning feelings depends on being able to recognize and identify them and an essential part of counselling might simply be helping the client to do just that.

Counselling is not a one-way process; it involves the client and the counsellor. Just as the client has to own his/her feelings, so does the counsellor need to acknowledge his/her part in the interaction and this would invariably involve owning one's feelings, which are generated within the relationship. It might not be appropriate to disclose all feelings to the client, although this would depend on the approach one is using, but certainly in debriefing or recording, or in supervision, one's feelings, unless owned, will interfere with the counselling relationship.

P

PACE IN COUNSELLING

Counselling is like travelling from London to Brighton. It can be done by express train, car, bicycle or on foot. For each of these modes of travel, the pace will be different. Some counselling interviews can proceed at a rapid pace; others are much slower. It is the person you are counselling who sets the pace. Any attempt to force the person to change from a walking pace to a run will, in all probability, result in 'client fatigue'. One person may be quite able to dash along quite happily; the nature of the problem and the emotional state may permit this. Another person may want to stroll, so as to view the countryside as it passes. If, somewhere along the road, this person decides to hasten the pace, so be it. The skilful counsellor will be able to adapt to this change and still remain alongside.

Further reading

Sutton, J. and Stewart, W. (1997) *Learning to Counsel: How to develop the skills to work effectively with others*. How To Books, Oxford.

PARABLE (*see also*: Bibliotherapy)

Parables, fables and allegories are forms of imaginative literature or the spoken word, so constructed that the reader or listener is encouraged to look for meanings hidden beneath the literal surface of the fiction.

A poet may describe the ascent of a hill in such a way that each physical step corresponds to a new stage in the soul's progress toward a higher level of existence.

An allegory is usually a long narrative full of symbols conveying a moral message. Well-known allegories include *The Pilgrim's Progress*, *The Divine Comedy*, *Animal Farm*, *Gulliver's Travels* and *The Picture of Dorian Gray*.

Fables and parables are short, simple forms of allegory, usually about animals or inanimate objects, who behave as though they are human. Fables tend toward detailed, sharply observed realism, sometimes satirical, and use impossible events to teach their lesson. The 200 or so fables of Aesop (6th century BC) is probably the best-known collection, although other writers have achieved acclaim: John Gay and Edward Moore (England) and La Fontaine (France) are three examples.

Parables also tell a simple story with a moral message, this time about humans, and depend heavily on analogy. The story of the Good Samaritan in the New Testament is an example. Only the elite can decipher the inner core of truth of the parable. Christ's disciples had 'ears to hear'.

Parables possess a certain mystery that makes them useful for teaching spiritual values. The counsellor can use stories (fictional or true, taken from literature or the Bible or from clinical experience) to draw analogies with some aspect of the client's life, to show how another client successfully solved a similar problem. Such a technique must be used with care, lest it put undue pressure on the client. The essential ingredient is the symbolic connection between the story told and the client's problem.

Further reading

Cade, B. W. (1982) Some uses of metaphor. *Australian Journal of Family Therapy*, 3, 135–40.

Felner C. (1976) The use of teaching stories in conjoint family therapy. *Family Process*, 15, 427–33.

Gunzburg J. C. (1997) *Healing Through Meeting: Martin Buber's approach to Psychotherapy*, Jessica Kingsley, London.

TeSelle, S. (1975) *Speaking in Parables: A study in metaphor and theology*, SCM Press, London.

PARANOIA

Paranoia, a type of psychosis in which a person suffers from logically consistent delusions (fixed, false beliefs) of persecution or grandeur. In the late 1890s, Sigmund Freud postulated that paranoia is an intellectual disorder in which the primary symptom is extreme distrust of others.

People suffering from paranoia think or believe that other people are plotting or trying to harm, harass or persecute them in some way. Trivial incidents in everyday life are exaggerated into menacing or threatening situations and sufferers cannot rid themselves of their suspicions and apprehensions. In addition, in paranoid schizophrenia the patient may have hallucinations in which famous persons from history or mythology appear and communicate messages; this manifestation is related to the patient's delusion of grandeur.

A paranoid personality disorder is characterized by excessive suspiciousness, hostility and sensitivity to accusations or even hints of accusation. This type is to be distinguished from paranoia by the absence of a fully developed persecutory system.

Psychoanalysis and other psychotherapies, which are based on developing insight into the presumed underlying emotional conflicts, are difficult to apply to psychotic patients.

The word 'paranoid' is used very loosely to mean 'suspicious' or 'obsessively concerned with'. For example, an athlete was heard to say on TV, 'Some runners become paranoid about what they eat'. This is a misuse of the word.

Counsellors should be aware of the connotations of labelling when they drop into the use of what is specific medical terminology.

PARAPHRASING

A paraphrase is a brief response, in the hearer's own words, that captures the main points of the content of what the other person has said. It may condense or expand what has been said.

In general conversation, many assumptions are made about what has been said. Counselling is not an 'ordinary' conversation. Effective paraphrasing is part of effective listening which ensures understanding.

Words carry feelings, so not only is it necessary to understand the client's words, we must also try to understand why particular words are used in preference to others. If clients have been expressing their thoughts with difficulty, then is a good time to paraphrase. Letting clients hear the meaning as understood by someone else may help them to clarify more precisely what they do mean. Paraphrasing may echo feeling words without responding to them.

Our response need not be a repetition of the details. Rather, we paraphrase the client's content by summarizing and using our own words. Paraphrasing is not parroting. A paraphrased response will capture the main points communicated by the client in a brief statement, thus ensuring that the client clearly understands our summary.

A useful format for responding to content is:

'You're saying....'

Or

'In other words,....'

Or

'It sounds as if....'

Such formulated responses can sound stilted unless freshness is retained.

Examples of paraphrasing

Example 1
Andrew says, in an emotionally flat voice, with short pauses between words and sentences, 'I used to ... enjoy going out and having ... fun. Now I have to really force myself and I – I ... don't enjoy myself any more. All the time I just have a – a ... feeling of [longer pause] sadness. I'm not really part of the group any more.'

The key words and phrases here are: **going out; fun, force, sadness, not part of.**

Paraphrase: 'In the past, Andrew, you had a great time socializing. Right now, however, you've lost your drive and don't get much pleasure from going out and meeting people.

'For a lot of the time you feel down and flat and not really part of what's going on around you.'

Example 2
Susan, a student colleague, says, over coffee, 'I don't expect Sam to help with the household chores, but he knows very well I need time to study for my

nursing finals. I can't spend all my spare time cooking and cleaning and waiting on him hand and foot.'

The key words and phrases here are: **expect, chores, time, exams, hand and foot.**

Paraphrase: Susan, you would like Sam to support you more, and take his share of the work around the house, so that you can find more time to study instead of running after him. You would like a bit more sharing.'

Example 3

Alex, a 17-year-old, talks about home. 'I'll have to leave home – not sure how I'll cope, though. Mum and Dad smother me and can't see why I want to lead my own life.'

The key words and phrases here are: **have to; cope, own life.**

Paraphrase: 'Alex, something is forcing you into making a break from your parents, even though living on your own might not be easy for you and you're not quite certain you can manage by yourself. You also have difficulty getting your parents to see that you need more independence.'

Example 4

James, aged 23, says, 'I want to take up nursing but my mates are giving me a hard time; they say it's only a job for women and queers, not for men. It's the job for me, though. What should I do?'

The key words and phrases here are: **nursing, mates, queers, hard time, really want, what should I do?**

Paraphrase: 'Life is not easy at the moment, James. Your mates are ribbing you because you want to become a nurse, yet you're convinced, in spite of what they think about you, that this is the career for you. You would like me to help you make up your mind.'

Further reading

Sutton, J. and Stewart, W. (1997) *Learning to Counsel: How to develop the skills to work effectively with others.* How To Books, Oxford.

PASTORAL COUNSELLING

Introduction

I have chosen to introduce Gerkin's hermeneutical model of pastoral counselling because in many ways it provides a balance to some of the other models included in this book. I also think that what Gerkin has to say develops some of the psychological concepts and principles introduced elsewhere in the book and introduces some new ones.

Although Gerkin writes from a Christian perspective, what he says is applicable to other religions. Although this article has a pastoral counselling emphasis and some counsellors and clients might not subscribe to Christian theology, the principles go far beyond doctrine and dogma. A study of Gerkin's model provides valuable insights across many different counselling approaches.

Charles V. Gerkin, a professor of pastoral psychology at Emory University, draws upon the work of another visionary, Anton Boisen. Boisen believed that a person's struggle must be interpreted in much the same way as a historic Bible text. Although pastoral counsellors make use of a number of secular theories, their work must essentially be founded in Christian faith.

Traditionally there has been a conflict of ideology between theological ministry and the psychodynamic theory of the person. Gerkin attempts to resolve this conflict by introducing a **hermeneutical** alternative.

Hermeneutics is the critical interpretation and the science of the Bible, used by both Jews and Christians to discover the truths and values of the Old and New Testaments.

Gerkin proposes that hermeneutical pastoral counselling can bring together the two language worlds of theology and psychology. Pastoral counselling needs to incorporate the insights coming from secular psychotherapy, although not to be so absorbed into the general stream of psychotherapy that it loses its own identity.

Pastoral counsellors: who are they?

Pastoral counsellors listen to and interpret other people's stories and help them make sense of what seems senseless. Clients, through counselling, are helped to change the plot and counterplot of the life story. The pastoral counsellor and client are likely to use different language systems, symbols and images to interpret the meaning of experiences. The counsellor must strive to understand the client's frame of reference and the personal meanings. Failure to do so will result in the client going empty-handed.

The more the counsellor understands the language of the client and helps the client to understand his/her own language, the more the distance between their worlds will be reduced. Gerkin sees people in crisis as being caught between despair on the one hand and an interpretation of hope and expectation on the other. Much of the problem of the crisis experience is seen as a loss of the sense of continuity, with accompanying difficulty in moving into the open-ended future of hope and faith.

Anton Boisen's vision

Anton Boisen is generally considered the spiritual ancestor of the development of the pastoral counselling movement. His term **living human document** was coined to highlight how essential it is that theory **about** people should be supported by direct experience **of** people. For Boisen, the soul's cure is fundamentally to do with the raw stuff of religious experience.

Boisen viewed the person in distress as a troubled soul whose inner world had become so disorganized that the world had lost its foundations. If we interpret and understand, the language and gestures of the troubled soul, we will gain understanding of the specific inner world of this particular client.

The troubled person's own reporting of his/her inner world of experience is to be respected and heard, as having authenticity and integrity of its own, no matter how peculiar its language. What the person needs is an interpreter and a guide. One event must be interpreted in the light of all other experiences in the life story.

Boisen's philosophy was that the pastoral counselling tenets of faith and salvation, sin and redemption, have been replaced by the psychological language of neurotic symptoms, identity conflicts and compensatory behaviour; useful, but sterilized of religious meaning.

The client cannot be read as a living document unless the counsellor is willing to be read by the client. In person-centred counselling, this is the process of empathy, rapport and acceptance.

Horizon of understanding (empathy)

Experiences, prejudices, previous understandings, personal meanings and biases all limit our horizon of understanding. Listening to someone's inner world of meaning involves extending our horizon of understanding to admit something of the other person's world. Change takes place in the transitional space between the two horizons of understanding. The integrated language worlds used in Gerkin's model may be imaged as bridges between what is known – the past – on the one hand and the unknown – the yet-to-be – on the other.

Psychological theory and pastoral counselling

Pastoral counselling is concerned with communicating the inner meaning of the Gospel to persons at their point of need. Pastoral counsellors search for clues to understand the nature and purpose of God in his relationship with people. Theological and biblical images, themes and symbols need to be part and parcel of the pastoral counsellor's self-understanding and self-expression. Pastoral counselling ministry – seen as the communication of the inner meaning of the Gospel – flows first out of that level of inner meaning that has been informed and influenced by the images of faith. Pastoral counsellors draw from biblical and theological tradition a broad range of images, symbols and narrative themes. These provide a language with which to broaden the horizon of understanding and move towards self-identity.

What pastoral counselling is not, according to Gerkin's model, is indiscriminate quoting of Bible verses to clients. That is not active listening, whereas what Gerkin is proposing is listening of the highest order.

Self-identity

Self-identify involves taking into self the contents of the world; to refuse to do so is to become an empty self. Yet to be too open to do so brings with it the risk of chaos. The Spiritual Presence is both a fundamental answer and a safeguard. Where the Spiritual Presence is effective, life is turned toward the ultimate direction of the Kingdom.

People who come for pastoral counselling are usually aware of the suffering that comes from being stuck in their history, although that awareness may be hazy. Counselling aims to liberate clients' inner resources so they can handle the suffering more positively and help to restore their identity.

For the pastoral counsellor, change involves the work of the Spirit. The Spirit is seen as an energy or power, whose subject is God or Christ. The counsellor cannot force change. Change is achieved through the mediating influence of the Spirit. The counselling relationship is undertaken in the hope, and with the expectation, that in the search for new directions the client will be accompanied by the Spirit.

Identity

Identity is the self's effort to maintain some level of consistent attitude in the face of forces that would cause fragmentation. It is both an individual uniqueness and something conferred upon the individual by the significant figures in the person's life.

Identity is received, in part, from the person's historic circumstances in which human life takes place and in part from the individual's participation in the coming kingdom of God. The ego, self and soul are analogous to the Trinity: Father, Son and Holy Spirit – functionally distinct but coexistent and indivisible.

Three force/meaning dimensions of the life of the soul

The task of the self is to hold in tension the three force/meaning dimensions, which come from three general directions in the life space of the individual.

- Self/ego
- Social context
- The interpretations of faith and culture.

Self/ego dimension

Self/ego tensions arise from conflicts that emerge in the course of psychological development.

Social context
This includes:

- Economic, cultural, class, race
- Immediate community, work, family
- Relationships
- Expectations, commitments, conformity.

Faith and culture

- Myths and symbols of a culture are shaped over time
- They provide languages by which behaviours and relationships are given meaning and the way an individual perceives self and the world
- They tell us what relationships should be and why

- They tell us what thoughts and behaviour should be assigned guilty, accusatory meaning and what should receive commendation.

The constant interaction between all three dimensions makes up the flow of life in which the soul is either nurtured or kept in bondage. Our relationship to God is part and parcel of the self in all our relationships, including our struggle to hold the tension between forces and meanings.

Gerkin identifies three approaches to counselling:

- A 'force approach', where the counsellor sifts truth from falsehood; searching for hidden memories, forgotten facts and unconscious forces
- A 'meaning approach', where the facts are considered to be secondary to the client's interpretation of the meaning attached to the facts – this relies on acceptance and affirmation, without questioning the truth or falsity of the statement, an approach closely allied to Carl Rogers's unconditional positive regard
- Gerkin's 'integrated approach' holds in either hand the languages of force and meaning, two parts of a whole that are in constant tension – to truly understand a human situation we must understand both force and meaning: what happened, what is happening the interpretation of those events.

The self as a story

The story creates a pathway between the known and the unknown, although it is often narrated as a muddle and portrayed in highly symbolic language. The self is a book of many chapters. When chapters remain open, we cannot fully move forward. Part of counselling is to enable the client to examine chapters that are still open, work through the contents and close the chapter.

Elements of a narrative

Atmosphere
Pastoral counsellors attune themselves to hear the hidden positive and negative forces that influence the way a story is portrayed.

Plot
The deep story of the soul has a plot with a beginning, a principal story line, minor lines and an anticipated ending. People who cannot construct their story line are in danger of losing their sense of self.

Characterization
Character is how the person describes her/himself and how significant others in the life story are described. We use both imagination and behaviour to characterize someone.

Tone

Tone has three interlinked facets:

- We select or choose material to tell
- Language is used in a certain way
- Certain attitude are used to tell the story.

The way counsellors listen reinforces how and what they interpret. Vital lines may be missed because we are blinkered. We need to ask, 'Why is this particular part of the story being told? What is being left out and why?'

Examples of languages the client may use:

- **Blame and accusation**: 'It's all my parents' fault'
- **Helplessness and weaknesses**: 'What can I do, I'm a failure'
- **Determination against odds**: 'I won't let this thing beat me'
- **Emotional or intellectual**: 'I feel...' or 'I think...'.

The changing tones in the reporting of a life story is often a reliable indicator of changes in the life of the soul.

Stage 1: Evoking the story

The story may be painful and difficult to tell. What is told may not be **the** story, but merely a connecting line. Many sidelines may be told before the central story emerges. The pastoral counsellor must constantly be alert to the line that will lead to the person's central line. Most stories indicate some sense of an obstruction, damming the flow. When the line of life is blocked, then is the time to seek the client's interpretation.

How we listen and interpret is influenced by the ego conflicts and object relationships of our own pre-understandings. These must be as soft wax, to allow our horizon of understanding to come somewhere near the client's inner world. In the gap between these two worlds, the Christian counsellor can work with an understanding enhanced by the Holy Spirit. Or, in humanistic terms, the counsellor can work with an understanding enhanced by the psyche.

Stage 2: Exploring the story

Psychoanalytic therapies regard the development of insight as a central principle. Gerkin's theory emphasizes not only insight but also the need for integration and wholeness, the development of an authentic selfhood to replace the fragmented and dissociated self-image.

The soul needs to integrate and hold in balance the tensions coming from the three dimensions of self/ego, social situations and belief; not to do so will result in fragmentation.

The fragmented soul is unable to achieve integration. The narrative account of the life of the self must achieve a certain unity and cohesion, so that the various subthemes and issues in the life of the soul hold together. Integration and wholeness are not static goals but an open-ended process of movement and change.

Stage 3: Changing the story

Changing the story involves working with two concepts: **the horizons of under-standing** and **the living human document**. Five ways of using language help to understand this process.

- Myth **establishes** the client's story: The counsellor risks immersion in the client's world in order to change the myth from within
- Apologue (moral fable) **defends** the client's story: Pastoral counselling defends the self-story and explores relationships, attitudes, feelings, behaviours, evaluations of self and others within it
- Action **investigates** the story, by asking questions and posing hypotheses about what is going on or will go on: Action language can be intrusive if it does not understand the language of images, symbolism and feeling-laden words; when we understand those, we begin to understand the client's story
- Satire **attacks** the story by mocking it and encouraging us to laugh at ourselves: If there is a place for satire in pastoral counselling it must be handled with every bit as much care as a physician administers a highly powerful but potentially dangerous medicine
- Parable **transforms** the client's story: The well-told parable is an ordinary story with a familiar ring. As the story progresses, it takes a new and unexpected turn and stretches the imagination, of the hearer. A well-told parable involves the person as **participant**, not just a passive hearer.

Levels of counsellor suffering

Counsellors who are involved in this gradual transformation process of another require a level of personal involvement and interpersonal engagement that taps the deepest suffering of the soul at a number of different but related levels.

- **Level 1: Anxiety.** No counsellor has foreknowledge of a client's journey.
- **Level 2: Vulnerability.** Certain themes of the client's life story may awaken unfinished business within the counsellor that require reworking.
- **Level 3: Balance.** As client and counsellor move in the transitional space between their worlds, a balance between objectivity and subjectivity is essential. This is the space where the Spirit works and transformation begins to take place. It is there where one's own vulnerabilities become open to challenge and change, in the light of the Spirit's work with the client.
- **Level 4: Transference** – the unconscious process whereby the counsellor becomes the focus of the client's unresolved feelings toward significant others.

The hermeneutical circle of understanding

Understanding is like a circular feedback system, taking in, interpreting data, then adding it to what already exists to produce new data. The circular flow moves from the present counselling relationship to the history of significant relationships, then back again. This leads to an ever-enlarging arena. A danger is that both counsellor and client may be so taken up exploring one line of the story that all other lines remain unnoticed.

The ending phase of counselling

Gerkin identifies four issues related to ending counselling:

- How to help people make the transition from an intense, therapeutic relationship back into everyday life without that relationship. The return to the community, for many, may not be an easy journey. Where, for them, the understanding, totally accepting, nonjudgemental person to whom they have said farewell?
- The degree of control the counsellor exercises as to the outcomes of counselling. Where the person already has allegiance to a community of faith, the aim of counselling will be to strengthen that commitment.
- How the pastoral counsellor handles the termination of clients who do not have a relationship with a community of faith. The pastoral counsellor can never ensure the moral correctness or lasting outcome of counselling.
- Issues concerned with care and service. The final phase of counselling is the turning away from the primary concern for self and its welfare, toward service and concern for others.

Indicators of the ending phase of counselling:

- **Signals of integration and wholeness**
  - Higher level of energy and the sense of well-being
  - Spontaneity of affect (feeling)
  - Evidence of shared involvement
  - Self-esteem and self-criticism are more realistic
  - Fragmentation is giving way to transformation of the life story
  - Realism is replacing fantasy
- **Signals of altered behaviour and altered relationships**
  - Increased understanding of behaviour and meaning
  - Congruency between behaviour in relationships
  - Signals of clearer understanding of soul issues
  - An awakening to the possibilities of the future
  - A growing awareness of one's relationship with other souls
- **Signals of openness to travelling beyond, and to, the story**
  - A style of openness to life experience involving faith
  - A growing ability to go beyond the obvious and explicit
  - An openness to the flow of events in the one's life
- **Signals of beginning to accept eschatological (ultimate) identity**
  - Claiming the Kingdom, not just mental assent to it
  - Changed attitude toward self and toward the world
  - No longer at war with one's life story
  - A realization that one is a pilgrim among pilgrims
  - A greater sensitivity to the suffering of others.

Summary of hermeneutical pastoral counselling

The summary seeks to answer five salient questions.

What is the precise relationship between dynamics and narrative patterns of meaning in both intrapsychic and interpersonal life?

- The hermeneutical theory seeks to hold in working harmony the dynamics of **force** and **meaning**. Force concentrates on the conflicts and the functions of the self/ego, particularly thinking, analysis and psychological interpretation. Meaning involves a theological interpretation, which stresses the symbolic, imagistic as they influence the life story of the individual.
- Hermeneutical theory emphasizes the development of insight through interpretation of the events and experiences of the life story. It uses the language of images, symbols and characterizations. The medium is narrative expression of life conflicts of both force and meaning.
- Hermeneutical theory also deals with soul work, allowing the Spirit to work within the transitional space between the horizons of understanding of counsellor and client.

Is pastoral counselling in the hermeneutical mode best seen as form of spiritual direction or is it best imaged as theologically oriented form of psychotherapy?

- The hermeneutical model of pastoral counselling lies somewhere between psychotherapy and spiritual direction. Like Janus, it faces both ways, drawing from both, but is distinct from either.
- The hermeneutical model is primarily concerned with the individual's pilgrimage through the problems and crises of everyday life. It is concerned with the person's relationship with God and claiming the Kingdom.
- It is spiritual direction because it is spiritual. It is psychotherapy because it takes account of psychological ways of attending to the client's inner world. At all times pastoral counsellors must be sensitive to the direction of the client's face. To manipulate a client to tread a spiritual path would be as psychologically damaging as pushing a client to perform some behavioural task for which s/he is unprepared.

What are the concerns about short-term versus long-term pastoral counselling?

- Time is probably the major enemy to be overcome.
- Hermeneutical pastoral counselling can only be developed over time.
- Many situations, problems and difficulties are best understood and resolved within the total life story.
- Whenever problem-solving techniques are used, they are best viewed as part of the resolution of the deeper soul issues.

Can a hermeneutical approach to a theory of pastoral counselling provide a comparable basis for a theory of pastoral care in the parish?

- Pastoral care involves establishing a pre-counselling relationship with persons and families as they go about their daily business of living and working. Caring provides a connection between the pastor's desire to help and the willingness of people to seek that help.
- The hermeneutical approach provides a structure for listening and responding to persons in a way that demonstrates deep caring, although such conversations may never reach the depth of long-term counselling.
- The hermeneutical, unified approach offers a ministry theory that is integrated and holistic.

Does the hermeneutic approach have broader implications than simply being a theory of pastoral counselling?

- The counsellor using such an integrated model must find ways of moving back and forth between the worlds of theology and personality without collapsing into one or violating the basic integrity of either.
- Hermeneutical pastoral counselling, with its emphasis on object relations and the transformation of self, within a larger context of meaning, has a contribution to offer both theology and psychotherapy.
- Pastoral counselling asserts the standard values of Christian images of what human life, under God, was meant to become and, as such, is an important Christian witness.
- Theology and psychotherapy together offer something more powerful than either could do if kept separated.

The ending of counselling brings the satisfaction of having been involved with the soul of another. This is often coupled with the humbling acceptance that perhaps not all that was hoped for has been achieved. Added to this is the knowledge that, in the helping, one has been helped; that in sharing the pain of another's wounds, one's own wounds have been touched and transformed. Above all, there is a sense of gratitude that whatever was changed was made possible by the Spiritual Presence.

Working with the life of the soul model

I find it helpful to present the model as a triangle then, together, client and counsellor identify the various factors. Having done that, they work out the tensions between them (Figure 2).

The task of the self is to hold in tension the three force/meaning dimensions, which come from three general directions in the life space of the individual.

Self/ego dimension

The tensions that arise from **psychological** development of the self/ego are

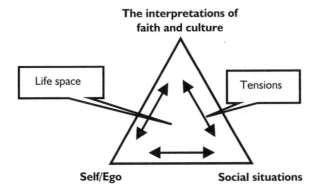

**The interpretations of
faith and culture**

Life space

Tensions

Self/Ego

Social situations

___

Figure 2

The Life of the Soul Model

conflicts that emerge in the course of development. Every individual has a certain 'set' or configuration that shapes a certain disposition and character.

Social context
This includes:

- Sociocultural, class, race
- Immediate community, work, family
- Relationships
- Expectations, commitments, conformity.

Faith and culture

- Faith and culture give rise to myths and symbol by which a tradition or way of life is shaped over time in a given location
- Faith and culture provide languages by which behaviours and relationships are given meanings and the way an individual perceives self and the world
- Faith and culture tell us what relationships should be and why
- What thoughts and behaviour should be assigned guilty, accusatory meaning and what should receive commendation.

There is constant interaction between all three dimensions that make up the flow of life in which the life of the soul is embedded and nurtured or kept in bondage. The individual's relationship to God is not separate from the life of the self in the world. It is part and parcel with the life of the self in all its relationships, its struggle to fine integrity at the connecting associations of a the meeting place of forces and meanings.

When working with clients, whether within a pastoral context or not, I have found the following guidelines helpful. Construct three boxes: Self, Society, Beliefs. Then, together, identify the questions the client could ask that would help both you and the client to achieve greater understanding. Put into the box all the things you have found out.

For example, under **Self**: What does this man think and feel about himself? What is his level of self-esteem? How does he relate to himself? Is he comfortable with himself and with others? What are his relationships like?

Under **Society**: How does he relate to society and what does he think of his place in society? What are his relationships with various significant sections of society; parents, siblings, friends? What are his views about society? What are his views about work? Does he fit easily with society or is he uncomfortable in it? Does he feel more at ease with certain groups in society than with others? If so, why?

Under **Beliefs**: What are his views of God? What is his relationship to God? What are the foundations of his beliefs? How do his beliefs relate to Self and Society?

Tensions: When you have examined the client's statement from all these angles, then you can start to piece them together. From each of the three boxes, take one thing at a time and contrast and compare it with those from the others. In this way you start to get some idea of the tensions that exist between them.

Further reading

Gerkin, C. V. (1984) *The Living Human Document*, Abingdon Press, Nashville.
Institute of Counselling (1995) *Introduction to Counselling, Lesson 8*. Institute of Counselling, 6 Dixon Street, Glasgow, G1 4AX.

PERSONALITY

Introduction

Personality is the enduring characteristics of an individual's behaviour, attitude and feelings in everyday social situations. Personality usually refers to that which is unique about a person, the characteristics that distinguish her/him from other people. Personality implies predictability about how a person will act or react under different circumstances. There are many influences on an individual's personality, including culture, genetic make-up and early family life. Personality psychology encompasses the whole person and the interface of that person with the world.

Type approaches (group 1)

According to the ancient Greeks, emotional equilibrium and general health depended on an appropriate balance among four fluids (humours) within the body.

- **The sanguine type**, associated with air (thought to have an excess of blood), was optimistic, enthusiastic, excitable, warm and hopeful
- **The melancholic type**, associated with earth (thought to have an excess of

black bile – congealed blood from the spleen), was full of foreboding and dark thoughts; now synonymous with the state of depression

- **The choleric type**, associated with fire (thought to have an excess of yellow bile – from the gall bladder), was irritable, touchy, easily angered and viewed the world with a jaundiced eye
- **The phlegmatic type**, associated with water (thought to have an excess of phlegm – the secretion of the throat) was stolid, apathetic, undemonstrative, unexcitable and unemotional.

The fact that these words are used today to describe personality characteristics is an indicator of just how much they still influence us.

Type approaches (group 2): constitutional psychology

One of the earliest works on body build is *Displaying the Secrets of Nature Relating to Physiognomy* by Aristotle (384–322 BC).

Ernst Kretschmer (1888–1964)

Kretschmer's best-known work, *Physique and Character* (1921), advanced the theory that certain mental disorders were more common among people of specific physical types. Kretschmer's ideas entered into popular culture to some extent and generated further psychological research.

William Herbert Sheldon (1898–1970)

In Sheldon's system, human beings can be classified as to body build in terms of three extreme body types:

- **Endomorphic** – tending toward roundness
- **Mesomorphic** – marked by greater than average muscular development
- **Ectomorphic** – tending toward being thin.

In practice, extreme types are rare or nonexistent and the person of normal build has a somatotype approaching an even balance between the extremes.

Trait approaches

The American psychologist Gordon Allport developed a trait theory of personality that has remained virtually unchanged. A trait refers to any characteristic that differs from person to person in a relatively permanent and consistent way. Like physical characteristics such as height, weight and hair colour, traits help to provide information about one person in relation to other people. Attributes of personality regarded as traits include sociability, dominance, impulsiveness and anxiousness. We are using trait terms when we use such adjectives to describe ourselves as 'aggressive', 'cautious', 'excitable', 'intelligent', 'shy'.

The most extensive study of personality traits has been conducted by Raymond Cattell and resulted in *Cattell's Sixteen Personality Factor Questionnaire* (16PF), the most widely used and influential of personality tests.

J. M. Digman's model identifies five relatively distinct groups of traits:

- **Extroversion** – talkative versus silent, dominant versus submissive
- **Agreeableness** – kind versus unkind, generous versus stingy
- **Conscientiousness** – hardworking versus lazy, reliable versus unreliable
- **Emotional stability** – relaxed versus tense, calm versus temperamental
- **Intellect** – intelligent versus unintelligent, creative versus uncreative.

Psychodynamic approaches

Psychodynamic approaches, based on the work of Sigmund Freud, look at personality not from what could be considered the 'public' side but from the inner world of the person – from the unconscious. Many of Freud's disciples departed from strict psychoanalytic theory to form their own approaches and theories of personality and generally introduced more of a social emphasis in their theories of personality. Underlying development of personality is the belief that it is necessary to understand what motivates the individual. Psychodynamic theories are more concerned with explaining existing neurotic behaviour than with predicting future behaviour.

Freud proposed that early experiences in eating, toilet training and sexual feeling are critical in shaping the developing personality structure. The structure is manifest throughout life in how we view ourselves, in relationships with others and in general ways of relating to the environment.

Psychodynamic theory describes how the structures of the id, ego and superego are in constant conflict and their interaction influences human behaviour. These structures become part of our personality in childhood and become manifest in adult behaviour.

Cognitive–behavioural approaches

Cognition refers to the manner in which we perceive, remember, think and make use of language and how we organize information about the world. What people think about themselves is an important influence on their behaviour. Other factors that influence personality, according to this model, are how we process information both about the self and the surrounding world; how we attempt to predict and control events; how some people tend to think in a complex, abstract way while others think in a simple, concrete way; how people organize information to make long-range plans and to regulate their behaviour in accordance with these plans.

The behaviourist view of personality is represented by thinkers such as the American psychologist B. F. Skinner, who place primary emphasis on learning. Skinner sees human behaviour as determined largely by its consequences. If rewarded, behaviour recurs; if punished, it is less likely to recur. A common theme running through the cognitive–behavioural approaches is the interplay between the external and the internal or between the person and the situation.

Situationism

Situationism is a theory of personality proposed by Walter Mischel. It emphasizes characteristics of the situation in which we are placed, rather than any personality types or traits within the person. According to the theory, human behaviour is determined by influences in each situation. Situationism suggests that people behave in response to changes in the situation.

Social-learning approach

Social-learning theory assumes that personality differences result from variation in learning experiences. Responses may be learned through **observation**, without reinforcement, but reinforcement is important in determining whether the learned responses will be performed. The leading social-learning theorist is Albert Bandura.

Social learning emphasizes the importance of environmental or situational factors in determining behaviour. Environmental conditions shape behaviour through learning; a person's behaviour, in turn, shapes the environment. Social-learning theory places much emphasis on cognitive factors such as memory.

The sorts of issue over which social-learning theorists are concerned are:

- **Competence** – What can you do?
- **Interpreting strategies** – How do you see it?
- **Expectancies** – What will happen?
- **Subjective values** – What the person believes.
- **Goals** – How can you achieve them?

Humanistic approaches

The existential-humanistic approach emphasizes the growth and self-actualization of the individual and his/her conscious subjective experience. Possibly the most influential figures in this field are Carl Rogers – originator of person-centred counselling – and Abraham Maslow.

Rogers's research has explored the conditions that promote positive developments of the self and enhance movement toward self-actualization. These approaches focus more on the future – what the person can become – than on what the person has been. For Rogers, the most important aspect of personality is the congruence between various aspects of the self and congruence between self and the ideal self.

Interactionism

The interactive approach is fundamentally eclectic and maintains that personality is a sum total of many influences, of some of which we are aware; others we have barely yet started to become aware of. Interactionism takes into account both a person's predisposition to a type of response and the variables of the situation. It says that both factors influence performance. Rather than being a precise and measurable 'thing', personality is truly a cover term for the complex patterns of interaction.

Personality theory applied to counselling

Type and trait theories complement each other. Type theories are concerned with that which is common among individuals; trait theories focus on that which differentiates them. Personality traits are ill-adjusted if they cause significant impairment in everyday life or if they lead to distress or discomfort. In such cases the personality characteristic is referred to as a **personality disorder**. These disorders are lifelong patterns of behaving that lead to maladjustment and an inability to cope with ordinary situations.

Personality disorders are not, strictly speaking, illnesses, since they need not involve the disruption of emotional, intellectual or perceptual functioning. In many cases, people with a personality disorder do not seek psychiatric treatment for such unless they are pressured to by relatives or by a court. There are many different types of personality disorder; they are classified according to the particular personality traits that are accentuated.

Personality disorders differ from personality change. However, the study of personality disorders is not without its difficulties, for it operates in the grey and ambiguous area between sickness and health, an area that abounds with personal opinion and value judgements. Where do we draw the line between, for example, characterizing someone as cautious and determining that s/he is paranoid? Where is the dividing line between a man who prefers his own company and the schizoid personality? When does a person cross the line from 'normality' to 'personality disorder'?

Personality disorder – also called character disorder – is a mental disorder that is marked by deeply ingrained and lasting patterns of inflexible, faulty or antisocial behaviour. A personality disorder is an accentuation of one or more personality traits to the point that the trait significantly impairs an individual's social or occupational functioning.

For a diagnosis of personality disorder to be made, there must be an evaluation of the person's long-term pattern of functioning. The particular personality features must have been evident from early adulthood. In addition, the disorder must be distinguished from changes that accompany other medical or psychiatric illnesses. Personality disorder tends to appear in late childhood or adolescence and continues to be manifest into adulthood. It is therefore unlikely that the diagnosis of personality disorder will be appropriate before the age of 16 or 17 years. General diagnostic guidelines applying to all personality disorders are presented below; supplementary descriptions are provided with each of the subtypes.

Personality disorders are treated with various forms of psychotherapy, sometimes by using drugs under the direction of psychiatrists, psychologists, social workers and many other mental-health professionals.

Counsellors who suspect that a client they are dealing with has a personality disorder are advised, in the first instance, to seek psychiatric advice as to the wisdom of continuing.

Further reading

Digman, J. M. (1990) Personality structure: emergence of the five-factor model. *Annual Review of Psychology*, **41**, 417–440.

Mischel, W. (1986) *Introduction to Personality*, 4th edn. Holt, Rinehart & Winston, New York.

Person-Centred Counselling (*see also*: Core conditions, Frames of reference)

Dr Carl R. Rogers (1902–87) an American whose study of theology convinced him that he was not suited to the ministry, turned to psychology and psychoanalysis. His study of children led him to question the validity of some of the fundamental tenets of psychoanalysis.

Rogers attached more importance to the counsellor's attitudes than to his/her technical training or skills. Accurate and sensitive understanding of the client's experiences and feelings is paramount, because it helps the client focus on the experience of the moment. (Rogers used the word 'client' instead of 'patient' to indicate that the treatment is neither manipulative nor medically prescriptive.)

Rogers developed the nondirective approach to counselling, based on his unshakeable belief that clients needed to have much more control over the therapeutic process than they were given in traditional therapy. In nondirective therapy, the aim of the therapist was to engage the client in an equal, participative relationship rather than in organized and structured therapy.

Rogers later replaced the term by 'client-centred' and it is now 'person-centred'. The term is often used to distinguish a process that is different from the directive therapies, particularly behaviour therapy. Rogers's move toward 'person-centred counselling' acknowledged the difficulties of being totally 'nondirective'. It is probably no more possible to be totally nondirective than it is to be totally objective. The very fact that time, venue and length of session are all set removes some of the credibility of being nondirective. What seems to be important is the intention of the counsellor and the underlying philosophy.

To be 'nondirective' means relinquishing some or most of the control to the client. The influence of the counsellor and the wish to help the client to change, some would argue, must in some way be directive, even although it is the client who decides what s/he wants to change.

The person-centred approach emphasizes the capacity and strengths of clients to direct the course and direction of their own therapy. The concept of self-actualization is at the centre of person-centred counselling, in common with other humanistic therapies, philosophies and approaches.

Fundamental to the method is the relationship established between therapist and client, based on the core conditions of empathy, genuineness or congruence, nonpossessive warmth and unconditional positive regard. (*See* Core conditions for full discussion.)

Person-centred counsellors prefer to talk about attitudes and behaviours and creating growth-promoting climates. Their view of their clients is that they are intrinsically good, capable of directing their own destinies and capable of self-actualization. Counsellor and client work within a partnership of equals who trust each other.

The focus is on entering the client's frame of reference and understanding and tracking the client's personal meanings. This does not mean that the counsellor is passive. Being able to enter the client's frame of reference means active listening and a continual struggle to lay aside preconceptions that would hinder the process. The person-centred counsellor also believes in the importance of rejecting the pursuit of authority or control over others. Power is there to be shared. Person-centred counselling is not a soft option; neither does it mean that the counsellor does nothing but listen. Not having a set model to work to, yet always remaining in touch with the client's feelings and what those feelings mean to this unique client, means that the counsellor has to be prepared to travel unknown roads, for the experience of every client is totally unique. If the core conditions are present, then growth and change will take place.

The answers to two basic questions are sought in therapy, 'Who am I?' and 'How can I become myself?'

The person-centred approach, in common with many other therapies, is less successful with severely disturbed psychotic clients. Person-centred principles have been applied in the classroom, in colleges, in organizations and in groups. Critics of the approach argue that it is naive and does not help the client face reality.

Stages in therapy

Stage 1

- Client communicates about externals
- Feelings are not owned
- Constructs are rigid
- The client is reluctant to engage in close relationships.

Stage 2

- Feelings are sometimes described but not owned
- Keeps subjective experience at a distance
- Problems are perceived as external to self.

Stage 3

- Feelings and personal meanings in the past are described, usually as unacceptable or bad
- Expressions of self are in objective terms
- Self tends to be seen as a part of others
- Personal constructs are rigid
- Some recognition that problems are personal and not external.

Stage 4

- Free and full description of feelings and personal meanings

- Intense feelings are not described in the present
- The possibility of feelings breaking through causes alarm
- Unwilling to experience feelings
- Personal constructs become more free
- What was absolute now becomes possibility
- Some recognition of self-responsibility.

Stage 5

- Easier to express feelings in the present
- Owning of feelings
- Immediacy of feelings is less fearful
- More able to tolerate contradictions and ambiguities
- Personal constructs and meanings are open to question
- More acceptance of self-responsibility.

Stage 6

- Acceptance and immediate expression of previously denied feelings
- Feelings expressed bring liberation through catharsis
- Acceptance of the validity of working in the present
- Self is real, not an object
- Flexible constructs replace flexible ones.

Stage 7

- The client feels comfortable with living in present experience
- The immediacy of feelings are experienced with enhanced richness
- Able to risk expressing feelings.

The counsellor's task is to facilitate clients' awareness of, and trust in, self-actualization. The therapeutic process is centred in the client and it is the client's inner experiencing that controls the pace and the direction of the relationship.

When clients are accepted and when the core conditions are present, they feel safe enough to explore their problems and gradually come to experience the parts of themselves they normally keep hidden from themselves and from others.

Thus counselling means helping the client to move away from what is less desirable toward something more desirable or, in Egan's terms, from the present scenario to the desired scenario. Much of the present scenario consists of not living to the fullness of what we are capable of; where we are frequently pulled away from what we want to be by what others want us to be. This is the scenario of the façade or what Jung calls the Persona, the mask. The desired scenario pulls us toward what we could become, where we know we are being real; where our feelings toward ourselves and others are genuine and positive, yet still being able to express negative feelings appropriately. Being authentic means that we can be real with ourselves and other people.

The person-centred counsellor has no model, structure, strategies or techniques to rely on, only his/her own unique self and the intense desire to be at one with the client and to feel with this client within a relationship in which the client feels upheld and able to become her/himself.

Within the person-centred relationship three stages can be identified:

1. **Trust.** This may take many sessions to develop. Trust can never be demanded, it can only be earned, and this will happen as the client feels safe to express whatever feelings need to be expressed without fear of judgement or their being slotted into some preconceived model. Trust is two-way: the counsellor has to trust the client. This does not mean trusting the 'truth' of what the client says, rather it means trusting the client's feelings. More than that, it means having trust in the client's ability to work toward self-healing.

2. **Intimacy.** Intimacy can only develop where there is trust. Intimacy does not mean physical closeness or even touch; intimacy means a sharing of feelings, experiences, thoughts, wishes, desires, which we normally do not share readily. When the client allows the counsellor to share in his/her inner world, to see something from the internal frame of reference, that is intimacy. When client and counsellor sit in silence, just having shared something deeply important, as if sharing in the communion, that is intimacy.

3. **Mutuality.** Brian Thorne speaks of this intimacy as the stage of complete trust and transparency, where 'neither is fearful of the other and intimacy comes easily in ways which are appropriate to the counselling setting'. Here the counsellor is likely to become more, but appropriately, self-disclosing. This enhances the counsellor's genuineness as a person, not just a counsellor responding from within a role. This is the stage when the client moves further into, as it were, being his/her own counsellor; where the client begins to trust his/herself; where the control is located within, not within the counselling relationship; where the core conditions have been internalized to become integrated within the personality; where acceptance by the counsellor has been replaced by self-acceptance; where healing, if not complete, is taking place.

Finally, being person-centred not only means having the client at the centre of the counselling relationship, it also means having one's self at the centre. This does not mean being self-centred or egotistical, it means that the core conditions reside deep within and find expression in our relationship with others. If, for example, we are not genuine within, can we be genuine with clients? If we do not accept ourselves as we are, yet never ceasing to change what is unacceptable to our self-image, can we unreservedly accept clients? Can we really listen to the feelings of others, track their meanings, if we do not understand ourselves?

Further reading

Mearns, D. and Thorne, B. (1988) *Person-Centred Counselling in Action*, Sage Publications, London.

Rogers, C. R. (1942) *Counselling and Psychotherapy*, Constable, London.

Rogers, C. R. (1951) *Client-Centred Therapy: Its current practice, implications and theory*, Constable, London.

Rogers, C. R. (1961) *On Becoming a Person: A therapist's view of psychotherapy*, Constable, London.

Rogers, C. R. (1980) *A Way of Being*, Houghton Mifflin, Boston, MA.

Thorne, B. (1985) *The Quality of Tenderness*, Norwich Centre Publications, Norwich.

Thorne, B. (1996) Person-centred therapy. In: *Handbook of Individual Therapy*, (ed. W. Dryden), Sage Publications, London.

PERSON-CENTRED COUNSELLOR ATTITUDES

This article is adapted from Nelson-Jones, R. and Patterson, C. H. (1974) 'Some effects of counsellor training'. *British Journal for Guidance and Counselling*, 2(2) and is used with permission. The original article, and this section in the second edition of this book, was designed as a questionnaire to be scored; in this edition the questions and answers have been merged.

The interpretations I give, resulting from several years in teaching counselling, are purely my views and may not be in agreement with more dedicated person-centred counsellors. Although this is specifically directed at person-centred counsellors, the concepts apply equally to most counselling.

I feel I must point out that you may disagree with some of the answers. In my work as a lecturer in counselling, there have been many students who could not accept the answers as given. The 'Agree' or 'Disagree' verdicts are taken from the original scoring, supplied by Richard Nelson-Jones. The rationale that follows derives from my attempt to help students arrive at a greater understanding of what is meant by person-centred counselling. Nelson-Jones and Patterson's paper was based on research and their validation of the questionnaire must be acknowledged. My comments are not research-based, but I hope this does not make them less valid.

1. *The counsellor's goal is to make people better adjusted to society*
   Disagree. The counsellor is there for the client, not primarily as an agent of society. To agree with this has implications of conformity and compliance, both of which most counsellors would certainly not agree to.

2. *It is the counsellor's job to solve the client's problems*
   Disagree. As with 1, most counsellors would agree that the client must solve the problem. The counsellor is there to help clarify and facilitate.

3. *A thorough diagnosis is necessary for effective counselling*
   Disagree. Unlike medicine, or indeed social work, diagnosing does not play an essential role in counselling. A dictionary definition of diagnosis is: determination of the nature of a cause of a disease and the opinion derived from such an examination. Diagnosis consists of observation, an essential facet of counselling, but it also implies examination by questions and applying preconceived principles and criteria and a process of elimination. Successful treatment is dependent on accurate diagnosis and cannot start until the process of diagnosis is completed. In person-centred counselling, and indeed

in most other counselling approaches, the word 'treatment' is not used and the process starts immediately, as counsellor and client begin to interact.

4. *The counsellor should plan each session carefully before the client comes*
Disagree. This question is related to the previous one. In person-centred counselling, the counsellor remains as open as possible and it is the client who determines where the session goes. Planning assumes that the planner knows where the session should go.

5. *In the session, clients may discuss any area of concern they wish*
Agree. If the client is in charge, then the client will know what to discuss. This may sound a contradiction; what I mean is that the person-centred counsellor has faith in the integrity of the client's psyche. The underlying belief is that the client's psyche is constantly seeking for wholeness and will direct the client accordingly. The counsellor's most difficult task is to make connections among what the client is exploring.

6. *The counsellor should be in control of the session at all times*
Disagree. I would imagine that this is self-explanatory, other than for the length of the session. Client and counsellor have an agreed time limit and either may draw it to a close at the appointed time, although normally it is the counsellor who does so.

7. *Clients understand themselves best when compared with other people*
Disagree. Comparisons are offensive and are generally either felt to be a put down or an attempt to offer reassurances.

8. *The counsellor should suggest reading material pertinent to the problem, whether it is requested or not*
Disagree. While some approaches recommend and some insist upon homework, this is foreign to the person-centred counsellor. I doubt even if reading material would be suggested, on the premise that, by so doing, the counsellor is giving direction.

9. *In order for clients to benefit most from counselling, they must be given unconditional acceptance by the counsellor*
Agree. I would think that this is self-explanatory, although putting it into practice is far from simple.

10. *If clients are unable to understand their problem, it is the counsellor's responsibility to explain it to them carefully and clearly*
Disagree. Explanations come from the counsellor's frame of reference and, as such, they could be interpreted as an attempt to convince or gain control.

11. *The function of the counsellor is to create and maintain an atmosphere in which clients may explore their feelings and attitudes however they wish*
Agree. When the core conditions are operating, the climate is conducive to exploration.

12. *Clients must first establish a dependency relationship upon the counsellor before they can become independent*
Disagree. Unlike some approaches, person-centred counselling works very hard to avoid dependency. The more one takes control and gives direction, the more risk there is of a relationship of dependency being created.

13. *The counsellor has the social and professional right not to interfere with the client's choice of an antisocial solution to the problem*
Agree. This often presents difficulty for student counsellors, where their view of themselves as citizens conflicts with their view of themselves as counsellors. The counsellor might hope that counselling might help the client not to be antisocial, but the counsellor cannot interfere. See similar questions 20, 32, 37.
14. *The counsellor is always the one to decide when the counselling relationship should end*
Disagree. See question 6. This sometimes causes confusion between the ending of a session and the ending of counselling. Here the meaning is the ending of the counselling relationship. In this instance, it is the client who determines when counselling ends.
15. *Clients have within them the capacities to work out a solution to their problem without manipulation by the counsellor*
Agree. I hope that this is self-explanatory, though it does take a great deal of faith in the client to work toward this.
16. *If, in the initial session, the counsellor has some negative feelings toward clients, the counsellor should firmly but gently refuse to continue with them*
Agree. I admit to having difficulty with the answer and it could be firmly disputed. The only rationale I can think of is that the counsellor is being truly genuine and open. If the counsellor feels unable to work with a certain client, then it is being genuine to say so. However, there are other points to be considered. If a client engenders negative feelings in me, I would feel it incumbent on me to explore with the client, and with my mentor, the reasons for these feelings. This provides a wonderful opportunity for growth. I find it difficult to believe that any of us can be so sure of our feelings that we could determine after one session if we could work with a client or not. If I have misunderstood the scoring, then I apologize to devoted person-centred counsellors, who may well feel outraged at my lack of perception.
17. *If counselling is to be successful, the counsellor must depend, for the most part, on the client's own potential for growth*
Agree. The discussion so far should pave the way for an affirmative.
18. *A complete case history is necessary before counselling starts*
Disagree. Similar to question 3. For my part, I prefer to build up the picture of the person gradually; otherwise the first session can seem like an interrogation. Very often, clients come for counselling because they are under stress; it would therefore seem inappropriate to deal with the history at the expense of dealing with the crisis.
19. *Clients should be permitted to solve their problems in their own way*
Agree. Although the answer is 'Yes', carrying it out may prove difficult for the counsellor. One of the major difficulties, as I see it, is the clash of values. My values are correct for me but I have no right to impose them on others. This question is also tied in with self-determination.

20. *The client has the right to choose goals that are antisocial or immoral*
    Agree. Similar to question 13. I think it is necessary to point out that, although the answer is 'Yes', the counsellor is not just a passive bystander. A client who disclosed that an immoral act was contemplated would be helped to explore the various pros and cons of that act so that the client would be making an informed choice.

21. *In the session, clients have the right to say anything they wish about the counsellor*
    Agree. This would be difficult for most counsellors to accept. I think what underlies this question is that very often clients vent their anger at the counsellor rather than at the person who generated that anger. On the other hand, if I am inept and continually fail to understand the client, then the client has a perfect right to say so. That is my interpretation.

22. *The counsellor should offer advice when it is clearly needed*
    Disagree. However, it is sometimes very difficult not to offer advice. In my style of counselling I do use advice, simply because I also use other approaches. A client who is stressed, for example, may be advised how to relax and what steps to take to reduce stress levels.

23. *The best way to understand clients is to see them as they see themselves*
    Agree. This refers to being able to enter the client's frame of reference. Understanding what something means to the other person is what person-centred counsellors call 'tracking the meanings'.

24. *People must work out their own solutions to their problems*
    Agree. Similar to question 19.

25. *If clients talk about a number of problems at the same time, the counsellor should tell them to concentrate on one problem at a time*
    Disagree. This is taking control and giving direction, both of which are anathema to person-centred counsellors.

26. *The counsellor should praise the client whenever appropriate*
    Disagree. This is a difficult one. The strict person-centred counsellor neither praises nor condemns, believing that both are evaluations and judgements. Most other counsellors would give praise appropriate to the situation.

27. *One of the counsellor's main functions is to try to convey to clients that their feelings and attitudes are accepted*
    Agree. There is generally no problem with this one. If the core conditions are present, then the client feels totally accepted.

28. *After clients have decided on their goals, the counsellor should then tell them how they can best be achieved*
    Disagree. Person-centred counsellors never tell their clients what to do. They will help them explore what the goals could mean.

29. *When clients feel their situation is hopeless, reassurance is in order.*
    Disagree. Reassurance is often no more than an attempt to diminish the problem. The mere fact that the counsellor is taking time to help the client explore the problem and is creating a climate conducive to foster exploration is adequate reassurance.

30. *When clients do not understand the meaning of a particular piece of behaviour, the counsellor should explain it to them*
Disagree. The meaning of behaviour would be from the counsellor's frame of reference. Explaining something puts the counsellor in a position of power and control.

31. *Clients should be permitted to express attitudes that are contrary to those of the counsellor*
Agree. If the aim of counselling is to encourage self-expression and client control, then this has to be a 'Yes'. Authority does not encourage expression; person-centred counselling is as opposite from authority as Australia is from Britain.

32. *Counsellors should try to discourage clients from making mistakes*
Disagree. The counsellor who does try is seeking to gain control.

33. *Counsellors should ask questions only when they do not understand what the clients have said*
Agree. The skill of person-centred counselling lies more in creating statements that reflect the client's statement rather than in asking questions. Questions, when asked, are best constructed as open questions.

34. *If clients present points of view that are obviously prejudiced or distorted, the counsellor should put them right*
Disagree. What is prejudiced or distorted is very much a question of perception from one's own frame of reference. What the counsellor can do is to present an alternative frame of reference. 'As I see it ... Is that something you would like to explore?'

35. *It is essential for client and counsellor to identify and discuss insights*
Disagree. This is another moot point. The strict person-centred counsellor probably feels that insights don't need to be discussed and that to do so would rob the experience of some of the thrill. However, I think that, if the client wishes to, then it's all right to do so, although I would never insist upon it. Insights have to be worked in before they can be worked out.

36. *The counsellor should interpret the client's unconscious attitudes and feelings*
Disagree. Interpretation of the unconscious is rarely advisable in counselling unless one is psychologically equipped so to do, by virtue of appropriate training and experience.

37. *The counsellor should discourage clients from their intentions to perform criminal acts*
Disagree. Similar to questions 13 and 20. Situations are rarely black or white and quite often counsellors are thrown into conflict. A major consideration must always be: Who is at risk if this action is carried through and how will I cope with the knowledge that I did nothing to stop it? I think another question must also be considered: Why is the client telling me? There may not be a simple answer to that, so my feeling is that the counsellor would be wise to discuss it with the client. Counsellors in the UK must always bear in mind that they can be subpoenaed to disclose information before a court of law.

38. *The counsellor's main function is to provide an accepting and permissive atmosphere in which clients are free to work out their problems*
Agree. Similar to question 11.

39. *When clients have stated their problems, the counsellor should offer one or more possible solutions to serve as a basis for further discussion*
Disagree. This would remove control from the client to the counsellor. 'What would you like to discuss?' leaves the client in control.

40. *Early in the counselling process the counsellor should reassure clients that their problems are not insoluble and thereby reduce their anxiety so that they can start working on their problem*
Disagree. This is false reassurance and puts the client in an inferior position. The anxiety is real and the client must work through it. The anxiety is part of the problem.

41. *The counsellor should feel free to ask clients questions in order to obtain pertinent information necessary for the solution of the problem*
Disagree. On the face of it this sounds as if it should be 'Agree'. On closer examination, however, the clue lies in the 'solving the problem'. By asking questions that 'investigate' the problem, the counsellor is taking control and showing superior knowledge.

42. *Clients should be free to discontinue counselling whenever they wish*
Agree. Although this may not suit the counsellor, can be very frustrating and may break all contracts, the decision must remain with the client. This may be the first decision the client has ever taken to assert his/her own authority.

43. *When counsellors see that clients are solving their problems realistically, they should encourage them*
Disagree. Similar to question 29.

44. *If the life situation of clients demands an immediate decision or some course of action and the clients feel unable to make a choice, the counsellor should make suggestions*
Disagree. The counsellor cannot take decisions on behalf of the client; to do so is removing responsibility from the client. However, in a crisis, when the client is immobilized, then the counsellor may have to take action. This course of action would probably be disputed by person-centred counsellors.

45. *Clients who wish to spend long periods in silence should be allowed to*
Agree. This may be a frustrating situation to be in, yet it must be the client's choice. Rogers tells a delightful tale of a college counsellor to whom a student was referred. The counsellor explained the process and the number of sessions and so on, ending with something like, 'Now the time is yours to do what you like with'. The student said nothing for the whole session. At the end, the counsellor said, 'See you next week,' and the student left, to reappear next week and to sit in silence again for the whole session. At the end of the contracted number of sessions, the counsellor said something like, 'Do you feel you need to come again?' 'No', said the student and left. During the six sessions, I think it was, not a word was exchanged. Some time later, the counsellor had a note from the student's teacher: 'I don't

know what you did with..., but she's really great now and she's been voted head of the class!'

46. *If clients threaten suicide, the counsellor should endeavour to help them explore their feelings*

 Agree. This seems logical – in fact it has been suggested that one way to show genuineness is not only to explore feelings, but to explore how the client plans to do it.

47. *The counsellor should end every session with some word of reassurance*

 Disagree. Similar to question 29. Rather than offer reassurance, here is what I do. Just before the end I usually (I would hesitate to say 'always') say, 'What do you think/feel you are taking away with you from today?' This invites the client to find his or own reassurance.

48. *When clients ask for advice, they should be given it*

 Disagree. Similar to question 22. This time it is if the client asks. The rationale for the 'disagree' is that once again it puts the counsellor in control and removes responsibility from the client. It increases the power of the counsellor and the helplessness of the client.

49. *The counsellor should give an explanation of the counselling relationship in the first session*

 Agree. There should be no problem with this. Personally, I give all new clients a one-page handout of who I am and my style of working.

50. *Resistance to counselling should be accepted, not interpreted*

 Agree. What is meant here is that an interpretation could be something like, 'You are resisting the process because you have a problem with authority figures'. Accepting the resistance could be something like, 'It seems that this is difficult to talk about'.

51. *In the initial contact, the counsellor should develop a friendly, social relationship with the client as a basis for counselling*

 Disagree. The reason for this being 'disagree' is that counselling is friendly but it is not a social exchange. It is a purposeful relationship which, when the client so decides, will end.

52. *The counsellor should assume the major responsibility for the content of discussion during the session*

 Disagree. If we do that, the client is no longer in charge.

53. *Most clients are unable to take the responsibility for the solution to their problems, otherwise they would not be in counselling*

 Disagree. This is the view of some therapies but certainly not person-centred counselling. The person-centred view would be that the person's inner powers have become temporarily 'frozen' and that within the warmth of the counselling relationship they will become 'unfrozen' and mobilized.

54. *The major contribution of the counsellor to the solution of clients' problems is providing an objective, external point of view*

 Disagree. Once again, this is linked with the counsellor's frame of reference. Objectivity comes with the way the client's statements are understood and reflected.

55. *The client should be allowed to indulge in self-pity*

Agree. It is one thing to recognize that the client is feeling self-pity and another to try to shake her/him out of it. Far more constructive to understand what self-pity means from the client's frame of reference.

56. *The counsellor should discourage long pauses in counselling, to keep the client from feeling embarrassed or uncomfortable*

Disagree. Similar to question 45. To break silence because we think the client might be embarrassed is putting us in a position of superiority. The truth is that we probably feel embarrassed, not the client. Again, the question could be asked, 'What does this silence mean?'

57. *When clients seem unable to talk about themselves, the counsellor should engage in 'small talk' to get them started*

Disagree. Small talk leads to small discussion. Pleasantries such as 'Hello, how have things been with you since we last met?' open the way for exploration. Small talk such as 'Well what did you think of the football yesterday?' may then make it difficult to get started on the 'real' business.

58. *It is rarely helpful for counsellors to tell clients what they would do when faced with the same problem*

Agree. Please notice the qualifying word, 'rarely'. It is tempting, when asked, 'Yes, but what would you do?' to provide an answer.

59. *The purpose of the first session is to diagnose the client's problem*

Disagree. Similar to question 3.

60. *If counsellors feel that clients persist in wasting interview time, they should be open with the client and tell them*

Agree. At first glance this may seem contradictory to the philosophy of person-centred counselling. As I interpret it, it is being genuine and open. 'John, there's something been bothering me for a few sessions; your time is precious to you just as mine is to me, yet it seems that you waste our time together by turning up late, then making excuses for wanting to get away before time. What do you think about that?'

61. *Counsellors should try to help clients see their problems logically*

Disagree. Similar to question 10. The word 'logically' implies head knowledge, rather than addressing feelings.

62. *The counsellor should never take a client's statements at face value, since the client is not fully aware of the hidden significance*

Disagree. Similar to question 30, 36 and 53. This question implies superior knowledge of the counsellor, based on presupposition and not understanding the client's frame of reference.

63. *The counsellor must remain objective and impersonal in the counselling relationship*

Disagree. This question may present difficulties to some counsellors. Part of the counselling process is to bring some objectivity to the relationship, yet too much objectivity creates distance while too little hampers progress. It means striving for a fine balance between involvement and over-involvement.

My own feeling is that one can be objective without being impersonal. At the same time, to become involved demonstrates our humanity. Being involved with another person has its risks. In one training session, Brian Thorne speaks of how at one stage in the interview he was in danger of losing his moorings, as he viewed the enormity of the client's isolation. For Brian, experiencing that isolation was temporarily terrifying. Yet it was probably that momentary identification that enabled him to really enter the client's world and make contact other than with words.

64. *The more prior information the counsellor has about the client, the better it will be to understand the client's problem*
   Disagree. Information that comes from other people may be biased at best and downright inaccurate at worst. Personally, I prefer not to know anything other than the barest of facts. 'Mr Jones is suffering from stress.' 'Miss Smith has had several abortions and can't come to terms with them.'

65. *Clients who deviate from the discussion of a significant problem area should be brought back to it in a gentle, subtle or round-about way*
   Disagree. This is very tempting to want to do. It can be very frustrating to stay with a client who appears to be going all around the houses – several times. I was facilitating a group for abused women. In the ninth session of 12, the discussion centred on one lady who was obviously angry about her current home situation. My thoughts were, 'What is the relevance to the subject of abuse?' When the penny dropped, I connected the discussion to the main issue by coining a phrase 'domestic abuse'. Having made the connection, we explored that issue which then allowed the group to once more look at other issues of abuse.

66. *Successful counsellors are those who are able to suggest solutions to clients' problems in such a way that the clients feel they are their own*
   Disagree. This is commonly called 'manipulation', behaviour from which most counsellors would recoil. However, situations are seldom clear cut. There is a fine line between legitimate influence and manipulation. Manipulation always carries with it some benefit to the manipulator. Influence is generally unconscious. In any case, suggesting solutions is not part of effective counselling. There is a difference between exploring alternatives and suggesting solutions.

67. *The counsellor should allow the client to make self-derogatory statements*
   Agree. This sounds wrong and the natural tendency would be to present a counter-argument. This would not be considered 'good practice'. The person-centred counsellor would probably reflect the feelings. 'I get the feeling that when you say you are a useless no-good that your self-esteem is at rock bottom.'

68. *The counsellor should make every effort to get at the true facts of a situation when the facts are in conflict*
   Disagree. Counselling is not detective work and counsellors are not investigators. I would draw attention to what appears to be a discrepancy without making a value judgement. Truth and untruth are value judgements. If the

client is presenting conflicting statements, this could be because of confusion.

69. *It is necessary for the counsellor to get a clear picture of the nature and origin of the problem before clients can be helped*

Disagree. Counselling is something like building a jigsaw. The whole picture only emerges as each piece is put into place. The client's problem is made clearer as each bit is put into place and connections are made between different parts of the puzzle.

70. *Counsellors should adapt the counselling relationship to the expectations of the client*

Disagree. Counsellors are not professional chameleons. If I were to adapt the counselling relationship with every client, what would happen to my professional judgement? Would I become emotionally fragmented and end up not knowing who I was or what I was supposed to be doing? At the same time, it is in the best interests of clients and for my personal and professional development to remain as open and flexible as I can be, so that I can address this client's needs in the most appropriate way for this client.

Finale

I have tried to give my interpretations of the person-centred approach. As I indicated at the start, I would not call myself a 'person-centred counsellor', I am person-centred. Therein lies a difference.

If one client finds it difficult to work with reflecting feelings, yet is able to work with images, then I will use images. Another client may prefer a behavioural approach. That, for me, is eclecticism. To be person-centred the client has to be the focus, rather than trying to fit the client into some preconceived therapeutic model. That for me has advantages and disadvantages. To work strictly to a model, to my way of thinking, is like trying to fit all people into size 6 shoes. That for me is an impossibility; I take size 12.

Person-centred counselling takes the client where s/he is and works really hard to stay alongside the client on the particular journey. For some clients, this approach works; others feel it is too woolly and nondirective. The approach does not rely on techniques, yet for some people 'techniques' are helpful.

Clients who are stressed may need help to relax. Marjory liked working with images and, although she was a 'thinker' and found difficulty speaking about feelings, the images she produced were full of feelings. Working with these, as they changed and developed, brought healing.

Every person who engages in counselling is advised to explore many approaches to find one that suits their personality. If there is not a good fit between approach and personality, the approach will sit uneasily and the counsellor will not do the best possible work.

PHENOMENOLOGY (*see also*: Existential therapy)

Phenomenology is a school of philosophy that arose in the early years of the 20th century. It is the study of all human experience as free as possible from presupposition or bias. Phenomenology is a way of showing the essential involvement of human existence in the world, starting with everyday perception.

Phenomenologists limit their study to conscious experiences without trying to elicit underlying, hypothetical, causes. The data they produce are formulated from the subject's point of view.

Phenomenologists, as a rule, reject the idea of the unconscious. They believe we can learn more about human nature by studying how people view themselves and their world than we can by observing their actions.

In that phenomenologists are more concerned with internal mental processes and the inner life and experiences of individuals – self-concept, feelings of self-esteem and self-awareness – than with behaviour, they have certain similarities to cognitivists.

Phenomenologists believe that we are free agents, that we are not acted upon by forces beyond our control, but that we have a great degree of control over our own destiny – the issue of free will versus determinism.

Phenomenological approaches view people as naturally evolving in the direction of psychological growth and maturity. Society may hinder this process by imposing false values and causing the individual to distort his/her awareness of experience – emotional disorder results from this distortion. The goal of therapy is to restore the patient's natural self-direction by helping her/him to become aware of distorted or denied feelings and emotions.

The counsellor attempts, as far as possible, to understand the subjective experience of the client and to communicate back – and thus clarify – this experience. The counsellor is an active, empathetic listener who provides an accepting atmosphere and helps the client to regain awareness and thus control of his/her emotions and behaviour. Emphasis is on present experience as opposed to recollections of early development. Person-centred counselling is a well-developed example of this type of approach. Fritz Perl's Gestalt therapy is a related technique that uses therapy exercises.

The existential approaches of Abraham Maslow and Rollo May can also be grouped here. Phenomenology has made strong contribution in the field of psychopathology, in which the German Karl Jaspers, a leading contemporary Existentialist, stressed the importance of phenomenological exploration of a patient's subjective experience. Jaspers was followed by the Swiss Ludwig Binswanger and several others. The phenomenological strand is also very pronounced in American existential psychiatry and has affected sociology, history and the study of religion.

Counsellors who use a phenomenological approach concentrate on what is happening now. Most personality theories look at the person from the outside; phenomenology attempts to enter the person's own psychological experience, to try to understand what something means to that person. A phrase often used by

Carl Rogers, 'from the internal frame of reference of the individual', sums up the phenomenological experience.

Further reading

Keen, E. (1982) *A Primer in Phenomenological Psychology*, Holt, Rinehart & Winston, New York.

PLATEAU

Frequently, especially during ongoing counselling, progress appears to have stopped; little or nothing seems to be happening. The plateau may be an indication of transference or counter-transference.

When I first experienced this I discussed it with my mentor and we could see no apparent reason why this should be; he said, however, that it was not unusual. He took me back over what had happened and the obvious progress that had been made. It just so happened that at about that time I was learning to touch-type and had experienced some difficulty in gaining extra speed. An experienced typist with whom I discussed this said that most students experienced the same difficulty but that with practice the speed would improve once the plateau was passed. Her use of the word 'plateau' brought back to my memory something from my psychology lectures about plateaux in the learning process and as I reread this I could see how it applied to counselling.

When a person is learning a new skill the learning does not take place in a straight line but in a series of uphill climbs followed by horizontal lines or plateaux, when, in the case of typing, the speed remains static. It is in this plateau stage that consolidation takes place. It is also the stage where discouragement frequently sets in because progress (which up to that time has been fairly rapid) has slowed down.

As I applied this idea to counselling, I could see that the client had made substantial gains; his upward climb had been quite marked and well sustained. Now he was on a plateau, resting, gaining new psychological strength ready for the next phase. We took a closer look at the process thus far, the gains he had made and the differences, however small, such gains had made in his life. I realized that we had both been in danger of trying to hasten the process and it was not until then that we had stopped to take stock. Any attempt on my part to push him could have created resistance because he was not yet ready to move on to the next stage. After one or two sessions, it became obvious from what he said that he was now ready.

When we have frequent contact with clients, we may not readily detect progress when it is made – like parents who don't observe their children's physical growth. Very often it needs someone else to draw attention to the change.

When I speak of behaviour change I do not mean a radical overnight conversion, but a gradual movement towards the desired, acceptable behaviour.

The change, when it does take place, may go unnoticed until someone says, 'What has happened to Tom? He no longer jumps down my throat when I speak to him.' It may be some time, however, before Tom is able to move from the safety of this particular plateau – only when he feels secure in the gains he has made will he have the confidence to move out and start on some other part of the problem, which will take him upwards to another plateau.

POST-TRAUMATIC STRESS DISORDER (*see also*: Crisis counselling)

The term first appeared in the third edition of the Diagnostic and Statistical Manual of Mental Disorders (DSM-111), grouped under anxiety disorders.

Post-traumatic stress disorder (PTSD) is an anxiety disorder brought about by exposure to an exceptional mental or physical event. The symptoms may be felt immediately, although the onset may be 3 months or more afterwards. The person is beset by persistent reliving of the event and avoidance of anything associated with the trauma. There maybe numbing of general responses and manifestations of increased anxiety to other situations.

During the First World War, this was known as 'shell shock'. After the Second World War, the condition became known as 'concentration-camp syndrome'. PTSD is a feature of many catastrophic events and is particularly linked to war conditions.

The essential feature is the development of characteristic symptoms following a psychologically traumatic event that is generally outside the range of human experience, where the symptoms persist for at least 1 month. The precipitating event would be distressing to almost anyone and would involve, for example:

- Serious threat to life or physical integrity
- Serious threat or harm to one's children, spouse or other close relatives and friends
- Sudden destruction of home or community
- Seeing another person who has recently been, or is being, seriously injured or killed as the result of accident or violence.

The traumatic event is persistently re-experienced in at least one of the following:

- Recurrent and intrusive, distressing recollections of the event – children often engage in repetitive play in which themes or parts of the trauma are expressed
- Recurrent, distressing dreams of the event
- Sudden acting or feeling as if the traumatic event was recurring – this may include reliving the experience, illusions, hallucinations and dissociative episodes (flashbacks), which may occur at any time
- Intense psychological distress at exposure to events that symbolize or resemble an aspect of the traumatic event, including anniversaries.

Avoidance of the topic or numbing of responses may show as:

- Strenuous efforts to avoid thoughts or feelings associated with the trauma or to avoid activities or situations that arouse recollections of the event
- Inability to recall an important aspect of the trauma
- Marked lack of interest in significant activities – in young children there may be loss of recently acquired skills
- Feelings of detachment or estrangement
- Restricted range of emotions
- Pessimism about the future.

Symptoms may persist and may show as:

- Difficulty falling or staying asleep
- Irritability or outbursts of anger
- Difficulty in concentrating
- Being ever on the alert
- Being easily startled
- Anxiety when exposed to situations that resemble the traumatic event.

Stressors in PTSD would include:

- Rape or assault
- Military combat
- Natural and manufactured catastrophes
- Physical or sexual abuse.

Planning for crises can reduce anxiety when they do occur. Dealing with a crisis demands fast decision-making and action, clear lines of communication and easy access to all available information. What is not always appreciated is that people who are in the front line of coping with the crisis need support and personal supervision during and following the incident. Suffering can be intensified by official obstruction and insensitivity.

Grief is a natural reaction to most traumatic events, particularly where there is loss of life. Relatives who have an opportunity to see the dead body usually grieve more constructively.

A proactive approach, reaching out to people to offer help, is often more helpful than waiting for people to ask for it. Offering help, however well-meaning the motive, does not guarantee acceptance of the offer. But it does show caring.

Early intervention and opportunity to talk through their experiences and their feelings is important, before defences start building up.

Survivor syndrome

The term was introduced in 1926 by R. J. Lifton, an American psychiatrist, for a pattern of reactions frequently observed in those who have survived some terrible ordeal such as an earthquake, a flood or a war. Aspects of the syndrome include chronic anxiety, recurring dreams of the event, a general numbness, withdrawal from and loss of interest in the pleasures of life and, often, **survivor guilt**.

Survivor guilt was first noticed in those survived the Holocaust of the Second World War. It has been observed since in people who have survived other severely traumatic events. Part of the sense of guilt seems to be linked to the feeling that those who survived did not do enough to save others who perished.

A crucial point about the survivor syndrome and survivor guilt is the clear link with grief and grieving – grief about the actual event and the event triggering off unresolved grief. It is also worth mentioning the link between guilt and anger – one explanation is that guilt is internalized anger. It would appear, therefore, that counselling should be addressing the feelings of grief.

Critical incident stress debriefing

Staff who provide support to traumatized and bereaved people need recognition, support, stress relief, adequate supervision and the chance to record their experience and to properly round off their participation when the time is right. Individual counselling may also be required, to help people work through their grief reactions.

Debriefing, ideally, should take place on day 2, 3 or 4 following the incident. Day 1 is too soon. After day 4, perceptions, feelings and reactions begin to harden and the debriefing begins to have less healing value.

The debriefing should be conducted by an experienced group facilitator who has experience of stress management. Only people with direct experience of the event should be present with the facilitator.

Debriefing is not an evaluation of behaviour but a time for sharing their feelings and experiences, not relating those of other people. It is necessary to warn participants that they may feel worse at first talking about these things, but that it will help to prevent more serious problems developing.

Further reading

Cohen, N. (1989) Lockerbie's other victims. *Independent*, 8 Feb., p. 15.

Cunningham, V. (1988) Herald disaster – from the shop floor. *Counselling*, **August**, 1–6

Davidson, J. R. (1995) Posttraumatic stress disorder and acute stress disorder. In: *Comprehensive Textbook of Psychiatry*, 6th edn, (eds H. J. Kaplan and B. J. Sadock), Williams & Wilkins, Baltimore, MD.

Figley, C. R. (ed.) (1985) *Trauma and Its Wake: The study and treatment of Post-Traumatic Stress Disorder*, Brunner/Mazel, New York.

Hodgkinson, P. E. (1988) Psychological after-effects of transportation disaster. *Medical Science and Law*, 28(4), 304–309.

Hodgkinson, P. E. (1989) Technological disaster – survival and bereavement, *Social Science and Medicine*, 29(3), 351–356.

McCann, I. L., Sakheim, D. K. and Abrahamson, D. J. (1988) Trauma and victimisation: a model of psychological adaptation. *Counselling Psychologist*, 16(4).

Morris, B. (1989) Hillsborough. *Insight*, 9, 8–9.

Oxfordshire Gulf War Psychosocial Support Group (undated) *Gulf War: Advice for staff caring for victims and their relatives*, Oxfordshire Gulf War Psychosocial Support Group, Oxford.

Woodruff, I. (1989) Major incident: impact on staff. *Hospital Chaplain*, **June**, 12–17.
Wright, M. (1990) Planning a trauma counselling service. *Counselling*, **August**.

PREJUDICE (*see also*: Authoritarianism)

The *Oxford English Dictionary* defines prejudice as: 'A previous judgement, especially a judgement formed before due examination or consideration; a premature or hasty judgement.' Prejudice, in social behaviour, is a pre-formed and unsubstantiated judgement or opinion about an individual or a group, either favourable or unfavourable in nature. A prejudiced person tends to believe that his/her own group is superior to others in intelligence, character or behaviour.

From a social psychological perspective, prejudice involves any or all of: derogatory attitudes or beliefs; the expression of negative feelings; the display of hostile or discriminatory behaviour toward members of a group, simply because they belong to that group.

Prejudice has existed for thousands of years and it can manifest itself in many aspects of human behaviour and has led to the most terrible atrocities in all parts of the world. It is often a way of giving expression to personal fears or insecurity. Sometimes prejudice can be extremely subtle and the discrimination may not be evident even to the person who discriminates. When unequal treatment takes the form of systematic abuse, exploitation and injustice, then it becomes **social oppression**.

Psychologists have sought the origins of prejudice in personality disorders, in the social environment and in attributes of normal thought processes. Prejudice often exists together with social institutions such as segregation, apartheid and other forms of discrimination. But segregation can also apply to the exclusion of a member of a minority group from social clubs or from access to particular jobs or educational opportunities. It is said not to be found among children under 3 or 4 years of age. Prejudiced attitudes have often proved extremely difficult to eradicate, even when integration is enforced by law. However, legislation does not readily change attitudes.

A prejudice may be either positive or negative and may be about a particular thing, event, person or idea. Prejudice is characterized by irrational, stereotyped beliefs and views and their accompanying emotions and values. Prejudice tells more about the bearer of the attitude than about the persons who are the objects of the prejudice. Prejudiced behaviour is discrimination.

An essential characteristic of prejudice is the need to separate people into acceptable and unacceptable groups. Our self-image is closely tied to the image of the group as a whole. Prejudice is failure to relate to people as unique individuals with distinct qualities and differences. Rather, people are lumped together as if they all possessed the same stereotyped qualities as one another. Generally, prejudice is an attitude of the majority towards a minority. Prejudice refers to attitudes; discrimination generally refers to behaviours.

Sexism

Sexism is prejudice under a different name; it is belief in (or a set of implicit assumptions about) the superiority of one's own sex, often accompanied by a stereotype or preconceived idea about the opposite sex. Sexism most commonly takes the form of an assumption of male superiority, regarding woman as inherently inferior intellectually, psychologically and physically to man. This view, shared by both men and women, has historically shaped institutions of world society. It has been perpetuated through the acculturation of generations of children, with resultant differences between the sexes.

Sexism was not effectively challenged until the 20th century, with the growth of the militant women's rights movements. The term, coined by analogy with racism, was first used in the 1960s by feminist writers to describe language or behaviour that implied women's inferiority. Examples include the contentious use of male pronouns to describe both men and women and the assumption that some jobs are typically or appropriately performed only by one sex.

Institutionalized sexism operates as social oppression. For example, minimum requirements for certain jobs might automatically screen women out, giving the advantage to male applicants. At first glance this might not be obvious discrimination but it becomes clearer when the requirements bear no relation to the ability to do the job.

Racial prejudice

Racial prejudice, or racism, consists of negative attitudes directed in blanket fashion against socially defined groups. It is important to distinguish between the psychological aspects of racism (prejudice) and the social aspects (discrimination), although the one is to the other as ink is to a pen. Societies set groups apart and subjects them to discrimination; this is racial prejudice. Conversely, people would not have become segregated unless there had already been widespread prejudice. Prejudice and discrimination feed upon each other. Attitudes can be moderated by experience, for example, when we move from one society to another. Many people keep their prejudices well-hidden but in times of stress and threat these prejudices surface.

Racial prejudice is often part of society's way of blaming minorities for its economic and social problems. Racism is the theory or idea that there is a causal link between inherited physical traits and certain traits of personality, intellect or culture and, combined with it, the notion that some races are inherently superior to others. This is prejudice on a grand scale. Technically, any prejudice with a racial basis constitutes racism, just as any based on sex is sexism and any based on ethnicity is ethnicism. This means that prejudice directed against men is sexist, just as prejudice directed by blacks against whites is racist. Some sociologists argue that, while minorities can be just as prejudiced as those who dominate them, concepts such as racism and sexism should be reserved for prejudice whose ideological function is to justify social oppression.

Racial prejudice takes three main forms: **xenophobia**, the fear of foreigners;

ethnic prejudice, the dislike of a person or race because of their different customs, beliefs and attitudes; and **colour prejudice**, which focuses upon skin colour and outward appearance.

Positive discrimination

Not all discrimination is based on prejudice. Positive discrimination is bias in favour of a particular individual or group of people precisely because they are often the object of prejudice and discrimination, where employment is actively sought out as applicants for jobs, government contracts and university admissions. Although this kind of positive discrimination has been quite controversial, it generally has had little effect on the overall distribution of men, women and members of different ethnic groups among occupations.

Values and beliefs

Prejudice and discrimination are very powerful and are bound up with values and beliefs. It is worth repeating: prejudice is an attitude; discrimination is acting out our prejudices. A prejudiced attitude influences relationships with the target group but a society in which prejudice exists must experience difficulty with other relationships and with other societies. Prejudice and discrimination show themselves in many ways.

Probably the most obvious manifestation of racial prejudice was in the millions of Jews who were slaughtered under the Nazi regime. Apartheid in South Africa and the colour-bar in America are other examples of prejudice in action. Those three examples are safe for most of us to talk about without feeling the finger pointing at us. But we don't need to go to those extremes. Taking up arms against an immigrant family coming to live next door or refusing to patronize a certain shop because the owner is from another country or giving preference to one person over another because of nationality are examples of discrimination.

Prejudice and discrimination have their roots in fear and in inferiority. Inferiority turned on its head becomes superiority. Superiority often accompanies a desire to ensure that the target person or group is kept at a inferior level in hierarchical relationships. For prejudiced people, equality of sorts exists only within their own 'in-group', yet even that semblance of equality is precariously balanced on the strictest conformity to the rules.

A possible reason for racial discrimination is based on the rarely articulated fear of losing one's cultural identity. That is one reason why immigrants, for several generations, tend to group together in communities, to keep alive their culture. Such community helps to cushion culture shock and the feeling of disintegration engendered in the transition from one culture to another.

People who are strongly prejudiced often see things in black and white terms, are closed-minded, do not tolerate ambiguity well and are generally intolerant and judgemental. Prejudices may be defences against feelings of inadequacy. Prejudice is closely linked to the idea of the scapegoat (see entry, below). Prejudiced people tend to see the world as being made up of **in-groups**, which must be supported, and **out-groups**, which must be avoided or rejected and attacked when they become threatening.

Counselling strongly prejudiced people can be very wearing, for there is often an accompanying lack of insight. If the premise is correct, that such people may be using prejudice as a defence against feelings of inferiority and inadequacy, then working to build up their self-esteem may be an effective way of lessening the prejudice, rather than tackling it head-on.

Further reading

Allport, Gordon W. (1954) *The Nature of Prejudice*, Addison-Wesley, Reading, MA.

Dovidio, J. F. and Fazio, R. H. (1986) *Prejudice, discrimination, and racism*, Academic Press, Orlando, FL.

Katz, J. H. (1978) *White Awareness: Handbook for anti-racism training*, University of Oklahoma Press, Norman, OK.

Lago, C. and Thompson, J. (1989) Counselling and race. In: Dryden, W., Charles-Edwards, D. and Woolfe, R. (eds) *Handbook of Counselling in Britain*, Tavistock/Routledge, London.

PRESENTING PROBLEM

The presenting problem is what clients complain of – the client's 'admission ticket' to counselling. The presenting problem may be in the nature of a 'trial balloon': not of primary importance, but of sufficient import to generate some anxiety. The presenting problem can be thought of, in musical terms, as an 'overture'. An audience does not judge the performance by the overture; they wait to hear the full work.

In psychoanalytic and humanistic therapies, the presenting problem is regarded as symbolic of the client's underlying difficulties.

In therapies that concentrate on behaviour, the presenting problem is regarded as significant and treated accordingly. The professional discipline and theoretical orientation of the therapist will influence how the presenting problem is handled.

Presenting problems should not be dismissed as unimportant, for they give a clue to whether or not the client is suitable for counselling or whether other specialist help would be more appropriate.

PROBLEM-SOLVING INTERVENTIONS (*see also*: Action plans, Goals and goal setting)

These are goal-directed techniques aimed at improving the abilities of an individual or a family. Symptoms such as anxiety and depression may be due to the client's inadequate attempts at resolving certain situations. When new problem-solving skills are learned, the symptoms may fade.

Effective problem-solving can only take place when well-defined phases are pursued:

1. Define the problem
2. Decide a method of attack for the problem
3. Generate alternatives
4. Test alternatives for reality
5. Choose an alternative
6. Plan for action
7. Implement the plan
8. Evaluate
9. Decide on next step.

Often, when confronted with a problem, we are deluded into a false sense of security by counterproductive activities:

- Denying the problem exists
- Ignoring it, hoping it will go away
- Blaming something or someone for it
- Blaming oneself.

Before we can start on the problem-solving process it is necessary to acknowledge that a problem exists and that we intend to do something about it.

Step 1 – Define the problem
This diagnostic stage helps to identify if there is conflict and if so, where.

- Whose problem is it?
- Who is doing what, to whom?
- Are the perceptions accurate?
- Is communication distorted?
- What is at stake?
- What decisions have to be made?

Defining the problem provides clarity, understanding and purpose.

Step 2 – Decide a method of attack

- Is there anyone else who can help?
- Do you need any more information?
- Do you know anyone else who has successfully solved this problem?
- What sources can you tap?

Step 3 – Generate alternatives

1. Brainstorm, if possible with someone else
2. Think through each alternative, looking at positive and negative aspects.

Step 4 – Test alternatives for reality

- Don't eliminate possibilities too quickly
- Try operating the 'detailed response' before rejecting something – this means

that, before a suggestion is rejected, you must have generated at least three positive statements about it
- Work out a 'for' and 'against' for each possibility
- When all possibilities have been filtered through the detailed response, arrange them in a hierarchy of feasibility.

Step 5 – Choose an alternative

- Use Force Field Analysis (see entry)
- The chosen alternative must be within one's capability and within available resources.

Step 6 – Plan for action
It is necessary to choose a planning process that is appropriate to the potential solution. There is a danger of becoming so engrossed in the planning that the original problem or the alternatives are lost sight of.

Step 7 – Implement the plan
Use Rudyard Kipling's 'six honest serving men', 5WH: Who? What? Why? When? Where? How?

Step 8 – Evaluation is at two levels.

- An evaluation of the action plan itself – how far did the plan meet the set goals and objectives? It may be necessary to go back to step 6
- The second level evaluates how effective the overall problem-solving was. Just how far did the plan contribute to the outcome?

Step 9 – Next steps
Follow-up is essential. If the original problem still exists, use 5WH. It may be necessary to go back to stage 1 and work through the process once more. Follow-up may also be helpful to consolidate the learning experience.

Problem-solving is aided by:

- Having a healthy self-respect, which also means accepting the consequences of one's own personal worth and contributions.
- A healthy other-respect. This may mean giving credit to those who think differently. It also means being able to listen to what others say.
- A healthy optimism that problems can be solved if everyone is willing to work at them to find an acceptable solution.
- A respect for, but not fear of, conflict as being potentially creative.
- A willingness to invest energy and to take risks.

Skills essential in problem-solving:

- Active listening, clarifying, paraphrasing, self-disclosure

- Diagnostic skills (steps 1–2)
- Decision-making skills (steps 2–5)
- Data-collecting skills (steps 5–6)
- Design and planning skills (steps 5–8)
- Organizing/administrative skills (step 7)
- Analysis skills (step 8).

Counsellors can help clients to develop their problem-solving skills and so reduce the helplessness they feel at being confronted with a problem that seems unsurmountable.

Further reading

Earley, L. C. and Rutledge, P. B. (1980) A nine-step problem-solving model. In: *1980 Annual Handbook for Group Facilitators*, University Associates, San Diego, CA.
Haley, J. (1976) *Problem-Solving Therapy*, Jossey-Bass, San Francisco, CA.

PSYCHE

The oldest and most general meaning of 'psyche' is that of the early Greeks, who regarded it as 'soul' or the very essence of life. In classical mythology, Psyche was the heroine of the story of Cupid and Psyche.

A certain Greek king had three daughters, of whom Psyche, the youngest, was so beautiful that people worshipped her and neglected Venus. Venus (Aphrodite) was so jealous she sent her son, Cupid (Eros), with instructions to make her fall in love with some ugly, old man.

Cupid, instead, fell in love with Psyche himself. He told her that she must never see him but one night she disobeyed and, while she was looking at him by the light of a lamp, he awoke and he fled.

Psyche was desolate and searched far and wide for him. She finally submitted herself to Venus who set her four impossible tasks: to sort a huge pile of different seeds into their respective piles; to acquire some golden fleece from the terrible rams of the sun; to fill a crystal container from an inaccessible stream; to descend into the underworld and fill a small box with beauty ointment. This last task was made all the more difficult because Psyche would have to harden her heart to compassion.

Psyche completed all her tasks, the first three with assistance from ants, an eagle and a green reed. The final task she accomplished by saying 'No'. Cupid persuaded Jupiter (Zeus), the Father of the Gods, to let him marry Psyche; he agreed and Psyche was made immortal.

In Greek folklore the soul was pictured as a butterfly – another meaning of both 'psyche' and 'soul' – the soul or spirit distinguished from the body.

The mind functions as the centre of thought, feeling and behaviour and consciously or unconsciously adjusting and relating the body to its social and physical environment.

In analytical psychology the psyche is the sum total of all the conscious and unconscious psychic processes. The soul is regarded as the sum total of personality, comprising the persona; the outward face or attitude, the mask; the Anima (in men) and the Animus (in women), the inward attitude or face.

The four main functions of the psyche are intuition, sensing, thinking and feeling. Each approaches reality from a different point of view and with a different question. Each grasps a different part of reality

Further reading

Jung, Carl G. (1958) *The Collected Works – Psychological Types* (vol. 6), Routledge & Kegan Paul, London.

PSYCHIC PAIN

Psychic pain is pain of the heart, mind and spirit. It is as real and powerful as any physical pain. Suppression of psychic pain very often leads to physical disorders.

Psychic pain is often the pain of the deepest sadness, where the person feels 'like a dried out husk' and where tears – normally therapeutic – dry up in the eyes before they can be shed.

Many people are taught that it is a worthy thing to endure physical pain. In the same way, there is the myth that to admit to psychic pain is a sign of weakness. Suppression of psychic pain drives it deeper into the mind and into the body and healing is therefore made much more difficult. Locked-in pain wastes valuable creative energy and leads to exhaustion.

Many people are now experimenting with new therapies to relieve physical pain. People who can be encouraged to express their psychic pain through counselling are likely to discover a generally improved state of physical health. Pain and anger are close companions. The ability to express anger is one way of expressing the underlying pain.

Psychic pain begins to be experienced at the moment of birth; it is the price we pay for separation. It is also the price we have to pay for forming relationships, for within every relationship lie the seeds of separation.

Speaking of the connection between depression and pain, Professor Lader says, 'If the depressive (person) already suffers from chronic pain, symptoms become much worse. This is particularly important in the management of the terminal patients where the very understandable reactive depression renders the patient miserable and increasingly symptomatic. The close relationship between depression and pain has lead some observers to refer to depression as "psychic pain".'

Psychic pain may be caused by such experiences as:

- Bereavement
- Divorce
- Enforced isolation
- Helplessness

- Loneliness
- Poverty
- Loss of purpose
- Loss of self-esteem.

C. S. Lewis said

> *Did you ever know, dear, how much you took away with you when you left?*
> *You have stripped me even of my past, even of the things we never shared. I*
> *was wrong to say the stump was recovering from the pain of the amputation.*
> *I was deceived because it has so many ways to hurt me that I discover them*
> *only one by one.*

Lewis, 1961

Further reading

Lader, M. H. (1981) *Focus on Depression*, Bencard, Great West Road, Middlesex.
Lewis, C. S. (1957) *The Problem of Pain*, Fontana, London.
Lewis, C. S. (1961) *A Grief Observed*, Faber & Faber, London.

PSYCHOANALYSIS (Sigmund Freud, 1856–1939) (*see also*: Psychodynamic counselling, Transference and counter-transference)

Introduction

Sigmund Freud, Moravian-born founder of psychoanalysis, studied medicine in Vienna, which became his home until 1938 when, with his daughter Anna, he went to live in London.

While working with patients under hypnosis (with Joseph Breur), Freud observed that often there was improvement in the condition when the sources of the patients' ideas and impulses were brought into the conscious.

Also, observing that patients talked freely while under hypnosis, he evolved his technique of free association. Noting that sometimes patients had difficulty in making free associations, he concluded that painful experiences were being repressed and held back from conscious awareness. Freud deduced that what was being repressed were disturbing sexual experiences – real or in fantasy.

Repressed sexual energy and its consequent anxiety finds an outlet in various symptoms that serve as ego defences. The concept of anxiety now includes feelings of guilt, fear, shame, aggression, hostility and fear of loneliness at the separation from someone on whom the sufferer is dependent.

Freud developed his psychoanalytic method and the technique of free association during the years 1892 and 1895. His basic theory was that neuroses are rooted in suppressed sexual desires and sexual experiences in childhood. He analysed dreams in terms of unconscious desires.

He maintained that many of the impulses forbidden or punished by parents are derived from innate instincts. Forbidding expression to these instincts merely drives them out of awareness into the unconscious. There they reside to affect dreams, slips of speech or mannerisms and may also manifest themselves in symptoms of mental illness.

Freud's view – that the conscious and the unconscious are sharply divided and that access to the unconscious is denied except by psychoanalysis – does not meet with universal acceptance. Rather, many believe that there are various layers of awareness.

In summary, Freud's view was that humans are driven by sex and aggression, the same basic instincts as animals. Society is in constant struggle against any expression of these.

Freud's Psychological Wednesday Circle – the 'inner circle' – was formed by invitation from him to several like-minded people to discuss psychoanalytic matters and later became the Vienna Psycho-Analytic Society.

Psychoanalysis, behaviourism and humanistic psychology is the trilogy of the main orientations of psychotherapy.

Psychoanalysis includes investigating mental processes not easily accessed by other means. It is a method of investigating and treating neurotic disorders and the scientific collection of psychological information. The main purpose of psychoanalysis is to make unconscious material conscious.

Overview of psychosexual (libidinal) development
See Stages of Freudian psychosexual development, for expansion.

- The first phase is the **oral phase**, which centres around feeding and the associated organs – mouth, lips and tongue
- The second phase is the **anal phase**, in which the main source of pleasure and libidinal gratification are the activities surrounding the retaining and passing of faeces
- Next is the **phallic phase**, in which the genital organs become the principal object of interest, with exhibitionist and voyeuristic wishes
- The **latency period** is a relatively quiescent period following the resolution of the Oedipus complex and the consolidation of the superego; the lull before the storm of puberty and adolescence
- The **genital phase** is the final stage of psychosexual development, usually around late adolescence.

The main techniques of psychoanalysis

- Free association (*See* entry, above)
- Interpretation of dreams, resistance and parapraxes (*See* Humour)
- Analysing and working through the transference (*See* entry, below).

Psychoanalytic assumptions

- The concepts are applicable to normal and abnormal behaviour
- There is a tripartite mental apparatus – id, ego and superego
- The idea of psychological adaptation – where the mental apparatus attempts to reduce conflict as much as possible

- The idea of psychic determinism – that all aspects of the mental life are determined, that nothing in the mental life is due to chance, any more than in the physical world
- There is both a conscious and an unconscious world.

Basic concepts

The pleasure and reality principles

Mental activity is governed by the pleasure and the reality principles. The term **pleasure principle** describes the basic human tendency of the person to maintain a pleasant, tolerable energy level through the relief of inner tension and in so doing to avoid pain and to seek pleasure. The terms 'pleasure' and 'pain' may be misleading – 'gratification' and 'unpleasure' may be more accurate. The pleasure principle is conspicuous in the first years of life and is moderated by the development of the reality principle.

The gratification of pleasure (or the avoidance of discomfort – the reduction of tension) is balanced by the ability of the **reality principle** (the leading principle in the ego) to accommodate to the facts of, and the objects existing in, the outside world.

The reality principle allows postponement of gratification to accommodate other immediate needs or to secure greater pleasure at a later time.

Normal development is seen as acquiring and strengthening the reality principle so that it acts as a brake on the more primitive pleasure principle.

It is not so much that pleasure is actively sought but that discomfort is actively avoided in order to keep instinctual tension in the best possible balance. Rather than regard the pleasure and reality principles as in opposition to each other, it might be advantageous to think of them as two integral parts that operate in different ways to keep the organism balanced, in much the say way as do the parts in a thermostat.

Instincts

Instincts are innate, inherited, unlearned and biologically useful behaviours. The presence of instincts does not indicate the absence of intelligence or learning. For Freud, instincts bridged the mental and organic spheres. Instinct theory plays a prominent role in psychoanalysis, although it has been modified and now the emphasis is on instinctual behaviour, rather than on the instincts themselves as fixed motivators of behaviour. Humans instincts is a fiercely contested topic.

The psychoanalytic classification of instincts are:

- **Ego instincts** are nonsexual, self-preserving and associated with repression.
- **Libido** is the sexual instinct, which has both mental and physiological manifestations. Libido shows itself in ways other than sexual union. Freud considered psychiatric symptoms to be the result of misdirection or inadequate discharge of libido. Jung used the term to encompass all life processes in all species.

- **Aggression**: Freud, unable to reconcile some of the self-destructive elements he observed in his patients, formulated the aggression instinct.
- **Life and death instincts**: With the modification of the instinct theory, Freud concentrated in later writings on the life and death instincts only.
  - *Life instinct (eros)*: Eros refers to the tendency of particles to reunite or for parts to bind to one another, to form greater unities. Sexual reproduction is an example.
  - *Death instinct (thanatos)*: Thanatos is defined as the tendency to return to an inanimate state. Because all organisms return to the inanimate state, Freud considered thanatos to be the dominant force.

The conscious and the unconscious

The **conscious** is the region of the mind that, with the preconscious and the unconscious, makes up the psyche. Freud described the conscious as the 'sense organ of the ego'. The conscious is open to immediate awareness, unlike the preconscious and the unconscious, which are not.

The functions of the ego – reality testing, perception, observation and evaluation – are all at a conscious level. Some of the superego functions – criticism and conscience – are also mainly conscious. The defence mechanisms and censorship are not within the conscious.

Some therapies emphasize working directly with what is conscious, as only what is observable or can be described can be accurately interpreted.

The **preconscious**, a region somewhere between the unconscious and the conscious known as 'the antechamber to consciousness', is also referred to as the descriptive unconscious or the foreconscious. The contents of the preconscious – knowledge, emotions, images – though not immediately in the conscious are accessible to it because censorship is absent. Material can be described as temporarily forgotten – suppressed and not repressed. The preconscious is important in the process of working through, a process necessary to consolidate the insight gained through interpretation.

The **unconscious** refers to mental processes of which the person is unaware. It is the storehouse of repressed material. Unconscious material is brought into the conscious only through dreams, word associations, free associations, parapraxes and symptoms. The unconscious has two levels: the unconscious proper, which contains repressed material admissible to the conscious only through analysis; and the preconscious, which refers to material that, though unconscious, is available and accessible.

The unconscious exists at the deepest level of the psyche, beneath the conscious and the preconscious. Only the id is entirely within the unconscious. Unconscious material comprises fantasies and images or representations that make their way into the conscious symbolically.

The discovery of the clinical importance of the unconscious became the cornerstone of psychoanalysis.

The mental apparatus

The **id** is one of the three parts of the psyche, a completely chaotic, primitive

reservoir of energy derived from the instincts, which demands immediate satisfaction. The id is not synonymous with the unconscious, although it represents a
major portion of it. Freud proposed that at birth the neonate is endowed with an
id with instinctual drives seeking gratification. It is entirely self-contained and
isolated from the world about it and is bent on achieving its own aims.

Characteristics of the id:

- It contains the psychic content related to the primitive instincts of the body,
  notably sex and aggression, as well as all material inherited and present at
  birth
- It is oblivious of the external world and unaware of the passage of time
- It functions entirely on the pleasure–pain principle
- It supplies the energy for the development and continued functioning of
  mental life.

The task of psychoanalysis is to make the ego function more effectively at the
expense of the id. Totally effective functioning is never totally achieved or even
desirable, for the id provides the creative energy to sustain the ego and superego.
The aim should be to integrate the id, not to overpower it.

The id is the oldest of these systems. It contains everything that is inherited
and fixed in the constitution. It is filled with energy from the instincts and strives
to operate the pleasure principle. It is a chaos, a cauldron of seething emotions.
It knows no judgement, values, good or evil and knows no morality. It is not
governed by logic.

The **ego**, literally meaning 'I', is the system of rational and realistic
functioning of the personality. The ego is one's perception of self. It is the part
that is in touch with reality, influenced by the external world and dealing with
simulation arising from without and within. Ego-psychologists are those who
give greater weight to ego processes, such as reality-perception, conscious
learning and voluntary control.

The characteristics of the ego:

- It has the task of self-preservation, which it achieves by developing defence
  mechanisms
- It gains control over the primitive demands of the id
- The ego remembers, evaluates, plans and interacts with the physical and social
  world around
- It gives continuity and consistency of behaviour
- It is separate from both personality and body
- It is capable of change throughout life.

The newborn infant has only the most rudimentary ego. The ego influences the
id by what happens in the external world and replaces the pleasure principle
with the reality principle. The ego is derived from bodily sensations and
mediates between the id and the outside world. It represents reason and
common sense and operates the reality principle to control the destructive

potential of the id's pleasure principle. It solves problems and perceives. Freud described the id as a horse and the ego as its rider.

An important dimension of the ego has been characterized as **ego-strength**. As we progress from immediate to directed behaviour, from pre-logical to rational thinking, we move slowly through a number of intermediate stages during childhood. Even in physical maturity, people differ considerably in the forms and effectiveness of ego functioning.

Some behavioural psychologists have adopted the psychoanalytic concept of ego strength – the degree of the ability to adapt oneself to reality. By measuring variables such as self-control, the ability to anticipate the future and the capacity to focus attention, they have found that a stable family life tends to produce greater ego strength in children.

Ego-strength is characterized by:

- Objective appraisal of the world and one's place in it
- Self-knowledge (insight)
- Ability to plan and organize
- Ability to choose between alternatives
- Not being overwhelmed by needs and desires
- Ability to pursue a chosen course
- Theoretically, the 'stronger' the ego, the more able the individual will be to withstand the trials of life, although this would be difficult to ascertain.

On the other hand, people with weak egos are more like the child:

- Their behaviour is impulsive and immediate
- Their perception of reality and self is distorted
- They are less capable of productive work because energy is drained into the protection of warped and unrealistic self-concepts
- They may be burdened by neurotic symptoms.

The **superego** is the last of the components of the psychic apparatus to develop. It has been called 'the heir to the Oedipus complex'. It is that part of the ego in which self-observation, self-criticism and other reflective activities develop. It is formed gradually within the ego as a mechanism for maintaining the **ego-ideal**.

The ego-ideal is the standard of perfection we create for ourselves and is derived from loved or admired (rather than judging and threatening) figures and images. It is responsible for the sense of guilt and self-reproaches so typical in neuroses. The ego-ideal consists of precepts ('You ought to be like this') and prohibitions ('You ought not to be like that') Both precepts and prohibitions result from the struggle to resolve the Oedipus complex, and also represent conscience.

The superego behaves as a moral judge, criticizing the thoughts and acts of the ego, causing feelings of guilt and anxiety when the ego gratifies or tends to gratify the primitive impulses of the id.

The superego evolves, to a large extent, as a result of repression of the instincts; it is thus more closely related to the id than to the ego.

In the developing process, standards, restrictions and punishments imposed by authority figures are internalized into the superego, which then becomes self-governing.

The immature superego tends to be rigid and punitive. Modification over time and with experience permits adult sexual behaviour.

The upheaval and aggressive acting-out behaviour of adolescence can be understood in terms of the instinctual release previously curbed by the superego. One of the major tasks of adolescence is to modify the development of the superego. Freud's first use of 'superego' related to his belief that obsessional ideas were self-reproaches for some sexual act performed with pleasure in childhood.

Some people suffer from excessive conscience, characterized by excessive work, earnestness and rituals, rarely allowing themselves pleasure. Only when we can achieve some separateness from superego can we live satisfactorily, even though sometimes the price of disobedience is guilt.

Anxiety

Anxiety is a reaction to actual danger or a signal involving the perception of impending danger which may be **realistic** (from the environment); **moral** (from conflict with the superego) or **neurotic** (from conflict with the id's impulses).

Psychical energy, cathexis and anticathexis

The id, ego and superego are charged with psychical energy, similar to an electric charge. Cathexis is a neologism invented by Freud, analogous to the flow of an electrical charge. Anticathexis is a blocking of the discharge of energy.

Bisexuality

Freud believed that all human beings are constitutionally psychosexually bisexual. As evidence of this he points to the biological fact that male and female have vestiges of the organs of the other sex and that libido is asexual. Both the woman and the man develop out of the child with a bisexual disposition.

Normal development

This may be viewed as:

- Passing through successive stages of sexual maturation without major fixations and regressions
- Developing an ego that copes reasonably effectively with the external world
- Developing a superego based on constructive identifications
- Not developing punitively, moralistic and evolving defence mechanisms.

Psychoanalytical belief is that neuroses are acquired only during early childhood. The neurotic person is unable to heal the disordered ego and the misery is perpetuated.

The ego pays the price of its defences by being denied access to repressed material by which neurotic conflict would be resolved and is weakened by its repression.

Personality functioning is impaired when psychical energy is used in harmful, defensive anticathexes. Neurotic symptoms will continue so long as the repressions continue.

Psychoanalytic therapy

- A neurotic person is someone who is incapable of enjoyment and efficiency
- To be capable of enjoyment and to live efficiently, the neurotic person needs to place the libido in real objects instead of transforming it into symptoms
- To live efficiently, the ego needs to have the energy of the libido at its disposal rather than wasting it in repressions; the superego needs to be allowed libidinal expression and the efficient use of the ego
- The objectives of psychoanalysis are to free impulses, strengthen reality-based ego-functioning and so to alter the contents of the superego that it operates less punitively
- The aim of therapy is to help a person become more self-aware and to achieve insight.

The stages of psychotherapy:

1. The opening phase
2. The development of transference
3. Working through
4. Resolution of the transference.

The process of psychotherapy:

- Free association
- Working with resistance
- Interpretation – the means whereby repressed, unconscious material is made conscious
- Interpretation of dreams.

'Schools' of psychotherapy using variations of psychoanalysis:

- **Freudian psychoanalysis** – followers of Sigmund and Anna Freud
- **Analytical psychology** – followers of Jung
- **Individual psychology** – followers of Adler
- **Interpersonal** – followers of Sullivan and Horney
- **Object relations or 'British School'** – followers of Balint, Fairbairn, Guntrip, Winnicott.

Each of the main schools has developed its own methods of training and accreditation. Knowledge derived from psychoanalysis has led to insights into:

- Art
- Religion
- Social organization
- Child development
- Education.

Major criticisms of psychoanalysis

- Self-fulfilling
- Overemphasizes sexuality
- Untestable and unscientific
- Deterministic and pessimistic
- Politically repressive
- Antifeminist
- Ignores social and interpersonal dynamics
- Elitist, costly and time-consuming.

Further reading

Karasu T. B. (1995) Psychoanalysis and psychoanalytic psychotherapy. In: *Comprehensive Textbook of Psychiatry*, 6th edn, (eds H. J. Kaplan and B. J. Sadock), Williams & Wilkins, Baltimore, MD.
Kernberg, G. S. (1976) *Internal World and External Reality*, Jason Aronson, New York.
Rycroft, C. (ed.) (1968) *Psychoanalysis Observed*, Penguin, Harmondsworth.
Smith, D. L. (1996) Psychodynamic therapy: the Freudian approach. In: *Handbook of Individual Therapy*, (ed. W. Dryden), Sage Publications, London.

PSYCHODRAMA

Psychodrama is a range of psychotherapeutic techniques, in which people dramatize their personal problems within a group setting. The technique was introduced in the 1920s by the Viennese psychiatrist Jacob. L. Moreno.

Although the situations in psychodrama are simulated, they can generate insight and release emotions through catharsis. It is a powerful method of working, which, in the hands of an experienced therapist, can be liberating. A stage setting is generally used, the therapist acting as the 'director', with group members playing various roles.

The roles

- **Director:** The group therapist or leader is both director and active participant in the drama, whose role is a catalyst.
- **Protagonist:** This is the person selected from the group and on whom the group focuses its attention. The situation may be chosen by the protagonist or by the director. The protagonist provides all the material, thoughts, feelings, historical details. The director helps the protagonist to work through toward a resolution.
- **Auxiliary ego or egos:** A member or members of the group act(s) out the roles of, for example, significant absent people, e.g. someone who has died.

- **Group**: Although only a few members of the group may be actively involved, all are involved to the degree that they are observers and are encouraged to identify with parts of what is taking place.

Some of the techniques are:

- **Soliloquy**: The person verbalizes his/her psychological reactions to various remembered or imagined situations.
- **Self-presentation**: The person plays the part of various significant others.
- **Self-realization**: the person enacts his/her past and future life plan.
- **Role playing**: This may be the impromptu enacting of some part of the protagonist's life – past, present or future. It might include acting out a stress-provoking situation.
- **Role reversal**: The person takes the part of someone else with whom interaction is difficult. Each is encouraged to act, speak, think like the other.
- **Mirroring**: a member of the audience attempts to copy the behaviour of the person, to enable that person to see her/himself through someone else's eyes.
- **Sculpting**: This is where one person is asked to describe, for example, his/her place within a group (often a family) by using space/position, not words.

Further reading

Moreno, J. L. and Ennis, J. M. (1950) *Hypnodrama and Psychodrama*, Beacon House, Boston, MA.
Greenberg, I. A. (ed.) (1974) *Psychodrama Theory and Therapy*, Behavioural Publications, New York.
Wong, N. (1995) Group psychotherapy, combined individual and group psychotherapy, and psychodrama. In: *Comprehensive Textbook of Psychiatry*, 6th edn, (eds H. J. Kaplan and B. J. Sadock), Williams & Wilkins, Baltimore, MD.

PSYCHODYNAMIC COUNSELLING (*see also*: Klein, Melanie, Psychoanalysis)

Almost every other approach derives from Freud's psychoanalysis, which gives rise to the word 'psychodynamic', meaning every psychological theory that uses the concept of inner drives and the interaction of mental forces within the psyche. Thoughts, feelings and behaviours are viewed as manifestations of inner drives. Psychodynamic counselling derives from psychoanalysis, but it is not psychoanalysis.

Thus a psychodynamic approach is the systematized knowledge and theory of human behaviour and its motivation. Inherent in this is the study of the functions of emotions. Psychodynamic counselling recognizes the role of the unconscious and how it influences behaviour. Further, behaviour is determined by past experience, genetic endowment and what is happening in the present.

In psychodynamic counselling the counsellor is far less active than in many other approaches and relies more on the client bringing forth material rather than reflecting feelings and inviting exploration, and what the client discloses will be interpreted according to the psychoanalytic model. Just as in psychoanalysis the patient is expected to report anything that comes to mind, so in psychodynamic counselling. Hesitation to reveal is interpreted as resistance, which must be worked through before progress is achieved.

While feelings are not ignored – for to ignore them would be to deny an essential part of the person – feelings are not the emphasis – insight is and that insight relates to the functioning of the unconscious. For the underlying belief is that it is the unconscious that produces dysfunction. Thus insight, in the psychodynamic model, is getting in touch with the unconscious and bringing what is unconscious into the conscious.

Although insight is usually worked toward in those approaches that focus on feelings, in the psychodynamic approach it is considered essential. Clients achieve insight when they understand what is causing a conflict. The premise is that, if insight is gained, conflicts will cease. Insight is often accompanied by catharsis, which is the release of emotion, often quite dramatic.

Insight refers to the extent to which clients become aware of their problems, origins and influences. It may be sudden – like the flash of inspiration; the 'eureka experience'. More usually it develops stage-by-stage as clients develop psychological strength to deal with what is revealed. The counsellor cannot **give** insight. Clients must arrive at it by themselves.

Psychodynamic counsellors are trained to interpret what clients say through the psychoanalytic model and, while the counsellor will not analyse clients, neither will s/he become as involved as in some other approaches. The psychodynamic counsellor can appear distant and detached, possibly even lacking in warmth, but this is because of the belief that the personal qualities of the counsellor should not intrude into the counselling relationship.

Further reading

Jacobs, M. (1992) *Psychodynamic Counselling in Action*, Sage Publications, London.
Smith, D. L. (1996) Psychodynamic therapy: the Freudian approach. In: *Handbook of Individual Therapy*, (ed. W. Dryden), Sage Publications, London.

PSYCHOSYNTHESIS (ROBERTO ASSAGIOLI, 1888–1974)

Psychosynthesis was developed by Assagioli, an Italian psychiatrist who broke away from Freudian orthodoxy early in the 20th century and developed an integrated approach to psychiatry.

Psychosynthesis is a synonym for human growth, the ongoing process of integrating all the parts, aspects and energies of the individual into a harmonious, powerful whole. Assagioli drew upon psychoanalysis, Jungian and existential psychology, Buddhism and yoga and Christian traditions and philosophies.

The fundamentals of psychosynthesis

- Psychological pain, imbalance and meaninglessness are caused where the various elements of the psyche are unconnected or clash with one another.
- When these elements merge, we experience a release of energy, a sense of well-being and a deeper meaning of life.
- Assagioli's map of the psyche:
  - The lower unconscious, which contains one's personal psychological past in the form of repressed complexes, long-forgotten memories and dreams and imaginations
  - The middle unconscious, wherein reside the skills and states of mind
  - The higher unconscious or superconscious, from where we receive our higher intuitions and inspirations – this is also the source of higher feelings and spiritual energies.
- The field of consciousness lies within the middle unconscious. It is the part of which we are directly aware and contains sensations, images, thoughts, feelings, desires and impulses. It also includes power to observe, analyse and make judgements.
- The conscious self or 'I' lies in the centre of the field of consciousness. One's task is to gain experience of the essence of self or 'I'. Awareness of the conscious self is essential for psychological health. The personal self is a reflection of the transpersonal self, in much the same way as the moon is a reflection of the sun.
- The higher or transpersonal self is the true Self, the permanent centre, situated beyond or above the conscious self. Identification with the transpersonal self is a rare occurrence.
- The psyche is bathed in the sea of the collective unconscious of dreams, myths, legends and archetypes.

The lines that delimit the various parts of the diagram are analogous to permeable membranes, permitting a constant process of 'psychological osmosis'.

Assagioli's map of the psychological functions (in diagrammatic form, star-shaped) is made up of three dimensions:

- Sensation – Intuition
- Thought – Emotion-feeling
- Impulse-desire – Imagination

At the centre is the personal self or 'I', surrounded by will. Of will, Brown says:

> *The experience and development of the will is basic to psychosynthesis. Our will is what separates us from being the conditioned automatons envisioned in Huxley's* Brave New World. *True, we are subject to conditioning, but we can transcend it through the skilful and harmonious use of the will. That is why the will is identified closely with the self in psychosynthesis models; conditioning is what our environment imposes on us, but the self can still express itself and its inner direction through acts of will.*

317

Assagioli's personality typology

The will type

The characteristics of the will type are prompt and decisive action, courage and the power to conquer, rule and dominate both physical surroundings and other people.

There is a strong tendency to suppress all emotions and, as a consequence, will types care little for their own or other people's feeling. This suppression of feelings often leads this person into committing heroic acts of courage.

Mentally this person is alert, with clear vision, unencumbered by emotions. Although not trusting of intuition, in the realm of abstract thinking this person excels, having a quick and sure grasp of principles, general laws and universal connections.

The love type

Love types are often attached to material possessions, money or property and the good things of life. The love may be expressed through the mind and emotions. Many love people are underdeveloped sexually, with a distinct possibility of egotistical love. The love type can be self-indulgent and a lover of comfort, with a tendency to laziness and to follow the crowd.

Intuition is highly developed in love types, who have an interest in psychology and a communion with the inner worlds of others.

Generally, love types are kind and receptive, sociable and often afraid of solitude. They are sometimes too readily influenced by others.

The active-practical type

The characteristics of this type are based on intelligent activity and the practical use of tools, coupled with highly developed manual dexterity. Active-practical types are comfortable in the 'real' world of things. Material objects, particularly money, interest them, so they often pursue activities for gain. Money is power.

This type wants immediate and lively reactions; to go slowly is a punishment. Feelings and all that requires psychic sensitivity are foreign to this type, as is the feminine principle of the psyche; the practical mind sees no relevance or meaning in it. Men of this type struggle to understand the psychology of women.

Mentally this type deals well with concrete and practical problems but the more abstract ones leave them cold.

The creative-artistic type

This type is characterized by the search for harmony, peace, union and beauty. Creative-artistic types have an excellent sense of colour and exhibit good taste. They are often beset by unsatisfied ambitions, internal and external conflict.

They are prone to mood swings – between optimism and pessimism; between uncontrolled happiness and despair. They are easily disturbed by violence, vulgarity and ugliness.

They are sensitive to psychic phenomena and rely on their intuition, which is well developed. They are always searching for the meaning hidden behind everything they perceive. They are imaginative, dreamy and impracticable and may live in a fantasy world. Men of this type feel at home with feminine psychological characteristics.

The scientific type
This type is characterized by an interest in the appearance of things, as perceived through the five senses. There is no real interest in moral, aesthetic or any other type of value.

The emotions of this type are totally directed toward impersonal objects. They are passionately attached to ideas and theories and their energies are directed toward intellectual ends.

Their minds are constantly on the alert, investigating, posing questions, solving problems, searching, probing, experimenting, proving and discovering.

The devotional-idealistic type
This type is attracted to an ideal, which is often an ideal personality. The ideal may be religious, political, social or philosophical. Sometimes their severely ascetic attitude turns to hatred of the body as a hindrance toward their spiritual ambition.

Devotional-idealistic types often love or hate with a passion that makes them narrow-minded, intolerant, critical and uncompromising. They generally lack a sense of proportion and humour and have a tendency to impose their views on others. At the same time they, are sincere and not egotistical. The Inquisitors are quoted as examples of such a type, torturing and killing in an effort to save the souls of their victims.

The high level of intuition that some develop is identified with the feminine principle. The active subtype does not develop the same degree of intuition and identify more with the masculine principle, with combativeness and aggression – the person who is always prepared to do battle for a just cause.

The organizational type
Organizational types express themselves in action and are thoroughly objective. They demonstrate will and purpose, a clear mind, constructive activity and practical ability and are methodical and persistent 'doers'. They organize the co-operation and work of other people to achieve the desired end.

This type like to formalize laws with meticulous care and they tend toward rigidity, which often manifests itself as bigotry. They are strong disciplinarians, both external and internal, and use discipline in order to eliminate loss and waste of time, energy and materials, to avoid friction and to establish, in the end, more productive co-operation.

The organizational type relies heavily on tradition, habit and custom and when these fail or break down organizational types are thrown into confusion; as if their anchor has gone.

The task of psychosynthesis

No person is exclusively one type; we are mixtures. Most of us could identify one or two types that are more of us than the others. When we have identified the type(s), our task is how to use the knowledge we have acquired to effect self-potential.

Expression, control and harmonization

Each person faces the three-point task.

Expression:

- Accepting the characteristics
- Recognizing the potentialities
- What our type can teach us
- The opportunities and dangers
- The kind of service to the world.

Control:

- Controlling and correcting excesses
- Working on the opposites.

Harmonization:

- Cultivating undeveloped faculties
- Develop the will-to-change
- Seek the company of people who demonstrate the desired attributes.

Psychosynthetic tasks

The will type

- To develop love, understanding, empathy and compassion in such a way that they become capable of expressing goodwill
- To develop sensitivity, intuition and the ability to co-operate with, rather than to solely dominate, compete with and direct, others
- To feel comfortable without solitude and to learn to live with others
- To transform egotistical will into service to others.

The love type

- To attain nonattachment and to eliminate from real love the elements of greed and possessiveness and allow for liberty of the other person
- To separate love from the egocentric elements
- To develop a stronger will to help them control their love.

The active-practical type

- To cultivate the qualities of the love and creative types

- To recognize the intangible world, intuition, psychological qualities, beauty
- To learn how to relax and be silent.

The creative-artistic type

- To learn to seek a mid path between polarities and extremes
- To work with reality and the practical
- To respect the limitations of others
- To develop more self-discipline, although not at the expense of inspiration
- To develop a more responsible attitude toward money.

The scientific type

- To control the thirst for knowledge and apply it to specific areas
- To approach relationships with warmth, compassion and goodwill
- To cultivate the appreciation of subjective qualities, of internal experiences and intuition, love and beauty.

The devotional-idealistic type

- To distinguish true from idealistic love and to transform devotion to an ideal into true love
- To learn to suspend judgement and to accept that there are other 'ways'
- To learn to be more impersonal and objective
- To develop tolerance and intellectual humility.

The organizational type

- To avoid becoming too identified with the formal and the predictable and to beware of the organization becoming an end in itself
- To work toward modifying the tendency to rely on the practical and the objective, the concrete and the visible, by developing loving service and the true good of all, free from officiousness and rigidity
- To apply the developed principles of co-ordination and synthesis to personal or transpersonal development.

Assagioli's concept of subpersonalities

Subpersonalities are distinct, miniature personalities, living together within the personality, each with its own cluster of feelings, words, habits, beliefs and behaviours. They are often in conflict with one another and engaged in a constant jockeying for position.

They are remnants of helpful and unhelpful influences left over from a time when they were needed for survival to meet lower level needs. For example, a policeman subpersonality is helpful in keeping one on the right side of the law, but becomes tyrannical when it always pushes one into punishing other people for minor breaches of one's self-imposed standards.

Examples of subpersonalities:

Boffin
Executioner
Gaoler
Granite
Monk/nun
Nurse
Playboy
Policeman
Professor
Rebel
Saboteur
Seducer
Spider
Tiger

The goals of psychosynthesis

- To free ourselves from the infirmity of illusions and fantasies, unrecognized complexes, of being tossed hither and thither by external influences and deceiving appearances
- To achieve a harmonious inner integration, true self-realization and a right relationship with others
- To recognize when we have identified with one or another subpersonality and disidentify from its control.

These goals are achieved through knowledge of one's personality, control of the various elements of the personality and working with the subpersonalities to free oneself from their tyranny. Psychosynthesis speaks of 'guiding', not therapy.

Principal methods and techniques:

- Catharsis
- Creativity
- Critical analysis
- Dialogue
- Dreamwork
- Evocative words and affirmation
- Free drawing
- Gestalten
- Guided imagery
- Homework
- Journal keeping
- Meditation
- Movement
- Subpersonality work.

Broad classification of techniques:

- **Analytical**: To help identify blocks and enable the exploration of the unconscious
- **Mastery** (*See* Assagioli's map of the psychological functions, in Psychosynthesis): The eight psychological functions need to be gradually retrained to produce permanent positive change
- **Transformation**: Creating a soil in which the seeds of change can blossom. The goal is the refashioning of the personality around a new centre
- **Meditative**: To awaken and integrate intuition, imagination, creativity and higher feelings
- **Grounding**: The learning and growth of a session is brought into the concrete terms of daily life – grounding makes use of:
  - Carrying out the choices made in the session, actively using imagination
  - Standing or moving in ways that express new qualities or attitudes
  - Mental images to evoke positive emotional states
  - Repeating key phrases or affirmations throughout the day
  - Practising chosen behaviours.
- **Relational**: To deal with the common obstacles within relationships and communication and to cultivate qualities such as love, openness, empathy.

Psychosynthesis is an evolutionary psychology, to help us to become increasingly aware of our vast potentials and to bring them into service in the world. It can help us to balance all aspects of the human personality; intellect, emotion, body, intuition and imagination.

Psychosynthesis can facilitate courage and patience, wisdom and compassion. It refers to the ongoing synthesis of the psyche, a process that transcends specific models and methods.

Further reading

Assagioli, R. (1965) *Psychosynthesis: A manual of principles and techniques*, Turnstone Press, Wellingborough.

Assagioli, R. (1969) *Symbols of Transpersonal Experiences*, Institute of Psychosynthesis, London.

Assagioli, R. (1974) *The Act of Will*, Wildwood House, London.

Assagioli, R. (1976) *Transpersonal Inspiration and Psychological Mountain Climbing*, Institute of Psychosynthesis, London.

Assagioli, R. (1983) *Psychosynthesis Typology*, Institute of Psychosynthesis, London.

Brown, M. (1983) *The Unfolding Self: Psychosynthesis and counselling*. Psychosynthesis Press, Los Angeles, CA.

Ferrucci, P. (1982) *What We May Be*, Turnstone Press, Wellingborough,

PUBLIC AND PRIVATE SELF

A social psychology concept, in which the self has both a private and public face. The private self consists of what we are inside. The public self is the face we present to others. The one is secret; the other is what we want other people to think of us. Both public and private selves influence our behaviour: the one in how we are when by ourselves; the other in how we react to others and how they will react to what we do.

Confronting ourselves makes us aware of who we are: if faced with a TV camera or an audience, we become more aware of the public self – as indicated by an increased tendency to change our attitudes to conform to the opinions of others.

Some people are prone to introspect, to examine their feelings and motives frequently. Some are habitually concerned with how they appear to others.

Characteristics of those high on private self (inner-directed):

- Tend to be prone to mood changes
- Prone to anger when provoked
- Suggestible
- Reasonably resistant to political propaganda
- Reasonably accurate in describing their own behaviour
- Seem to have more self-awareness
- Able to disclose private aspects of selves to their spouses or intimate partners
- Tend to behave in accordance with their own attitudes and beliefs.

Characteristics of those high on public self (other-directed):

- Tend to be sensitive to group rejection
- Usually good at predicting the kind of impression they make on others
- Place importance on their 'social' identity
- A tendency to conform to the values of society
- A tendency to comply with the expectations and preferences of other people
- Tend to tailor their actions to fit the social demands of changing situations.

Examples of private self-consciousness statements:

- My reflections are often about myself
- I listen to my inner feelings
- I'm always trying to work myself out
- Examining my motives is important to me
- I'm aware of changes in my mood
- I like to think I am aware of myself
- I know how my mind works when I'm thinking through a problem
- I feature a lot in my own fantasies
- I am aware that I often watch myself.

Examples of public self-consciousness statements:

- My behaviour is influenced by about what other people think of me
- Making a good impression is important to me
- It is important to me to present myself favourably to other people

- I'm self-conscious about the way I look
- My appearance is an important part of me
- I always check how I look in the mirror before leaving the house.

It needs to be stressed that however 'accurate' personality tests are, they are not absolute. These are not precise instruments but rather indicators of what might be. With reference to this specific indicator, a person's behaviour is likely to be modified by the situation and circumstances – in the real-life world, not in the laboratory. For example, a person who tips the 'private person' scale might be totally different in a group where s/he is accepted and feels at ease, or when in position of being in control.

Clients may be caught in the trap between these two opposing parts of themselves and not really be sure which of them is the 'real me'. In reality, of course, the majority of people have both private and a public self. Where it might prove a problem is in having to 'put on a brave face' when caught up in grief, for example, or where one's profession 'demands' a certain attitude, such as happens with doctors and nurses.

The question to be asked is: For whose benefit is the public self? It is possible that putting on a brave face is a defence mechanism; something that maintains our self-esteem (in our own eyes). Being seen to be 'strong' is more important than showing one's feelings. Like all defences, counsellors should recognize them for what they are but not try to break them down. Teasing out the various strands of the two selves might allow the client to develop insight and resolve any conflict there might be.

Further reading

Fenigstein, A., Scheir, M. F. and Buss, A. H. (1975) Public and private self-consciousness: assessment and theory. *Journal of Consulting and Clinical Psychology*, **43**, 522–524.

Q

QUESTIONS

The appropriate use of questions is essential, both in communication and in counselling. Once understood and mastered, your counselling style will be enriched and enhanced.

A guide to using questions

Examples of *experiencing* **questions:**

- What is going on?
- How do you feel about that?
- What do you need to know to...?
- Would you be willing to try...?
- Could you be more specific?
- Could you offer a suggestion?
- What would you prefer?
- What are your suspicions?
- What is your objection?
- If you could guess at the answer, what would it be?
- Can you say that another way?
- What is the worst/best that could happen?
- Would you say more about that?
- What else?
- And?

Examples of *sharing* **questions:**

- Would you like to share?
- What went on/happened?
- How did you feel about that?
- Who else had the same experience?
- Who reacted differently?
- Were there any surprises/puzzlements?
- How many felt the same?
- How many felt differently?
- What did you observe?
- What were you aware of?

Examples of *interpreting* **questions:**

- How did you account for that?
- What does that mean to you?
- How was that significant?

- How was that good/bad?
- What struck you about that?
- How do those things fit together?
- How might it have been different?
- Do you see something operating there?
- What does that suggest to you about yourself/other people?
- What do you understand better about yourself/other people?

Examples of *generalizing* **questions:**

- What might we draw from that?
- What might that be connected to?
- What did you learn/relearn?
- What does that suggest to you about ... in general?
- Does that remind you of anything?
- What principle is being applied there?
- What does that help to explain?
- How does that relate to other experiences you've had?
- What do you associated with that?
- So what?

Examples of *application* **questions:**

- How could you apply that?
- What would you like to do with that?
- How could you repeat this again?
- What could you do to hold on to that?
- What are the options?
- What might you do to help/hinder yourself?
- How could you make it better?
- What would be the consequences of doing/not doing that?
- What modifications can you make to get it to work for you?
- What could you imagine/fantasize about that?

Examples of *processing* **questions:**

- How was this for you?
- What were the pluses/minuses?
- How might it have been more meaningful?
- What's the good/bad news?
- What changes would you make?
- What would you continue?
- What are the gains/losses?
- If you had it to do over again, what would you do?
- What would you add/take away?
- Any suggestions?

Summary of helpful types of question

Elaboration questions give the person the opportunity to expand.

- Would you care to elaborate?
- What else is there?
- Could you expand what you've just said?

Specification questions aim to elicit detail.

- When you say he upsets you, what precisely happens?
- When?
- How many times?

Questions that focus on feelings aim to elicit how the other person feels about something.

- How do you feel about that?
- What would you say your feelings are right now?
- Is it possible that you're feeling...?

Personal responsibility questions imply that the other has a responsibility not only for owning the problem but also for making the choices that contribute to solving it.

- How do you see your part in the break up?
- What skills do you need to develop to help solve the problem?
- What other ways are there to improve the situation?

Wrongly used, questions can create an expectation that we will provide solutions to other people's problems. The emphasis in counselling is on using questions as aids to problem-solving. We may find it expedient to ask questions to fill certain 'gaps' in our understanding. Should we find ourselves asking two consecutive questions without getting a response, then, in all probability, we have asked inappropriately and should return to responding accurately.

Using open questions

Open questions are an open invitation to continue talking, particularly about feelings.

- 'What would you like to talk about today?'
- 'What happened then?' ('What' questions tend to bring out the specific facts of a problem)
- 'How did you feel about the situation?' ('How' questions often lead toward discussion. When the word 'feel' is included, the client is usually more ready to talk about feelings). This does not mean that every minute or so the counsellor should say, 'How do you feel about that?' That can become nothing more than a stereotyped response, almost guaranteed to irritate the client.

- 'Why do you think it happened?' ('Why' questions tend to lead clients to talk about their past or present reasoning around an event or situation). 'Why' questions often take the client away from feeling into thinking and away from the present into either the past or the future and discourage exploration of feelings in the here and now. Sometimes this is helpful – not, however, in this context. If it's information you want, a 'why' question is fine. Another point about 'why' questions is that they are more to do with the counsellor's knowledge than with the client's feelings. 'Why' is not as important as 'how'. 'Why' is investigative; 'how' is facilitative.

Open questions should:

- Seek clarification
- Encourage exploration
- Establish client understanding
- Gauge feelings
- Establish counsellor understanding
- Make effective use of 5WH: Who? What? Why? When? Where? How?

> *I keep six honest serving-men*
> *(They taught me all I knew);*
> *Their names are What and Why and When*
> *And How and Where and Who.*
>
> Rudyard Kipling, 'The Elephant's Child', *Just So Stories* (1902)

Guidelines on questions

- Avoid closed questions unless you want to elicit information or establish facts. Closed questions can usually be answered with a few words and usually begin with 'Is', 'Are', 'Do' or 'Did'. When we preface a statement with 'Could it be?', 'Do you think/feel?', 'Does this mean?', 'Have you considered?', 'Is that...?', 'Am I (would I be) right?' or 'Don't you think?' it usually means a closed question.
- Avoid leading questions, where the desired answer is implied in the question
- Avoid curiosity questions about areas not yet touched on
- Avoid too many questions, which give the impression of an interrogation
- Avoid probing questions that the client is not yet ready to answer
- Avoid poorly timed questions that interrupt and hinder the helping process.
- Think of responding to what the client has said rather than asking questions
- Responding is like building a wall, brick by brick. In this way, the counsellor does not rush ahead of the client and cause anxiety by pushing indelicately into sensitive areas not yet ready to be explored.

Closed questions derive from a desire to know, to seek information, rather than from an ability to help the client explore or clarify. Closed questions often move the client from the present into the past or from the present into some direction chosen by the counsellor.

QUESTIONS

However, although it is generally agreed that closed questions stop exploration and the more so if two such questions are asked in succession, creating open questions is sometimes not easy.

Examples of changing closed questions to open ones
Joe, aged 28 says, 'Honestly, I don't know what to do. It sounds really silly, but I'm afraid of women. I like them, I think, but I never know what to do. Maybe it's because I like them too much. I start to get to know a girl and it's OK. Then I just fall head over heels for her. It scares me. I always end up getting hurt. That's how it's happened before and that's how it is with Emma.'

Closed: 'How many times has this happen before?' **Open**: 'This has happened to you a few times before, Joe.'

Closed: 'Are you in love with Emma?' **Open**: 'There seems to be some doubt in your mind that you're in love with Emma.'

Closed: 'When was the last time this happened to you?' **Open**: 'It's happened many so many times before and you don't really know why.'

Closed: 'Are you afraid of girls hurting you or you hurting them?' **Open**: 'You don't want to end up hurting girls or getting hurt yourself.'

Closed: 'Is she in love with you?' 'You feel fairly sure how you feel, Joe, but not so sure how Emma feels.'

Amanda, aged 42, married to Charles, says, 'I don't know what to do. Charles is going out to China on contract. He wants me to go with him but I'm afraid. I've never been away from this country. If I stay here I can carry on working and earn some extra money, which we desperately need. But if I don't go, I shan't see him for months on end. What should I do?'

Closed: 'What part of China?' **Open**: 'The prospect of going to China doesn't appeal to you.'

Closed: 'How long will he be away for?' **Open**: 'The idea of being separated from Charles doesn't appeal to you.'

Closed: 'What are you afraid of? **Open**: 'There's a fear within you that holds you back from even thinking about going.'

Closed: 'How much money will you be able to earn while he's away? **Open**: 'Both the money you might earn and being with Charles are equally important.'

Closed: 'What sort of work does Charles do?' **Open**: 'Your work, Amanda, is just as important to you as Charles's work is to him.'

In rephrasing these closed questions, instead of questions that seek information, each of the 'questions' is in fact a statement with a question mark hanging on the end. Because it is phrased as a tentative statement it encourages the client to continue. It is as if, at the end of every open question, there is an implied phrase, 'How do you feel about that?' This has not been added, for when that sort of phrase is overdone, it can become very irritating to the client and does little to enhance the counsellor in the client's eyes.

However, it must be pointed out, that if clients have a mind not to respond,

330

no matter how open the counsellor's response, then they have the right not to. Generally speaking, though, the more open the counsellor's response and the more empathetic, the more likely it will be for the client to build upon what the counsellor has said.

Closed questions have more of a tendency to be impersonal than open questions. This is probably because open questions have a basis of empathic warmth in them.

Further reading

Sutton, J. and Stewart, W. (1997) *Learning to Counsel: How to develop the skills to work effectively with others.* How To Books, Oxford.

R

RAPE COUNSELLING

Definition (the Sexual Offences (Amendment) Act 1976): A man commits rape if:

1. He has unlawful sexual intercourse with a woman who at the time of intercourse does not consent to it; and
2. At that time he knows that she does not consent to the intercourse or he is reckless as to whether or not she consents to it.

Rape was traditionally considered an act that occurred only against females and only outside marriage. Traditionally, a man was incapable by law of raping his wife; the argument was that a married woman had given her consent to intercourse by marrying her husband and could not retract it. This interpretation was challenged in the House of Lords in 1992 and no longer applies in most jurisdictions. Until 1994 the rape of a man came under the offence of nonconsensual buggery, rather than rape. The law was changed to reflect the general perception that nonconsensual buggery is a form of rape.

Sexual intercourse is taken to mean the penetration of the labia by the penis to any degree – full penetration and ejaculation need not take place in order to prove rape. A man can be guilty of rape if he takes advantage of a woman by false pretences, e.g. by impersonating her sexual partner and approaching her just as she wakes from sleep.

Rape can involve the following:

- Intimidation with threats or weapons
- Beating, choking, knifing
- Sexual and mental humiliation
- Urination or spitting on the victim
- Forced oral sex
- Multiple rape by one or more assailants
- Injury to genitals, e.g. bottles, sticks pushed up vagina.

If a woman or child is raped or sexually assaulted, there are very few people to whom she feels she can turn. Some women find it impossible to tell anyone what has happened; those who do sometimes meet with anger, suspicion, recriminations and hostility from those closest to them. And a large number of raped women suffer in silence. Rape remains a highly unreported crime and not all women report the crime to the police. It doesn't matter how long ago the attack took place. A raped woman will still need to talk.

Rape is a violation of the person and of human and legal codes of behaviour. It is an anger and a pathological assertion of power. Although rape is a sexual assault, it has more to do with aggression than with sexuality. In fact, one-third of rapists experience either erectile or ejaculatory dysfunction during the assault.

Studies of convicted rapists suggest that the crime is committed to relieve pent-up anger against persons of whom the rapist is in some awe. The feminist theory proposes that the woman serves as an object for displacement of aggression that the rapist cannot express directly toward other men. This theory could be borne out by the incidence of rape during times of war – frequently gang rape – which serves to demoralize the male enemy, relive pent-up aggression and fear, enhance male bonding and increase feelings of power.

Convicted rapists seem to be part of a general subculture of violence and a great many of them have previous convictions for other offences like burglary and robbery.

Victims of rape can be any age. The greatest danger exists for females aged 10–29. Rape most commonly occurs in a woman's own neighbourhood, frequently inside her own home. The woman being raped is frequently in a life-threatening situation. During the rape she experiences shock and fear approaching panic. Her prime motive is to stay alive. There is a high incidence of submission, as can be expected, when the rapist uses a knife or a gun. In most cases, rapists choose victims slightly smaller than themselves.

Many women experience the symptoms of a post-traumatic stress reaction. The rape overwhelms them with a sense of vulnerability, fear of living in a dangerous world and loss of control over, their own lives. They become preoc-cupied with the trauma and it colours their future actions and day-to-day behaviour.

Some typical reactions are:

- A feeling of being unable to wash themselves clean
- Fear of walking out
- Fear of remaining alone in the house
- Fear of being followed
- Fear of being alone – ever
- Nightmares
- Insomnia
- Work problems
- Changes in eating patterns
- Somatic symptoms – headache, nausea, exhaustion, all-over tension
- Sexual difficulties – lack of desire, inhibited orgasm, inhibited excitement, vaginismus.

Few women emerge from the assault completely unscathed. The manifestations and the degree of damage depend on the violence of the attack itself, the vulner-ability of the woman and the support systems available to her immediately after the attack. Rape treatment centres that co-ordinate psychiatric, gynaecological and physical trauma services in one location and with close police co-operation are most helpful to the victim.

The rape victim experiences a physical and psychological trauma when she is assaulted. She is not always believed, in much the same way as the child who discloses incest is not believed. Statements such as 'She was asking for it' or 'She wanted it to happen' are common and they haunt and intimidate the rape victim. If a fruit and vegetable stall-holder displays his wares openly and a thief steals them, would the defence dare to say of the stall-holder 'He provoked my client' and expect the thief to be acquitted on that defence?

Rape is such a terrible experience that the shock itself can distort a person's memory in the immediate period after the attack. The help of experienced counsellors is valuable at this stage, especially if the listener is not connected with anyone who might be concerned with asking necessary questions and making examinations for legal reasons. Long-term counselling is often wise because of the frequency of delayed psychological effects, which can cripple a woman years after the original event.

The rapist

(Taken from Trimmer E. (1978) *Basic Sexual Medicine*, Heinemann, London.)
Three types of rapist can be identified:

- The well-adjusted heterosexual who has enjoyed an unusual amount of heterosexual activity, including mouth to genital contact, at an early age. Such men are unusually prone to fantasy, particularly sado-masochistic fantasies, and have a marked tendency to behave aggressively towards and feel a pronounced hostility to women. They are also subject to erectile failure.
- The amoral delinquent or sociopathic personality – in other words, a criminally, inclined man who takes what he wants.
- The incestuous rapist who uses his daughter as a convenient sex object.

Sometimes custodial sentences are necessary for the protection of society and for the safety of the perpetrator. But rapists need skilled help as well as their victims.

This article has concentrated on women who have been raped by men. It should be remembered that men and boys who are sexually assaulted by men and women who are forcibly attacked by other women can suffer very similar trauma. Several incidents of male rape have hit the headlines, as have rape by husbands and the more newly reported occurrence of 'date-rape'.

Rape prevention

- Help men to learn to find strength through expressing what are called the 'softer' emotions such as fear, sadness, vulnerability and tenderness. When we hear men talking about women in an abusive, derogatory or dismissive way, take it upon ourselves to make them aware of what they are doing.
- Do not condition children by filling them with our own fears and depriving them of their own self-reliance. Let us not lay down blanket rules of dos and don'ts but rather try to instil within them a foundation of resourcefulness by

our own openness and willingness to explore the topic of sexuality as one facet of self-awareness.

- For those of us who are older, let us value our age, for it is a tremendous treasure-chest of wisdom and experience. Let us make it available to those with a need to draw from such wisdom and experience.
- Let us help others to learn to say 'no' when that is what they mean; and to say 'yes' only when they are convinced that they do not want to say 'no'.
- Let us not be silent partners to violence and violation. Let us not accept things as 'the way they are'; without making our protests heard.
- Let us value ourselves, then we will value others too.

Further reading

Allison, J. A. and Wrightsman, L. S. (1993) *The Misunderstood Crime*, Sage Publications, London.
Sadock, V. A. (1995) Physical and sexual abuse of the adult. In: *Comprehensive Textbook of Psychiatry*, 6th edn, (eds H. J. Kaplan and B. J. Sadock), Williams & Wilkins, Baltimore, MD.

RAPPORT (*see also*: Bonding, empathy, in Core conditions)

Generally, rapport is a comfortable, relaxed, unconstrained, mutually accepting interaction between people. More specifically, when applied to counselling it is the feeling of accord, harmony or quality that is the foundation for any therapeutic relationship, without which healing and growth cannot take place. The term was originally used to describe the relationship between hypnotists and their subjects.

Rapport develops in the presence of:

- Active listening
- Accurate, sensitive responding
- Reflecting feelings
- Clear demonstration of the core conditions of empathy, warmth, genuineness and unconditional positive regard
- A sincere desire to understand
- An ability to be fully present with the client, wherever that might be
- Compassion for the client's suffering and distress.

Rapport has three essential ingredients:

- **Harmony,** something for which we strive, sometimes achieve and so easily lose. It is an elusive shadow that somehow we must turn into substance.
- **Compatibility,** which is influenced by such factors as:
  - Personality
  - Appearance
  - Intelligence
  - Emotional stability

- Understanding
- Kindness/tenderness
- Common interest.

- **Affinity**, which is the quality of the relationship. Counselling forms a significant bond between counsellor and client who have become bonded together for a specific purpose. When that purpose has been fulfilled, the relationship, the bond of affinity, will be severed. The more one invests in a relationship, the stronger the bond grows; and the breaking of it may bring pain.

Rapport is not something a person gains, like a certificate of competence. It is a transient state, more easily lost than achieved, always under threat from misinterpretation, lack of awareness of the interaction with the client and ineffective listening. The more one is able to engage the client's frame of reference, the deeper will be the rapport.

RATIONAL EMOTIVE COUNSELLING

Rational emotive counselling (RET) is a comprehensive, cognitive-behavioural method of psychotherapy developed by Albert Ellis. RET (also called rational emotive behaviour therapy) considers dysfunctional behaviour to be the result of faulty beliefs and irrational and illogical thinking. The method has elements in common with both cognitive and behavioural counselling.

The method uses an A–B–C–D sequence:

A = Activating event
B = Beliefs, which influence C
C = Consequences
D = Dispute.

Highly charged emotional consequences are invariably created by our belief systems. Undesirable emotional consequences can usually be traced to irrational beliefs. When irrational beliefs are disputed (D), disturbed consequences disappear.

Basic RET propositions:

- We are born with the potential to be rational as well as irrational
- Our tendency to irrational thinking, self-damaging habits, wishful thinking and intolerance is influenced by culture, community and family group
- We tend to think, feel and behave at the same time
- RET therapists believe that a highly cognitive, active–directive, homework-assigning, hard-headed and discipline-oriented system is likely to more effective than other systems
- A warm relationship is neither necessary nor a sufficient condition for effective personality change

- RET makes use of a variety of techniques to achieve a deep-seated cognitive change rather than a removal of symptoms
- All serious, emotional problems can be attributed to magical and faulty thinking; logical, observable and experimental thinking will eliminate these problems
- Insight is cold comfort if all it does is to let us see we have problems; we must accept that the real difficulty is in ourselves, not in other people nor in what happens to us.

Three basic principles:

- While present behaviour is related to the past, it is beliefs about the events and not the events themselves that cause problems in the present
- Although we may have been emotionally disturbed in the past, our faulty beliefs continue the process; we actively reinforce them by the way we think and act
- Only repeated rethinking of our irrational beliefs and repeated actions designed to undo those beliefs and the crooked thinking that goes with them are enough to create lasting change.

Aspects of personality

Physiological basis of personality

- We are born with a strong tendency to want, and to insist, that everything should happen for the best in our lives
- We condemn ourselves and others when we do not get what we want
- We tend to think childishly all our lives and only with great difficulty achieve and maintain realistic and mature behaviour
- Self-actualizing capacities are frequently defeated by our inborn and acquired self-sabotaging strategies.

Social aspects of personality

- When others approve of us and accept us, when we love and are loved, we tend to approve of ourselves as 'good' and 'worthwhile'
- Emotional disturbances are often caused when we care too much about what others think – this leads us to believe that we can only accept ourselves when others accept us
- A corollary of this is that we have an exaggerated compulsion to do anything to be liked.

Psychological aspects of personality

We become psychologically disturbed when we feel upset at C, after experiencing a disturbing event at A. Beliefs at B could run something like:

'I can't stand this'
'It's awful'

'I'd just as soon be dead'
'I'm worthless'
'It's all your fault'.

The illogicality of this is that:

- We may not like what has happened, but we can stand it
- Why can't we?
- What is awful?

It would be more precise to say:

'It may be very inconvenient' or
'It may be unhelpful'.

Being precise aids logical thinking. To think we can control the world is magical, irrational thinking. When we upset ourselves we then start to condemn ourselves for being upset.

To help people change, concentrate on B. A is past. The feelings of C, although real, are strongly influenced by B. Concentrating attention on B diverts attention from both A and C.

Counselling tasks

Dryden identifies the following counsellor tasks:

- To help clients see that their emotional and behavioural problems are rooted in faulty thinking
- To train clients to identify and change what is irrational to rational
- To teach clients that thoughts, behaviour and feelings can be changed by cognitive, behavioural and emotive methods, including imagery.

The client's tasks are:

- To identify the feelings and behaviours that disturb them
- To relate these disturbances to their faulty thinking
- To use behavioural and emotive methods, including imagery, to work at changing their irrational beliefs.

The therapeutic process

- No matter what feelings the client brings out, the counsellor tries to get back to the irrational ideas that lie beneath the feelings
- The counsellor does not hesitate to contradict and may use personal experience or experience from other people
- The counsellor never misses a chance to draw attention to and attack 'shoulds', 'oughts', 'musts'
- The counsellor will use the strongest philosophic approach possible, saying something like, 'If the worst think possible happened, would you still be worthless?'

- The counsellor does not dwell on feelings but uses them to point to irrational beliefs and ideas
- While showing acceptance, unconditional regard and confidence in the client's abilities, the counsellor, when necessary, is stern and insists that the client is capable of doing better
- The counsellor at all times tries to get the client to see the irrational ideas, without telling or explaining
- The counsellor may use strong, confrontational language to give the client an emotional shock
- The counsellor is empathetic but not sympathetic
- The counsellor constantly checks the client's understanding of what is being taught and does this by getting the client to repeat and clarify what has just been said
- Unlike some therapies, the RET counsellor does a lot of the talking and taking the lead.

In all of this, the client is understood and, although deep feelings are there, the client is given little chance to become immersed in them or to abreact strongly to them.

The client experiences:

- Full acceptance
- Renewed confidence
- Self-responsibility
- Hope of recovery
- Reduction in defences.

RET is used in numerous settings with individuals and groups.

Behavioural methods used

- *Cognitive homework assignments*, e.g.:
  - Making lists of current problems
  - Recording irrational beliefs and how to dispute them
  - Filling out RET self-help reports, showing how the client will combat these dysfunctional ideas
- *Activity homework assignments*, e.g.:
  - Client and counsellor devise desensitizing assignments that are specific to the unique situation of the client
  - Working out a step-by-step plan for overcoming faulty thinking, feeling or behaviour
  - Performing tasks that they dread doing, thereby facing the fear
- *Skills training*, e.g.:
  - Communication, intimate relationships, satisfying sex, job-seeking, business relations and time-management
  - Clients are shown how to reinforce what they do and penalize themselves

for what they do not do or when they regress to what they know to be dysfunctional.
- *Physical methods of therapy*, e.g.:
  - Encouraging clients to engage in health-developing activities, which includes diet, exercise, relaxation, biofeedback.

Techniques commonly used

- Repeating forceful, rational, coping statements, e.g.:
  'I do not need people's approval. That is a desire'
  'I am not annihilated when people don't approve of me'
- Rational emotive imagery to change inappropriate feelings to appropriate ones
- Unconditional acceptance, even when the client's behaviour is stupid or blameworthy
- Role-play of difficult situations, during which the counsellor will interrupt to draw attention to faulty thinking
- Clients learn to conduct forceful dialogue with themselves; to express irrational beliefs and then to dispute them
- These dialogues may be tape-recorded and played back for the counsellor to hear
- When clients feel strongly ashamed for doing what they want to do, for fear of disapproval, they are encouraged to accept a 'shame-attacking exercise', like doing something ridiculous in public; they work on themselves until they no longer feel ashamed or embarrassed
- RET uses humour to attack people's over-sensitiveness and dogmatic 'musts'
- RET discourages dependence by teaching clients to help themselves; to monitor their thoughts, feelings and behaviours; not to blame events or people; to restructure their perceptions and evaluations; and to stand on their own feet.

Major irrational beliefs

- I must do well and must win approval for all my performances or else I rate as a rotten person
- You must act kindly and considerately toward me or else you are a thoroughly bad person
- I must live under good and easy conditions, so that I get practically everything I want without too much effort and discomfort – if I don't, the world is doomed and life hardly seems worth living.

Examples of irrational ideas and their reworking

As you work through these, try to identify any that you use, either in the form given or some variation of it.

- **Irrational**: I must have love and approval almost all the time. **RETional**: I can please some people all of the time; all the people some of the time, but I know I shall never please everybody all of the time. There are times when I will fail – I can accept that.

- **Irrational**: Certain people are evil, wicked and villainous and should be punished. **RETional**: People do behave antisocially or inappropriately. I would like it better if they changed their behaviour. But they are themselves and I am me.
- **Irrational**: I feel awful when people and things are not how I would like them to be. **RETional**: I will not act like a spoiled child. I refuse to get stressed about trivial events. I refuse to 'awfulize' everything.
- **Irrational**: External events cause most human misery – people simply react as events trigger their emotions. **RETional**: I am not responsible for controlling external events. I cannot create universal happiness or eradicate suffering. At times I might feel helpless and anxious because I cannot change or control things. I can only control my own emotions and behaviour.
- **Irrational**: I should be afraid or anxious about what is unknown, uncertain or potentially dangerous. **RETional**: If I rehearse catastrophes, I only increase the fear or anxiety. I make coping more difficult and increase stress. The fear response is for actual danger.
- **Irrational**: It is easier to avoid difficulties than to face life and responsibilities. **RETional**: I know that avoiding responsibilities is only putting off what I must do. I must not make excuses to myself or blame others for what I don't do.
- **Irrational**: I need something or someone stronger or greater than myself to rely on. **RETional**: I know I'm not an island, but my independent judgement and my specific needs could be undermined if I rely too much on higher authority.
- **Irrational**: I am what I am today because of the past and I can't change that. **RETional**: Just because I once experienced something, that does not mean that I must keep playing the old, worn out tapes, to cope with a situation that is no longer real.
- **Irrational**: Happiness can be achieved by endless leisure and pleasure. **RETional**: I refuse to dwell in the Elysian Fields as an escape from reality. There is more to happiness than illusion. I resist the lure of the Lotus Eaters. I refuse to be a slave to pleasure.
- **Irrational**: I am helpless and have no control over what I experience or feel. **RETional**: I can exercise a degree of control over my relationships and I can control how I interpret and emotionally respond to each life event. To believe I have no control will lead to helplessness, depression and anxiety.
- **Irrational**: People are fragile and should never be hurt. **RETional**: I do not set out to hurt people, but if I refuse to say or do anything, lest it inadvertently hurt someone, I will feel frustrated, helpless and trapped.
- **Irrational**: I must never ask for what I want from people. **RETional**: I cannot expect others to be psychic and to anticipate and provide for my needs. If I do this I will indulge in self denial and being a martyr.

- **Irrational**: I must be a people-pleaser or else I will be abandoned or rejected. **RETional**: I will offer people my true, natural self. They can take it or leave it. If they respond to the real me, I don't have to worry about being rejected. That does not mean I have to be a steamroller, crushing people.
- **Irrational**: When people disapprove of me, it is because I am wrong or bad. **RETional**: I know I am not perfect, but my imperfections do not make me all bad.
- **Irrational**: I cannot be truly happy or find pleasure and fulfilment on my own. **RETional**: I like being with people, but I also need my own space at times.
- **Irrational**: Somewhere there is perfect love and a perfect relationship waiting for me. **RETional**: Finding the perfect relationship is like chasing the elusive butterfly.
- **Irrational**: I shouldn't have to feel pain; I'm entitled to a good life. **RETional**: Pain is an unavoidable part of human life. I know that pain may be a part of the decisions I make. Pain is a part of healthy growth. Life is not fair and sometimes I will feel pain no matter what I do.
- **Irrational**: My worth depends on how much I achieve and produce. **RETional**: My real worth depends on my capacity to be fully alive, feeling everything it means to be human.
- **Irrational**: Anger is bad and destructive. **RETional**: Anger is one of my feelings. It only becomes destructive when I attack someone, myself or some object.
- **Irrational**: In every circumstance and at all times, I must be:
  - Cheerful
  - Comfortable
  - Compassionate
  - Competent
  - Confident
  - Consistent
  - Controlled.

    The seven great illogical Cs.

Five steps to help clients towards RETional thinking

Start by selecting a situation that consistently generates stressful emotions.

1. Write down the objective facts of the event as they occurred at the time. Do not include subjective impressions or value judgements.
2. Write down self-talk about the event: 'My subjective impression, value judgements, assumptions, beliefs, predictions and worries are....' My irrational ideas are....'
3. Focus on the client's emotional response. Make a clear one- or two-word label to describe it, e.g. 'Angry', 'Depressed', 'Felt worthless', 'Afraid'.
4. Dispute and change the irrational self-talk identified at step 2.
   - 'The irrational idea I am going to dispute is...'
   - 'The rational support for this idea is...'

- 'The evidence that this is a false idea is . . .'
- 'The evidence for the truth of this idea is . . .'
- 'If what I want to happen, doesn't, the worst consequence could be . . .'
- 'If what I don't want to happen, does, the worst consequence could be . . .'
- 'If what I want to happen, doesn't, the benefit could be . . .'
- 'If what I don't want to happen, does, the benefit could be . . .'

5. Substitute RETional self-talk.

Making use of RETional imagery

1. Get the client to imagine a stressful event in detail; emotions; sight, smell, sound, dress, conversation
2. Encourage the client to feel the main emotion, then transform it
3. Transform anxiety into concern; depression into disappointment; rage into annoyance; guilt into regret; helplessness into discomfort
4. Get the client to examine how to achieve this transformation. Instead of saying, 'I can't handle this . . .. This will drive me crazy', the client may now say, 'I've dealt successfully with situations like this before'.

Insight

Three levels of insight are necessary to change:

- Knowledge that we have a problem and awareness of some of the events that may have caused the problem
- Seeing clearly that the irrational ideas we acquired early in life are creating the emotional climate we live in now and that consciously or unconsciously we work fairly hard to perpetuate them
- We will find no other way of eliminating the problem other than steadily, persistently and vigorously working to change your irrational ideas.

Without commitment, altering habitual, irrational responses will prove difficult.

Further reading

Dryden, W. (1996) Rational emotive behaviour therapy. In: *Handbook of Individual Therapy*, (ed. W. Dryden), Sage Publications, London.
Ellis, A. (1977) *Reason and Emotion in Psychotherapy*, Secauces, Citadel, NJ.
Ellis, A. (1989) *Why Some Therapies Don't Work*, Prometheus Books, New York.
Ellis, A. and Harper, R. A. (1975) *A New Guide to Rational Living*, Prentice-Hall, Englewood Cliffs, NJ.
Eschenroeder, C. (1982) How rational is rational emotive counsellor? A critical appraisal. *Cognitive Counsellor and Research*, 6, 381–391.

REASSURANCE

Reassurance is a verbal attempt by the therapist to relieve anxiety by trying to prove to the client that things are not as bad as the client thinks. Unwarranted, and false reassurances are a violation of respect, for they are an attempt to diminish the problem in the eyes of the client.

Verbal reassurances given inappropriately may make the client 'dry up'. Sometimes it is essential for clients to experience the depths of their feelings in order to work through them toward understanding and insight.

Unwarranted reassurances are very often attempts to minimize the feelings or the problem. They may reflect therapists' inability to handle their own anxiety and frustration. Reassurances may be a refusal to acknowledge the reality of the client's perceptions. If the client perceives something as a mountain, then a mountain it is. Unwarranted reassurances can frighten the client off. If the therapist, the expert, can't handle feelings, what hope has the client? For example, the client says, 'I wonder if there is something in me that made my husband go off with another woman?' The counsellor, not wishing to confront that issue, says, 'You mustn't blame yourself. He's the one who couldn't stand the heat.' This is unwarranted reassurance and will get in the way of effective counselling because the counsellor does not provide the opportunity for exploring the client's feelings.

On the other hand, when clients make statements that indicate that they are seeking reassurance, it is sometimes difficult not to drop into the trap. Advanced empathy will hear the plea but will use that to draw out the implied request. For example, when Amy said, 'Is it always going to be as painful as this?' the counsellor replied, 'I hear the anxiety in your voice that you will never get back to feeling OK again and you want me to reassure you, maybe even to take away some of the pain.' This is not falling into the trap.

Positive reassurance is conveyed indirectly through the skills of active listening and responding, within a relationship in which the core conditions are demonstrated. The more closely we enter another person's frame of reference, the less likely we shall be to offer empty, unwarranted and false reassurances.

Further reading

Foskett, J. (1984) *Meaning in Madness*, SPCK. London.
Jacobs, M. (1982) *Still Small Voice*, SPCK. London.

RECORDS

Counselling records serve four main purposes:

- To aid good counselling practice
- Help administration
- Training
- Research.

The record should show how you set out to help this particular client. It is the first step in evaluation. It is through the record that hypotheses can be tested, characteristic patterns of behaviour perceived and progress assessed. A good record should be readable. A good recording style is plain, clear and as brief as treatment will permit. We cannot record accurately if we have not heard and observed accurately. Clarity and brevity indicate analytical thinking. The record will be a thoughtful reflection of what took place in the interview.

In certain situations, some notes are essential, if only to keep the key issues before your eyes. Before starting a session, if you say something like, 'What do you feel about me taking some notes?' you will rarely meet with a refusal. Such notes need only be single words, enough to act as refreshers later in the session. Single words or short sentences can usually be written without taking your eyes off the client for too long.

Process recording is a term borrowed from social work, in which an interview is recorded as nearly verbatim as possible. It includes not only what both you and the client said, but also significant reactions of the client and changes in mood and response. It preserves the sequence in which the various issues were explored. This is a tremendous discipline, yet an exercise that brings with it great rewards.

Sureness of what material to select grows with experience, if the process is seen as a necessary discipline requiring time and thought. Accurate recording is also an analytical look at the meanings behind the facts and words used.

The early stages of counselling generally require longer records than later sessions. At all times you should be both forward-looking and backward-looking, trying to tie up what took place in past sessions with the present session.

Good observation and perception in the interview will be reflected in the record and, from time to time, particularly with long-term counselling, summaries are recommended.

Suggested items to include:

- How and why the client came to you: was it a referral or self-referred?
- The presenting problem (*see* entry)
- The facts
- The relationship between the client and any significant others
- Personal history
- Any significant quotes made either by you or the client that bring out important feeling, attitudes, opinions or refer to the 'larger problem'
- Your own activity within the session; thoughts, feelings, behaviours, interactions
- As counselling continues, the record should reflect development and include your periodic evaluations and statements of aims
- Future dates for sessions
- Referrals if any.

However, it is not essential that all these data be gathered in the first session, although some counsellors do work with a 'history' sheet completed in the first session.

To be serviceable, a record must be orderly in its arrangements; this hinges on thinking through what has to be included, even although how it was presented may not be logical. A page with margins for headings can be a useful way of making quick reference to material. Counselling records are not an end in themselves; they are tools, not works of art, yet they should be legible, readable and logical. You may wish to refer to your notes for research purposes. Records often provide evidence changes which need to take place within an organization or a community.

Finally, you may wish to consider using a tape recorder. Although some clients may refuse your request to do so, I have never had a client refuse. Taped sessions are useful because they are an accurate record of what took place and although the listening and transcribing time is considerable, the benefits are a tremendous compensation.

When I first started using a tape recorder, in the early 1970s, John, the client I was then working with, asked if he could listen to the tapes when I had finished with them. So, before the next session, I would have listened, transcribed and analysed the session; he then had the tape, listened to it in the intervening week and we would discuss any particular points raised by listening to the tape. There were many times when he said something like 'I hadn't remembered saying that' or 'I've had some new thoughts on that' or 'Listening again to that made me quite upset'. Our relationship lasted 9 months and, in the evaluation, he said how much he had gained from listening to the tapes. In effect, he was having two counselling sessions a week – one he paid for, one for free!

For one's own professional development, some time should be devoted to making a summary of what has taken place throughout counselling. It is possible that what is included in the summary may never be read by anyone else. But the fact that you have taken time and effort to commit it to paper may at some time be a useful resource for you when pondering on a particular point in counselling.

Experience can never be wiped out but, when experience is reinforced by evaluation, many of the interactions, the words, the nuances that so quickly fade from the memory are captured in a way that experience by itself cannot do. If you feel that the final evaluation is proving too difficult, that may be because evaluating your own part in the process is eluding you. It is possible, for example, that some aspect of the relationship between yourself and the client is proving a stumbling block. If the stumbling block is not removed it will remain an obstacle in the way of effective counselling. Stumbling blocks can be turned into stepping stones by an honest and in-depth evaluation assisted by honest recording.

A final point should be made about computer-kept records. The whole issue of record-keeping presents difficulties of confidentiality; counsellors certainly must consider the implications of keeping client records on computer. Such questions as: storing (on hard disk or on floppy); security of material (where is it kept?); access (password; who has access?); how long the records are kept and for what purposes; and, if you are part of a computer network, how you protect the material all have to be considered. Computer-kept records can save an enormous amount of time and space but client confidentiality must always be uppermost in our minds.

Further reading

Sutton, J. and Stewart, W. (1997) *Learning to Counsel: How to develop the skills to work effectively with others.* How To Books, Oxford.

REDUNDANCY COUNSELLING (*see also*: Dying – stages of, Retirement)

The effects of redundancy can be devastating to the person, to the immediate family and also to society. It may be the most psychologically mutilating event the individual has ever experienced.

Redundancy affects the person concerned and the one having to give the news. The whole organization is subjected to the trauma. Whatever the reasons, when the axe falls the innocent often feel they have a hand in the execution.

A disturbing fact is that people, particularly managers, who have once been made redundant are more at risk of a second or third redundancy.

The stages of redundancy:

1. Planning in secret; often accompanied by rumours and suspicion
2. Announcement of redundancy and selection of personnel to go
3. Individuals leave the organization and enter a period of unemployment
4. Search for new jobs.

The psychological phases of redundancy:

1. **Shock**: 'I can't believe it', 'I won't survive'
2. **Optimism**: 'Something is bound to turn up'
3. **Pessimism (or depression)**: 'Nobody wants me'
4. **Fatalism**: 'I might as well give up.'

Redundancy can also be regarded as a bereavement – the loss of something precious, suggestive of the Kubler-Ross model. All models have their limitations and it does not mean that every person will follow the model through as presented. Neither does it mean that there is a logical progression through the stages. It is more likely that the person will fluctuate between the various stages and perhaps experience all of them within a short space of time and return to a previous stage many times before 'acceptance'. In many cases of redundancy, acceptance only comes with being re-employed.

Stress following redundancy is to be expected for the following reasons:

- Expectations have been cut short
- Being unemployed is not the norm.

People may not find the answer to the question 'Why me?' It is possible that the individual does have a part to play in what has happened, e.g. s/he may not have kept abreast of personal development, something expected by many organizations. This expectation may be justified, particularly where the organization provides opportunity for self-development. At the same time, effective management might have detected the lack before and been able to take constructive action, not redundancy.

Redundancy counselling, which covers dismissal or other severance, is concerned mainly with helping people change in order to improve their chances of new employment. New employment may have to be different from the previous one but it should feel psychologically good, according to the following criteria:

- Provides an opportunity to use one's special abilities
- Permits one to be creative and original
- Enables one to look forward to a stable and secure future
- Provides one with a chance to earn a reasonable income
- Gives one an opportunity to be of service to others.

Some people want only practical advice; others need an opportunity to explore their feelings before they can make a decision, having explored various options.

The stages of redundancy counselling

1. Dealing with the crisis
2. Careers advice
3. Coaching (interviewing skills, preparing CVs and presentation)
4. Where to look, whom to approach, coping with rejections and follow-up after reemployment.

Counselling should be an integral part of the organization's redundancy package. Some people have the necessary coping skills and have an already established network of support and contacts, but may need some help with the practicalities. Some, because of their stress levels (which may, of course, involve the family), may need more personal counselling before they are able to think clearly enough to take action. Some are so devastated that they experience a full-blown grief reaction and will need a lot of personal counselling.

Redundancy counselling benefits the organization by:

- Taking the problem off the organization's shoulders
- Showing concern, thereby keep up morale
- Enabling difficult decisions to be made
- Helping to keep confidence in the organization.

Services usually offered by companies specializing in redundancy counselling:

- Negotiating the 'golden handshake'
- Financial, pensions and investments advice
- Legal advice

- Health check-up
- Crisis/personal counselling
- Vocational/career guidance
- Analysis of interests and skills, strengths and weaknesses, aptitude and psychometric tests and advice from clinical psychologists
- Self-marketing skills; interviewing, presentation, preparing CVs and letters
- Exploring new opportunities; working abroad, self-employment, retraining
- Getting lists of vacancies and contacting recruiting agencies
- Providing office facilities, including secretarial assistance
- Advice on handling offers of work.

An important step forward is when the person can say, 'My job is redundant, I am not.'

Further reading

British Association for Counselling (1983) *Redundancy and Unemployment*, BAC, Rugby.
Burrows, G. (1985) *Redundancy Counselling for Managers*, Institute of Personnel Management, London.
De Board, R. (1983) *Counselling People at Work*, Gower, Aldershot.
Weatherley, M. J. (1982) Counselling in career self-management courses for the mature executive. *British Journal of Guidance and Counselling*, **10**(1), 88–96.
Webb, S. (1984) *Guidelines for the Redundant Manager*, British Institute of Management, London.

REFERRING A CLIENT

Not every counsellor is the best person for all clients, so from time to time it may become necessary for the client's development that s/he is referred to another counsellor or counselling agency.

It may become necessary, therefore, to refer a client for one or a combination of the following reasons:

- Medical
- Social
- Pastoral
- Psychiatric
- Psychological
- Emotional
- Spiritual
- Legal.

It is helpful, therefore, to know the resources available in your own locality, agencies as well as people. In addition, it might become necessary to refer clients because:

- You are moving to a different area
- The client requests it

- The client requires more in-depth work than you feel comfortable with
- The agency you work for does not take on clients with this type of difficulty
- The problem is outside your competence
- Your style of counselling does not suit the client
- You discover that you and the client share a relationship with a third party and there is a conflict of loyalty or confidentiality
- It becomes apparent that the client might do better in couple counselling or group counselling
- The client wants to explore sensitive areas such as sexuality and needs a counsellor of the same sex
- The client is of a different culture and this is creating difficulty in the relationship – this might also apply to people whose first language is not the same as yours.

Referral is likely to be delayed because of:

- The counsellor's hurt pride at not being able to continue with the client until completion
- Not creating an awareness in the mind of the client from the start that referral is a possibility
- Not admitting limitations
- Not working through and helping the client understand why referral is indicated
- Not being able to separate from the client.

The client might see referral as rejection rather than development. Sometimes there is the tendency to refer too quickly. Perhaps the counsellor may see a need for referral but this is totally rejected by the client. The limitations should then be brought into the open and discussed. The counsellor then may need to seek expert help if work with the client is to be productive. Working with a client who refuses to be referred is both demanding and exciting but the counsellor will need a great deal of support.

Referral is particularly difficult for clients who feel they have already been pushed from one counsellor to another; this could lead to a feeling that they are beyond help. It is certainly true that the longer the relationship the more difficult referral might be, even though the need is recognized by the counsellor and accepted by the client. But just as it is possible to work toward separation at the end of counselling, so it is equally possible to achieve this in referral.

You should do all you can to make the transition easy – talk about the other counsellor or agency, arrange a visit, let the client make contact, work with the client to prepare a summary of what has been achieved so far. Clients who feel totally involved in the referral are likely to get the most out of the new relationship.

Further reading

Jacobs, M. (1982) *Still Small Voice*, SPCK, London.

REFLECTING (*see also*: Paraphrasing)

Reflecting concentrates on the feelings within a statement. Paraphrasing and reflecting are invariably linked and it may be artificial to try to separate them. Reflecting feelings accurately depends on empathic understanding.

Pity = feeling for
Sympathy = feeling like
Empathy = feeling with.

Neither pity nor sympathy is constructive. Reflecting involves both listening and understanding then communicating that understanding. If understanding remains locked up within us, we contribute little to the helping process.

Being able to reflect feelings involves viewing the world from the clients' frame of reference – what their thoughts, feelings and behaviours mean to them.

Effective responding shows that we accept people. It does not act as a 'stopper' on their flow of talk and their emotions. They do not feel inadequate, inferior or defensive talking to us or as though they are being talked down to.

To respond effectively:

- Observe facial and bodily movements
- Listen to words and their meanings
- Tune into your own emotional reactions to what the client is communicating
- Sense the meaning of the communication
- Take into account the degree of client self-awareness
- Respond appropriately
- Use expressive, not stereotyped language
- Use vocal and bodily language that are in agreement with each other
- Check the accuracy of your understanding.

Paraphrasing mirrors the content of a statement; reflecting mirrors the feelings of a statement. It is a clarification of the emotional content. Accurate paraphrasing and reflecting communicate empathy. Accurate mirroring of feelings will demonstrate deeper empathy.

Examples of reflecting feelings:

Example 1: Alex says, 'I'll have to leave home – not sure how I'll cope, though. Mum and Dad smother me and can't see why I want to lead my own life.'

Counsellor says, 'Alex, you sound confused and very uncertain that you would be doing the right thing, moving away from home. Your parents are getting on your back and perhaps you feel like a racehorse, champing at the bit. At the same time, you want your independence and it seems as if the price of this is having to separate from your parents.'

Example 2: Mary says, 'I will be a success. I can do it if I work hard. If it takes 18 hours a day chained to a VDU, I'll do it. If husband and family suffer, too bad. I hope they don't, but it'll be worth it all in the end. Success is what matters.'

Counsellor says, 'Mary, you're on the ladder of success and very determined to reach the top. So desperate is your desire to succeed that, no matter what it costs, you're going to slave away and, if necessary, burn the midnight oil to get what you want. You fully realize that this stiff climb could be painful and that you may put your relationships at risk, yet so strong is the drive that you won't let anything stand in the way.'

Example 3: Sam, married to Susan and in business partnership with his brother Bill, says, 'I can never find the time to do the things I enjoy. I'm just getting ready to go out for a swim or go jogging when Bill reminds me there's some letters to write to customers or Susan collars me to help with some household chores. It's getting more difficult to get the fun out of life I expect to have. It's depressing.'

Counsellor says, 'It seems to me, Sam, that no matter what you do, other people always find something else for you to do. It's really bugging you, to the extent that you feel life is just one long chore. You long for some recreation, to have time to enjoy yourself doing what you want for yourself, yet all the time you're being driven into the ground by the pressure from Bill and Susan.'

REGRET

The usual meaning of this word is that in retrospect we might have behaved differently in the past or that things might have turned out better had events gone differently. In many ways, regrets are negative feelings and often pointless, mainly because there is nothing we can do to change the past. The only positive thing is that we can learn from the past.

Paradoxically, one way to help clients move from regrets is to get them to talk about them *ad nauseam*, to explore them in the light of where they are now and then to get them to think of how different their life would have been had they followed a particular path, which they regret not following. Bringing fantasy into reality is one way of defusing regrets.

Hearing the client's regrets means hearing the underlying feelings, which, for example, may be anger, blame, guilt or loss. In psychology, **anticipatory regret** is a vague feeling of worry when a person contemplates a certain course of action, particularly when thinking about the negative elements of the choice.

People who have been bereaved often express regret: 'If only I had done…', 'If only I had been…'. The underlying feeling there is likely to be guilt. 'If only I hadn't done…'. There the feeling is likely to be shame.

The following quotation is attributed to the comedian Woody Allen: 'My one regret in life is that I am not someone else.' He may have said that with tongue in cheek but, taking it at face value, he is expressing what many people feel; they regret who they are. Exploring that feeling with the client could help them close a particular chapter of their past to enable them to move forward.

REJECTION (*see also*: acceptance, in Relationship principles of counselling, Approval)

Rejection is the opposite of acceptance: someone has failed to accept us as we are. The body may reject something like an implant; a parent can reject a child; an adult, a lover; a committee, an idea. Rejection is a refusal to incorporate something.

If we take the analogy of the body, rejection leads to pain and maybe death. While clients seldom face death as a result of feeling rejected, the feelings may be just as powerful – a cutting off, separation.

Some of the synonyms for rejection are: cold shoulder, denial, dismissal, rebuff, refusal, renunciation, repudiation, spurning, turn-down. All of these portray something of great pain and distress, a feeling akin to bereavement, of a cutting off of a part of one's self.

An aspect of social anxiety is hypersensitivity to rejection and criticism. Such a person over-reacts emotionally and their response portrays that they feel devastated and almost feel destroyed by what to other people is insignificant.

This hypersensitivity to rejection is closely related to the client's feeling of self-worth, self-acceptance and self-esteem. Clients who are low in self-acceptance set themselves up for rejection by the way they relate to people. If we don't value ourselves, then we will find it difficult, if not impossible, to recognize when someone values us. If we cannot accept ourselves, then accepting other people is asking too much; hence we reject others because we reject ourselves. Then we feel victimized and rejected.

In counselling language, rejection is a very overused word and, as a consequence, has lost much of its power. One way to bring freshness to the feeling is to use another word or to get the client to think of other words to describe it.

A behavioural approach in helping a client who fears rejection would be to get the client to perform some task that would open the client to the possibility of rejection, like asking a friend for a loan.

RELATIONSHIP PRINCIPLES

To work effectively with people we need to be able to:

- Build on other people's ideas
- Express warmth and affection
- Handle personal anger constructively
- Be aware that we influence others
- Listen with understanding
- Receive warmth and affection
- Tolerate conflict and antagonism
- Tolerate conflicting views of others
- Tolerate other people's behaviour
- Have aspirations for self

- Be aware of our own feelings
- Have an awareness of other people's feelings
- Be willing to continue developing self-awareness
- Have close personal relationships
- Value independence
- Value innovativeness
- Strive to be open-minded
- Show peace of mind
- Maintain physical energy
- Work towards maintaining high self-esteem/self-worth
- Be self-expressive
- Tolerate differences in others
- Trust people
- Be versatile
- Be willing to discuss our own feelings.

RELATIONSHIP PRINCIPLES OF COUNSELLING

Individualization

- Individualization means recognizing and respecting the other person's uniqueness
- It recognizes not just a human being but this human being – just as s/he is
- Every person has the need and the right to be related to as unique
- Clients need our undivided attention and privacy, to be able to discuss their unique problem
- People whose uniqueness is not respected react by only giving information and not disclosing feelings
- When people are related to with uniqueness, when they feel understood, they will enter more willingly into the helping relationship
- Relating to others in this way may not come easily
- Training is essential to:
    - Recognize and deal with our biases and prejudices
    - Acquire knowledge of human behaviour
    - Develop listening and responding skills
    - Learn to move at the client's pace
    - Learn to respond with empathy
    - Develop perspective
    - Develop a flexible approach
- We can enhance individualization by:
    - Thoughtfulness and care
    - Privacy
    - Preparation
    - Engaging the client
    - Flexibility.

Expressing feelings

- Every client has the right to be permitted, and indeed encouraged, to express both positive and negative feelings within an atmosphere of understanding and acceptance and without feeling judged
- We should neither discourage nor condemn feelings – it is often therapeutic to encourage the expression of feelings
- Any problem, however practical its focus, has an emotional component
- The expression of feelings is encouraged:
  - To relieve pressures and tensions and free the client for positive, constructive action
  - To understand more clearly the client and the problem
  - To help us assess the client's strengths and weaknesses
  - To provide psychological support – feelings shared brings closeness
  - Because when feelings are brought into the open there is more chance that something constructive can be done with them
  - Because feelings shared help to deepen the counselling relationship
  - To create a safe environment
- Feelings are facts
- Feelings have a voice; they will speak for themselves – we must ensure that we listen to them
- We can enhance the expression of feelings by:
  - Being relaxed
  - Adequate personal preparation
  - Active and purposeful listening
  - Not trying to rush the process.

Some cautions:

- Psychological awareness is essential to deal constructively with other people's feelings and the feelings generated within us
- The relationship must encourage true expression of feelings
- Give free time and space to the client
- Keep your foot on the emotional brake – feelings expressed too soon, too much, may be destructive
- Clients' feelings should not become our burden
- Do not fall into the trap of offering premature or empty verbal reassurances.

Thinking and feeling

Trainee counsellors learn quickly that beginning sentences with 'I think' is bad form, so they preface their remarks with 'I feel' and go on to report thoughts. This use of 'I feel' often results in muddled communication. Thinking (head talk) seeks to explain interaction – the prose of communication. Feeling (heart talk) seeks to understand interaction – the poetry of communication.

Thinking:

- 'Think' statements refer to what the environment means to us
- They attempt to define, assert, offer an opinion, rationalize or make cause and effect connections between different events
- 'Think' statements are bound by the rules of logic and scientific inquiry; they may be true or untrue
- A 'think' statement can generally be proved or disproved
- 'Think' statements require words to be communicated
- Most of us have been trained to make 'I think' statements exclusively
- We are constantly engaged in cognitive work: observing, inferring, categorizing, generalizing and summarizing
- Occasionally we report to others what goes on in our head
- Frequently we are asked for:
  - Facts: 'Where did you put the car keys?'
  - Opinions: 'Which tastes better, French or Spanish wine?'
  - Speculation: 'What happens when we achieve population saturation?', What are you thinking about?'
- Human beings like to think and our ability to do it is usually on the short list of characteristics that distinguish us from other species.

Feeling:

- 'Feel' statements refer to what is implied, internal affective, immediate, non rational, emotional – a 'gut' response to something personal and distinctive happening within
- Like dreams, feel statement are neither true nor false, good nor bad; they can only be honestly or dishonestly communicated
- Many of us have conditioned ourselves to screen out our internal reactions: we allow ourselves to say we feel 'interested', 'uncomfortable' but are scared to disclose our more intense feelings
- By getting in touch with what is happening within us, we enrich our own lives and those with whom we communicate
- Internal changes provide direct cues to the feelings we are experiencing: a change in bodily functioning – muscle tightness, restlessness, frowning, smiling, inability to stay with a conversation – tell us how we are reacting to what is happening.

Watch yourself when you say 'I feel that...'. The 'that' is a tip-off that you are making a think statement with a feel prefix.

Examples of thinking and feeling statements:

Example: 'I feel like having a drink'. **Rephrased:** 'I'm thirsty, so I think I'll have a drink'.

Example: 'I feel your brashness is a cover for your insecurity'. **Rephrased:** 'It's my opinion that you cover up your insecurity with brashness'.

Example: 'I feel that all men are created equal'. **Rephrased**: 'I believe that all men are created equal'.

Involvement must be controlled

- No emotional involvement means separation
- Controlled emotional involvement means effective contact
- Over-involvement leads to feelings of being engulfed
- Over-involvement/over-identification is caused by a deficiency of self-awareness. The components of controlled involvement are:
  - **Sensitivity**: Listening to feelings, verbal cues, nonverbal cues, paralinguistic cues
  - **Understanding** what these feelings mean to this person: Getting inside the client's frame of reference, seeing through the client's eyes, hearing through the client's ears, feeling through the client's experience
  - **Responding**: Responses convey understanding – a response may be internal, founded on attitudes, feelings and understanding, or external; verbal or nonverbal
- Avoid empty phrases such as: 'I know how you feel', 'This must be hard on you'. We can never know how another person feels. We only know how we feel, how we felt. We trust that our level of understanding is helping us get somewhere need the client's feelings.

Self-determination (self-direction)

- Self-determination is our basic right of freedom to choose our own direction, even though that decision may clash with the values, beliefs and desires of other people
- We all have the responsibility to live our one life and achieve life's goals as we perceive them
- One of the functions of counselling is to help clients mobilize their inner resources so that they are more able to make balanced decisions
- Many people feel helpless to make decisions because the alternatives are unclear; helping them tease out what is involved often enables them to make a decision and to take responsibility for what they decide to do
- We may face a dilemma: if, in our view, a proposed course of action is destructive, could we still be objective and positive toward the client? If our values clashed, could we continue counselling without trying to persuade, manipulate, take responsibility or try to control the client?
- Clients need help to:
  - See their problem in a new perspective
  - Explore alternatives and the possible consequences
  - Express their thoughts and feelings about choices
  - Explore their thoughts, feelings and behaviours within a relationship in which they feel safe

    The counsellor, as it were, helps clients clear some of the mist away from the window, thus allowing them to look out and see a little more clearly.

- Self-determination is not licence. It is influenced by:
  - The rights of others
  - The client's capacity to make informed decisions
  - Civil and criminal law and the client's own moral law
  - In work, the contract of employment
  Clients who violate their own moral law do spiritual harm to themselves. If a decision would be so contrary to the client's own moral law as to be destructive, it is questionable if we are really helping to solve a problem if we do not challenge that decision.

For every individual right of choice there are accompanying duties and responsibilities in our relationship with others. When we practise self-determination it does not mean that we are indifferent to what clients do; neither does it mean that we have to approve. We accept their basic right.

However, being able to work with a client who challenges our willingness not to interfere might also challenge how willing we are not to control or to possess the client. Possessiveness refers to any tendency to attempt to gain and hold ownership over things; however, it is generally applied to possessiveness of people. It is the tendency to maintain power and control over others, to treat them as though they were one's owned possessions. It is most commonly observed in parents' attitudes toward their children and husbands and wives toward each other. Possessiveness – the opposite of self-determination – is anathema in counselling.

Confidentiality (*see also*: Counselling ethics)

Counselling touches human lives intimately, possibly more so than any other helping relationship. The counsellor is frequently the observer and, often the recipient, of confidential material about people, their life situations and intimate details of their families. Confidentiality is both an ethical consideration and an element in the counselling relationship. At first glance, it is deceptively simple.

- Confidentiality means not passing on secret details about another person disclosed during counselling
- Everything said in a counselling interview is confidential; not everything is secret – what are secrets?
  - The **private secret** is that which, if we reveal it, would libel, injure or cause great sadness to the person concerned
  - The **pledged secret** is when one person shares something with another and is assured that it will remain in confidence
  - The **entrusted secret** is the explicit or implicit understanding that the confidant will not divulge the information
- A belief that absolutely everything the client says must never be shared with anyone else can lead to problems
- If it becomes imperative that some information must be passed on, full discussion with the client is essential
- The professional counsellor is bound by certain ethics, which are not

applicable in their totality to people using counselling skills as part of their repertoire of work skills. People who use counselling at work, as distinct from independent counsellors, must consider the rules of professional conduct of their organization. It is helpful to ask: Is this information concerned mainly with the client as a person with the organization? Purely personal material, unless it impinges on the client's working life and influences performance, is of no concern to anyone else. The dividing line between 'personal' and 'organizational' is finely drawn. Only after a weighing up of all the pros and cons will we realize why the balance is tipped the way it is and so make our decision to keep something or pass it on.

- Wherever possible agreement to disclose should be received, to avoid feelings of betrayal
- Feelings as well as facts should not be shared indiscriminately
- Confidentiality is limited by:
  - Whose needs predominate
  - Who would be harmed
  - The organizational needs
  - The needs of the wider society.

Counsellors need to be quite clear what information gleaned during counselling they may pass and to whom. Some clients need to be reassured of confidentiality and counsellors should take time to clarify precisely what the client understands by confidentiality.

The person's right to secrecy is never absolute. Counsellors may be required by a court to disclose secret information. Failure to do so may lead to imprisonment for contempt of court.

Acceptance (*see also* entry, above)

- Acceptance is:
  - A warm regard for people as persons of unconditional self-worth
  - Valuing people no matter what their condition, thoughts, behaviours or feelings
  - Respect and liking for people as separate, unique persons
  - Willingness to allow people to possess their own feelings
  - Regard for the attitudes of the moment, no matter how negative or positive; no matter how much such attitudes may contradict other attitudes the person held in the past
- Inherent in the idea of acceptance is that the counsellor does not judge the client by some set of rules or standards
- Counsellors who are unable to suspend their own judgement will find that they intrude on the interaction and influence their impartiality
- Acceptance is a special kind of loving that moves out toward people as they are – warts and all; maintaining their dignity and personal worth, with their strengths and weaknesses, with their likeable, unlikeable qualities; with their positive and negative attitudes, constructive and destructive wishes, thoughts,

feelings and behaviours. There is no wish to apply pressure to make the person to be someone else, no wish to control, criticize or condemn and attaching of 'if' clauses; e.g. 'I will love you if...'. Clients will test our unconditional acceptance.

- When we accept clients just as they are, they accept us – just as we are and this helps them to accept other people as they are
- Acceptance is dependent on self-awareness: the more psychologically aware we are, the more able we shall be to help others mobilize their feelings and energies and to direct them toward change, growth and fulfilment
- Obstacles to acceptance are:
  - Lack of knowledge of human behaviour
  - Blockages within self
  - Attributing one's own feelings to the client
  - Biases and prejudices
  - Unfounded reassurances
  - Confusion between acceptance and approval
  - Loss of respect for the client
  - Over-identification with the client.

Acceptance is the feeling of being accepted as we really are, including our strengths and weaknesses, differences of opinion, no matter how unpleasant or uncongenial, without censure. We do not feel accepted unless the very worst in us is accepted too. We never feel accepted when judgement is passed on us.

If we want to guide someone, even one step of the way, we must feel with that person's psyche. We may not put our judgements of other people into words; we may keep them to ourselves; this makes not the slightest difference. Judgement in the heart will be revealed.

We cannot change anything unless we accept it. Condemnation (which lies at the heart of rejection) does not liberate, it oppresses. We can only truly accept when we have already seen and accepted ourselves as we are.

Acceptance enables the counsellor to distinguish between the client's 'self' and 'behaviour'. It means maintaining all the while a sense of the client's innate dignity and personal worth. Unconditional acceptance demonstrates to clients that no matter how badly they act – toward us or toward others – we can still accept them and teach them to unconditionally accept themselves.

Acceptance does not mean approval of deviant attitudes or behaviour. The object of acceptance is not the 'good' but the 'real'.

Acceptance is not an all-or-nothing phenomenon like perfect sight or total blindness. Rather, every counsellor has a certain degree of acceptance, which may vary from day to day or from client to client. No counsellor has or is expected to have **perfect acceptance**, for that would require godlike wisdom and an immunity from human frailties.

Acceptance is based upon the conviction that we have an innate dignity and worth and that acceptance cannot be lost by any weakness or failure on our part. It is possible that, in counselling, the client can lose this consciousness and feeling of personal dignity and value if the counsellor loses respect for the client.

Acceptance requires the quality of love. In real love, of whatever variety, the two persons know each other; they know their weaknesses and strengths, their successes and failures, and in spite of them, possibly even because of them, mutual respect continues and even increases. Love and acceptance cease with a loss of respect. Respect for other people necessarily implies a recognition of their innate dignity and value. This internal attitude is expected of a professional helping person and is the result of self-awareness and philosophy of life.

Nonjudgement

- People who are troubled need help, not judgement.
- An attitude of nonjudgement is based on the firmly held belief that assigning guilt or innocence, or the degree to which the client is responsible or not for causing the problem, has no place in the therapeutic relationship.
- Judgement without the appropriate authority is a violation of basic human rights.
- Clients who are nurtured within a relationship of nonjudgement learn not to pass judgement upon themselves.
- When in such a relationship, people find the courage and the strength to change.
- When we pass judgement upon others, if we examine ourselves, we will find the very thing on which we pass judgement also present within us.
- 'Nonjudgement' does not mean being valueless or without standards. It does mean not trying to mould others to fit into our value systems. Our values may be right for us, but totally wrong for other people. Counsellors, however, are not human chameleons. They must remain true to their own values and standards.
- Guilt or innocence, blame, condemnation and punishment are all part of judgement.
- People feel attacked when judgement is passed on them and less attacked when their observed behaviour is questioned.
- We communicate the unspoken judgement lurking within; when we feel nonjudgement, that feeling is communicated.
- We may not like all clients, but it is our duty to strive toward freedom from prejudices that will lead us into passing judgement.
- We can work toward nonjudgement by:
  - Recognizing and carefully scrutinizing our own values and standards, some of which we may need to jettison
  - Trying to see the world from the client's frame of reference
  - Not jumping to conclusions
  - Not saying, 'I know how you feel'
  - Not comparing the client to someone else
  - Not becoming over-involved
  - Not responding to the client's inappropriate feelings toward us, which may indicate transference.

Judgement is to do with law, blame, guilt or innocence and punishment. If relationships are to work, we must learn to suspend judgements and standards and not to impose them on others. Judgementalism takes no account of feelings. It is critical and condemns others because of their conduct or supposed false beliefs, wrong motives or character. Judgementalism is arbitrary, without room for negotiation or understanding. It is an evaluation and rejection of another person's worth.

The result of judgementalism is that it dims, divides and fragments relationships. Judgementalism seeks to elevate one person above another. Within it are the characteristics of self-exaltation, self-promotion and the determination to be first on every occasion. Judgement invariably attacks the person rather than the behaviour. It creates massive blind spots in our relationships. We cannot relate to people effectively while we are judging and condemning them.

Judgementalism can often be detected by such words as 'should,' 'ought', 'must' and 'don't' and by such phrases as 'In my opinion', 'I think...' and 'This is what you should do'. It is moralistic, based on norms and values, warnings, approval/disapproval, instruction. Judgementalism induces inferiority and evokes inhibition, guilt and distress. Judgementalism is often associated with authority, control, hierarchy, rules and regulations that impose standards of behaviour.

Judgementalism and acceptance are opposites – judgementalism paralyses: acceptance affirms and encourages action. People with a strong attitude of judgementalism are very often highly critical of themselves and find it almost impossible to forgive others or themselves.

Judgement does not fit with being judgemental. If judgement is the opposite of acceptance, then to judge is to reject and that negates the whole idea of counselling. Counsellors might not **like** what a person is or does, but acceptance goes far beyond liking; it goes beyond the surface and makes contact with the real person.

Further reading

Biestek, F. P. (1957) *The Casework Relationship*, George Allen & Unwin, London.
Billheimer, P. E. (1981) *Love Covers: a viable platform for Christian Unity*, Christian Literature Crusade, Arlesford, Hampshire.
Dryden, W. (1988) *Therapists' Dilemmas*, Harper & Row, London.
Friedman, M. (1972) *Touchstones of Reality*, E. P. Dutton, New York.
Rogers, C. R. (1961) *On Becoming a Person*, Houghton Mifflin, Boston, MA.
Rogers, C. R. (1980) *A Way of Being*, Houghton Mifflin, Boston, MA.

RESISTANCE (*see also*: Transference and counter-transference)

In psychoanalysis, resistance describes the client's unconscious efforts to thwart the aims and process of therapy, sometimes referred to as 'sticking points'. The client does this by blocking unconscious, repressed material from breaking through into the conscious. This may take the form of being unwilling to continue exploring a particular theme, with its thoughts and feelings. This might be due to anxiety about the disclosure or fear of how the counsellor will react. If the client deliberately blocks something, then this is more avoidance than resistance, which, in its original sense, is an unconscious mechanism.

Because of the client's resistance, access to the unconscious can be gained only by indirect means, the chief of which is free association. Resistance must be overcome if the client is to integrate unconscious material into the conscious and move forward toward the loss of symptoms. However, this 'overcoming' is not an aggressive breaking down of the defence; rather it is achieved as client and counsellor work through the need for resistance. Neither does resistance mean that the client does not comply with what the counsellor wants or desires.

Resistance is not a 'once-and-for-all' phenomenon; it is continually being experienced. By analysing the resistances, the client gains freedom from them. The analyst uses positive transference to overcome resistance.

The paradox is that many people who engage in counselling experience resistance to it. Most people would experience resistance if they felt, for example, censured and judged.

Anticipated change may also create resistance. Clients are more likely to undertake change with less resistance when in a supportive relationship than when they feel undesired change is being forced upon them.

Resistance occurs as the client's unconscious senses that something is waiting in the wings to be disclosed and this something is likely to increase the client's distress or anxiety. It may be concerned with guilt over some 'forgotten' experience or some feeling of shame or disgrace, or just some vague feeling of something not quite right.

Overcoming resistance cannot be hurried, it can be helped by:

- The client's need for recovery
- The client's intellectual interest
- Positive transference
- Making the expression of resistance as safe as possible
- Honouring the resistance by careful listening, without discounting what is revealed
- Acknowledging the resistance, not by agreeing with it but by recognizing the difficulty the client is experiencing
- Reinforcing that there must be valid reasons for resisting at this time.

Exploring the resistance

- Distinguish between valid and invalid resistance. Valid resistance is directed at the specific topic; invalid resistance is a smokescreen of feelings to divert the counsellor's attention. Invalid resistance is often linked to generalities and bringing up the past.
- Any probing of the resistance must be carried out with extreme caution. The probing is carried out with the express consent of the client.

- The aim is to reduce needless resistance that interferes with the client's healthy functioning.

Indicators of resistance include:

- A tendency to argue
- Avoidance of new learning
- Refusal to co-operate in suggested programmes
- Refusal to look at new possibilities
- Always wanting to generalize and not deal with specifics
- Intellectualizing and refusing to work with feelings
- Rudeness, antagonism, anger or any other strongly negative feeling
- Silences and passivity
- Verbal aggression
- Projecting feelings on to the counsellor
- Denial, without desire to explore
- Insistence that there is no improvement
- Talking about trivia
- Talking about external events and other people
- Premature ending of counselling
- Refusal to terminate counselling.

Resistance may be created by the counsellor, either from what is said or done or from what is not said or done. The counsellor whose empathy has lapsed and who is no longer relating to the client from the internal frame of reference is in danger of creating the conditions in which resistance will flourish.

Further reading

Karp, H. B. (1988) A positive approach to resistance. In: *1988 Annual: Developing Human Resources*, University Associates, San Diego, CA.

Jacobs, M. (1988) *Psychodynamic Counselling in Action*, Sage Publications, London.

Jacobs, M. (1993) Client resistance. In: *Questions and Answers on Counselling in Action*, (ed. W. Dryden), Sage Publications, London.

Rosenthall, L. (1980) Resistance in group psychotherapy. In: *Group and Family Therapy*, (eds L. Volberg and M. Arunsen), Brunner/Mazel, New York.

Wachtel, P. L. (ed.) (1982) *Resistance: Psychodynamic and Behavioural approaches*, Plenum Press, New York.

RETIREMENT

Retirement is more than a date on the calendar when we become entitled to the state pension.

An estimate of the likely total stress of retirement, using the life change units (*see* Stress management) is made up of:

- Retirement from work   45
- A significant change in financial state   38

- Significant change in living conditions 25
- A revision of personal habits 24
- Change in residence (perhaps) 20
- A significant change in the person's usual type and/or amount of recreation 19
- A significant change in social activities 18

This does not take into account many other items, not included in the chart, such as:

- Loss of friends and colleagues
- Disrupted routine
- More contact with spouse – this may produce friction, as neither is used to having the other around for so long
- Time hangs heavily
- Loss of status – joins the ranks of the 'retired'
- A new status, which has overtones of ageing
- Loss of purpose and meaning
- Reduced income.

All is not negative. The retired person does have more time to 'do all those things that, over the years, have been left'. Yet this can produce strain. Over the years at work, the body has become accustomed to a certain routine of sleep, work, rest, diet and recreation.

Many people go hell-for-leather at redecorating the house, carrying out major structural alterations to the garden, etc. These new activities use different groups of muscles and very often the result is strain and frustration.

There are definitely many positives: being able to please oneself as to where to go and when; being able to resume activities such as walking and swimming, which are thoroughly recommended.

Many people, with more time on their hands, turn to developing hobbies that have lain dormant and discover another 'career'. Sadly, however, many feel that when the work gate closes (symbolically, if not actually) life stops and all they can see is the scrap heap.

When retired people complain of feeling stressed, what they complain of is associated with the ageing process. They show a higher tendency to leave things until the last minute and may also exhibit anxiety, heart trouble, fear of health breakdown, loss of temper, irritability, sleeplessness and periods of depression.

Counselling might mean helping such a person find a new direction in life, for with retirement often come feelings similar to grief, grieving over what has been lost and can never more be. Recognizing that the client is grieving, although this might not be acknowledged, might be the first step toward something new.

S

SADNESS (*see also*: Depression, Psychic pain)

This article will consider sadness within depression, because there is no sadness as profound as that experienced by a person caught in the grip of depression. Grief and the sadness of depression are close relatives; indeed it could be said that depression has many elements of unresolved grief. One of the differences is that in grief the sadness has a focus – the loss of someone treasured. In the sadness of depression there is no such identifiable focus. A parallel can be drawn between specific anxiety and free-floating anxiety, where no known cause can be identified.

Sadness is unhappiness brought down a degree. Most people know the feeling of unhappiness. Many know the feelings of sadness. Not everyone understands the deep, lasting, incapacitating sadness of a person depressed to the point of feeling like a dried out husk and where tears – therapeutic in normal sorrow – dry up in the eyes before they can be shed.

Depending upon the particular theoretical approach, the sadness of depression is considered to have its genesis in:

- The loss of some valued person, possession or status
- The way we attribute meaning to our ideas, feelings, ideals and circumstances – the sense of lack or loss of positive emotions, such as love, self-respect and feelings of satisfaction
- A sense of deprivation, pessimism and self-criticism.

While sadness is a normal and healthy response to any misfortune and is common, sorrow that does not lessen with the passage of time is pathological. People who experience normal sadness are usually able to talk about it, to know why they are sad and still feel hope that the sadness will lift. Depression sets in when normal exchanges are absent or greatly diminished. The words that would express how a depressed person feels are blocked in the well by the dried up tears. Sadness is also referred to as 'psychic pain' – pain that is not physical but mental (*see* entry, above).

If sadness is psychic pain, is the psyche able to tolerate only so much pain? Is it possible that excess psychic pain is transformed into other feelings – anxiety, anger, rage and psychosomatic manifestations? Sadness, particularly when it follows a definite event such as a death, is reparative, but renewal may take a long time. Are people who pass from normal sadness to depression those in whom the reparative work of sorrowing has not taken place? Is it that they have not been able to do 'sorrowing work'? Such people are psychologically ill-equipped (because life experience has not prepared them) to solve their sorrow or their sadness.

People consistently use figurative language to describe the feelings of depression such as: the heart is heavy, dark, constricted, sunk; they may feel they have a stone in their heart; a dark cloud hangs over their head; if they pray, they may feel that the heavens are as brass.

Loss of joy and lack of pleasure feature as much as actual feelings of sadness and there is an increasing inability for depressed people to enjoy themselves. This affects relationships with their families; hobbies become boring; art and music, which they previously enjoyed, lose their appeal; the world of nature and sound is dull and insipid. The fact that life is dull and cheerless causes them concern. They know the joy has gone but they cannot find out where or how to recapture it. The fact that they find no pleasure in things or people has the effect of cutting them off emotionally from activities and people who would normally stimulate them.

That such a feeling of joylessness causes problems should come as no surprise. When any mood separates husband from wife, parent from children, work colleague from mates, neighbour from neighbour, and when all these relationships are affected **all at once**, the emotional world shrinks so much that even they themselves are reduced to nothing.

One of the characteristics of depression is that it is contagious. We may well find ourselves 'picking up' the sadness and reacting to it by ourselves becoming sad and losing some of our own joy. The effect that depressed people have on others is an important factor in their increasing isolation. On the one hand, depressed people desperately need human contact, yet there is very little that they can offer to establish or maintain affectional relationships. Indeed, depressed people's ability to love and be loved is impaired. A measure of this – which reinforces the feeling of isolation – is a decrease of libido. The decrease may range from 'little desire' to total inability and impotence. For couples who have hitherto enjoyed satisfactory and fulfilling sex, loss of desire or inability may put their relationship under great strain.

Another part of an 'affectional relationship' is communication. Yet the profound feeling of isolation usually makes communication burdensome. One of the difficulties expressed by depressed people is that the conversations of others jar; their normal laughter seems totally out of place; their attempts to 'keep things going' become sources of irritation. The wave bands of communication have become distorted by depressed feelings. Communication – of any meaning – virtually ceases.

Counselling: an intervention in sadness and depression

The role of confidant – spouse or someone else – is significant in depression and in working through sadness. If it is important to share intimacies within a caring relationship, then the lack of such a relationship could be conducive to developing depression. Everything must be done to foster an atmosphere in which intimate feelings may be shared. But one of the enemies of intimacy is impersonality.

There is no doubt that having opportunity to talk with someone, to express one's feelings, is a safeguard, not only against loneliness and isolation, but against weaving, out of one's defensive mechanisms, a blanket to suffocate all feelings. Counselling offers the sort of support that avoids smothering feelings.

Some people, because of the severity of their depression, require 'in-depth' psychotherapy but many people remain depressed simply because they have no one to support them and afford them an opportunity to explore their feelings. Support enhances a person's ability to cope with depression, particularly when one remembers that self-doubt, hopelessness and isolation are cardinal features of depression.

Theories and therapies dealing with depression are legion but when all else fails, when theories fall flat and when techniques fail to satisfy, all we have left are our relationship skills. It is surely upon these, and through these, that theories become fact and techniques become reality. Rapport, immediate and intense, must be established immediately.

Depressed people often feel themselves to be 'losers'. It is important that we help them to feel 'winners'. A small task accomplished is infinitely more beneficial than an unrealistic task that is doomed to failure. The change in self esteem that comes with even small successes is essential if the person is to step out of his/her depression. Maintaining self-esteem is vital if the ill or disabled person is to stop her/himself from sliding into depression.

This may sound easy. But, as with all counselling, working with those who are depressed is not always easy or successful. Some people construct their lives and relationships on a purely negative foundation and are very resistant to change. It seems that they need to be 'poorly'. In a curious way it makes them feel 'good'. This is the construct of the 'martyr' (*see* The martyr attitude). Such people resist giving up their suffering. What they gain from being 'ill' is more than they would gain from being well. Thus, counselling – of even the most intense sort – may not always work. Moving away from illness would mean that we could no longer regard ourselves as helpless victims of circumstances imposed upon us by others.

One theme that repeats itself throughout this article is the isolation felt by depressed people, cut off as they are from emotional contact. In a sense, depressed people pre-empt and pre-experience their own death – the final isolation. The relationship between client and counsellor is crucial in maintaining contact and thereby reducing the risk of isolation. Human contact has a calming effect on the cardiovascular system of a person under stress. Thus it is quite feasible that our very presence achieves as much, or more, than our words of counsel, however profound. What we do when we counsel is to offer ourselves in a relationship that makes no demands for itself. When we reach out to make emotional contact with depressed people, we break through the invisible barrier that keeps them isolated. This emotional contact builds a bridge across which they may walk towards health.

SCAPEGOATING

Although the idea of the scapegoat is commonly associated with early Jewish history, the use of scapegoats has a long and varied history involving many kinds of animals, as well as human beings.

In ancient Greek religion, the ritual of the scapegoat was associated with the festivals of Apollo at Athens, celebrated on the sixth and seventh days of Thargelion (May–June). This festival was a vegetation ritual named after the first fruits or the first bread from the new wheat. On the first day of the festival, one or two men (or a man and a woman), representing the deity but also acting as scapegoats for community guilt, were chosen. After being feted, the couple was led around the town, beaten with green twigs, driven out of the city and possibly even stoned. In this way the city was supposedly protected from ill fortune for another year. Occasionally, as in times of heavy calamity, they were sacrificed, being either thrown into the sea or burned on a funeral pyre. On the second day of the festival, there was a thank-offering, a procession and the official registration of adopted persons.

During the Roman feast of Lupercalia, priests (*luperci*) cut thongs from the sacrificial animals (goats and a dog), then raced around the walls of the old Palatine city, striking women (especially) as they passed with the thongs. A blow from the hide of the scapegoat was said to cure sterility. In early Roman law an innocent person was allowed to take upon himself the penalty of another who had confessed his own guilt.

In the Old Testament it is stated that, on the Day of Atonement, Aaron would sacrifice two goats, a ram and one bullock. One goat and the bullock would be sacrificed immediately as a sin offerings. The second goat was allotted to the demon Azazel, symbolically burdened with the sins of the Jewish people and driven off into the wilderness and abandoned (Leviticus 16:7–10 and 20–22.).

The same ritual was carried out in the purification of lepers but using two birds (the variety is not named but in Leviticus 14:22 two pigeons are mentioned as sin offerings, so the 'birds' might have been pigeons). One of the birds was killed and the leprous person was sprinkled with its blood. The second bird was sprinkled with the blood and was allowed to fly free, carrying with it, symbolically, the remnants of the disease.

In *The Golden Bough*, Sir James Frazer, drawing attention to variations on a theme, quotes cases of certain African Moors who, when experiencing a headache, would beat a lamb or a goat until it falls down, believing that the headache will be transferred to the animal. Similarly, in Morocco, wealthy Moors were known to keep a wild boar in their stables in order than the jinn and evil spirits would be diverted from the horses and enter the boar.

In certain South African tribes, when all known remedies have failed to cure a sickness, a goat will be brought in and the sick person will confess his/her sins over it. Then the animal is turned out to fend for itself. When plague hits Arabia, the people have been known to lead a camel through all the quarters of the town in order that the animal may take the pestilence on itself; then the animal is strangled in a sacred place. Similarly, in Taiwan, to get rid of smallpox, the people used to drive the demon of disease into a sow, then cut off the animal's ears and burn them or it.

In all these rituals, the belief is that the 'curse' will be averted, the illness cured or sins will be forgiven.

By extension, a scapegoat has come to mean any individual or group that innocently bears the blame of others. Christianity reflects this notion in its doctrine of justification and in its belief that Jesus Christ was the God-man who died to atone for the sins of all mankind. Christ's death and atonement reflects the notion of the innocent suffering for the guilty.

The concept of scapegoating applied to counselling

In groups, scapegoating describes the way in which one person can be isolated and excluded in order to relieve group tension and stress. The scapegoated person usually possesses one or more characteristics that influence the process, such as:

- Mental or physical disability or illness
- Racial, sexual, colour or language difference
- Vulnerability – difference in rank or status or, in families, low rank order.

Scapegoating can be seen within societies, where minority groups are blamed for everything that goes wrong in the community, which relieves the others from having to take any responsibility. Scapegoating uses the defence mechanisms of displacement (where emotions, ideas or wishes are transferred from their original object to a more acceptable substitute), projection (where what is emotionally unacceptable in the self is unconsciously rejected and attributed – projected – to others) and projective identification (attributing unacceptable parts of self – feelings, thoughts and impulses – on to another).

Scapegoating is also seen in family therapy, where one member is designated as 'the sick one', the one in need of being 'cured'. Then the family would be 'normal'. It is also seen in therapy groups or, indeed, in any growth group, where one member will be ganged up against and blamed from the nonprogress of the group task. If the group leader does not draw attention to what is happening, the 'scapegoat' can be demoralized and psychologically destroyed. In individual counselling, clients may engage in this as they lay blame at the door of someone else. Scapegoating is thus an effective way of avoiding dealing with something relevant in counselling; if it goes unrecognized, counselling will cease to be effective.

Further reading

Frazer, J. (1993) *The Golden Bough*, Wordsworth Reference, London.
Gaskell, G. A. (1981) *Dictionary of All Scriptures and Myths*, Random House, New York.

SELF

Self refers to the organized, consistent perceptions of the 'I' and the relationship of 'I' to others. In modern psychology, the notion of the self has replaced earlier conceptions of the soul. The concept of the self has been a central feature of many personality theories, including those of Sigmund Freud, Alfred Adler, Carl

Jung, Gordon W. Allport, Karen Horney, Carl Rogers, Rollo May and Abraham H. Maslow.

The self is a relatively stable set of perceptions of who we are in relation to ourselves, to others and to social systems. Personality and ego are commonly used synonyms, although they do not have exactly the same meaning. The personality is more outwardly observable (by others, that is) and the ego, as a psychoanalytical term at least, contains unconscious elements that the self does not recognize.

The development of self is shaped through interaction with other people and draws upon social materials in the form of cultural imagery and ideas. We are not passive participants in this process of socialization; we exert a powerful influence over how this process and its consequences develop.

Self-concept

The self is organized around a self-concept, the ideas and feelings that we have about ourselves. Charles H. Cooley referred to the **looking-glass self**, based on how we think other people see and evaluate us (which, of course, is not necessarily how they actually see us).

The self is also based on cultural ideas about the social statuses and roles that we occupy. In this way, for example, a man who is a father will draw upon cultural ideas about fathering in constructing his idea of who he is. This component of a self-concept, which is based on the social positions that a person occupies, is known as a **social identity**. Self experiences are the basic material from which the self-concept is formed.

Confusion and tension result in a state of vulnerability when there is incongruity between the self-concept and actual experience. Lack of awareness of incongruity between self and experience makes us vulnerable to anxiety and disorganization. Many people resist feedback that would alter their views of themselves, even rejecting feedback of a flattering nature that tells them they are better than they thought. On the other hand, some people seek positive flattering feedback in order to make a good impression on others.

Ideal self

We all possess an **actual** self and an **ideal** self. The ideal self is what we know we could be, should be or would like to be. Low self-esteem operates in the gap between the actual self and the ideal self. The ideal self is influenced by three major factors:

- Parental expectations instructions received on how to behave
- The values of parents
- The values of heroic figures from real life, biography and fiction.

A related concept is that of **undesired self**, that which we would not like to become, similar to Jung's concept of the Shadow. This motivates us to do all we can to avoid becoming that person.

Self-esteem

Self-esteem is the positive and negative evaluation we make of and apply to ourselves. Self-esteem indicates the extent to which we believe ourselves to be significant, capable and worthy. Self-esteem is generally applied to feelings of worthiness. We may have a good, average or bad opinion of ourselves; the views we hold about ourselves are not always held by other people.

Self-esteem is also affected by evaluations that are part of the looking-glass self. Generally we see our value mirrored in the eyes of society, a process that starts in childhood. To some extent, our self-esteem is derived from a comparison between ourselves and other people. On the other hand, we may think well of ourselves if we occupy positions of high status, because other people look up to us. Comparison with the peer group, for example, is important and is based on popularity, power over others, task competence and honour or virtue.

A surprising point about self-esteem is the enormous variation that exists between individuals. Some people think the whole world is theirs for the taking; others almost feel they have no right to exist. Some people attempt to bolster their self-esteem at the expense of that of others but this, in the long-term, is not fruitful.

There is a general need to regard one's self favourably and one way we do this is to exaggerate our good points. Another way is to alter our behaviour so that we conform to the expectations and standards of our ideal self. Self-esteem includes self-significance, self-competence and self-like.

Freud believed that the male child who has been the mother's favourite will forever keep the feeling that he is a conqueror. Yet other children, even within the same family, grow up with the feeling that their very existence is a terrible mistake. There is no 'self-esteem blueprint' for parents to work on.

At the highest level, self-esteem depends on making sense of our relationship to the rest of the universe. Low self-esteem operates in the gap between the actual self and the ideal self. Low self-esteem is often associated with:

- Abuse
- Anxiety states
- Delinquency
- Depressive illness
- Disability, disfigurement
- Prejudice
- Psychosomatic disorders.

Self-esteem rating scales correlate strongly with scales measuring anxiety, depression and neuroticism and in many cases there is overlap of items. Low self-esteem is an enormous public health problem. People who report low self-esteem usually say that it has been present since early childhood or at least since adolescence.

Self-significance refers to feelings of being significant, important, worthwhile and meaningful as opposed to feeling unimportant, meaningless and of no value.

Self-competence refers to feelings of competence, intelligence, ability and strength as opposed to weakness, incompetence and the inability to cope.

Self-like refers to feeling good in the presence of the self, i.e. when alone, as opposed to not enjoying one's own company.

Self-attentiveness (also called self-consciousness). People differ in the degree to which they habitually attend to themselves as well as in the focus of their self-preoccupations. For example, some people are prone to introspect, to examine frequently their feelings and motives. Some are habitually concerned with how they appear to others.

Public and private self

The self has both a private and public face. The private self consists of our personal thoughts, feelings values and beliefs. The public self is what we present to others – the behaviour, mannerisms and ways of expressing ourselves that create people's impressions of us. Both aspects of the self influence behaviour: our actions are guided by our personal feelings and beliefs as well as by the social context in which we find ourselves, i.e. by considering how others will react to what we do (*see also*: Public and private self)

Private and public self-consciousness

Persons who score high in private self-consciousness (i.e. the disposition to introspect) tend to be more responsive to transient affective states than do persons who score low in that category. They show more behavioural signs of anger when provoked and are more affected by viewing pleasant and unpleasant slides. They are also less suggestible, more resistant to political propaganda and more accurate in describing, their own behaviour. It seems they know themselves better than do those low in private self-consciousness. They are also more likely to disclose private aspects of selves to their spouses or intimate partners.

People who score high on the scale of public self-consciousness seem more sensitive to group rejection than those who score low on this dimension. Individuals high in public self-consciousness also are better at predicting the kind of impression they make on others and place more importance on their 'social' identity in describing themselves – e.g. their physical characteristics, gestures and mannerism and group memberships. If they are female, they are apt to wear more make-up than are those who score low on public self-consciousness.

The dimensions of private and public self-consciousness have implications for the question of personality consistency. Individuals who score high on private and low on public self-consciousness have greater consistency in behaviour over different situations than do people who score low on private and high on public self-consciousness. People high in private self-consciousness tend to behave in accordance with their own attitudes and beliefs rather than tailoring their actions to fit the social demands of changing situations.

It needs to be stressed that however 'accurate' personality tests are, they are not absolute. They are not precise instruments, but, rather, indicators of what might be. For example, a person who tops the 'private person' scale might be totally different in a group or in a one to one relationship, where s/he is accepted and feels at ease or when in position of being in control.

The self in counselling

Self-esteem is part of the ego and, when the ego suffers, self-esteem suffers with it. Difficulties with self-esteem are present in many clients. Self-esteem is at the very core of our personality and low self-esteem is characteristic of depressive personality. Loss of self-esteem often accompanies depression and may result from the symbolic (and symbolic does not mean worthless) losses of, for example, power, status, roles and values, all of which influence, to one degree or another, the way we live our life. When we feel good about ourselves, it is almost certain that most of our activities will be successful. We derive great joy from them. People who feel good about themselves:

- Take risks with confidence, they do not have to be either foolhardy or over-cautious
- Can keep on being what they are, confident and likeable, the thought of not being liked or supported does not shatter them
- Can take orders without resentment and give orders without guilt or without fearing punishment
- Can take criticism and make constructive use of it
- Can take a compliment graciously without suspecting the sincerity of the giver
- Can give compliments without being afraid that they will gain an advantage; they do not think that others need to feel the same way about them
- Can speak directly and honestly to people with whom they have a problem instead of talking behind their back.

The basic components of self-awareness are:
- **The reality and integrity of self**: I am one person
- **The continuity of self**: I am the same person now that I was yesterday and that I will be tomorrow
- **The boundaries of self**: I can distinguish between myself and the rest of the world as being nonself
- **The activities of self**: I know that I am thinking, feeling and doing
- **Body-image**: my mental representation of my body
- **Ego ideal**: the positive standards, ideals and ambitions that according to psychoanalytic theory form a person's conscious goals.

Disturbances of these basic components are seen in certain mental illnesses and indicate the urgent need for psychiatric help.

Further reading

Becker, J. (1979) Vulnerable self-esteem as a predisposing factor in depressive disorders. In: *The Antecedents of Self-esteem*, (ed. S. Coopersmith), W. H Freeman. San Francisco, CA.

Lowry, R. J. (ed.) (1973) *Dominance, Self-esteem, Self-Actualisation: Germinal papers of A. H. Maslow*, Brooks/Cole, Monterey, CA.

Stewart, W. (1998) *Building Self-esteem: How to replace self-doubt with confidence and well-being.* How To Books, Oxford.

SELF-DISCLOSURE

Self-disclosure is the process by which we let ourselves be known to others. In the process, we enhance our self-awareness.

Disclosures may be:

- Intentional (mainly conscious)
- Unintentional (mainly unconscious)
- Verbal (mainly conscious)
- Nonverbal (mainly unconscious)
- Thoughts, feelings and behaviours.

Clear verbal and nonverbal disclosures increase the chance of accurate reception without the need for complicated decoding.

Appropriate disclosure is critical in relationships, for it enhances them, keeps them alive and helps to avoid alienation. One person's low disclosure is likely to block another person's willingness to disclose.

People who are genuine, in touch with their own inner empathy, are also in touch with what they are experiencing and send authentic messages to others.

Disclosure involves both negative and positive aspects of self. Not everyone finds it easy to disclose positive aspects of themselves, possibly because of low self-esteem.

Disclosing means that we have to anticipate:

- Our own feelings
- The other person's reactions
- The possible effect on the relationship.

We may interfere with people's genuine self-disclosure by:

- Being secretive; this leads to a high degree of information control
- Colluding with them, in which case fantasy and reality become confused
- Faking disclosures, which prevents the other person from making genuine disclosures.

Questions of appropriateness of disclosure:

- How much can I disclose?
- What area can I disclose?
- How many areas should I disclose?

- How intimate should the disclosures be?
- To whom could I disclose?
- In what context could I disclose?
- Why am I disclosing?

Encouraging self-disclosure

- **Assertion**: Learning to express, where appropriate, positive and negative feelings
- **Challenging**: To give feedback nonaggressively
- **Development of relationships**: Breadth and depth of disclosures tend to increase naturally as relationships develop
- **Expressiveness**: To be able to express feelings appropriately (or not express them, but recognize and acknowledge them), not just talk about them
- **Feedback options**:
  - To agree
  - To restate the initial disclosure
  - To reflect the other person's message
  - To send an 'I' message
  - To remain silent
- **Immediacy**: To be able to respond immediately and say what otherwise would remain unsaid
- **Positive/negative disclosure**: Genuine intimacy is characterized by a willingness to let ourselves be known genuinely
- **Questions**: Questions often avoid having to disclose; they should be used with discrimination
- **Reciprocity**: Relationships can be prevented from becoming shallow by matching levels of disclosure
- **'I' messages**: Recognizing, owning and expressing one's own feelings, not someone else's
- **Specificity**: Generalizations are too vague for people to relate to
- **Verbal and nonverbal disclosures**: People can be taught to disclose by such means as:
  - Modelling/teaching
  - Rehearsal/practising
  - Homework
  - Audio-visual aids.

Self-disclosure (client)

This is where the client makes a conscious decision to disclose feelings, thoughts, attitudes, behaviours – past or present – to the therapist. Client disclosure is an essential element of most types of psychotherapy.

Where this is not happening, counselling is seriously impeded. The degree of disclosure is related to the degree of trust within the relationship. Counsellor trustworthiness, a nonjudgemental attitude and acceptance all facilitate disclosure.

Exploring how disclosure could facilitate or hinder counselling may help those clients who have difficulty disclosing. Clients may be helped toward disclosure by considering the potential gains and risks.

Possible gains:

- Lessened loneliness and alienation
- Greater intimacy
- More friendships
- Self-responsibility
- More assertive
- Makes it easier for others to disclose
- Discovering others
- Self-acceptance
- More control of own life.

Possible risks:

- Rejection
- Not liking self
- Feelings of shame
- Being misunderstood
- Wary of confidentiality
- Feeling tense/vulnerable
- Too much intimacy, too soon
- Too many close relationships
- Too much self-knowledge
- Equilibrium of relationship disturbed
- Breaking taboos about disclosures.

Reluctance to disclose may also be related to ethnic or religious influences. It may also be an indication of resistance.

Self-disclosure (counsellor)

Where counsellors are open and use disclosure appropriately, clients are more likely to be equally disclosing. Counsellor disclosure involves appropriate sharing of:

- Attitudes
- Experiences
- Feelings
- Reactions to the client
- Views.

Appropriate self-disclosure is critical in relationships; it helps to keep us real.

One of the dangers of self-disclosure is that it can remove the focus from the client, particularly if the disclosure goes into too much detail. This can be an effective way of the client engaging the counsellor as a defence against exploration and of the counsellor avoiding challenging the client. Being clear about the motive for disclosing is essential.

Counsellor disclosure may be more appropriate in well established relationships. Disclosures should reflect the needs of the client, not of the counsellor.

It is also useful to distinguish between supplying information requested by the client and choosing to disclose something that is designed for the client's benefit. Asking for information may indicate that the client wants to reduce the client-counsellor distance, effecting a change in the relationship.

Self-disclosure is embraced in humanistic therapies but seldom in psychoanalytic therapies, where to self-disclose would get in the way of working through the transference.

Inappropriate or mistimed disclosures may increase rather than decrease the client's anxiety. The focus may be removed from the client if the disclosure is lengthy or inappropriate.

The counsellor must always remember who is the client; any discussion of personal problems is inappropriate and will lead to confusion of roles, because the boundaries have been blurred.

While the counsellor might feel that disclosing something could deepen empathy, and there is no doubt that it could, unless the disclosure is brief and to the point and the focus is returned to the client, any empathy could be destroyed.

Disclosure is appropriate if:

- It keeps the client on target and does not distract
- It does not add to the client's burden
- It does not occur too often.

The greatest block to self-disclosure is fear of not being accepted; of thinking oneself to be different, odd, unworthy, fit only to be judged. Cautious, ritualized communication inhibits self-disclosure.

To build self-disclosure skills:

- Be direct
- Be sensitive
- Be relevant
- Be nonpossessive
- Be brief
- Be selective.

Example
Peter was talking to his counsellor, Roy, about his father's recent death. He was having difficulty expressing himself until Roy said, 'My father died 4 years after

mother. When he died I felt I'd been orphaned. Maybe that is something like how you feel.'

Peter sat for several minutes in deep silence before saying, 'You've put into words exactly how I feel. May I talk about my childhood and how Dad and I got on?'

Further reading

Johnson, D. W. and Noonan, M. P. (1972) The effects of acceptance and reciprocation of self-disclosures on the development of trust. *Journal of Counselling Psychology*, **19**, 411–416.

Jourard, S. M. and Friedman, R. (1970) Experimenter–subject 'distance' and self-disclosure. *Journal of Personality and Social Psychology*, **15**, 278–282.

Jourard, S. M. and Friedman, R. (1971) *The Transparent Self*, Van Nostrand Reinhold, Toronto.

Segal, J. (1993) Against self-disclosure. In: *Questions and Answers on Counselling in Action*, (ed. W. Dryden), Sage Publications, London.

SELF-FULFILLING PROPHECY

The self-fulfilling prophecy is a concept developed by the sociologist R. K. Merton in 1948. Merton mainly focused on self-fulfilling prophecies related to such social problems as discrimination against Jews and other minorities. Merton's work was furthered by Rosenthal and Jacobson in their influential Pygmalion study (1968), related to self-fulfilling prophecies in the classroom (*see* Pygmalion effect, below, and Stereotypes).

Self-fulfilling prophecies occur when a false social belief leads to its own fulfilment because people act as if it is true already. The father who continually predicts that his son will fail increases the likelihood of failure. Another example would be where parents who fear a child will turn against them bring it about by constantly predicting to the child what will happen, and *vice versa*. When teachers treat certain students as if they will do better than others, the favoured ones will tend to perform better and achieve more than they otherwise would. It is worth thinking about, as young people are often the most vulnerable in the area of self-concept and, as a corollary, the most likely to be involved in negative self-fulfilling prophecies. Such major events as changing school class, changing schools or entering a new job all make us more vulnerable.

When minorities are denied educational opportunities based on the belief that they lack ability and motivation, the denial itself may produce just that result. In some cases, a self-fulfilling prophecy takes the form of a genuine prediction, as when rumours about stock markets set off waves of selling that produce the very collapse that has been predicted.

The Pygmalion effect

In his play *Pygmalion*, written in 1912, George Bernard Shaw describes the transformation of a Cockney flower girl, Eliza Doolittle, into a fine lady at the hands of a cynical misanthrope. (The play is the basis of the film of the same name and the musical *My Fair Lady*.) In Greek mythology, Pygmalion was the king of Cyprus who sculpted an ivory statue of a woman and then fell in love with it. In answer to his prayers Aphrodite gave life to the statue, whom Pygmalion called Galatea. She bore him a son, Paphos. Ovid tells this story in *Metamorphoses*.

The 'effect' is observed in people who come to behave in ways that correspond to other people's expectations of them. The term also describes a pathological condition in which the creator falls in love with his own creation, rather like the toymaker in *Tales of Hoffman* who fell in love with the doll he made and was thrown into despair when she did not return his love.

The term self-fulfilling prophecy is also used in a psychological sense, usually in a negative way, in cases where clients put themselves down. Whatever we believe tends to occur. Whatever we dwell on thrives. If we dwell on problems, we find more problems. If we dwell on happiness, we find more happiness. These beliefs become self-reinforcing in that, the more often one of them comes true, the more absolute it becomes in the subconscious and the less we question it. These beliefs become self-limiting as they become more absolute because they cause us to select experiences that will provide support for existing beliefs.

An unclear self-perception leads people to become more vulnerable to social influences and to self-fulfilling prophecies. For example, the client who believes he is destined to be large or that he does not have time to exercise creates an inner dialogue that says, 'Don't do anything about your weight', and is engaging in a self-fulfilling prophecy. It would be far more responsible were he to tell himself that he will not lose weight or make time to exercise. We also allow 'shoulds' and 'oughts' to govern our lives and thus set ourselves up for frustration and disappointment. Shoulds and oughts lead to unrealistic expectations of ourselves or others and to dysfunctional behaviours.

Where do these beliefs come from?

Imagine the subconscious mind as a kind of computer that takes every input quite literally. Whatever the 'software' tells it to do, it does and behaviour is affected. In order to change our behaviour, we need to rewrite the software. The foundations of our beliefs are established by the repeated messages we heard in childhood from parents, teachers, doctors, and so forth. We maintain these premises with our own inner dialogues and by associating with people who received similar programming in their childhood. Change the software by choosing new, more desirable behaviours, suggesting them to ourselves often enough to overwrite the old programme. It is important to note that we do not need to believe that this is so for it to work. Merely acting as if it is so for a month or two and paying close attention to subtle changes in what we are getting out of life can make the difference.

Having a clear sense of our purpose in life is another key element to attaining the results we most want to attain. People who are aware of their personal purpose are better able to select goals and to focus efforts in areas that serve that purpose and to change negative self-fulfilling prophecies into positive ones.

Further reading

Gascoigne, B. (1994) *Encyclopedia of Britain*, Macmillan, London

SEX THERAPY

Psychological problems constitute by far the largest category of sexual diffi-culties. They may be the product of socially induced inhibitions, faulty attitudes and ignorance, but sexual myths held by society are powerful influences. An example of the latter is the idea that good, mature sex must involve rapid erection, protracted coitus and simultaneous orgasm. Magazines, novels and sexual folklore reinforce these demanding ideals, which cannot always be met and hence give rise to anxiety, guilt and feelings of inadequacy.

Sexual dysfunction is a disturbance of the sexual response cycle – desire, excitement, orgasm and resolution – or pain associated with sexual intercourse.

Sex therapy involves the treatment of sexual disorders, variances and dysfunc-tions. In particular, sex-therapy programmes are directed toward the solution of such sexual problems as impotence, premature ejaculation, retarded ejaculation, painful coitus, sexual unresponsiveness and orgasmic dysfunction.

A common assumption underlying many modern sex-therapy programmes is that sexual problems are often learned and hence can be alleviated or corrected through relatively brief intervention measures. Intensive psychotherapy and medical treatment may be given when emotional disturbances and/or physical disorders compound sexual difficulties.

Sex-therapy programmes generally attempt to help people by providing appro-priate sex information, alleviating anxieties and fears about sexual performance and facilitating verbal, emotional and sexual communication between sex partners. Sex instruction, followed by private home assignments in which a couple practises newly learned, healthier ways of interacting, is an integral part of many sex-therapy programmes.

Both partners in the couple are often included in sex-therapy programmes. Sometimes, however, it is reasonable for a single person or only one member of a couple to be counselled alone, depending upon the nature of the sexual problem. Group-therapy techniques, including groups of individuals and/or groups of couples, are often used in sex-therapy programmes.

Some sex therapists believe that sex problems can be treated best if one therapist counsels both partners. Other therapists believe that a therapy team composed of a male and a female therapist is the best way to help couples overcome their difficulties. Still other therapists believe that couples with sexual difficulties can engage in self-treatment if given instructions through books, films and tapes, along with brief intensive counselling.

Physicians, psychiatrists, psychologists, social workers and marriage and family counsellors can usually either provide effective sex therapy or make referrals to other sources that can provide such therapy.

The couple approach recognizes that sexual dysfunction results from the interaction between two people and is not the exclusive problem of one member of the pair. Individual counselling is employed for those without co-operating partners and may involve the use of a surrogate partner or may focus on exercises that can be practised by an individual to improve his/her sexual interactions. Group therapy, in which individuals discuss feelings about sex, is also employed for both single-sex and male–female groups.

S<small>EXUAL HARASSMENT</small>

Sexual harassment is a subject which, like child abuse, has hit the headlines as if it was something new, yet it has been around for centuries. Sexual harassment is abuse, perpetrated often, although not exclusively, by men. The discussion centres on harassment by men, because this is what is most reported. Perhaps the next decade will reveal the prevalence of sexual harassment of men by women. What has come to light in recent years is that boys are abused by women more than was imagined. So if men are being harassed, they can take heart from women and disclose it. Then perhaps that might alter the balance of power somewhat.

It could be conjectured that, just as men who have themselves been abused as children are said to turn into abusers of children, so boys who have been abused by women may turn into adults who harass women sexually.

Whatever the dynamics of sexual harassment, we still have to struggle with the stereotypes of the macho man and the compliant, weaker woman who has no rights except to satisfy the sexual desires of men. These are powerful stereotypes to break. It can be done, but it will only come about as we all relate to one another as people, with respect and regard, and not through the sexual male and female stereotypes.

Sexual harassment in the workplace has received increased attention lately in the general press and in professional journals. Sexual discrimination is sexual harassment. Discrimination is any action that does not extend to people of one gender the same job conditions, courtesy, benefits, salary, training and development and advancement opportunities that are extended to the other.

Who is vulnerable?
Sexual harassment is often based on men not being willing to share power or control with women. It is more to do with 'keeping women in their place' than with 'sex'. Women are most vulnerable to being sexually harassed:

- When they are the first of their sex to break into an area of employment
- When they make up less than 25% of the work force
- When they enter hitherto male-dominated positions, e.g. female police officers, fire fighters, factory workers, maintenance and repair workers.

Many of the harassing behaviours are intended to actually cause the woman to be fired or to resign from the job.

Men who are pioneers in occupations typically held by women are also more vulnerable to harassment:

- Male nurses may still experience discrimination and harassment
- Telephone operators
- Bus conductors, in days when buses had them
- Those who want to work as baby-minders or *au-pairs*.

Sexual harassment may be motivated by feelings of power, anger or cruelty, while other harassment is motivated by sexual desires.

Harassment can include:

- Insulting, degrading, hurtful or rude comments
- Offensive talk, language, pictures or physical actions
- Bad reviews and appraisals
- Attempts to force the person out of the job.

More recently, stalking, which is harassment by another name, has become a criminal offence.

Costs of harassment at work:

- Effects on the victim:
  - Psychological damage
  - Loss of productivity
  - Loss of wages and benefits
  - Loss of employment and future benefits
  - Claims to a court or tribunal may result in further victimization
- The effects on others in the work force:
  - Psychological damage (such as anger, resentment, fear)
  - Loss of productivity
  - Loss of esteem for the persecutor and/or supervisors involved
  - Divisions, as people 'take sides'
  - Demoralization of the work force.
- Investigating or dealing with a complaint:
  - Inquiries or in-depth investigations create tension
  - If in-house personnel carry out the investigation, they may be accused of bias and 'cover-up'; if outside people are brought in, they may meet a stone wall of silence and passive aggression
- Other costs:
  - Loss of morale and absenteeism
  - Administrative
  - Counselling
  - Impact on other workers, supervisors
  - Personnel relationships

- Rescheduling of tasks
- Redeployment
- Training of new employees.

Sexual harassment may amount to indecent assault (a hostile act accompanied by circumstances of indecency). In this instance, 'hostile' means that the person receiving the act is an unwilling victim and the act is a criminal offence. In the USA, sexual harassment (which applies to men and women) means:

- Unwelcome sexual advances
- Requests for sexual favours
- Other verbal or physical conduct of a sexual nature.

And sexual harassment exists when:

- Submission to such conduct is made – either explicitly or implicitly – a term or condition of an individual's employment
- Submission to or rejection of such conduct is used as the basis for employment decisions affecting the individual
- Such conduct has the purpose or effect of unreasonably interfering with an individual's work performance or creating an intimidating, hostile or offensive working environment.

A third party also may file a complaint if behaviour offends her/him, even if the victim has not complained. For example, if two men are telling sexual jokes in the work setting in the presence of female employee and a third person who overhears them is offended, that person may complain.

What we can do about harassment

- Help people distinguish between what is acceptable and what is offensive behaviour
- Help people to deal with offensive behaviour, **when it happens,** in an assertive manner that gives a clear, unambiguous message
- Help people to recognize when they are sending mixed messages
- Undertake experiential training in how to handle harassment.

Experiential learning helps people to:

- Develop their listening skills
- Become aware of their own values and assumptions
- Learn about the values and assumptions of others
- Practise constructive confrontation techniques
- Learn to use third-party intervention
- Learn to use direct statements and 'I' statements
- Distinguish between 'thinking' and 'feeling' statements
- Explore and understand different social styles
- Understand other people's motivations to work.

In mixed gender, experiential-learning groups, people can explore underlying issues at first-hand and develop interpersonal skills. Within the safety of an experiential group, people can sort through their feelings, assumptions and values as they hear about and relate to the values of others. Participants learn from their own experiences, including their emotional responses, reflections, insights and discussions with others.

Summary of sexual harassment

- We must all do everything possible to reduce and eliminate sexual discrimination and sexual harassment. Managers must effectively resolve each instance of sexual harassment in the workplace.
- Legislation cannot remove personal prejudices but it requires that we do not act out those prejudices and persecute other people.
- We all have a responsibility to ensure that others do not use discriminatory behaviour.
- We all have a responsibility to behave in ways that do not intentionally cause offence.
- We must demonstrate, not only by policy but also by example, that sexual harassment is not appropriate nor is it to be tolerated in our society.
- At a personal level, when people believe in equality and work hard to put their belief into practice, when they work hard not to exert undue power over other people, then sexual harassment will cease to exist.
- On a counselling level, helping a client deal with sexual harassment is akin to helping a client deal with sexual abuse. It is embarrassing to disclose, frightening in its consequences and likely to arouse feelings of helplessness, similar to feelings experienced in childhood over bullying. Above all, the complainant has to be believed and, as with the rape victim, who is often not believed, the counsellor must believe. The counsellor is not in the position of proving or disproving a client's statement. That is for the court to decide. Counselling may provide the psychological strength for the client to confront the harasser.

Further reading

Carbonnell, J L., Higginbotham, J. and Sample, J. (1990) Sexual harassment of women in the workplace. In: *1993 Annual: Developing Human Resources*, University Associates, San Diego, CA.
Lee, C. (1992) Sexual harassment: after the headlines. *Training*, **March**, 25.
Mills, H. (1992) *The Independent*, **2 March**.
Pattinson, T. (1991) *Sexual Harassment*, Futura, New York.
Summers, D. (1992) *Financial Times*, **19 March**.

SILENCE

- Silence is referred to in psychotherapeutic literature as:
  - An indicator of resistance

- A necessary and productive part of the therapeutic process
- An intervention by the counsellor
- An integrating process

- Silences enable the client to make associations and connections and engage in problem-solving; breaking the silence may interfere with the client's internal processes
- The positive value of silences is stressed in the person-centred and humanistic approaches, as a means of adding depth to the relationship
- Silence enables clients to hear what they and the counsellor have said and releases attention to observe nonverbal behaviour
- Silences give clients the opportunity to explore their own inner world without the pressure of having to respond
- Counsellors who are never silent deprive themselves and their clients of the opportunity to listen to the deeper meanings that lie beyond words
- Silence happens between people, rather than within one of them, and is an essential characteristic of the relationship
- Silences may arise from resentment, through not having been listened to, being argued with, put down or given incorrect, mistimed or unacceptable interpretations
- In family therapy, 'dysfunctional silence' is used by one member of the family in order to sabotage change
- Silence, on the other hand, is essential in techniques such as meditation, relaxation and imagery
- When silence is thought to be resistance or blocking, the counsellor may use a prompt, by repeating something previously said or by drawing attention to the nature of the silence
- Counsellors may have to work hard on their ability to tolerate silence – what could be a constructive silence is easily ruined by too quick an intervention
- Some silences are as deep as communing with another spirit.

Further reading

Biestek, F. P. (1961) *The Casework Relationship*, George Allen & Unwin, London.
Buber, M. (1958) *I and Thou*, T. & T. Clark, Edinburgh.

SIX CATEGORY INTERVENTION

Six category intervention is a method developed by John Heron It is client-directed, with counsellor interventions directed toward catharsis and support.

The six interventions

Prescriptive
Prescriptive interventions aim to influence and direct the client's behaviour in such a way that:

- The client is free to accept or reject them
- They do not interfere with the client's freedom of choice.

Prescriptive interventions take the form of:

- Advice, in a specific area of expertise
- Suggestions or commendations
- Requests
- Demands or commands
- Modelling behaviour
- Giving a lead
- Verbally and nonverbally directing the client's behaviour
- Attitudes and beliefs about behaviour
- Particular goals to be achieved.

Informative

Informative interventions aim to impart new knowledge:

- That the client sees as relevant
- That does not increase dependence
- In such a way that the client is encouraged to be an active partner in the learning process.

Informative interventions give:

- General knowledge
- Information specific to the client's situation
- Information about the client's behaviour.

Confronting

Confronting interventions:

- Challenge attitudes, beliefs and behaviours
- Support the client while highlighting the defences being used
- Enable the client to achieve insight.

Confronting interventions include:

- Direct, descriptive, nonjudgemental, personal-view feedback
- Interrupting the pattern of negative thinking or acting by:
  - Distraction
  - Introducing a new topic
  - Contradicting
  - Proposing a total change of activity
- Mirroring, in a supportive way, the client's negative verbal or nonverbal behaviour
- Using direct questions to get at what is being defended
- Challenging restrictions – e.g. the use of 'shoulds' and 'oughts' and generalizations

- Unmasking, which uses information not given by the client
- Interpretation of the client's defences
- Discharge feedback, which is demonstration by the counsellor, in sound and movement, of pent-up anger and frustration.

Confronting interventions that are punishments or attacks cause the client to counter-attack. They only succeed when clients feel that the counsellor is attacking their defences, not them.

Cathartic

Cathartic interventions aim to help the client release repressed emotions:

- Anger, through storming
- Grief, through tears and sobbing
- Fear, through trembling
- Tension, through yawning
- Embarrassment, through laughter.

Cathartic interventions include:

- **Literal description,** where, in the first person and in the present tense, the client describes a traumatic event in detail. Detail would include sounds, sights smells, what people said and did.
- **Repetition,** where the client repeats emotionally charged words or phrases. Nonverbal cues indicate emotionally charged content such as faltering tone, sudden emphasis, puckering of mouth or eyes, twitching of fingers or limbs, sudden change of posture, change in breathing pattern.
- **Association,** when the client is encouraged to verbalize a sudden, unbidden thought or to repeat a slip of the tongue. Unbidden thoughts may be detected mainly by the eyes looking anywhere but at the counsellor and by hand movements, indicating discomfort.
- **Acting into** means encouraging the client to deliberately act out the sounds and movements of the emotions, to tap into a genuine discharge of emotion.
- **Self-role-play** is a basic cathartic intervention. Clients become themselves in a past traumatic scene, with its words and wishes and feelings. The counsellor becomes the recipient of the client's emotionally charged message.
- **Monodrama** (*see also*: Gestalt counselling) is where the client has a different chair for each role in the conflict. The client switches from chair to chair and creates a dialogue between the characters in each chair.
- **Primary contact:** The counsellor gazes into the client's eyes and, at the same time, holds the client's hands and gives total attention.
- **Touch:** When the client is on the verge of tears and sobbing, touch is supportive and may allow the floodgates to open.
- **Body work,** with breathing and exaggerated movements.
- **Contradiction** encourages the client to use phrases that:
  - Contradict the negative self-image, accompanied by voice tone and body language that agree with the verbal message

- Express negative views with voice and body language that contradict the feelings
- Use a double negative to exaggerate tone of voice, facial expression and body language.
- **Fantasy** may be used in a number of ways to bypass intellect.
- **Relaxation** and reverie to work on associations.
- **Transpersonal work,** e.g. meditation.

Balance of attention: Old, painful emotions cannot be discharged unless the client has sufficient attention outside the traumatic experience. The counsellor may help to generate attention by directing the client's attention to something in the immediate environment or to the counsellor, by getting the client to describe a recent, pleasant experience, to relax or do controlled breathing.

Catalytic

Catalytic interventions are those that:

- Enable the client to work toward self-determination and self-discovery
- Convey to the client that the counsellor is paying attention, is supportive and is trying to understand.

Catalytic interventions include:

- **Free attention,** not being distracted either by the external or by internal thoughts and feelings, using gaze, posture, facial expressions and touch, being totally supportive, waiting and expecting with hope, being nonanxious, being tuned into the client
- **Active listening skills,** such as:
  - Reflecting the last words after a pause, selective reflecting, where attention is focused on significant words or phrases
  - Paraphrasing, putting into one's own words the gist of what the client has said
  - Empathy building, making every effort to work within the client's frame of reference; checking for understanding is a summary that reinforces understanding, aids empathy building and encourages further elaboration
  - Discreet self-disclosure by the counsellor, which encourages trust and acceptance
  - Open questions by the counsellor, which encourage further exploration
  - Problem-solving structured exercises, which work logically from identifying symptoms toward an agreed action plan
  - Self-discovery, through reality games and growth games
  - Theoretical structure, where the counsellor offers relevant theories and conceptual models
  - Analysis of variables as they relate to how the counsellor perceives the possible causes
  - Examination of options: how the counsellor perceives the various alternatives to the client's decision.

Supportive

Supportive interventions are those that:

- Affirm the person's worth and value
- Are given unconditionally
- Are caring and authentic
- Do not collude with the client's defences and negative self opinions.

Supportive interventions include:

- Free attention
- Touch
- Expressing positive feelings
- Expressing care and concern
- Validation. and positive affirmation
- Sharing what is happening in the relationship
- Self-disclosure.

A negative self-image makes it difficult for some clients to accept supportive interventions. Productive interventions fall into one or other of the six categories. No one intervention is superior to another. To be productive, any intervention has to be caringly supportive. All interventions must have a catalytic element.

Counsellors who are not drawn to using the full-blown model may find some of the interventions worth including in their repertoire of skills.

Further reading

Heron, J. (1972) *Experience and Method*, Human Potential Research Project, Guildford.
Heron, J. (1973) *Experiential Training Techniques*, Human Potential Research Project, Guildford.
Heron, J. (1974) *Reciprocal Training Manual*, Human Potential Research Project, Guildford.
Heron, J. (1975) *Six Category Intervention Analysis*, Human Potential Research Project, Guildford.

STAGES OF FREUDIAN PSYCHOSEXUAL DEVELOPMENT (*see also*: Complexes, Libido, Psychoanalysis)

Oral stage

The oral stage is the earliest phase of both libidinal and ego development, extending from birth to approximately 18 months. The mouth is the main source of pleasure and centre of experience and the libido is satisfied through oral contact with a variety of objects, biting and sucking.

Oral needs are also satisfied by thumb-sucking or inserting environmental objects, such as dolls, other toys or blankets, into the mouth.

The infant's needs and means of expression are centred in all the organs related to the oral zone. Oral sensations include thirst, hunger and pleasurable tactile stimulation, which come by way of the nipple (or substitute). Although the oral stages clearly begins at birth, it is not clear if it ends with weaning.

According to psychoanalytic theory, people who have an oral fixation retain the mouth as the primary erotogenic zone, have a mother-fixation, are prone to mood swings and tend to identify with others rather than relating to them. Fixation is the process by which a person becomes or remains ambivalently attached to an object. Fixation, then, is failure to progress through the appropriate stages of development and is characterized by:

- Infantile and outmoded behaviour patterns, particularly when under stress
- A compulsive tendency to choose objects that resemble the one on whom the person is fixated
- Feeling drained of energy, because the energy is being invested in a past object.

Traits said to be associated with incomplete resolution of the oral phase are:

- Excessive optimism or, conversely, pessimism
- Narcissism
- Being demanding of other people
- Dependency, characterized by needing to be looked after
- Weakened self-reliance and self-esteem
- Envy and jealousy.

Freud believed that the oral phase begins to shift toward the end of an infant's first year to the anal region.

Anal stage

This describes the second stage of psychosexual (libidinal) development. In the anal phase the anus and defecation are the major sources of sensuous pleasure. The anal stage, generally the second and third years of life, is held to be significant for the child's later development because the way the infant responses to parental demands for bowel control may have far-reaching effects on personality.

The desire of the parent means control over the infant and this develops into a struggle over retaining or expelling the faeces. This results in ambivalence, together with a struggle over separation and independence. Loss of control often brings with it feelings of shame and fear of displeasure or punishment.

This phase is also important in the development of ego, as the infant begins to exercise sphincter control, something so obviously important to the parents and which brings mutual pleasure. Should a person become fixated or locked in the anal stage, s/he may develop what has been termed an anal character.

The **anal expulsive** character typically is said to be excessively pliant, untidy and generous; the **anal retentive** to be obstinate, orderly and miserly.

The theory proposes that the anal character may be either of these two extreme forms; more commonly, the traits are combined. The theory also says that the anal character is an unconscious reaction formation against finding erotic pleasure in excretion. Although the term was first used by Freud, it still offers a valuable insight into the obsessive-compulsive personality.

People who have resolved the conflicts of this stage are:

- Certain of their own autonomy
- Independent
- Self-determined
- Not overwhelmed by guilt, shame or self-doubt
- Able to co-operate without the need to comply.

Phallic stage

This describes the third stage of psychosexual development, in which there is interest in the sexual organs. The phallic stage occurs between the ages of 3 and 5 years. Sexual gratification occurs through direct experience with the genitals – the penis or the clitoris.

The penis becomes the primary focus for both sexes; lack of a penis in the female, giving rise to penis envy, is evidence of castration. It is at this stage that we unconsciously desire sexual involvement with the parent of the opposite sex, the Oedipus complex. The guilt over masturbation and oedipal wishes, coupled with the threat of castration, result in castration anxiety. Successful resolution of the phallic stage provides the foundation for a sexual identity. Resolution of the oedipal conflict releases energy to be channelled into constructive purposes. It is at this stage that the superego – or conscience – starts to regulate the child's conduct and behaviour.

Latency period

This is the period of sexual development between the age of 4 or 5 years and the beginning of adolescence, separating infantile from normal sexuality. During this – relatively quiescent – waiting time, memories and wishes remaining from the earlier infantile period are repressed. The latency period is marked by an absence of any great sexual development. Ego and superego development allow the person greater control over potentially destructive impulses.

This is the period of affiliation with others of the same sex and sublimation of energies into learning, play and exploration of the world around, as well as the development of important relationship skills.

Some psychoanalysts, e.g. Erikson, who focus less on sexual development, point to the great social and cognitive developments of this period. The development of social skills, within the education system, may provoke the development of new feelings of inferiority.

This is a period of consolidation and integration, when the child looks forward to adulthood; where industry means growing independence.

Where there is insufficient sublimation into learning and activities, the child might lack internal control, resulting in precocious sexual behaviour or aggression.

Genital stage

This describes the final stage of psychosexual (libidinal) development, usually from the onset of puberty until the person reaches young adulthood. In some models this stage is divided into pre-adolescence, early adolescence and late adolescence.

Physiological maturation, with its hormonal changes, increases libidinal drive While on the one hand this reawakens conflicts of previous stages of development, it also provides opportunity for these conflicts to be resolved and the achieving of a mature sexual identity.

The aims of this stage are:

- Successful integration of the previous stages
- Independence from parents
- To establish successful sexual relationships, free from the oedipal complex
- To establish a mature personal identity
- To accept a set of adult roles with their accompanying responsibilities
- To accept social expectations and cultural values
- To work toward self-set goals.

Further reading

Erikson, E. H. (1963) *Childhood and Society*, Penguin, Harmondsworth.
Gabbard, G. O. (1995) Theories of personality and psychopathology: psychoanalysis. In: *Comprehensive Textbook of Psychiatry*, 6th edn, (eds H. J. Kaplan and B. J. Sadock), Williams & Wilkins, Baltimore, MD.

STEREOTYPES

Introduction

Britain, as with many other nations, is now a society made up of people from many different races, with their languages and cultures. This makes interaction at the same time both interesting and frustrating – for everyone. Living in close proximity to people whose language and customs are different from ours can present many problems of daily living and interaction. When engaged in the counselling relationship, these differences are brought sharply into focus, as we both struggle to make sense out of two totally different sets of values and beliefs.

One of the ways we cope with differences is to create stereotypes. Stereotyping is a behaviour that classifies groups of people, generally in unfavourable terms. We know we are using a stereotype when we use generalizations and attribute to everyone the characteristics that we have observed in only a few.

One of the points about stereotyping is that we lump everybody together; this has come to be known as the halo effect – a tendency to allow an overall impression of a person or one particular outstanding trait to influence the total impression of that person. 'All nuns are kind' would be a positive statement to demonstrate the halo effect. 'No politician ever speaks the truth' would be a negative application. Both are stereotypes and would not stand up to close scrutiny.

A very potent application of stereotypes is how we place people in social classes and attribute certain characteristics to them, simply on the basis of their occupation. The idea of social class being linked to occupation is the basis of much of the snobbery in our society. While it may not be so obvious as it was 50 years ago, it is still there.

What are stereotypes?

A stereotype has the following characteristics:

- It is a belief about people
- It is a pattern of behaviour
- It is relatively fixed
- It is simplistic
- It is unjustifiable
- It allows for no individuality
- It allows for little or no variation
- It is often negative.

Stereotyping is similar to labelling (*see* entry, above), a process whereby certain negative attributes are bestowed upon people or groups. Very often such people are the weak, infirm, disabled or mentally ill. Stereotyping pushes us into precon-structed cages. The bars of the cages have been created out of inflexible and yet often invisible rules and regulations that govern the way we think, feel and behave. The very invisibility of the bars makes it difficult to attempt to break out and change things. At the same time, the bars control every part of our person-ality, so that we find ourselves thinking, feeling and behaving, not as we would wish, but as if we are controlled by some power outside of ourselves. That power is society.

How stereotyping starts

- **Before birth**: The programming starts before birth – examples: 'Blue for a boy, pink for a girl', 'I want my daughter/son to be . . .'.
- **Occupational roles** are often chosen (albeit as wishful thinking) according to gender. Girls are programmed to play with dolls and to be domesticated; boys are programmed differently.
- **School** strengthens the process – different activities are scheduled according to gender. It is possible to arrange such activities as sports along a female–male dimension. Towards the middle of the dimension there are some 'mixed gender' sports but at either end there are others that are definitely not mixed, at least not unless the people involved want to be considered 'strange'.
- **Education** encourages boys and girls to go in different directions. The girl

who wants to study civil engineering, for example, is certainly out of the ordinary and as for boys who want to be carers...!

- **Peer pressure** is a potent force in maintaining the stereotypes. Fear of being regarded as the 'odd one out' can put the young person under a great deal of pressure to conform. Peer pressure does not stop at adulthood. Many of the difficulties between people at work are created by peer pressure. Sexual harassment is one such behaviour that is largely influenced by the group. Peer pressure is not always negative. When there are sufficient numbers of men with a positive attitude towards women, a climate is created in which sexual harassment will not flourish.

- **Prejudice and discrimination** are very powerful and are bound up with values and beliefs. Prejudice and discrimination have their roots in fear and in inferiority. Inferiority turned on its head becomes superiority. Superiority often accompanies a desire to ensure that the target person or group is kept at a inferior level in hierarchical relationships. For prejudiced people, equality of sorts exists only within their own 'in-group', yet even that semblance of equality is precariously balanced on the strictest conformity to the rules.

- **Occupational status**: Stereotypes show themselves in the emphasis we place on a person's occupational status, which, in turn, is a reflection of social class, e.g. the house and area in which people choose to live, the cars they drive and the schools their children attend. The reason we do this is mainly to create a distance between them and us, in much the same way as skin colour creates distance. Prejudice is prejudice whether directed at skin colour, religious differences or property.

Equality, the antidote to stereotyping

Stereotyping seeks to create difference and division; this article has been written from a firm belief in equality. Equality does not mean conformity and standardization; it means recognizing individual differences instead of uniformity. Being pushed into conformity against our will creates stress, which may cause us to rebel. Equality is a high ideal that brings with it certain responsibilities, which some men and women find too frightening. It seems much easier to perpetuate the stereotypes than to struggle towards relative independence.

Equality means that men are liberated as well as women for, as Adler pointed out, men are trapped in the **myth of masculine superiority**. Although Adler (*see* Individual psychology) was writing almost a century ago, his words have a powerful message for us today. When men feel trapped within the stereotyped image of masculinity it means that vital parts of themselves are also trapped. For some men, to express tenderness and caring would be totally unacceptable, to themselves and to the various groups of society to which they belong. They may not realize that this is a source of stress, yet having to live up to a myth does seem to be an obvious and powerful stressor.

An undeniable fact is that between the occupations of men and women there is still a gulf as wide as the Pacific Ocean. Pioneers who cross that great divide encounter many trials and tribulations. For centuries women and men have been 'kept in their occupational place' by the pressures from society.

This century has witnessed changes, yet women are still under-represented in many occupations, particularly those that have been traditionally male-dominated. The civil service, the judiciary and Parliament are but three. The underlying assumption is that women are incapable of or unsuitable to hold such posts. This is insulting and inaccurate and is a clear example of prejudice and discrimination.

An anecdote

I pride myself on not being prejudiced. This anecdote shows how deep-rooted many of our stereotyped responses are.

When working with a group of students and explaining a complex point, I became confused and what was clear in my mind came out jumbled. I jokingly said, 'Sorry about that, it sounded really Irish, didn't it?' then continued to clarify the point. On noticing some of the group looking at one another and smiling wryly, I realized what I'd done. At least half the group were Irish! I stopped trying to explain and apologized for what I then knew to be a racist remark. The Irish contingent were kind and forgiving and what they said is important. 'We get used to it.' Perhaps they get used to it in the same way as other groups are discriminated against – they don't let it show. From that day on, I have made a conscious effort never again to use that expression.

Further reading

Dovidio, J. D. and Gaertner, S. L. (1986) *Prejudice, Discrimination, and Racism,* Academic Press, New York.

STIGMA

The term stigma (plural, stigmata) arises from the Greeks, who burned or cut signs into the bodies of people to denote something bad about the moral status of the person. These signs drew attention to the fact that the bearer was a slave, a criminal, a traitor; a blemished person ritually polluted, to be avoided, especially in public places.

Stigmata, in Christianity, are marks on a person's body resembling the wounds suffered by Jesus Christ during the Crucifixion that are presumably inflicted by a supernatural agency. They are manifested on the hands, on the feet, near the heart and on the head and shoulders. They are often presumed to accompany religious ecstasy.

Erving Goffman, in the introduction to his now classic essay, *Stigma: The management of a spoiled identity,* states that stigmatization is an attitude where the stigmatized person is considered to be different from others, tainted and not a whole person.

People who suffer from mental illness are often on the receiving end of the stigmatizing attitudes of others. If one reflects on the origins of stigma it is easy to see how people would wish to separate themselves from and not be associated with stigmata. If those bearing these marks were criminals or morally depraved or, in the case of the leper with his bell, calling 'Unclean', it is understandable that people not so distinguished would regard these people as different from themselves. They might well have feared that contact with the tainted would have tarred them with the same taint. It is possibly significant that the only people who did not fear such contact (or if they did experience fear they did not let it act as a barrier) were those devoted to charitable works. Perhaps they did not fear contamination because they were secure in their identity and knew that the stigmata of others would in no way compromise their identity.

We may no longer brand people with stigmatizing marks, nor are they required to carry a bell and declare themselves 'unclean'. But just as indelibly we stigmatize physically and mentally handicapped people, people with psychiatric illness, people who are blind or deaf and many others who do not conform to the norms of society. Their presence threatens our identity. When we feel threatened we very often isolate the person or group by highlighting some difference that we ourselves do not possess, which we call a defect. This makes us feel superior: by implication they are inferior. And while the stigmata are not visible – as they once were – they are no less felt by the people who are subjected to the same feelings that the outcasts experienced when they were branded as slaves, criminals or lepers.

Although much has been done in recent years to remove stigma from people who are disabled, the fear of being stigmatized is deeply rooted in our psyche. This is important when thinking of counselling, for many people (not necessarily with disabilities) may not wish to engage in counselling for fear of what other people might think. More than that, what people themselves think is of equal, if not greater importance and the fear of branding oneself 'weak' or 'different' may be enough to stop someone from seeking counselling. If they do, then within the counselling relationship the client, hopefully, will experience so much that is positive that the imagined stigmatization will not happen and the client can walk away feeling whole and clean.

Further reading

Goffman, E. (1973) *Stigma: the management of a spoiled identity*, Penguin, Harmondsworth (original American edition (1963), Prentice-Hall, Englewood Cliffs, NJ).
Stewart, W. (1985) *Counselling in Rehabilitation*, Croom Helm, London.

STRESS MANAGEMENT (*see also*: 'A' type personality, Anxiety, Fight/flight response, Post-traumatic stress disorder)

Stress is the result of any change that a person must adjust to. It is an effect and not a cause; the effect is felt only within the individual and is essentially the rate of wear and tear in the body. The subjective sensations of stress are feeling tired, jittery or ill.

Hans Selye says that stress produces 'adaptive reactions' as a defence. He refers to this as the 'general adaptive syndrome'.

The general adaptive syndrome has three stages:

- Alarm reaction
- Resistance
- Exhaustion.

When we interpret something as threatening, the body prepares us to fight or run away:

- Blood flow to the brain increases
- Blood is redirected from the extremities to the trunk and head
- Hands and feet become sweaty
- Hearing becomes more acute
- Heart and respiratory rates increase
- Muscles tense
- Thought processes speed up
- Vision becomes clearer.

Chronic stress is the result of the body not being given relief from the biochemical changes that occur during the 'fight or flight' response.

What produces stress in one person may have no effect whatsoever in someone else. One person cannot make assumptions about what is not 'distressing' for another person.

Only when something is perceived as hostile does it have the power to act as a stressor, although stress events are not necessarily negative or unpleasant.

Stress has been found to be related to many physical ailments and every organ of the body may become the focus for felt stress.

Sources of stress

- **Environmental**: Crowds, time pressures, noise, work demands, finance, weather
- **Physiological**: Ageing, illness, diet, endocrine, poor sleep, pregnancy
- **Emotional**: Ambitions, relationships, desires, drives
- **Mental**: Thoughts, judgement, reason, intelligence, memory
- **Behavioural**: Outgoing/withdrawn, quiet/excitable, aggressive/placid
- **Transpersonal**: Values, attitudes, ideals, beliefs, spirituality.

The 'social readjustment rating scale' of Holmes and Rahe identifies 10 significant areas related to life events and stress:

- Economics
- Education
- Family
- Group and peer relationships
- Health

- Marriage
- Occupation
- Recreation
- Religion
- Residence.

Holmes and Rahe developed a scale of 43 'life change units' (LCUs). People who accrue 200 or more points at any one time, over a period of about a year, are prone to physical disease or psychiatric disorder.

The top ten LCUS

Death of spouse (partner)	100
Divorce	73
Marital/partner separation	65
Death of close family member	63
Detention in prison or other institution	63
Significant personal injury or illness	53
Marriage	50
Being dismissed from work	47
Reconciliation with partner	45
Retirement from work	45

Measures to reduce life events stress:

- Become familiar with life events and their degree of change
- Display your life change chart in a prominent place and review it frequently
- Practise recognizing significant life events
- Identify feelings about significant events
- Learn to control events, not *vice versa*
- Do not make decisions in a hurry
- Plan significant events well in advance
- Practise keeping calm.

Helping people recognize and deal with stress
How many of the following phrases do you regularly use?

- I'm just as tired when I wake up
- I can't face another day
- I'll take another day off sick
- Oh God! Another dreary day
- I couldn't care less
- If I sit down, I'll never get started again
- I'm bad tempered lately; it's not like me
- Life's one long, boring slog
- Life's maddening, nothing's ever right
- I need a drink.

Mind indicators of stress

- Frequent headaches
- Lapses in memory
- Ringing/buzzing in the ears
- A particular thought that won't go away
- Inability to settle down to get on with things
- Constantly putting tasks off
- Great difficulty in concentrating
- Head feels full of cotton wool
- A feeling as if thinking through a fog.

Social indicators of stress

- People are more difficult than usual
- People make too many demands
- Too much change is happening
- No one to confide in
- Life is nothing but work and sleep
- Family problems
- Don't really know anyone really well.

Body indicators of stress

- Legs twitch in bed
- Frequently have cramp in bed
- Aches and pains in the back of the neck
- Shoulders, neck and back ache a lot
- Hands often tremble
- Sigh often
- Can't get enough breath in the lungs
- Suffer from diarrhoea
- Rings on fingers get very tight
- Tummy feels knotted
- Tummy gets very gassy
- Bladder needs to be emptied a lot
- Sleep is difficult
- Wake in the early hours
- Difficulty getting back to sleep
- Get very hot at night
- Heart-beat seems loud and fast at night
- Heart seems to skip a beat.

Emotional indicators of stress

- Often very near to tears
- Rarely laugh these days

- Can't react with the same feeling
- Life is flat
- Upset by the least little thing
- Feel as taut as violin string
- Don't feel or care about anything/anybody.

'A' type personality and stress (*see also*: 'A' type personality):

- Undertakes more than one job at any one time, which results in poorly done work
- Tries to cram too much work into a given time, which results in a race against the clock
- Competitive about almost everything, sometimes with hostility and aggression
- An intense, sustained drive to achieve self-selected but usually poorly defined goals, coupled with extraordinary mental alertness.

Categories of occupational stress:

- Workload
- Occupational frustration
- Occupational change.

The stress levels of people caught on the occupational treadmill of long hours, intensive study, promotion and relocation (usually with increased financial commitments) will inevitably increase. The spirit of work of the new century is geared toward the 'A' type personality.

Assertiveness and stress (*see also*: Assertiveness)
Assertive behaviour is a middle way between passive and aggressive behaviour. People who behave passively feel humiliated, put down, worthless, not appreciated and stressed because they have allowed someone to walk all over them. People who behave aggressively feel stressed because of the angry feelings generated within themselves and in other people.

When people feel good after communicating with others, it is usually because:

- They have said what they want to say
- They have listened and been listened to
- They have maintained their self-esteem.

Making decisions often causes stress and conflict because of the way difficult events are perceived and interpreted. Fears about making a faulty decision add to the stress.

Symptoms of decisional stress:

- Feelings of imminent loss if a wrong decision is made – losses may be material, social or affecting reputation or self-esteem.

Effects of stress on decision-making

- One's ability to handle information is undermined
- Crisis management becomes the norm
- There is a tendency to make irrational/hasty decisions
- Sometimes the inability to make a decision is total.

Helping people reduce decisional stress

- Explore and evaluate alternative choices
- Explore and evaluate risks
- Encourage action, however small
- Don't overload with information
- Don't encourage making 'any old decision'
- Teach relaxation and positive imagery
- Use a 'for and against' approach.

Helping people manage time

Time is a conveyor belt of small and large decisions, all of which shape our lives. Some decisions produce frustration, lowered self-esteem and stress. Inappropriate decisions give rise to the symptoms of ineffective time management:

- Rush and hurry
- Chronic hesitation between alternatives
- Fatigue or apathy alternate with nonproductivity
- Deadlines are often missed
- Few periods of rest or companionship
- Sense of being overwhelmed by demands and details
- For most of the time having to do what they don't want to do
- Often no clear idea what they would prefer to be doing.

People can be helped toward effective time management by:

- Establishing goals
- Establishing goal priorities
- Creating time by constructing a realistic and practical programme to take care of essential tasks
- Taking time to learn how to make decisions.

Encourage them to take time to reflect on:

- How their day has gone
- Were intervals between work genuine times of recreation?
- Was their eating healthy?
- Did they eat/drink more than they could handle?
- What mood are they in at bedtime?
- Are they on the emotional treadmill of anxiety about some aspect of work?
- Are they having a relationship problem?

Helping people set goals (*see also*: Goals and goal-setting)
One step toward a goal is one step behind. Focus on the goal, not on the route. Help them to think how not to spend 80% effort to get 20% reward.

Some golden do's to help people avoid stress

- Learn to say 'No' assertively – the consequences of saying 'No' have to be weighed against the consequences of saying 'Yes' when it's really 'No' you want to say
- Tackle high-priority tasks first – low-priority tasks may go away
- Don't become so schedule-conscious that interruptions create more stress
- Create personal time and space every day – everyone around benefits
- Make one decision every day – start with something small but significant
- Practise deep relaxation daily.

Stressful thinking (*see also*: Cognitive therapy)
Many people are caught in the trap of negative thinking. A sense of inferiority or inadequacy puts a stumbling block in the pathway of achievement. Negative thinking is destructive and wasteful of precious energy. Negative thoughts interfere with relaxation and increase stress. Self-confidence leads to self-realization and successful achievement.

Aids to thought control:

- Explore and list negative thoughts
- Use imagination positively
- Use 'thought stop'
- Substitute a positive thought to replace the invasive negative thought
- Make positive thinking an ally.

Irrational ideas and stress (*see also*: Rational emotive counselling)

- Negative thinking uses irrational ideas
- Negative thinking creates stress
- Negative self-talk leads to negative feelings
- Many irrational ideas are based on impossible standards, generally imposed on us by other people and taken on board, lock, stock and barrel
- Rationality enhances goal attainment
- Irrationality hinders goal attainment.

Main stress-management techniques

- Assertiveness training (*see* Assertiveness)
- Autogenic training (a series of mental exercises designed to reduce the 'fight/flight' response and switch on to rest and relaxation)
- Body awareness
- Biofeedback (a technique of body awareness designed to reduce stress)
- Breathing (as practised in yoga)

- Coping skills training
- Exercise
- Imagination (*see* Imagery)
- Meditation
- Nutrition
- Relaxation – can be learned in one week, practising two 15 minute sessions a day
- Rational emotive counselling (*see* entry)
- Self-hypnosis
- Thought stopping (*see* Cognitive therapy)
- Time management.

Helping clients to relax

Relaxation is a state of low tension in which emotional level is diminished, especially the level of emotions such as anxiety, fear, anger and the like. Relaxation therapy, generally, is any psychotherapy that emphasizes techniques for teaching the client how to relax, to control tension. The procedure used is based upon Jacobson's progressive relaxation techniques, in which the client learns how to relax muscle groups one at a time, the assumption being that muscular relaxation is effective in bringing about emotional relaxation. Jacobson's techniques are often used in various forms of behaviour therapy, e.g. desensitization procedure.

Relaxation quietens our physical and psychological internal worlds and therefore aids in reducing arousal level. One can relax immediately and quickly by starting to breathe slowly and deeply.

It is essential that the person using a particular technique is not only familiar with it but adheres to the underlying principles. If the counsellor attempting to instruct a client in relaxation does not appear to be someone who uses such a technique, it will be perceived as not being authentic and will lack purpose. Counsellors cannot justifiably proclaim the virtues of relaxation if they do not practise it and have not proved the benefits of it for themselves.

There are many excellent tapes on the market that teach progressive relaxation techniques. A regular programme of relaxation is preventive as well as curative. The routine is as follows:

- Choose a comfortable position
- Close your eyes
- Relax your muscles
- Become aware of your breathing
- Maintain a passive attitude when thoughts surface
- Continue for a set period of time (20 minutes is recommended)
- Practise the technique twice daily.

If the above technique is practised with a phrase or word that reflects your basic belief system, then relaxation and its curative powers will be enhanced. Some examples of phrases used in teaching the expanded relaxation response are: 'My peace I give unto you' or 'Shalom' (the Hebrew word for peace).

Relaxation for better health and well-being

Rewards:

- A person who uses regular relaxation needs less sleep
- Body and mind have more energy and consciousness has more clarity
- Concentration improves
- Living is more joyful and fulfilling
- The journey toward self actualization is made easier.

Medical findings about regular relaxation:

- Heart rate decreases by about 3 beats a minute
- The body's consumption of oxygen decreases
- The metabolism reduces by around 20%
- Anxiety is reduce
- Blood pressure is reduced
- The brain produces alpha and perhaps theta waves – beta waves denote activity whereas others produce a relaxed condition.

Clients who are stressed and anxious can be taught to control their anxiety by learning how to relax. This is more than a technique, for it gives the client a strong element of control over what they feel is something out of control. Another bonus for relaxation is that, if behavioural counselling is indicated to help with panic attacks or phobias, relaxation is vital.

Further reading

Cooper, C. L., Sloan, S. J. and Williams, S. (1988) *Occupational Stress Indicator*, NFER Nelson, Windsor.

Davis, M., Robbins, E. and McKay, M. (1982) *The Relaxation and Stress Reduction Workbook*, New Harbinger Publications, Oakland, CA.

Holmes, T. H. and Rahe, R. H. (1967) The social readjustment rating scale. *Journal of Psychosomatic Research*, 11, 213–218.

Livingstone-Booth, A. (1985) *Stressmanship*, Severn House Publishers, London.

Lovelace, R. T. (1990) *Stressmaster*, John Wiley, Chichester.

Sutton, J. (1998) *Thriving on Stress: How to manage pressures and transform your life*, How To Books, Oxford.

SUICIDE

Definition

Suicide is any deliberate act of self-damage that the person cannot be certain to survive and which, to some degree, carried the intention of causing death.

Attempted suicide is where such an act has failed or has been prevented. **Parasuicide** is where there is little or no intention that death should result.

Historical perspective

In ancient Greece, convicted criminals were permitted to take their own lives but the Roman attitude toward suicide hardened toward the end of the empire as a result of the high incidence among slaves, who thus deprived their owners of valuable property.

To St Augustine, however, suicide was essentially a sin. Several early church councils decreed that those who committed suicide should be deprived of the ordinary rites of the Church and by the Middle Ages the Catholic church condemned all suicides. Until the Reformation, suicides were condemned by both Church and state and burial in consecrated ground was prohibited. The state confiscated the suicide's possessions. Traditionally, suicides were buried at a crossroads with a stake through their bodies. Even until 1823 burial was carried out at night, without a burial service and with a stake through the heart.

Following the French Revolution of 1789, criminal penalties for attempting to commit suicide were abolished in European countries, England being the last to follow suit in 1961. The change in the legal status of suicide, however, has had no effect on the suicide rate.

Many countries and numerous American states also adopted laws against helping someone to commit suicide. Under English law, to aid and abet another's suicide is an offence and euthanasia or mercy killing may amount to aiding in this context. Where there is a suicide pact and one partner survives, s/he may be charged with manslaughter.

Sociological perspective

Suicide is an important subject in sociology, because of the systematic study of suicide by Émile Durkheim (1858–1917) that was published in 1897. He argued that suicide was not simply a result of individual pathology and psychology but that weak social ties resulted in higher rates of suicide. He predicted that Protestants would have higher rates of suicide than Catholics, since Protestantism emphasized personal autonomy and achievement more than did Roman Catholicism.

Durkheim's classification of suicide is:

- **Egoistic suicide** results from a deep sense of personal failure coupled with a lack of concern for the community, with which the person was inadequately involved. Persons not involved in society and its institutions are not constricted by its rules, including those that regulate – and often prohibit – suicide. Instead they are regulated only by their own rules of conduct and act in terms of their own private interests.
- **Altruistic suicide** results from excessive integration into society and insufficient individuation. The behaviour of the individual is almost

completely determined by the social group. Such an individual may commit suicide as a sacrifice to benefit the collective good.

- **Anomic suicide** (*see also*: Anomie, Alienation) is based on the belief that life no longer has meaning, resulting from a sense of anomie, loneliness, isolation and loss of contact with the norms of society. When changes – usually of an abrupt nature – occur in the situation of an individual or culture, equilibrium is disrupted and a state of deregulation exists. Under such circumstances the anomic individual is left without clear norms to guide behaviour. Suicide is one possible result.

Social influences
Social conditions frequently result in a marked increase in the suicide rate. This happened, for instance, among young people in Germany after the First World War (1914–18). Many social scientists believe that the various pressures on young people to succeed in school and the inevitable failure of some of them are leading to significant increases in suicides among students. Some psychologists think that growing feelings of loneliness, rootlessness and the meaninglessness of life are contributing to more suicides in industrialized nations.

Psychological perspective
Freud viewed suicide as an instinctual human tendency toward aggression and destruction. In suicide the death instinct (thanatos) somehow manages to overcome the life instinct (eros). Freud's second explanation was based on the notion that an individual who commits suicide feels aggression and anger over the loss of love objects but turns these feelings inward on himself or herself.

Psychic pain: One of the characteristics of people who feel they want to commit suicide is the amount of psychic pain they experience, an unbearable psychological pain from which the person desires to escape (*see* entry, above).

Who is at risk?
Married couples and those in stable couple relationships have the lowest rates of suicide, while single people have twice the rate and the rates for divorced, separated and widowed people are considerably higher. Family and religious affiliations influence the suicide rates: Catholics and Jews have lower rates than Protestants. People of higher social class have a higher incidence of suicide than those from lower classes, although the risk does increase at the lower end of the scale, possibly because of socioeconomic conditions and stressful life circumstances.

Many people experience feelings of loneliness, depression, helplessness and hopelessness from time to time. The death of a family member, the break-up of a relationship, blows to our self-esteem, feelings of worthlessness and/or major financial setbacks are serious blows that all of us may have to face at some point in our lives. Because each person's emotional makeup is unique, each of us responds to situations differently.

In considering whether a person may be suicidal, it is imperative that the crisis be evaluated from that person's perspective. What may seem of minor importance to one person can be extremely distressful to another. Regardless of the nature of the crisis, if a person feels overwhelmed there is a danger that suicide may seem an attractive solution.

Depression is the chief cause of suicide. Some depressive conditions do respond to counselling, for example where there is a definite known cause, such as depression following bereavement. Major depressive illness is difficult to handle with psychotherapy but usually responds to medical intervention. Loneliness often leads to what is known as situational depression. Relationship difficulties may also lead to depression and are a common cause of suicide and parasuicide. Chad Varah of the Samaritans says that befriending often swings the ambivalent person in favour of living and toward finding an alternative to death.

The effects of suicide

Recognition of suicide today exists within the context of wider awareness of mental health problems, so that there is a decreased tendency to moralize and condemn suicide. Frequently, however, stigma and shame are still associated with such deaths. Surviving family members and friends of the suicide are particularly affected and may experience altered grieving and bereavement associated with the mode of death of their loved one.

The common link among people who kill themselves is the belief that suicide is the only solution to a set of overwhelming feelings. The attraction of suicide is that it will finally end these unbearable feelings. The tragedy of suicide is that intense emotional distress often blinds people to alternative solutions, yet other solutions are almost always available. Suicide is often used as an escape from painful circumstances or as an act of revenge on another person who is blamed for the suffering that led to the suicide. These feelings are sometimes revealed in suicide notes and in the place where the suicide takes place.

The ambivalence of suicide

Almost all people in the 'presuicidal' state experience ambivalent feelings. They want to die and also to be saved. They want to escape from an intolerable situation and they also wish that the intolerable situation could be so transformed that they could continue living. Prevention may be possible in the presuicidal state because of the ambivalence, but people of immature personality may not experience ambivalence.

Many people are now experimenting with new therapies to relieve physical pain. People who can be encouraged to express their psychic pain through counselling are likely to discover a generally improved state of physical health. Pain and anger are close companions. The ability to express anger is one way of expressing the underlying pain.

Myths about suicide

Myth: 'You have to be crazy even to think about suicide.'
Fact: Many people have thought of suicide from time to time. Most suicides and

suicide attempts are made by intelligent, temporarily confused individuals who are expecting too much of themselves, especially in the midst of a crisis.

Myth: 'Once a person has made a serious suicide attempt, that person is unlikely to make another.'

Fact: The opposite is often true. Persons who have made prior suicide attempts may be at greater risk of actually committing suicide; for some, suicide attempts may seem easier a second or third time.

Myth: 'If a person is seriously considering suicide, there is nothing you can do.'

Fact: Most suicide crises are time-limited and based on unclear thinking. Persons attempting suicide want to escape from their problems. Instead, they need to confront their problems directly in order to find other solutions – solutions that can be found with the help of concerned individuals who support them through the crisis period until they are able to think more clearly.

Myth: 'Talking about suicide may give a person the idea.'

Fact: The crisis and resulting emotional distress will already have triggered the thought in a vulnerable person. Your openness and concern in asking about suicide will allow the person experiencing pain to talk about the problem, which may help reduce his/her anxiety. This may also allow the person with suicidal thoughts to feel less lonely or isolated and perhaps a bit relieved.

Myth: 'People who commit suicide are people who were unwilling to seek help.'

Fact: Studies of suicide victims have shown that more than half had sought medical help less than 6 months before their death.

Recognizing potential danger

- At least 70% of all people committing suicide give some clue as to their intentions before they make an attempt – becoming aware of these clues and the severity of the person's problems can help prevent such a tragedy
- If a person is going through a particularly stressful situation – perhaps having difficulty maintaining a meaningful relationship, having consistent failure in meeting goals or even experiencing stress at having failed an important test – watch for other signs of crisis
- Many persons convey their intentions directly with statements such as 'I feel like killing myself' or 'I don't know how much longer I can take this'
- Others in crisis may hint at a detailed suicide plan, with statements such as 'I've been saving up my pills in case things get really bad' or 'Lately I've been driving my car like I really don't care what happens'
- In general, statements describing feelings of depression, helplessness, extreme loneliness and/or hopelessness may suggest suicidal thoughts; it is important to listen to these 'cries for help' because they are usually desperate attempts to communicate to others the need to be understood and helped
- Often persons thinking about suicide show outward changes in their behaviour – they may prepare for death by giving away prized possessions, making a will or putting other affairs in order; they may withdraw from those around them, change eating or sleeping patterns or lose interest in prior activities or relationships

- A sudden, intense lift in spirits may also be a danger signal, as it may indicate that the person already feels a sense of relief at knowing the problems will 'soon be ended'.

How you, the counsellor, can help

Most suicides can be prevented by sensitive responses to the person in crisis. If you think someone you know may be suicidal, try to:

- Remain calm. In most instances, there is no rush. Sit and listen to what the person is saying. Give understanding and active emotional support for his/her feelings.
- Deal directly with the topic of suicide. Most individuals have mixed feelings about death and dying and are open to help. Don't be afraid to ask or talk directly about suicide.
- Encourage problem solving and positive actions. Remember that the person involved in an emotional crisis is not thinking clearly; encourage her/him to refrain from making any serious, irreversible decisions while in a crisis. Talk about the positive alternatives that may establish hope for the future.
- Get assistance. Although you want to help, do not take full responsibility by trying to be the sole counsellor.
- Seek out resources that can lend qualified help, even if it means breaking a confidence.
- Let the troubled person know you are concerned – so concerned that you are willing to arrange help beyond that which you can offer.
- Tell the person, 'The suicidal crisis is temporary. Unbearable pain can be survived. Help is available. You are not alone.'

Further reading

Roy, A. (1995) Suicide. In: *Comprehensive Textbook of Psychiatry*, 6th edn, (eds H. J. Kaplan and B. J. Sadock), Williams & Wilkins, Baltimore, MD.

SUMMARIZING

Summarizing is used to:

- Focus scattered facts, thoughts, feelings and meanings
- Prompt the client to further explore a particular theme
- Close a particular theme
- Help the client to find direction
- Help to free a client who is stuck
- Provide a 'platform' to view the way ahead
- Help the counsellor when feeling stuck
- Help clients to view their frame of reference from another perspective.

A summary:

- Outlines the relevant facts, thoughts, feelings and meanings
- May include a mixture of what was said and what was implied
- Gives a sense of movement
- Requires checking with the client for accuracy
- Should be simple, clear and jargon-free.

Example of a summary

Jane had come to a 'drop-in' counselling agency and it was likely that this would be a 'one-off' session. She had been brought up by her puritanical, elderly grandmother from birth, when her own unmarried mother had 'disgraced the family'. Jane's grandfather had died very soon afterwards, so her grandmother was her main influence. She had done well at school, was bright and achieved good academic grades that took her to a convent grammar school and then on to university to study English language. She was now 20 and approaching her final year of study. She was head-over-heels in love with Alan, another English student. As she started talking about Alan and their love for each other, the tears that had been hovering on the brink spilled over, although she didn't seem too embarrassed by them. She went on to tell the counsellor that she had a strong religious belief that premarital sex was wrong. Alan had tried to persuade her to have sex because he wanted her to have a baby. He had said, 'If you do this, I'll know you truly love me'. But the whole idea of sex and having a baby outside marriage was too much for her. Alan said he wasn't yet ready for marriage and settling down, he just wanted to do it for her. Jane wanted to carry on with a career in teaching. She ended with 'If I do what he wants I'm not being true to myself and if I don't I'll probably lose the only person who loves me'.

Summary

'You said you're very confused, Jane, with all that's happening in your life right now. Your boyfriend wants you to have a baby, but you're not sure about that. You would like to carry on with your career; it means a great deal to you. At the same time, you do want to have children, but not yet. You would like to get married before you start a family but your boyfriend doesn't think like that. You're afraid that if you stick to your principles you may lose your boyfriend.'

Further reading

Sutton, J. and Stewart, W. (1997) *Learning to Counsel: How to develop the skills to work effectively with others.* How To Books, Oxford.

SUPERVISION (*see also*: Evaluation)

Why counsellors need supervision

For counselling to be productive, counsellors must be continually moving forward towards increased understanding of themselves in relation to other people. Time and again they will be brought into contact with clients whose problems will awaken within them something that will create resistance or conflict **within that relationship and specific to it**. The client's difficulty will not be adequately resolved until the counsellor's own resistance or conflict is resolved.

The client may seek help from other sources, but if s/he does the counsellor's personal development may be retarded. When faced with a situation where their own emotions are thrown into turmoil or where counselling appearing to have reached stalemate, there are three courses of action that counsellors may take. They can pull the blanket over their heads and hope that the problem will go away, they can work at it on their own or they can seek help.

In counselling we hope that clients will achieve a degree of insight in order to see their problem more realistically. If insight is essential for the client, how much more is it essential for the counsellor? If it is necessary for clients to seek help from someone to work through their problems, it is equally important for the counsellor.

Supervision helps counsellors to increase their skills and develop understanding and sensitivity of their own and the clients' feelings. The supervisory relationship is not primarily a therapeutic one. The task of the supervisor falls somewhere between counselling and tutoring. Supervision is developmental, helping the counsellor examine his/her relationship with particular clients and the counselling process.

The supervisory relationship forms a three-way relationship of client, counsellor and supervisor. Supervision is often resisted, because people don't use it fully. Counsellors who disregard the supervision relationship will lose out and run the risk of their counselling becoming stale.

Supervision is a requirement of membership of the British Association for Counselling.

The components of supervision:

- Support and encouragement
- Teaching and integrating theoretical knowledge and practice
- Assessment in the maintenance of standards
- Transmission of professional values and ethics.

Approaches to supervision

Characteristics of case-centred supervision

- Exploration of case material
- Concentrated mainly on what took place
- Little exploration of the counselling relationship
- A teacher/pupil relationship
- Discussion is more in the 'then-and-there', than in the 'here-and-now'.

Characteristics of counsellor-centred supervision

- The counselling relationship and what is happening within the counsellor
- Feelings are more readily acknowledged
- Carried out in an uncritical atmosphere
- Transference and counter-transference are more openly explored.

Characteristics of interactive supervision

- Takes into account both the case and the counselling relationship
- The interaction between client and counsellor may, in some way, be reflected in the supervisory relationship. Recognizing the interaction and working with it, is likely to provide the counsellor with invaluable first-hand experience.

Supervision can be achieved in a number of ways:

- One-to-one, supervisor and counsellor
- Co-supervision between peers – usually recommended for experienced counsellors
- Group supervision, where a supervisor works with a number of counsellors
- Peer supervision, where a group of experienced counsellors meet on a regular basis.

Further reading

British Association for Counselling (1987) Supervision. *News-Letter of the Counselling at Work Division*, **Spring**.
Marteau, L. (1976) *Ethical Standards in Counselling*, British Association for Counselling, Rugby.

SYMPATHY (*see also*: empathy, in Core conditions)

This article compares and contrast sympathy with empathy. Sympathy is the quality or state of being affected by the condition of another with a feeling similar or corresponding to that of the other; the fact or capacity of entering into or sharing the feelings of another or others; fellow-feeling. Also, a feeling or frame of mind evoked by and responsive to some external influence. The quality or state of being thus affected by the suffering or sorrow of another; a feeling of compassion or commiseration (*Oxford English Dictionary*).

Empathy, on the other hand, is the power of projecting one's personality into (and so fully comprehending) the object of contemplation (*Oxford English Dictionary*).

In both sympathy and empathy we permit our feelings for others to become involved. The difference is the degree of involvement of feelings. Theodor Reik points out that an essential element in empathy is being able to vibrate unconsciously in the rhythm of the other person's impulse and yet be capable of grasping it as something outside oneself and comprehending it psychologically, sharing the other's experience and yet remaining above the struggle. This does not happen in sympathy. In sympathy we become immersed, engulfed in the other person's experience and thereby lose our own moorings. Empathy is objective, standing with one foot in one's own world; sympathy is passive and means that we have lost contact (albeit momentarily) with our own world. Sympathy often leads to an inability to take appropriate action, even although counselling action may be no more than accurately reflecting the client's feelings.

T, U

Tavistock method (*see also*: Groups)

The Tavistock method originated with Bion, working with small study groups at the Centre for Applied Social Research in the Tavistock Institute of Human Relations, London. Bion's experience in military psychiatry convinced him that the individual could not be considered except as part of a group. The emphasis later gradually shifted from the roles adopted by people in groups to the dynamics of leadership.

Basic assumptions of groups
- A group is formed from a collection of people when there is interaction between members who are aware of their shared relationship, from which a common group task emerges
- Various forces bring groups into being, such as external threat, collective regressive behaviour and attempts to satisfy needs for affection, dependency, safety and security
- When a collection becomes a group it behaves as a system and is greater than the sum of its parts, though the primary task may be masked
- The primary task of any group is to survive
- The fantasies and projections of its members give the group a life of its own
- Group members are used in the service of the primary task
- A person's present behaviour is an expression of that person's individual needs and also the needs of the group
- Whatever the group says or does, the group is always talking about itself
- Knowledge of the group process increases people's insights into their own and other people's behaviour in the group
- Groups have manifest (overt) and latent (covert) aspects
- People always have hidden agendas – parts of themselves that they consciously or unconsciously do not intend to reveal
- The basic assumption group is composed of the combined hidden agendas of:
  - Unconscious wishes
  - Fears
  - Defences
  - Fantasies
  - Impulses
  - Projections
- The basic assumption group is in conflict with the task
- The tension between the task and the basic assumption group is usually balanced by:
  - Individual defence systems
  - Ground rules

- Expectations
- Group norms
- Survival assumptions:
  - Dependency
    The aim is to gain security and protection from either the designated leader or the assumed leader
    The group behaves in such a way that it hopes it will be rescued, controlled and directed by the leader
    The group expresses disappointment and hostility when the leader does not rescue
    Authoritative leaders often fall foul of the dependency assumption
  - Fight/flight
    Fight is characterized by active aggression, scapegoating and physical attack
    Flight is characterized by withdrawal, passivity, avoidance and ruminating on past history
    Fight leadership is bestowed on the person who mobilizes the group's aggressive forces but this leadership is generally short-lived
    Flight leadership is bestowed on the person who successfully moves the group away from the 'here and now' to the 'then and there' and so reduces the importance of the task
  - Pairing, characterized by warmth and affection, creating intimacy and closeness and by mutual support that excludes others in the group
  - Oneness exists when the group surrenders self to some outside cause or all-powerful force, in order to feel a sense of well-being and wholeness.

Organizations seek to satisfy one or other of the survival assumptions. Examples are:

- Dependency, e.g. the Church
- Fight/Flight, e.g. the military and industry
- Pairing, e.g. the political systems
- Oneness, e.g. mysticism and cosmic consciousness.

The function of the facilitator

- To confront the group without intentionally offending group members
- To draw attention to group behaviour but not to individual behaviour
- To point out how the group uses individuals to express its own emotions
- To show how it exploits some members so that others can excuse themselves
- To focus on what is happening in the group
- To present observations in such a way as to increase the group's awareness.

Facilitator interventions may be:
- Description of what is observed
- Process observation – how the group pursues its task

- Thematic development – interactions that threaten the performance of the task, often drawing analogies from myth, legend and fairy tale
- Enlightenment – remarks aimed at instant enlightenment
- Shock – remarks that point to absurdities, aimed at producing shock and immediate awareness.

Issues confronting group members

- **Authority**
- **Responsibility**
- **Boundaries**: A fundamental precept of group relations is that work is not possible unless some boundaries – known to all members – are established and maintained. Boundaries must be strong yet permeable.
- **Projection** occurs in all human relationships and is particularly observable in groups in the form of:
  - Scapegoating
  - Hostility, often directed at the facilitator
  - Struggles for power
    People who project their weaknesses on to others are also in danger of giving away their strengths.
- **Group structure**
  - Control: the group objectives and contract
  - Restraints: ground rules
  - Selected emphasis: expectations and assumptions of both facilitator and members
  - Elaborate structures hinder the group process
  - Minimal structures enhance the group process
  - Visible structures build trust
  - Invisible structures open the door to manipulation.

Further reading

Bales, R. F. and Cohen S. P. (1979) *SYMLOG: A system for the multiple-level observation of groups*, Free Press, New York.

Brown, R. (1988) *Group Processes: Dynamics within and between groups*, Basil Blackwell, Oxford.

TELEPHONE COUNSELLING

The telephone, a central feature of many crisis intervention agencies, is seldom used for counselling over longer periods. Potential clients, those who have not yet plucked up courage to engage in a more formal counselling relationship, can use the telephone.

The telephone allows for anonymity, gives control to the client and reduces intimacy, something that many clients find frightening.

Difficulties of telephone counselling mainly arise from the lack of visual contact and total reliance on verbal language.

Listening, essential in any counselling, is crucial in telephone counselling. Effective listening is listening to what is said, the way it is said (paralinguistics) and what is not said, and being aware of silences.

The way the person responds helps to build rapport and is aided by the frequent (but not habitual, nor unrelated) use of minimal responses such as 'Hmm', 'Yes', 'Right', 'OK', 'Carry on'.

Nonverbal language is always being transmitted, so we should avoid doing anything we would not normally do in face-to-face counselling. Taking notes or doodling may create an intuitive distraction.

Telephoning advice:

- Look welcoming
- Imagine you are looking the speaker in the eye
- Try to convey warmth by avoiding a clipped, crisp, business-like, hurried approach
- Avoid looking at the clock, aware of a pressing engagement – be honest, tell the caller and arrange a return call
- If the telephone is held in your left hand, you are more likely to use your right brain function for feelings and to explore
- If the telephone is held in your right hand, you are more like to use your left brain to analyse and to be precise
- Empathy is more right- than left-brain-oriented.

Further reading

CEPEC, N16 (1.87C) (1987) *Notes on the Use of the Telephone in Counselling*, CEPEC, London SW1Y 6NY.

Kennedy, E. (1981) *Crisis Counselling: The essential guide for non-professional counsellors*, Gill & Macmillan, Dublin.

THERAPEUTIC HOUR

In some texts the session is referred to as the '50-minute hour'; this allows the counsellor time to make any notes before seeing the next client, although it may be more or less; beyond this time, efficiency begins to drop off rapidly.

Most counsellors advise a time limit, and certainly during training this aspect is always stressed. Counselling can be emotionally draining and exhausting. The knowledge that there is a time limit can be a positive safeguard for both client and counsellor.

When clients are being seen over several sessions, they themselves quickly learn to draw the interview to a close. Clients also may feel less anxious if they know there is a time limit; it also gives a sense of urgency to the interview that can be positively helpful.

If the session has been well structured, the client will instinctively feel when the counsellor is starting to draw to a close. This stage is important, for the client is able, mentally, to pick up the threads, ready to move out into the 'real' world. A clock strategically placed is an aid and 'I see time is just about up' alerts the client to the ending.

There is a phenomenon known as 'the hand on the door' – the client, just leaving, halts and discloses something quite dramatic. This immediately thrusts the counsellor on to the horns of a dilemma – should s/he extend the time or leave the disclosure hanging around for another week? Is the client seeking more of the counsellor's time? Has the disclosure really only come to mind? Has the client been trying to pluck up courage and the counsellor has not picked this up? Does the client really want to discuss it? Whatever the reason, the counsellor has to make a decision – continue with the session or close it. A simple 'I heard what you said, however, our time has gone, we will explore it next time, if you wish' will leave the client knowing that the counsellor did hear and the matter is clearly in the client's control.

TOLERANCE

The *Oxford English Dictionary* gives two definitions of tolerance. The first is rather negative, the second is more positive.

> *The action or practice of enduring or sustaining pain or hardship; the power or capacity of enduring; endurance.*
>
> *The disposition to be patient with or indulgent to the opinions or practices of others; freedom from bigotry or undue severity in judging the conduct of others; forbearance; the universality of spirit.*

Tolerance is also an attitude of liberal acceptance of the behaviours, beliefs and values of others. Tolerance embodies vigorous defence of others' values and accepts ambiguity. Truly tolerant people will resist any attempt to inhibit their free expression. Other people use the word in the sense of the first definition – implying a kind of strained forbearance, a sort of gritting of one's teeth while putting up with the behaviour, beliefs and values of others. Understanding and open-mindedness characterize a tolerant person and through accommodating other people and genuine acceptance of them we demonstrate tolerance in a practical form.

The aim of tolerance is peaceful living. Living cheek by jowl with people of different standards, races and religions demands tolerance and an acceptance of the idea that difference does not mean superiority or inferiority. Tolerance provides opportunity to discover and remove stereotypes and stigmas associated with people perceived to be different. As a result, relationships blossom. Tolerance is inner strength that enables us to face and transform misunder-standings and difficulties.

Tolerance does not mean concession, neither is it indifference. Tolerance means that we have reached some mutual respect and understanding of the other. Fear and ignorance are the root causes of intolerance and its patterns can be imprinted on the human psyche from an early age.

Counsellors aim for tolerance in the positive, rather than the negative sense. Tolerance is clearly linked with many of the counsellor qualities, such as empathy, acceptance and genuineness. Tolerance is clearly linked with being open-minded, which means being as free as we can from bigotry or prejudice. None of us can be entirely free but, as the text says, fear and ignorance are the root causes of intolerance and intolerance is one of the characteristics of both bigotry and prejudice. In order to be able to relate to other people with under-standing, counsellors have to strive to suspend anything that will get in the way and this includes judgements, values and prejudices. However, suppressing them is not enough, we need to understand them **as they affect our own lives**. Thus, confronting and reaching new understanding increases our self-awareness and our effectiveness.

TOUCH

The touch of significant others, especially the mother or principal caregiver, plays an important part in the development of security in the infant. Through its senses the infant learns that it is loved and develops a confident personality.

Deprivation of touch can give rise to neurotic or psychotic behaviour in later life, such as 'touch hunger' or 'touch revulsion'.

The psychoanalytic approach, which is exclusively verbal, operates a 'nontouch' rule, which affords no escape for the client and frees the counsellor from possible collusion and self-gratification. On the other hand, full expression of thoughts, feelings and fantasies are encouraged.

Body therapies, however, use a great deal of touch. For them, touch is healing. The cardinal guideline is that the counsellor is not 'touch hungry' or seductive. The touch should be for the benefit of the client, not the counsellor.

Touch can soothe and also inflame great passion. Touch can relax tired and tense muscles; it may also cause a person to shrink away in fear. We can enjoy being touched, embraced, hugged, cuddled or we can detest these touchings.

Rowan, speaking of humanistic therapies and the part touching plays, says, 'As babies we all had strong needs to be touched and cuddled. If these were not met, we may go through life looking for the touch we missed.' In another part of the same book, *The Reality Game*, he says:

> *Many humanistic practitioners touch the bodies of their clients, whether out of ordinary human sympathy, encouragement to regress, provocative massage designed to bring out feelings, re-enactment of birth, etc. In opening up the whole inner world which has been blocked off, we use a lot of gratification (whole body massage, cuddling and comforting, giving of bottles or breasts, immersion in warm water, group rocking and lullabies, affirmation of good qualities and general loveableness and so on) because we find it to be highly therapeutic and very effective in producing real change, if used in the right way.*

Thus on the one hand there is the psychodynamic counsellor who avoids any touch and, on the other, the body-awareness counsellor who will use any or all of the approaches mentioned by Rowan. Touch, like any other response, needs to be carefully used and we need to know why we want to touch the client. It can convey warmth but it may also evoke feelings of the parent–child relationship. Touch can be welcoming but it may also be perceived as threatening, an invasion of personal space. Touch can be encouraging; it may also have the effect of drying up emotions, almost like the patronizing 'There, there; everything will be all right'.

Further reading

Rowan, J. (1983) *The Reality Game*, Routledge & Kegan Paul, London.

TRANSACTIONAL ANALYSIS (E. BERNE, 1910–70) (*see also*: Drama triangle)

Transactional analysis (TA) is a system of analysis and therapy developed by Berne. The theoretical framework comprises:

- Various 'selves' or ego states – Parent, Adult, Child – that form the personality (Parent, Adult, Child are capitalized to identify them as distinct states)
- Transactions between people and between one's various selves
- An individual existential position
- A preconscious life-plan or 'script'.

TA is also a method of group work that emphasizes the person's ability to change, the role of the inner Parent in the process of change and the person's control of the ego states.

Theoretical framework – the ego states expanded

The critical Parent
- The basic need of the critical Parent is power
- Critical Parent functions are to set limits, discipline, make rules and regulations about how life should be; the do's and don'ts
- The critical Parent ego state criticizes and finds fault and is contrasted with the nurturing Parent
- The critical Parent may also be assertive and self-sufficient
- The critical Parent uses such words as 'always', 'never', 'should', 'should not', 'must', 'ought to', 'have to', 'cannot', 'good' and 'bad'
- The critical Parent judges and criticizes and uses such language as 'Because I said so', 'Brat', 'Childish', 'Naughty', 'Now what?', 'what will the neighbours say?'
- Some typical gestures and postures: Eyes rolling up in disgust, finger-pointing, folded arms, tapping of feet in impatience
- Some typical voice tones: Condescending, punishing, sneering

- Some typical facial expressions: Angry frown, disapproving, furrowed brow, hostile, pursed lips, scowl, set jaw.

The nurturing Parent

- The basic need of the nurturing Parent is caring
- Nurturing Parent functions are to give advice, guide, protect, teach how to and keep traditions – group work helps people become aware of the influence of Parent, then to sort out what makes sense and what does not
- The nurturing Parent ego state is characterized by warmth, support, love
- Some typical words and phrases: 'Don't worry', 'Good', 'Darling', 'Beautiful', 'I'll take care of you', 'Let me help you', 'Smart', 'There, there'
- Some typical gestures and postures: Consoling touch, head nodding -'Yes', pat on the back
- Some typical voice tones: Encouraging, supportive, sympathetic
- Some typical facial expressions: Encouraging nod, loving, sympathetic eyes.

The Adult

- The basic need of the Adult is rationality
- Adult functions are to work on facts, to compute, store memories and feelings, to use facts to make decisions
- The Adult decides what fits, where, and what is most useful
- The Adult gathers data on the Parent and the Child, makes decisions based on available data and plans the decision-making process
- The Adult is an analytical, rational and nonjudgemental ego state
- The Adult problem-solves and obtains information
- Some typical phrases: 'According to statistics', 'Look for alternatives', 'Check it out', 'Have you tried this?', 'What do the results suggest?', 'How do you arrive at that?'
- Some typical gestures and postures: Active listening; checking for understanding; giving feedback; pointing something out
- Some typical voice tones: Calm; clear, with appropriate emotion; confident; informative; inquiring; straight
- Some typical facial expressions: Attentive; confident; eyes alert; direct eye contact; lively; responsive; thoughtful.

The Child ego state
A basic ego state consisting of feelings, impulses, spontaneous acts. As a result of learning, the Child ego state takes the form of the adapted Child or the natural Child.

The natural (or free) Child

- The basic need of the natural Child is creativity
- The natural Child is loving, spontaneous, carefree, fun-loving and exciting

- The natural Child is adventurous, curious, trusting and joyful
- The natural Child describes the spontaneous, eager and playful part of the personality
- People whose natural Child is too dominant generally lack self-control
- Some typical words: 'Eek', 'Gee whiz', 'Gosh', 'I'm scared', 'Let's play', 'Look at me now!', 'Wow!'
- Some typical gestures and postures: Joyful, skipping, curling up, pretending
- Some typical voice tones: Belly-laughing, excited, giggling, gurgling, whistling, singing
- Some typical facial expressions: Admiration, wide-eyed and curious, excited, flirty.

The adapted Child

- The basic need of the adapted Child is for approval
- Adapted Child functions are being angry, rebellious, frightened and conforming
- The adapted Child functions are to conform to, or rebel against, what another person wants
- Some typical words and phrases: 'Can't', 'Did I do all right?', 'Do it for me', 'I didn't do it', 'It's all your fault', 'It's all my fault', 'Nobody loves me'
- Some typical gestures and postures: Batting eyelashes; dejected; nail-biting; obscene gestures; temper tantrums
- Some typical voice tones: Asking permission; annoying; spiteful; sullen silence; swearing; whining
- Some typical facial expressions: Eyes directed upward/downward, helpless, pouting, woebegone.

The Adult can turn off either or both of the other ego states. Control is not repression; it means changing the ego state. Control is about choice and decisions.

Transactions

Transactions are the basic units of human communication; any exchanges between the ego states of any two people. Transactions may be verbal and nonverbal. Transactions operate at an overt social level and at a covert psychological level.

Transactions may be:

- Parallel, e.g. Parent to Parent and Parent to Parent
- Crossed, e.g. Parent to Parent and Parent to Child
- Ulterior, e.g. Adult to Adult and Child to Adult.

Contamination

This is where the Child takes on the values, prejudices, opinions and feelings of significant others without filtering them through the Adult.

Strokes

Strokes describe the recognition we receive from others. Strokes can be verbal, nonverbal or both. A wave of the hand. 'Hello, how are you today?' A slap.

- Positive strokes are warm and enhance self-esteem and evoke the feeling of 'I'm OK, you're OK'. Expressing love, caring, respect and responding to an expressed need are all positive strokes.
- Negative strokes are cold and knock self-esteem and evoke the feeling of 'I'm not OK'. Expressing hating is a negative stroke. 'I can't stand you' is a negative stroke.
- Conditional strokes are given to get something in return. 'I will love you if...' (*see also*: unconditional positive regard, in Core conditions).
- Unconditional strokes are given without any attached strings; with no hidden motives.

We need positive strokes to maintain physical and mental well-being. Institutionalized infants have been known to die when deprived of stroking. As we grow, words are often substitutes for the physical stroking we received as children.

So often, strokes are given when we have done something. We also need strokes just for being who we are. We also need to learn to ask for strokes when we need them. 'I'd really appreciate a big hug right now.' 'Give me a kiss, darling.'

A positive self-esteem makes it in order to stroke oneself. 'I did a really good job and I'm pleased with myself.'

Recognition from others may be:

- Positive, evoking the feeling of 'I'm OK, You're OK'
- Negative, evoking the feeling of 'I'm not OK, You're OK'
- Conditional strokes are given for something done – 'I will love you if...'
- Unconditional strokes are given just for being.
- Positive, unconditional stroking benefits the giver as well as the receiver.

People whose Child feels 'not OK' become more used to negative strokes than to positive ones. They may yearn for compliments, but cannot accept them and cannot trust the person who gives them.

Existential or basic positions (scripts)

A script is one's preconscious life-plan, decided by the age of 6 or 7 years. It is based on injunctions ('Don't do...') and counter-injunctions (usually in the form of slogans). A counterscript is a preconscious life-plan decided by the child's Parent. The aim of therapy is to free people from following their scripts and counterscripts.

Transactional analysis recognizes four basic life positions (Table 1).

Stamps and Rackets

'Stamp collecting' is storing bad feelings as an excuse for doing things you might

Table I Transactional analysis's four Life Positions

I'm OK, You're not OK The basic attitude is: 'I'm going to get what I can, though I'm not much. Your life is not worth much; you are dispensable. Get out of my way.' This is a distrustful position and is taken up by a Child who is suspicious of people	Words to describe this state: Arrogant, Do-gooder, Distrustful, Bossy
I'm not OK, You're OK The basic attitude is: 'My life is not worth much; I'm nothing compared to you.' The position of the Child who usually feels low or depressed.	Words to describe this state: Depression, Resignation, Suicide
I'm not OK, You're not OK The basic attitude is: 'Life is not worth anything at all; we might as well be dead. So, it doesn't matter what we do or who we hurt.' Such people may yearn for warmth, but cannot accept it and cannot trust the person who gives it. The position of a Child who feels that life just isn't any good and that there is no escape from it.	Words to describe this state: Futility, Alienation, Severe withdrawal
I'm OK, You're OK The basic attitude is: 'Life is for living; let's live it to the full.' Only this state puts people on equal terms. The healthy position.	Words to describe this state: Good, Healthy, Successful, Competent, Confident, Challenging, Creative

not otherwise do. Stamps are not needed if the basic position is I'm OK; You're OK.

Rackets is a term to describe the habitual ways of feeling bad about oneself, learned from parents and other significant people. They are the feelings of our parents, they do not rightly belong to us, but we act as if they do.

An example would be that, when our parents were under pressure, they may have become anxious, depressed, confused or nervous. If they did not take appropriate Adult action to eliminate the tension or pressure, the likelihood is that we learned a racket by responding in the same way. Rackets originate from the 'not OK' Child of our parents; our Child then repeats these to avoid taking constructive action.

Time structuring

We fill our time depending on which of the four basic positions our Child has taken and what kind of stroking our Child wants.

- **Withdrawal**: No overt communication, e.g. in a railway carriage
- **Rituals**: Socially prescribed forms of behaviour, e.g. the 'Hello – Goodbye' sequence
- **Activities**: These are socially significant because they offer a framework for various recognitions and satisfactions
- **Pastimes**: Semi-ritualistic – topical conversations that last longer than rituals but are still mainly socially programmed, e.g. 'Let's talk about cars/babies/the weather'
- **Games** (over 90 have been described): These are unconscious (a conscious game is manipulation) and involve stamp-collecting
- **Intimacy**: The most satisfying solution to the need for positive stroking. To be able to enter intimacy, a person must have awareness and enough spontaneity to be liberated from the compulsion to play games.

Games

- Games describe unconscious, stereotyped and predictable behaviours. When games are conscious, it is manipulation. The transactions in games are partially ulterior and result in negative payoffs for the players.
- Games are classified as first-, second- or third-degree depending on the seriousness of the consequences. They allow the player to collect 'stamps'. Stamps are stored up feelings, positive or negative. When we have amassed enough stamps we may cash then in for a 'prize': letting fly at someone with whom we have been really tolerant over a long period; allowing oneself a period of relaxation, for example.
- Brown stamps are for negative feelings; gold stamps are for positive feelings
- Stamp collecting is a way of trying to help the Child to feel OK.

A game consists of:

- An apparent (conscious) transaction (usually Adult–Adult)
- A hidden (unconscious) transaction (usually Parent–Child or Child–Child)
- A sudden and unpleasant reaction (a stamp).

The most common games are:

- 'If it weren't for you'
- 'Kick me'
- 'I'm only trying to help'.

Injunctions, attributions and discounts

Injunctions are irrational negative feeling messages expressed preverbally and nonverbally. They are restrictive, reflecting fears and insecurities.

Examples of injunctions:

- 'Don't be you, be me or someone else'
- 'Don't grow up'
- 'Don't count, be unimportant'.

Examples of slogans as injunctions:

- Be a man, my son
- God helps those who help themselves.

Attributions:

- Are being told what we are, what we must do and how we must feel
- Are generally approving of obedience and disapproving of disobedience.

Injunctions and attributions lie at the heart of a judgemental attitude. The developing child's autonomy may be sacrificed on the altar of parental control.

Scripts

- A script is a preconscious set of rules by which we structure our life plan
- Scripts are decided before the age of 6 or 7 years
- Scripts are based on injunctions and attributions
- Scripts determine how we approach relationships and work
- Scripts are based on childlike illusions that automatically influence our lives.

Berne proposed that the parent of the opposite sex tells the child what to do and the parent of the same sex demonstrates how to do it.

Considerations for counselling

TA helps clients to become aware of how they hurt themselves, the changes they need to make and the inner forces that hinder change. Therapeutic change is based on decisions and action. If we do not decide or act, no one will or can do it for us. When we accept a 'can't' we agree with clients that they are helpless. Clients make a contract with themselves to work toward specific changes in behaviour. Change is for the purpose of the client assuming responsibility for his/her life and achieving a degree of self-actualization.

TA is an ideal model for eclectic counsellors to add to their repertoire, mainly because it does not clash with other models and secondly because clients readily understand the basic principles of the Parent–Adult–Child ego states and are normally adept at identifying which ego state they are speaking from.

Intimacy is the most satisfying solution to the need for positive stroking. To be able to enter intimacy, a person must have awareness and enough spontaneity to be liberated from the compulsion to play games. Intimacy is like a harp. The music it produces comes from all its strings. Intimacy means discovering the particular harmony and melody that is enjoyed by the people involved. Sometimes the melodies will vary. Sometimes a minor key will be more appreciated than a major one. But, as with music, it is all there to be enjoyed. Within the intimacy of the counselling relationship the client will learn how to ask for and receive positive strokes.

Further reading

Anderson, J. P. (1973) A transactional primer. In: *1973 Handbook for Group Facilitators*, University Associates, San Diego, CA.

Berne, E. (1961) *Transactional Analysis in Psychotherapy*, Grove Press, New York.

Berne, E. (1964) *Games People Play*, Grove Press, New York.

Berne, E. (1972) *What Do You Say After You Say Hello?*, Grove Press, New York.

Harris, T. A. (1969) *I'm OK – You're OK*, Harper & Row, New York.

Pareek, U. (1984) Interpersonal styles: the SPIRO instrument. In: *1984 Handbook for Group Facilitators*, University Associates, San Diego, CA.

Pitman, E. (1984) *Transactional Analysis*, Routledge & Kegan Paul, London.

Stewart, I. and Joines, V. (1987) *TA Today*, Lifespace Publishing, Nottingham.

Stewart, W. (1998) *Building Self-esteem*, How To Books, Oxford.

TRANSFERENCE AND COUNTER-TRANSFERENCE (*see also*: Bonding)

Transference describes the situation in therapy in which the client displaces on to the counsellor feelings, attitudes and attributes that derive from previous figures in the client's life. The client then responds to those feelings as though the counsellor were a significant figure in his/her past. Transference is a form of memory in which repetition in action replaces recollection of events.

Qualities that distinguish transference:

- Inappropriateness
- Intensity
- Ambivalence
- Inconsistency.

Transference may be positive, e.g. feelings of liking or love, or negative, e.g. feelings of dislike, insecurity, nervousness, anger, hostility.

The term is also used to describe the tendency to transfer on to any current relationship feelings and emotions that properly belong to a previous relationship.

Transference allows old conflicts to resurface and to be worked through. The counsellor is careful to avoid responding to the displaced feelings and behaviour.

Negative transference will interfere with therapy. It shows in direct attacks on the counsellor or in acting out negative feelings rather than exploring them and unwillingness to work through resistances.

Intense positive transference may make excessive emotional demands on the counsellor and prevent exploration of feelings.

Freud's position

- Transference is a resistance to true remembering
- Transference produces a conflict between getting better and getting the better of the counsellor
- Negative transference feelings are more likely to occur in male clients
- Narcissistic people are not likely to experience transference
- Transference means wanting to change the therapeutic relationship into something else.

In positive transference the counsellor is:

- All-important to the client
- A constant topic of conversation
- Idealized
- Constantly praised
- A significant person of dreams and fantasies.

Transference, if not recognized and worked through, may lead to a deterioration in the relationship, little progress and a plateau in therapy.

Jung's position

- Almost all cases requiring lengthy treatment involve transference
- Transference, of some degree, is present in any intimate relationship
- Transference is natural, it cannot be demanded
- Accurate empathy reduces transference.

Carl Rogers's position

- Understanding the client is easier than handling the transference
- Strong transference (in person-centred counselling) occurs in a relatively small number of cases, although some is present in all
- When the displaced feelings become realistically placed, transference attitudes disappear because they have become meaningless
- The more the counsellor interprets, controls, questions, directs, criticizes, questions and evaluates, the more dependency is created and the stronger the degree of transference
- Transference is likely to develop where the counsellor is perceived as 'the authority'.

Transference patterns

Idealizing the counsellor
This is characterized by:

- Profuse complimenting
- Agreeing
- Bragging about the counsellor to others
- Imitating the counsellor's behaviour
- Wearing similar clothes
- Hungering for the counsellor's presence
- Dreams that involve the counsellor.

Attributing supernatural powers to the counsellor
This is characterized by regarding the counsellor as:

- All-knowing
- Godlike
- The 'expert'
- Able to grant requests for advice
- Someone to be afraid of.

Regarding the counsellor as provider
This is characterized by the client:

- Displaying out of place emotion and weeping
- Displaying helplessness and dependence
- Being indecisive

- Asking for advice
- Asking for touch, to be held
- Professing to have no strength without the counsellor
- Being effusively grateful.

Regarding the counsellor as one who thwarts
This is characterized by being:

- Self-protective
- Watchful
- Reticent
- Resentful
- Annoyed at lack of direction
- Hostile.

Regarding the counsellor as unimportant
This is characterized by:

- Always changing the subject
- Talking and never listening
- Being unwilling to explore
- Being dismissive of ideas.

Working with transference
Working with transference means focusing directly on the expressed feelings and making them explicit. Re-evaluation counselling provides a useful two-part way of working with transference.

- Getting the client to identify and verbalize just how the counsellor is like someone else towards whom feelings are directed. This is repeated until no more likenesses remain.
- Getting the client to identify and verbalize just how the counsellor is not like the other person, so that the counsellor is perceived as the person s/he really is.

Counter-transference
Counter-transference refers to unconscious needs, wishes or conflicts of the counsellor evoked by the client, which are brought into counselling and influence the counsellor's objective judgement and reason.

Possible indicators of counter-transference:

- Altering the length of sessions or forgetting sessions with certain clients
- Being overly strict with certain clients and lenient with others
- Being preoccupied with certain clients
- Developing fantasies about the client
- Dreaming about certain clients

- Emotional withdrawal from the client
- Experiencing unease during or following sessions
- Feeling drowsy without cause
- Needing the approval of certain clients
- Not being willing to explore certain issues
- Not wanting the client to terminate
- Promising unrealistic rescue
- Reappearance of immature character traits in the counsellor
- Using the client to impress someone.

Theoretical perspectives

- **The classical viewpoint**: The counsellor displaces on to the client feelings that would be more appropriately directed at another person, either in the present or, more probably, in the past. Counter-transference feelings thus arise from the counsellor's own needs and are not directed to meet the needs of the client. Counter-transference interferes with counsellor neutrality and therefore has an adverse effect on therapy.
- **An integrated viewpoint**: Counter-transference is not pathological but is inevitable and an integral part of the relationship. How the counsellor uses feelings and thoughts all help to increase understanding of the counsellor and client within the relationship.
- **A 'totalistic' viewpoint**: All the counsellor's thoughts, feelings and behaviours are indicators of counter-transference.
- **A realistic viewpoint**: The counselling relationship possesses both positive (constructive) and negative (destructive) elements. Research supports the point of view that the client influences the counsellor much more than the literature would suggest.

Over-identification or disidentification

Counter-transference may be either over-identification or disidentification and may be one of four forms:

- **Overprotective** (over-identification): Characterized by Parent–Child interaction, collusion (allowing the client to blame others), cushioning the client from pain
- **Benign** (over-identification): Characterized by talk–talk, as friends, where distance is closed
- **Rejecting** (disidentification): Characterized by being cool/aloof with minimal involvement and increased distance, failure to intervene, allowing client to struggle and stumble – the counsellor fears demands and responsibility
- **Hostile** (disidentification): Arises from fear of contamination and is characterized by the counsellor being verbally abusive, curt or blunt.

Aids to managing the transference:

- Self-analysis

- Personal therapy
- Supervision
- Genuineness and self-disclosure
- Refer the client.

The counsellor and counter-transference

Working with clients who have deeply ingrained personality problems or those who display self-defeating behaviour may provoke similar behaviour in the counsellor. Counter-transference behaviour may take the form of:

- Anger
- Losing concentration
- Wishing to control
- Feeling defensive
- Denying the truth.

Anticipation, understanding and adequate supervision allow counsellors to avoid becoming engulfed in counter-transference. Concern over counter-transference is especially warranted when dealing with people who are depressed or manic, and those contemplating suicide.

Further reading

Jacobs, M. (1988) *Psychodynamic Counselling in Action*, Sage Publications, London.
Jung, C. G. (1946) *The Psychology of the Transference*, Routledge & Kegan Paul, London.
Klein, M. (1952) The origins of transference. In: *Envy and Gratitude and Other Works*, Hogarth Press, London.
Patterson, C. H. (1985) *The Therapeutic Relationship: Foundations for an eclectic psychotherapy*, Brooks/Cole, Monterey, CA.
Rogers, C. R. (1951, reprint 1981) *Client Centred Therapy*, Constable, London.
Watkins, C. E. (1989) Transference phenomena in the counselling situation, and Counter-transference: its impact on the counselling situation. In: *Key Issues for Counselling in Action*, (ed. W. Dryden), Sage Publications, London. Originally published (1983) in *Personnel and Guidance Journal*, **62**, 206–210 and **63**, 356–359.

TRANSPERSONAL PSYCHOLOGY (*see also*: Existential therapy, Psychosynthesis)

Sometime referred to as the 'fourth force', transpersonal psychology is the successor to humanistic psychology. It seeks to expand or extend consciousness beyond the usual boundaries of the ego personality and beyond the limitations of time and/or space. It is concerned with the ultimate questions about human existence.

Transpersonal psychotherapy is concerned with traditional concerns but includes personal awareness and growth beyond the reaches of the traditionally accepted limits of health. What matters is the experience of being at one with humanity.

Transpersonal experiences are distinguished from 'religious' or 'spiritual' experiences in that they are not required to fit into some prearranged pattern of dogma.

A transpersonal view of the world goes beyond ego boundaries and sees all parts as being equal in their contribution to the whole and all humans as having the same needs, feelings and potentials.

Transpersonal counsellors have trained themselves to see the light within themselves and others. Transpersonal work is not about learning something new but unlearning distorted knowledge already acquired.

Transpersonal psychology is not without its critics. Transpersonal counselling is at the opposite end of the scale from behavioural counselling. Ellis maintains that transpersonal counselling adds to people's burdens rather than relieving them. This criticism is applied to handling such florid conditions as phobias, obsessions and compulsions. This criticism is probably fair, for there is little doubt that these conditions fare better with a cognitive/behavioural approach.

Possibly one of the major criticisms is that that transpersonal counselling does not have one core theory (see Eclectic counselling), but is a hotchpotch of what some consider 'way-out' theories and techniques.

One example must suffice – anger. The transpersonalist will encourage the client to get in touch with the feelings – experience the feelings – but this is often an end in itself. If the person does not end up knowing what to do with the feelings, if there is no change, then the question must be asked: What use has it been? This is the argument of those who work from a cognitive/behavioural perspective.

On the other hand, for people who want to develop their creativity, imagination and intuition, rather than just to control dysfunctional behaviour, transpersonal work has much to offer. Many people are searching to know more of themselves; transpersonal psychology is one of the possible avenues, as are any of the other forms of therapy and counselling. Insight and self-awareness are not exclusive to one method.

A transpersonal counsellor would assist a client, not to come to terms with a dysfunctional society, for example, but to discover inner potential in order to transcend the difficulty. In addition to using techniques from all the traditional approaches, the transpersonal counsellor may use:

- Meditation
- Voluntary disidentification to provide a means of avoiding the effects of stress
- Learning to enter altered states
- Bodywork
- Breathing exercises
- Movement.

Core concepts in transpersonal psychology:

- **Self:** I am not defined by others; neither do I define myself; I am defined by the other

- **Motivation**: My motivation is not to satisfy need nor to exercise choice; it is to surrender
- **Personal goal**: My personal goal is not adjustment nor is it self-actualization; it is union
- **Social goal**: My social goal is not socialization nor is it liberation; it is salvation
- **Process**: The process I go through is not healing, ego-building or ego-enhancement; it is enlightenment and ego-reduction
- **Role of helper**: The role of my helper is not that of analyst or facilitator; it is guide
- **Focus**: The focus of my attention is not toward the individual nor toward the group; it is toward a supportive community.

Some transpersonal counselling beliefs:

- To do therapy is to receive therapy
- We cannot help anyone; we can only help ourselves
- Therapy is a day-by-day process
- We demonstrate what we believe
- What a counsellor is saying is only a small part of the therapeutic effort
- Everyone has the potential to be someone else's counsellor, client or both
- Therapy focuses on internal rather than on external resources
- Focus is on self-energy, not allowing others to invalidate us
- Thoughts determine outcome
- We have to find our own unique pathway, then tread it
- We need to learn to trust our internal voices.

Criticisms of transpersonal psychology

Ellis criticizes transpersonal counselling methods because they ignore effective, planned behavioural methods, relying instead on what he calls 'temporary distractions'. Ellis maintains that transpersonal counselling is not effective against many of the more florid disturbances of obsessions, phobias and compulsions, working rather with methods such as yoga, which often create their own rituals.

Thus there are many differences between transpersonal and behavioural psychology and between the two approaches to counselling. Yet to ignore one without exploring it might be closing one's mind to something that will help a particular client. While working exclusively with a transpersonal approach might do what Ellis says, perhaps it is appropriate for other cases where behavioural methods are not.

Further reading

Ellis, A (1989) *Why Some Therapies Don't Work*, Prometheus Books. New York.

Hendricks, G. and Weinhold, B. (1982) *Transpersonal Approaches to Counselling and Psychotherapy*, Love Publishing, Denver, CO.

Maslow, A. H. (1964) *Toward a Psychology of Being*, Van Nostrand, Princeton, NJ.
Maslow, A. H. (1971) *The Farther Reaches of Human Nature*, Viking Press, New York.
Rowan, J. (1983) *The Reality Game*, Routledge & Kegan Paul, London.
Tart, C. (1969) *Altered States of Consciousness*, John Wiley, New York.
Tart, C. (1983) *Transpersonal Psychologies*, Psychological Processes, California.
Walsh, R. and Vaughan, F. (1980) *Beyond Ego: Transpersonal dimensions in psychology*, J. P. Tarcher, Los Angeles, CA.

Trust (*see also*: Attachment)

Trust is the basis of many human experiences and relationships. For Erikson, trust develops gradually and requires consistent and concentrated effort to maintain it. Trust is associated with creativity, personal growth and productivity.

Characteristics of trusting people:

- Acceptance of values and attitudes
- Belief in equality
- Concentration on problem-solving
- Co-operation with others
- Decisions are arrived at more easily
- Freedom of expression
- Spontaneity
- Highly dependable
- Highly genuine
- Openness in communication
- Recognized competence
- Relate with warmth and empathy
- Respect for others
- Self-accountability
- Supportiveness towards others
- Treat others with regard
- Understanding of thoughts, feelings and behaviours
- Willingness to take risks.

Characteristics of mistrust:

- Always wanting to 'play it safe'
- Closed communication
- Cold/rejecting
- Concern with hierarchy and status
- Desire to control
- Feelings of superiority
- Focus on solutions
- Highly competitive

- Hostile behaviour
- Incompetence
- Inconsistent standards and behaviour
- Lack of respect for others
- Not consistently reputable
- Suspicion
- Unwillingness to give credit
- Unwillingness to take risks.

When trust is destroyed, hurt and anger develop and a fear of ever trusting again. Effective counselling hinges on developing a trusting climate.

Building trust:

- Accepting the feelings of others
- Being consistent
- Being present and involved
- Communication that is unambiguous
- Effective eye contact
- Empathic listening
- Expressing feelings
- Giving and receiving feedback
- Initiating action
- Initiating communication
- Respecting trusting behaviour in others
- Using 'I' talk
- Using affirming language and behaviour.

Trust is highly emphasized in counselling literature, especially in person-centred counselling, particularly as it relates to congruence

Behaviours of trusting/open people:

- Personal, not hiding behind roles
- Respond to current feelings and perceptions
- Focus on relationships
- Spontaneous
- Sharing of self
- Respond to the uniqueness of others
- Concerned for self-growth and growth of others
- Not afraid to follow hunches and impulses
- Focus more on positive than negative behaviours
- Focus on the 'here and now'
- Focus on strengths
- High congruence between verbal and nonverbal communication.

Further reading

Chartier, M. R. (1991) Trust-orientation profile. In: *1991 Annual: Developing Human Resources*, University Associates, San Diego, CA.

Johnson, D. W. (1986) *Reaching Out: Interpersonal effectiveness and self-actualization*, 3rd edn, Prentice-Hall, Englewood Cliffs, NJ.

V

VALUES

Values are what we consider good or beneficial to our well being. Values are learned beliefs, largely culturally determined, and show in our attitudes. Values are part of our personality, direct how we behave and think, and therefore influence how we feel. Values are acquired through experience; needs, on the other hand, are innate.

Six basic value systems:

- **Political**: The pursuit of power, characterized by:
  - Influence
  - Personal prestige
  - Control
  - Authority
  - Strength
  - Money as evidence of success
  - Social status and recognition
- **Aesthetic**: The pursuit of beauty, symmetry and harmony, characterized by:
  - Artistic expression
  - Style and charm rather than practicality
  - The dignity of people
  - Self-sufficiency and individuality
  - Taste, appearance and elegance
  - Money as a means to an end
  - Perhaps regarded as 'snobs', with expensive tastes
- **Social**: The pursuit of humanitarianism, characterized by:
  - Love of fellow beings
  - Being kind, sympathetic, warm, giving
  - Charity, unselfishness
  - Belief in freedom
  - Readiness to offer aid and assistance
  - Consequences of actions carefully considered
  - Frightened off by cold, unsympathetic people.
  - Social does not mean 'outgoing'
- **Theoretical**: The pursuit of truth and knowledge, characterized by:
  - Thinking, learning, probing, analysing, explaining
  - Being critical, logical, empirical
  - Science, research, information, theory
  - Organization of material
  - Detachment, lack of emotion
  - Problem-solving, development of theories, formation of questions
  - Knowledge is power

- Often a low tolerance of people who do not place the same value on knowledge
- **Economic:** The pursuit of what is practical and useful, characterized by:
  - Belief that knowledge is useful only if it can immediately be applied to produce something useful
  - Efficiency and effectiveness measured by profit and prosperity
  - Extreme frugality, giving the impression of being stingy or selfish
  - A feeling that we must conserve resources and use them wisely
  - May judge the success of others by their wealth
- **Religious.** The pursuit of faith, characterized by:
  - Renunciation of experience and logic
  - Seeking the mystic, unity with nature
  - Life is a divine creation
  - Life is ordained and planned
  - Self-denial, prayer, meditation.

Values clarification

In counselling, the following questions are useful to help clients understand full values:

- How freely was it chosen?
- What alternatives were there?
- What effects would any alternatives have?
- How has the value been acted upon?
- Is the value acted upon repeatedly?
- How does the value help reach potential?
- Has the value been publicly affirmed?

A full value must satisfy all seven criteria.

Some work values

Work values are the degree of worth a person attributes to particular aspects of work. Dimensions of work include the opportunities offered by the work for a person to satisfy the following needs:

- To be creative
- To earn money
- To be independent
- To enjoy prestige and status
- To serve others
- To do academic work
- To have a stable and secure job
- To enjoy one's colleagues
- To have good working conditions.

The counsellor's values are an important part of his/her frame of reference, just as the clients' values are to them. Values are closely linked to judgementalism and probably our values are one of the major areas that will bring us into conflict with clients. Just as we have to suspend our judgements, if counselling is to be effective, so must we learn that our values are right for us but we have no right to try to impose them on other people, let alone on clients.

Values are incredibly difficult to work with. As counsellors we need to have our own value-system firmly established and yet not let our values get in the way. This requires something of a balancing act. If there is one thing that will get in the way of understanding the client, of really being in empathy, it is our values. At the same time, it is part of our professional duty to explore our values. Many of us take on our parents' (and others') values lock, stock and barrel, then in counselling training comes the painful process of re-evaluating our values and perhaps getting rid of some of them. That process of evaluating and getting rid of outworn values should never stop and every new client presents the opportunity to take another look at what we value.

Moira Walker raises an interesting point: If there is value clash, what does the counsellor do? She says, 'My contract with [him] did not have an exclusion clause allowing me to withdraw if I found it I did not like his views'. She goes on to say that it is her professional duty to 'work on and with my own counter-transference'. Thus another factor has been introduced – counter-transference. Every clash of views, values, ideology gives us a wonderful opportunity to get to know more of ourselves.

Walker goes on to say that many people in the caring professions do not have the choice of who they work with; their clients (or patients) are chosen for them, so they cannot opt out of a relationship simply because their values clash.

Clients can feel trapped between two opposing sets of values. For example, Sandra is experiencing a value-clash with her mother because Sandra is living with her boyfriend and mother won't let them sleep together when they visit the parental home. A useful way of working with Sandra would be to get her to itemize the various values and their consequences in two columns – hers and her mother's. This might then lead to a discussion of how compromises could be reached. However, compromise can only be arrived at if both sides are willing to seek a middle path.

Further reading

Oliver, J. E. (1985) The personal value statement: an experiential learning instrument. In: *1985 Annual: Developing Human Resources*, University Associates, San Diego, CA.

Rao, T. V. (1991) Managerial work-values scale. In: *1991 Annual: Developing Human Resources*, University Associates, San Diego, CA.

Walker, M. (1993) When values clash. In: *Questions and Answers on Counselling in Action*, (ed. W. Dryden), Sage Publications, London.

W, X, Y, Z

WORKING THROUGH

Working through is a psychoanalytic term to describe the period that elapses between one part of counselling and another. It may be between interpretation and its acceptance and integration or the transference, in which the client moves from resistance to insight and permanent change.

The concept, although introduced by Freud and central to psychoanalysis, is common to most of the psychodynamic therapies. The term is also used to describe the gradual acceptance of loss in the process of grief and mourning.

Working through, according to psychoanalytic theory, comes as a result of the client confronting the particular mental event that is causing the difficulty, clarifying the various components of the particular event and interpreting the conflict. Constant and repetitive exploration is made until unconscious material is fully integrated into the conscious. For example, interpreting someone once is not enough; the interpretation has to be repeated, albeit focusing on different aspects as the client achieves insight. Working through means giving the client time for the interpretation to take root, then to deal with the resistance invoked by the interpretation.

WOUNDED HEALER

This is a Jungian term used to describe the potential healing power of the therapist's own suffering, pain and loss. Therapist and client are both part healer and part sufferer, the one for the other.

Counsellors draw on their own experience of being wounded in order to know the clients in an emotional sense. Counsellors who do not acknowledge their own woundedness erect barriers between themselves and their clients instead of being channels. When the counsellor's vulnerability is acknowledged, the client becomes an active partner in the process and not just a passive recipient of help. The counsellor is not then perceived as the perfect, healthy expert and the client as sick and unskilled.

The concept of the wounded healer finds an echo in Hephaestus (Vulcan), the mythical lame son of Zeus and Hera, queen of Olympus. Ridiculed in the hostile world of Olympus because of his club foot and rolling gait, he found refuge in his work. As a craftsman at the forge fire, he transformed raw material into beautiful objects.

Hephaestus, the only imperfect major deity, is the archetype of the wounded healer whose creativity cannot be separated from his/her emotional wounds. The motivation to heal comes from our own sense of being wounded.

Hephaestus could never (in his eyes) be beautiful, so he created beauty. His body didn't work perfectly, but what he created was perfect.

People who come for pastoral counselling may have only a hazy awareness of the suffering that comes from being stuck in their history. Counselling aims to liberate the clients' inner resources so they can handle the suffering more positively and help to restore their identity. For the pastoral counsellor, change involves the work of the Spirit.

The Spirit is seen as an energy or power, whose subject is God or Christ. The counsellor cannot force change; change is achieved through the mediating influence of the Spirit. The counselling relationship is undertaken in the hope, and with the expectation, that in the search for new directions the client will be accompanied by the Spirit. Jesus is the perfect example of the wounded healer whose work of healing cannot be separated from his/her own emotional wounds. Our motivation to heal comes from our own sense of being wounded and having travelled some way along the road towards healing.

The 'wounded healer' suggests a cost to the counsellor. Counsellors who are involved in this gradual transformation process of another require a level of personal involvement and interpersonal engagement that taps the deepest sufferings of the soul at four different but related levels:

- **Anxiety**: No counsellor has pre-knowledge of a client's journey and cannot plan the way.
- **Vulnerability**: Certain themes of the client's life story may awaken unfinished business within the counsellor, which require reworking. The experience of the client may be just the catalyst that the counsellor needs, at that moment, to be able to move one step forward towards his/her own healing.
- **Balance**: As client and counsellor move in the transitional space between their worlds, a balance between objectivity and subjectivity is essential. This is the space where the Spirit works and transformation begins to take place. It is there that one's own vulnerabilities become open to challenge and change, in the light of the Spirit's work with the client.
- **Transference**: This is the unconscious process whereby the counsellor becomes the focus of the client's unresolved feelings toward significant others.

The client who works through his/her woundedness with the help of the wounded therapist can then become the wounded healer for someone else. Generally the counsellor is aware of significant movement in the client when the client starts to relate to the suffering of other people.

COUNSELLOR TRAINING

There are too many organizations offering counsellor training to include in this book. The following information might help those who wish to embark on such a course.

Most colleges and universities offer counsellor training from Certificate to Master's degrees. The Universities Handbook will contain information on which courses are available.

In addition, counselling and related courses are offered by:

- The National Extension College
- The Open University
- The Institute of Counselling, Clinical and Pastoral Counselling, 6 Dixon Street, Glasgow G1 4AX, tel: 0141 204 2230. In addition to many distance learning counselling skills courses, the Institute offers Psychology for Counsellors, and an Introduction to Stress Management, which includes a relaxation instruction tape.
- The British Association for Counselling produces a Training in Counselling and Psychotherapy Directory. This would probably be the best one-book resource. You may find it in your local library. You can find out more details on the BAC website: www.counselling.co.uk. The following information is taken from the Association's website. 'The Directory has 400 pages of information to help you make a decision about Counselling and Psychotherapy training, with useful tips on funding, open learning and setting samples. Courses listed on a regional basis of Institutions with brief notes on course duration and entry requirements. BAC Code of Ethics & Practice for Trainers in Counselling & Counselling Skills. Another excellent nationally recognized reference book in the Training world of Counsellors & Psychotherapists.'
- The Westminster Pastoral Foundation, 23 Kensington Square, London W8 5HN, tel: 0207 937 6956, is a well-established and respected training organization.

Useful contact details

Age Concern, Astral House, 1268 London Road, London SW16 4ER, tel: 0208 679 8000.

Al-Anon, 61 Great Dover Street, London SE1 4YF, tel: 0207 403 0888. Help for families with relatives who have alcoholic problems.

Alcoholics Anonymous, PO Box 1, Stonebow House, Stonebow, York YOl 2NJ, tel: 01904 644026.

Association for Post-Natal Illness, 7 Cowen Avenue, Fulham, London S26 6RH, tel: 0207 386 0868.

British Agencies for Adoption and Fostering, 200 Union Street, London SE1 0LX, tel: 0207 593 2000.

British Association for Counselling, 1 Regent Place, Rugby, Warwickshire CV21 2PJ, tel: 01788 550899. Information Line, tel: 01788 578328.

British Association of Psychotherapists, 37 Mapesbury Road, London NW2 4HJ, tel: 0208 452 9823.

British Association of Sexual and Marital Therapists, PO Box 13686, London SW20 92H, tel: 0208 543 2707.

British Migraine Association, 178A High Road, West Byfleet, Surrey KT14 7ED, tel: 01932 352468 (24-hour answer phone).

Centre for Stress Management, 156 Westcombe Hill, London SE3 7DH, tel: 0208 293 4114.

Childline (for children in danger or trouble), tel: 0800 1111 (freephone).

CRUSE (Bereavement Care) Cruse House, 126 Sheen Road, Richmond, Surrey TW9 1UR, tel: 0208 332 7227.

Depression Alliance, 35 Westminster Bridge Road, London. SE1 7TB, tel: 0207 633 0557.

Drinkline (National Alcohol Helpline), tel: 0345 320202 (11 am–11 pm).

Institute of Family Therapy, 24–32 Stephenson Way, London N1 2HX, tel: 0207 391 9150.

Miscarriage Association, Head Office, c/o Clayton Hospital, Northgate, Wakefield, West Yorkshire. WF1 3JS, tel: 01924 200799.

National Council for One Parent Families, 255 Kentish Town Road, London NW5 2LX, tel: 0207 267 1361.

NSPCC, tel: 0800 800500 (free helpline).

RELATE Marriage Guidance, National Headquarters, Herbert Gray College, Little Church Street, Rugby CV21 3AP, tel: 01788 573241.

SAMARITANS (for your nearest branch consult your local telephone directory).

United Kingdom Council for Psychotherapy. 167–169 Great Portland Street, London 1N 4HJ.

BIBLIOGRAPHY

PRINCIPAL REFERENCE SOURCES

The following books form the core of the references and, therefore, are not listed under the various subjects.

American Psychiatric Association (1994) *Diagnostic and Statistical Manual of Mental Disorders*, 4th edn (DSM-IV), American Psychiatric Association, Washington, DC.

Arieti, S. (ed. in chief) (1974) *American Handbook of Psychiatry*, vol. 2, Basic Books, New York.

Atkinson, R. L., Atkinson, R.C., Smith, E. E. and Hilgard E. R. (1987) *Introduction to Psychology*, 9th edn, Harcourt Brace Jovanovich, Orlando, FL.

Bayne, R., Horton, I., Merry, T. and Noyes, E. (1994) *The Counsellor's Handbook*, Chapman & Hall, London.

Biestek, F. P. (1957) *The Casework Relationship*, George Allen & Unwin, London.

Campbell, A. V. (ed.) (1987) *A Dictionary of Pastoral Care*, SPCK, London.

Catholic Encyclopaedia (1913) The Encyclopedia Press, New York

Chetwynd, T. (1984) *Dictionary for Dreamers*, Paladin, London.

Chetwynd, T. (1986) *A Dictionary of Symbols*, Paladin, London.

Compton's Interactive Encyclopedia (1995) Compton's Learning Co., USA

Corsini, R. (ed.) (1973) *Current Psychotherapies*, 3rd edn, F. E. Peacock, Itasca, IL.

Drever, J. (1979) *A Dictionary of Psychology*, 2nd edn, Penguin, Harmondsworth.

Edgerton, J. E, Campbell, R. J. (eds) (1994) *American Psychiatric Glossary*, American Psychiatric Press, Washington DC.

Egan, G. (1976) *Interpersonal Living*, Brooks/Cole, Monterey, CA.

Egan, G. (1986) *Exercises in Helping Skills*, Brooks/Cole, Monterey, CA.

Egan, G. (1986) *The Skilled Helper: A systematic approach to effective helping*, Brooks/Cole, Monterey, CA.

Encarta Multimedia Encyclopedia (1995), Microsoft Corporation, California.

Encyclopedia Britannica (1998, electronic edition).

Everyman's Encyclopaedia (1989), J. M. Dent, London.

Great Illustrated Dictionary, Reader's Digest.

Grolier (1996) *The 1996 Grolier Multimedia Encyclopedia*, Version 8, Grolier, USA

Harré, R. and Lamb, R. (1983) *The Encyclopedic Dictionary of Psychology*, Blackwell Reference, New York.

Hastings J. (1908–24) *Encyclopaedia of Religion and Ethics*, T & T Clark, Edinburgh

Infopedia, UK 96, Softkey International, USA

Johnson, A. G. (1995) *The Blackwell Dictionary of Sociology*, Blackwell, Oxford.

Kaplan, H. I. and Sadock, B. J. S. (eds) (1995) *Comprehensive Textbook of Psychiatry/ V*, Williams & Wilkins, Baltimore, MD.

Manstead, A. S. R. and Hewstone, M. (1996) *The Blackwell Encyclopedia of Social Psychology*, Blackwell, Oxford.

Miller, B. F. and Keane, C. B. (1978) *Encyclopedia and Dictionary of Medicine, Nursing, and Allied Health*. W. B. Saunders, Philadelphia, PA.

Nelson-Jones, R. (1983) *Practical Counselling Skills*, Holt, Rinehart & Winston, New York.

Nelson-Jones, R. (1983) *The Theory and Practice of Counselling Psychology*, Holt, Rinehart & Winston, New York.

Nelson-Jones, R. (1986), *Human Relationship Skills*, Holt, Rinehart & Winston, New York.

Patterson C. H. (1986) *Theories of Counselling and Psychotherapy*, 4th edn, Harper & Row, New York.

Reber, A. S. (1985) *A Dictionary of Psychology*, Penguin, Harmondsworth.

Rycroft, C. (1972) *A Critical Dictionary of Psychoanalysis*, Penguin, Harmondsworth.

Samuels, A., Shorter, B. and Plant, F. (1986) *A Critical Dictionary of Jungian Analysis*, Routledge & Kegan Paul, London.

Stewart, W. (1985) *Counselling in Rehabilitation*, Croom Helm, London.

Tschudin, V. (1991) *Counselling Skills for Nurses*, Baillière Tindall, London.

Walrond-Skinner, S. (1986) *A Dictionary of Psychotherapy*, Routledge & Kegan Paul, London.

World Health Organization (1992) *International Classification of Diseases-10: Classification of Mental and Behavioural Disorders*, WHO, Geneva.

INDEX

Entries in upper case refer to the subjects

and alienation, 6
clients who feel alienated, 6
goals, Adlerian, 205
in sadness and depression, 367
tasks, RET; 338
, and internalization, 209
, and intimacy, 213
, ending, indicators of, 270
, observing, 258
counsellors, and burnout, 59
counsellors, and competition, 88
counterscript, TA, 424
counter-transference, 430
, and the counsellor, 432
, and values, 440
, classical viewpoint, 431
, dealing with, 106
, in therapeutic bonding, 55
, indicators of, 430
, integrated viewpoint, 431
, realistic viewpoint, 431
, totalistic viewpoint, 431
courage, and altruism, 7
crafts, right brain function, 229
creative-artistic type, Assagioli, 318
tasks, 321
CREATIVITY, 106
, and transpersonal counselling, 433
, barriers to developing, 107
, challenge of, 184
, characteristics, 107
, envy of, Klein, 221
, psychosynthesis, 322
, right brain function, 230
, work values, 439
credibility, essential elements of, 105
crises, examples of, 108
CRISIS COUNSELLING, 108
crisis intervention, types of, 108
criteria, counselling, Kleinian, 225
critical
analysis, psychosynthesis, 322
incident stress debriefing (CISD), 297
Parent, TA, role of, 421

, theoretical value systems, 438
cross cultural counselling, aids to, 247
cross-gender counselling, 150
cultural barrier, and creativity, 107
cultural estrangement, and alienation, 6
cultural identity , and prejudice, 300
Cupid and Psyche, 304

D

Dante's, *The Divine Comedy*, and guided imagery, 194
dark/eclipsed sun, as archetype, 19
data-collecting skills, and problem-solving, 304
Day of Atonement, scapegoat, 369
death
instincts, Klein, 221
, counselling guidelines, 172
, existential therapy, 141
debriefing, 109
decisional stress, reducing, 402
decision-making
skills, and problem-solving, 304
, effects of stress on, 402
deepening - descent, and guided imagery, 194
DEFENCE MECHANISMS, 110, 309
humour as, 189
in action, 152
outlined, 111
, characteristics of, 110
defences,
group, 415
, highlighting, confronting intervention, 387
, interpreting, confronting intervention, 388
defending, non-therapeutic interventions, 210
defensiveness, in indirect communication, 82
DEFINITION OF COUNSELLING, 122
definitions, grief and bereavement, 168

dehumanizing the individual, and anti-psychiatry, 227
delinquent family, 147
delusion of grandeur, 261
delusional disorder, and pathological jealousy, 216
delusional jealousy, 'Othello syndrome', 216
demandingness, and oral phase, 391
demands, prescriptive intervention, 387
denial,
and grief, 169
, and loneliness, 241
, defence mechanism, 114
, non-therapeutic interventions, 211
, terminal illness, 130
dependency, and oral phase, 391
dependency, survival assumption, 416
DEPRESSION, 123
and anomie, 20
and psychic pain, 305
, and bereavement, 173
, and bulimia, 58
, and grief, 124
, and learned helplessness, 228
, and loneliness, 240
, and problem-solving, 301
, and suicide, 408
, reactive, 125
, symptoms, 123
, terminal illness, 130
, treatment of, 125
depressive idealization, Klein, 222
depressive position, Klein, 222
descriptions, encouraging therapeutic techniques, 210
design and planning skills, and problem-solving, 304
desired scenario, Egan, 281
detached, resigned, Karen Horney, 93
devaluation, defence mechanism, 114
development and evolution, and guided imagery, 194
development, stages of, Erikson, 232

psychotherapy
and spiritual direction, 271
, and depression, 125
, trilogy of, 307
PTSDM characteristic
symptoms, 295
PUBLIC AND PRIVATE
SELF, 323, 373
public, versus private self, 325
self-consciousness
statements, examples
of, 324
self-consciousness,
dimensions of, 373
purpose, loss of, and psychic
pain, 306
Pygmalion effect, 379
Pygmalion study, Rosenthal
and Jacobson, 379

Q
question, the fundamental,
205
questioning, non-acceptance,
238
QUESTIONS, 326
personal responsibility
types, 328
, application types, 327
, closed, 329
, closed, transforming, 330
, demand or command, 82
, elaboration types, 328
, eliciting feelings, 328
, experiencing types, 326
, generalizing types, 327
, guide to using, 326
, guidelines on asking, 329
, helpful, 328
, hypothetical, 82
, interpreting types, 326
, leading, 82
, limiting, 82
, non-genuine, 81
, open types, 328
, open, 106
, open, aim of, 329
, processing types, 327
, punishing, 82
, screened, 82
, sharing types, 326
, specification types, 328
, trick, 82
, use with caution, 104
, direct, confronting
intervention, 387

R
race, and scapegoating, 370
racial prejudice, 299
racism, 299
RAPE COUNSELLING, 332
rape or assault, and PTSD,
296
prevention, 334
, and post-traumatic stress,
333
, defined, 332
, reactions to, 333
, what is involved, 332
rapist, profile of, 334
RAPPORT, 335
, aids to, 335
, and body language, 256
, and telephone counselling,
418
, essential ingredients, 335
RATIONAL EMOTIVE
COUNSELLING (RET),
336
, and stress management,
404
rationalization, defence
mechanism, 119
, in challenging, 64
rationality, left brain function,
228
reaction formation, defence
mechanism, 119
reactive attachment disorder,
38
reading between the lines, 106
realization, and grief, 169
reality
principle, 308
testing, Klein, 223
, denial of, Klein, 223
REASSURANCE, 343
, non-therapeutic
interventions, 211
rebirth – regeneration, and
guided imagery, 194
re-birthing, and catharsis,
63
recognition, strokes, TA, 424
reconciliation, and guided
imagery, 193
RECORDS, 344
, what to include, 345
recovery from anorexia, 24
REDUNDANCY
COUNSELLING, 347
, benefits of, 348

, services offered by
companies, 348
, stages of, 348
redundancy, in
communication, 78
, psychological phases of,
347
, stages of, 347
re-enactment, family therapy,
147
REFERRING A CLIENT, 349
, reasons for delay, 350
REFLECTING, 106, 351
feelings and interpretation,
211
feelings, examples of, 351
, therapeutic techniques,
210
regression, defence
mechanism, 120
REGRET, 352
, anticipatory, 352
Reik, Theodor, empathy, 413
, third ear listening, 237
reincarnation, 171
rejecting, and counter-
transference, 431
REJECTION, 353
versus acceptance, 353
, non-therapeutic
interventions, 211
relational, technique,
psychosynthesis, 323
RELATIONSHIP
PRINCIPLES, 353–354
relationship, family therapy,
144
relationships,
hierarchical, and prejudice,
300
, horizontal and Adler, 202
, levelling, 85
, vertical, and Adler, 202
relaxation and type B, 1
relaxation therapy, grief
work, 173
, outlined, 404
training, and Type A, 2
, and stress management,
404
, cathartic intervention,
389
, medical findings, 405
, rewards of, 405
religion, and cross-cultural
difficulties, 246